The SCHOOL LEADER'S
GUIDE TO

STUDENT
LEARNING
SUPPORTS

*Treat people as if they were what they ought to
be and you help them become what they are capable of being.*

—Goethe

Howard S. Adelman ▪ Linda Taylor

The School Leader's Guide to
Student Learning Supports

New Directions for Addressing Barriers to Learning

Corwin Press
A SAGE Publications Company
Thousand Oaks, California

For information:

Corwin Press
A Sage Publications Company
2455 Teller Road
Thousand Oaks, California 91320
www.corwinpress.com

Sage Publications Ltd.
1 Oliver's Yard
55 City Road
London EC1Y 1SP
United Kingdom

Sage Publications India Pvt. Ltd.
B-42, Panchsheel Enclave
Post Box 4109
New Delhi 110 017 India

Printed in the United States of America

Library of Congress Cataloging-in-Publication Data

Adelman, Howard S.
The school leader's guide to student learning supports: New directions
for addressing barriers to learning / Howard S. Adelman & Linda Taylor.
     p. cm.
Includes bibliographical references and index.
ISBN 1-4129-0965-1 (cloth)—ISBN 1-4129-0966-X (pbk.)
   1. School failure—United States—Prevention. 2. School administrators—United States.
I. Taylor, Linda (Linda L.) II. Title.
LB3063.A34 2006
371.9—dc22

                                          2005003092

This book is printed on acid-free paper.

05   06   07   08   09   10   9   8   7   6   5   4   3   2   1

Acquisitions Editor:	Faye Zucker
Editorial Assistant:	Gem Rabanera
Production Editor:	Melanie Birdsall
Copy Editor:	Marilyn Power Scott
Typesetter:	C&M Digitals (P) Ltd.
Proofreader:	Cheryl Rivard
Indexer:	Kathy Paparchontis
Cover Designer:	Tracy E. Miller

Contents

List of Guides:
Tools for Analyses
and Capacity Building

Preface

When it comes to enhancing learning supports, widespread agreement exists for moving in new directions. It is easy to agree that change is needed. It is harder to agree on what the changes should look like. And it is even harder to get from here to there.

Our intent on the following pages is first to underscore the importance of learning supports and clarify what's wrong with the way such supports currently are provided; then we offer frameworks for rethinking programs and policy. Our approach involves analyses and commentary about the state of the art, and we offer conceptualizations, examples, and opinions.

The analyses and frameworks presented are based on our many years of work in classrooms and schoolwide and from efforts to enhance school-community collaboration. Some of what we have learned comes from our direct efforts to introduce, sustain, and scale up innovations. Other insights come from theory and the large body of relevant research. And equally instructive is what we have derived from lessons learned and shared by many school leaders and on-the-line staff who strive every day to do their best for children experiencing learning, behavior, and emotional problems.

Our analyses clearly indicate the need for systemic changes. This in no way is meant to demean anyone's current efforts. We know that the demands placed on those working in the field go well beyond what common sense says anyone should be asked to endure. And we know that they often feel as if they are swimming against the tide and making too little progress. One of our objectives in writing this guide is to highlight some of the systemic reasons it feels that way, and the other is to move programs and policy forward to improve the situation and enhance school outcomes.

Some of what we propose is difficult to accomplish. Hopefully, the fact that there are schools, districts, and state agencies already trailblazing the way will engender a sense of hope and encouragement to those committed to improving how schools address barriers to learning. Throughout the book, we have included a variety of "tools" to guide analyses and capacity building for new directions. These can be used as training aids and handouts in explaining the need and frameworks for moving forward.

And as a major companion aid for leaders to use in building staff capacity, we have prepared *The Implementation Guide to Student Learning Supports in the Classroom and Schoolwide* as a companion volume. That work highlights concepts and frameworks presented in this book and goes on to detail teacher and learning support staff practices for making new directions a reality every day.

Acknowledgments

It will be obvious that our work owes much to many.

We are especially grateful to those who are pioneering major systemic changes across the country; so many in the field have generously offered their insights and wisdom. And of course, we are indebted to hundreds of scholars whose research and writing is a shared treasure, to Perry Nelson and the host of graduate and undergraduate students at UCLA who contribute so much to our work each day, and to the many young people and their families who continue to teach us all.

PUBLISHER'S ACKNOWLEDGMENTS

Corwin Press acknowledges with gratitude the important contributions of the following manuscript reviewers:

Linda Miller, Consultant
Strategic Systems Development
Iowa Department of Education
Des Moines, Iowa

Sandra Screen, Director
Office of Psychological Services
Detroit Public Schools
Detroit, Michigan

Jane Belmore, Assistant Superintendent
Madison Metropolitan School District
Madison, Wisconsin

Susan Wooley, Executive Director
American School Health Association
Kent, Ohio

About the Authors

Howard S. Adelman is professor of psychology and codirector (along with Linda Taylor) of the School Mental Health Project and its federally supported national Center for Mental Health in Schools at UCLA. He began his professional career as a remedial classroom teacher in 1960 and received his PhD in psychology from UCLA in 1966. He directed the Fernald School and Laboratory at UCLA from 1973–1986 and has codirected the School Mental Health Project since 1986. His research and teaching focus on addressing barriers to students' learning (including educational, psychosocial, and mental health problems). In particular, he is interested in system variables (e.g., environmental determinants and interventions, models and mechanisms for system change) and intrinsic motivational factors (e.g., self-perceptions of control, competence, relatedness) relevant to the causes and correction of emotional, behavioral, and learning problems. In recent years, he has been involved in large-scale systemic reform initiatives to enhance school and community efforts to address barriers to learning and promote healthy development.

Linda Taylor is codirector of the School Mental Health Project and its federally supported national Center for Mental Health in Schools at UCLA. Throughout her career, she has been concerned with a wide range of psychosocial and educational problems experienced by children and adolescents. Her early experiences included community agency work. From 1973 to 1986, she was assistant director at the Fernald Laboratory School and Clinic at UCLA. In 1986, she became codirector of the School Mental Health Project. From 1986 to 2000, she also held a clinical psychologist position in the Los Angeles Unified School District and directed several large-scale projects for the school district. These projects led to her involvement in systemic reform initiatives designed to enhance school and community efforts to address barriers to learning and enhance healthy development.

Introduction

What the best and wisest parent wants for his [or her] own child that must the community want for all of its children. Any other idea . . . is narrow and unlovely.

—John Dewey

L ack of success at school is one of the most common factors interfering with the current well-being and future opportunities of children and adolescents. Thus those concerned about the future of young people and society must pay particular attention to what schools do and do not do with respect to students who are not performing well.

The good news is that there are many schools where the majority of students are doing just fine, and in any school, one can find youngsters who are succeeding. The bad news is that in any school, one can also find youngsters who are failing, and there are too many schools, particularly those serving lower income families, where large numbers of students and their teachers are in trouble. The simple but profound truth is that many schools are ill-prepared to address the needs of those who are in trouble. Moreover, in some instances, the schools themselves are part of the reason some students and teachers are performing poorly.

Every day, a wide range of learning, behavioral, physical, and emotional problems interfere with the ability of students to participate effectively and fully benefit from the instruction teachers provide. Even the best schools find that too many youngsters are growing up in situations where significant barriers regularly interfere with their reaching full potential. And we all recognize the urgency arising from federal legislation. For example,

- Many schools are being designated as low-performing.
- Increasing accountability demands require that schools demonstrate progress for students who are "economically disadvantaged, [are]

from racial and ethnic minority groups, have disabilities, or have limited English proficiency."

- All schools are being evaluated on criteria designed to identify sites that are "persistently dangerous."

The notion of *barriers to learning* encompasses both external and internal factors. Some children bring with them a wide range of problems stemming from restricted opportunities associated with poverty, difficult and diverse family conditions, high rates of mobility, lack of English language skills, violent neighborhoods, problems related to substance abuse, inadequate health care, and lack of enrichment opportunities. Some youngsters also bring with them intrinsic conditions that make learning and performing difficult. As a result, at every grade level there are students who come to school each day not quite ready to perform and learn in the most effective manner. And students' problems are exacerbated as they internalize the frustrations of confronting barriers to learning and the debilitating effects of performing poorly at school. All this interferes with the teachers' efforts to teach. Good teaching is essential, but it clearly is insufficient under such circumstances.

Good teaching, and indeed all efforts to enhance positive development, must be complemented with direct actions to remove or at least minimize the impacts of barriers, such as hostile environments and intrinsic problems. Without effective direct intervention, such barriers continue to get in the way of development and learning for many students. Are we taking a deficit orientation? No! As we will emphasize, addressing barriers is not at odds with the paradigm shift that emphasizes strengths, resilience, assets, and protective factors.

Clearly, major systemic changes are in order. Schools must move forward in proactive and positive ways if they are to effectively address student needs. And they must do so with a fundamental appreciation of what causes problems and motivates learning and appropriate behavior. With increasing accountability for student outcomes and dwindling budgets, it is essential to rethink the use of existing learning supports resources to maximize a school's capability for addressing barriers to student learning and teaching. This is especially the case with respect to dealing with learning, behavior, and emotional problems.

There is growing concern about the wholesale misuse in educational circles of terms such as *learning disabilities* (LD) and *attention-deficit/hyperactivity disorder* (ADHD). Widespread misdiagnoses and inappropriate prescriptions have compromised special education and clinical practice, confounded regular education, and undermined research. For example, in the last part of the twentieth century, about 50% of those assigned a special education diagnosis were identified as having a learning disability. Such numbers are far out of proportion with other disability diagnoses, and this has led to a growing policy backlash.

Probably 80% of those who were diagnosed as having LD actually did not. This is not to deny that they had problems learning at school or to suggest that they didn't deserve assistance in overcoming their problems. This also in no way is meant to underappreciate the difficulties experienced by those who have true disabilities. We must approach learning, behavior, and emotional problems within the context of changing schools and a changing world. And we must do so with a sense of urgency because too many youngsters are having trouble in and out of school.

In what follows, we emphasize frameworks and strategies for dealing with the entire range of learning, behavior, and emotional problems seen in schools. Threaded throughout the book is an emphasis on four fundamental concerns leaders must address in moving in new directions to address barriers to learning and teaching. At the core of these concerns is the complexity and range of problems that must be addressed. It is clear that advancing the field requires adopting an *intervention framework* that is comprehensive, multifaceted, and cohesive. Such a framework encompasses systems to promote healthy development and prevent problems, provide assistance as early as feasible after the onset of problems, and address the needs of students with chronic and severe problems. Evolving such a continuum of interventions at a school and throughout a district requires *rethinking infrastructure* and *policy* and using a sophisticated approach to facilitating major *systemic changes.* In focusing on these fundamental concerns, we also highlight the importance of incorporating the invaluable understanding of human motivation that intrinsic motivation scholars have developed over the past 40 to 50 years.

In Part I, we address why learning supports are imperative and what's wrong with the way we're doing it now. The imperative stems from analyses of the scope of need and the limitations of what is happening. In effect, we do a gap analysis based on how many students need learning supports and are not receiving them and from the perspective of the type of comprehensive, multifaceted, and cohesive approaches that should be in place. We also underscore how important motivational factors are in understanding and correcting learning and behavior problems, particularly for students who have become disengaged from classroom learning. In this context, cautions are raised about the trend toward overreliance on techniques that overemphasize social control at the expense of engaging and reengaging youngsters in classroom learning.

In Part II, we outline new directions for student support to better address barriers to learning in schools. The emphasis is on enhancing classroom approaches and establishing a schoolwide component to enable all students to have an equal opportunity to succeed at school. Using the concept of an *enabling or learning supports component,* the "curriculum" for such an approach is outlined, as is the infrastructure that must be established so that such a component is not marginalized in school policy and practice.

The focus then expands to explore the potential of school-family-community collaboration for strengthening students, families, schools, and neighborhoods. And because moving forward requires a good research base, the available science base for developing comprehensive, multifaceted approaches is highlighted. Part III provides some additional resources that others around the country have found useful.

The orienting questions at the beginning of each chapter reflect the concerns of a growing group who have a stake in public education. As stakeholders explore these concerns, they are coming to understand that enabling all students to benefit more fully from their schooling depends on program and policy agendas that go well beyond current instructional reforms.

Before starting to read a chapter, use the orienting questions to create a picture in your mind about how they apply to a specific school and district with which you are familiar. The questions can also be used as a stimulus to guide discussions with concerned colleagues and as a focus for staff development sessions.

Our primary aim throughout the book is to present analyses and implementation frameworks that can enable leaders in the field to guide the pursuit of new and better directions for addressing barriers to learning and teaching.

We just missed the school bus.

Don't worry. I heard the principal say no child will be left behind!

PART I

Why Learning Supports Are Imperative and What's Wrong With the Way We're Doing It Now

Changing the individual while leaving the world alone is a dubious proposition.

—Ulric Neisser (1976)

Most school staff can detail both the external and internal factors that interfere with effective learning and teaching at their school. They aren't making excuses, they're stating facts.

School leaders and policy makers are aware of the need to address such barriers. This is reflected in the considerable expenditure of resources for student support programs and services and the growing number of initiatives for school-community collaboration. And the No Child Left Behind Act of 2001 (2002) set in motion events requiring even more attention to providing "supplemental services."

Currently, most districts offer a range of programs and services oriented to student needs and problems. Some are provided throughout a school district; others are carried out at or linked to targeted schools. Some are owned and operated by schools; some are from community agencies. The interventions may be for all students in a school, for those in specified grades, for those identified as "at risk," and/or for those in need of compensatory or special education.

Looked at as a whole, a considerable amount of activity is taking place, and substantial resources are being expended. However, it is widely recognized that interventions are fragmented and poorly coordinated. And the whole enterprise is marginalized in policy and practice. Schools confronted with a large number of students experiencing barriers to learning pay dearly for this state of affairs. Moreover, it is common knowledge that such schools don't come close to having enough resources to meet their needs. For these schools in particular, the reality is that test score averages are unlikely to increase adequately until student supports are rethought and redesigned. More broadly, schools that ignore the need to move in new directions related to providing learning supports remain ill-equipped to meet their mission.

The process of leading others in new directions begins with an appreciation of the imperatives for change. To this end, we begin with a gap analysis that leaders can use as a basis for articulating why it is imperative to move forward. In Chapter 1, we underscore what schools are doing to "leave no child behind" and why it isn't enough. Chapter 2 provides frameworks for describing the range of students who need learning supports and places the concept of addressing barriers to learning into a broad context. Chapter 3 offers an overview of the type of comprehensive and multifaceted continuum of intervention that is needed but has not been developed. Part I ends with a discussion of motivation with an emphasis on the need to reverse trends in classrooms as well as schoolwide that pursue behavioral control at the expense of student engagement or reengagement in classroom learning.

Do not follow where the path may lead.
Go instead where there is no path and leave a trail.

—Anonymous

REFERENCES

Neisser, U. (1976). *Cognition and reality: Principles and implications of cognitive psychology.* San Francisco: W. H. Freeman.

No Child Left Behind Act of 2001, Pub. L. No. 107–110, § 2, 115 Stat.1425 (2002).

Why New Directions Are Imperative

1

School systems are not responsible for meeting every need of their students. But when the need directly affects learning, the school must meet the challenge.

—Carnegie Task Force on
Education of Young Adolescents (1989)

What did you learn   Not enough, I guess; they told me
in school today?   I have to go back tomorrow!

ORIENTING QUESTIONS

? How many students are not doing well at school?
? What are schools doing about this?
? What's wrong with the way most schools provide learning supports?

*A*sk any teacher: "Most days, how many of your students come to class motivationally ready and able to learn what you have planned to teach them?" We have asked that question across the country. The consistency of response is surprising and disturbing.

In urban and rural schools serving economically disadvantaged families, teachers tell us that about 10% to 15% of their students fall into this group. In suburbia, teachers usually say 75% fit that profile.

Talk with students: Student surveys consistently indicate that alienation, bullying, harassment, and academic failure at school are widespread problems. Discussions with groups of students and support staff across the country suggest that many students who drop out are really "pushed out." Ironically, many young teachers who burn out quickly also could be described as *pushouts.*

TOO MANY KIDS ARE BEING LEFT BEHIND

Although reliable data do not exist, many policy makers would agree that at least 30% of the public school population in the United States are not doing well academically and could be described as having learning and related behavior problems. In recent years, about 50% of students assigned a special education diagnosis were identified as having a learning disability (LD). Such numbers are far out of proportion with other disability diagnoses. If estimates were correct at the turn of the 21st century, about 80% of those diagnosed as having LD actually did not. They certainly were having problems learning at school, and they undoubtedly needed and deserved assistance in overcoming these problems.

Given the above, it is not surprising that teachers, students, and their families continuously ask for help. And given the way student supports currently operate, it is not surprising that few feel they are receiving the help they need.

Schools must be able to prevent and respond appropriately each day to a variety of barriers to learning and teaching. This, of course, is not a new insight. It has long been acknowledged that many factors can negatively and profoundly affect learning. Moreover, the resulting problems are exacerbated as youngsters internalize the debilitating effects of performing poorly at school and are punished for the misbehavior that is a common correlate of school failure. Because of all this, school policy makers have a lengthy, albeit somewhat reluctant, history of trying to assist teachers in dealing with factors that interfere with schooling. Schools that can't effectively address barriers to learning and teaching are ill-equipped to raise test scores to high levels.

WHAT SCHOOLS DO TO MEET THE CHALLENGE

Currently, there are about 91,000 public schools in about 15,000 districts in the United States. Over the years, most (but obviously not all) schools have instituted programs designed with a range of learning, behavior, and emotional problems in mind. Some directly budget for student support programs and personnel. Some programs are mandated for every school; others are carried out at or linked to targeted schools. In addition to those that are owned and operated by schools, community agencies are bringing services, programs, and personnel to school sites. Interventions may be offered to all students in a school, to those in specified grades, or to those identified as at risk. The activities may be implemented in regular or special education classrooms or as pullout programs and may be designed for an entire class, groups, or individuals.

Across a district, one can find a wide range of efforts to address concerns such as school adjustment and attendance problems, substance abuse, emotional problems, relationship difficulties, violence, physical and sexual abuse, delinquency, and dropouts. As a result, most schools have some support programs and services.

School-based and school-linked programs to address barriers generally focus on responding to crises, early intervention, and some forms of treatment. There also may be a focus on prevention and enhancement of healthy development (e.g., promotion of positive physical, social, and emotional development) through use of health education, health services, guidance, and so forth—though relatively few resources usually are allocated for such activities. As we emphasize in Chapter 9, the science base supporting the promise of much of this activity is large and growing.

Student and teacher supports are provided by various divisions in a district, each with a specialized focus, such as curriculum and instruction, student support services, compensatory education, special education, English language learners, parent involvement, intergroup relations, and adult and career education. Such divisions usually are organized and operate as relatively independent entities. For example, many school-owned and school-operated services are offered as part of what are called pupil personnel or support services. Federal and state mandates tend to determine how many pupil services professionals are employed, and states regulate compliance with mandates. Governance of their work usually is centralized at the district level. In large districts, counselors, psychologists, social workers, and other specialists may be organized into separate units, overlapping regular, special, and compensatory education.

Staffing and Delivery Systems

School districts use a variety of personnel to address student problems. These may include resource teachers, special education staff, "pupil services" or "support services" specialists, such as psychologists, counselors, social workers, psychiatrists, and nurses, as well as language-hearing-speech, occupational, physical, recreation, art, dance, and music therapists and paraprofessionals. Federal and state mandates play a significant role in determining how many personnel are employed to address problems.

As outlined in Guide 1.1, their many *functions* can be grouped into three categories:

1. Direct services and instruction

2. Coordination, development, and leadership related to programs, services, resources, and systems

3. Enhancement of connections with community resources

Prevailing direct-intervention approaches encompass responding to crises, identifying the needs of targeted individuals, prescribing one or more interventions, offering brief consultation, and providing referrals for assessment, corrective services, triage, diagnosis, and various gatekeeping functions. In some situations, however, resources are so limited that specialists can do little more than assess for special education eligibility, offer brief consultations, and make referrals to special education and/or community resources.

Delivery Mechanisms and Related Formats

Key delivery mechanisms and formats for providing student support can be grouped into five categories:

1. School-financed Student Support Services

Most school districts employ pupil services professionals to perform services related to psychosocial and mental and physical health problems, including those designated for special education students. The format for this delivery mechanism tends to be a combination of centrally based and school-based programs and services.

Guide 1.1   Types of Interveners and Functions

I. Interveners Who May Play Primary or Secondary Roles in Carrying Out Functions Relevant to Learning, Behavior, and Emotional Problems

Instructional Professionals

(e.g., regular classroom teachers, special education staff, health educators, classroom resource staff, and consultants)

Administrative Staff

(e.g., principals, assistant principals, deans)

Health Office Professionals

(e.g., nurses, physicians, health educators, consultants)

Counseling, Psychological, and Social Work Professionals

(e.g., counselors, health educators, psychologists, psychiatrists, psychiatric nurses, social workers, consultants)

Itinerant Therapists

(e.g., art, dance, music, occupational, physical, speech-language-hearing, and recreation therapists; psychodramatists)

Personnel-in-Training

Others

- Aides
- Classified staff (e.g., clerical and cafeteria staff, custodians, bus drivers)
- Paraprofessionals
- Peers (e.g., peer/cross-age counselors and tutors, mutual support and self-help groups)
- Recreation personnel
- Volunteers (professional/paraprofessional/nonprofessional—including parents)

II. Functions Related to Addressing Mental Health and Psychosocial Needs at the School and District Levels

Direct Services and Instruction

(based on prevailing standards of practice and informed by research)

- Crisis intervention and emergency assistance (e.g., psychological first aid and follow-up; suicide prevention; emergency services, such as food, clothing, transportation)
- Assessment (of individuals, groups, classroom, school, and home environments)
- Treatment, remediation, rehabilitation (incl. secondary prevention)
- Accommodation to allow for differences and disabilities
- Transition and follow-up (e.g., orientations, social support for newcomers, follow-through)

- Primary prevention through protection, mediation, promoting and fostering opportunities, positive development, and wellness (e.g., guidance counseling; contributing to development and implementation of health and violence reduction curricula; placement assistance; advocacy; liaisons between school and home; gang, delinquency, and safe-school programs; conflict resolution)
- Multidisciplinary teamwork, consultation, training, and supervision to increase the amount of direct-service impact

Coordination, Development, and Leadership
Related to Programs, Services, Resources, and Systems

- Needs assessment, gatekeeping, referral, triage, and case monitoring/management (e.g., participating on student study/assistance teams; facilitating communication among all concerned parties)
- Coordinating activities (across disciplines and components; with regular, special, and compensatory education; in and out of school)
- Mapping and enhancing resources and systems
- Developing new approaches (incl. facilitating systemic changes)
- Monitoring and evaluating intervention for quality improvement, cost-benefit accountability, research
- Advocacy for programs and services and for standards of care in the schools
- Pursuing strategies for public relations and for enhancing financial resources

Enhancing Connections
With Community Resources

- Strategies to increase responsiveness to referrals from the school
- Strategies to create formal linkages among programs and services

2. Classroom-based Curriculum and Special "Pullout" Interventions

Most schools include in some facet of their curriculum a focus on enhancing personal and social functioning. Specific instructional activities may be designed to promote healthy physical, social, and emotional development and/or prevent learning and psychosocial problems, such as behavior and emotional problems, school violence, and drug abuse. And of course, special education classrooms always are supposed to have a constant focus on such concerns. Three formats have emerged:

- Integrated instruction as part of the regular classroom content and processes
- Specific curriculum or special intervention implemented by personnel especially trained to carry out the processes
- Curriculum integrated into a multifaceted set of interventions designed to enhance positive development and prevent problems

3. School District Specialized Units

Some districts operate units that focus on specific problems, such as safe and drug-free school programs, child abuse, suicide, mental and physical health (which sometimes include clinic facilities as well as providing outreach services and consultation to schools), newcomer processing centers, and so forth.

4. Formal Connections With Community Services

Increasingly, schools have developed connections with community agencies, often as the result of school-linked services initiatives (e.g., full-service schools, family resource centers), the school-based health center movement, and efforts to develop systems of care ("wraparound" services for those in special education). Four formats have emerged:

- Co-location of community agency personnel and services at schools
- Formal linkages with agencies to enhance access and service coordination for students and families at the agency, at a nearby satellite office, or in a school-based or school-linked family resource center
- Formal partnerships between a school district and community agencies to establish or expand school-based or school-linked facilities that include provision of various services
- Contracting with community providers to provide needed student services

5. Comprehensive, Multifaceted, and Integrated Approaches

Some school districts have begun to restructure their student support services and weave them together with community resources. The intent is to develop a full continuum of programs and services encompassing efforts to promote positive development, prevent problems, respond as early after onset as is feasible, and offer treatment regimens. Efforts to move toward comprehensive, multifaceted approaches are likely to be enhanced by initiatives to integrate schools more fully into systems of care and the growing movement to create community schools. Three formats are emerging:

- Mechanisms that are established to coordinate and integrate school and community services
- Initiatives to restructure student support programs and services and integrate them into the school improvement agenda
- Community schools

Use of Resources

At the school level, analyses of the current state of affairs find a tendency for student supports to be highly fragmented (see Guide 1.2). It is commonplace for support staff to function in relative isolation from each other and other stakeholders, with a great deal of the work oriented to

Guide 1.2   Talk About Fragmented!

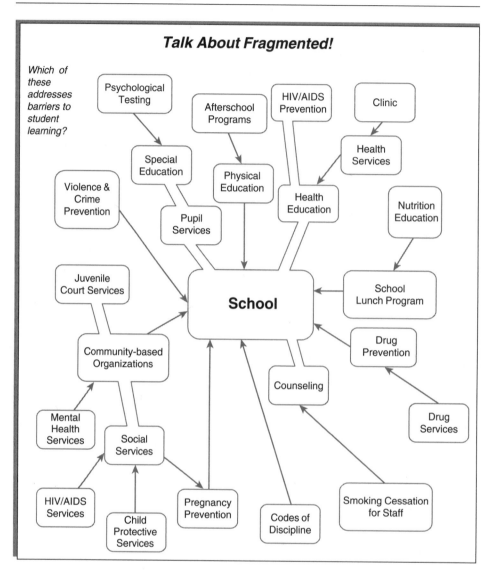

SOURCE: Adapted from Marx and Wooley (1998).

discrete problems and with an overreliance on specialized services for individuals and small groups. In some schools, a student identified as at risk for grade retention, dropout, and substance abuse may be assigned to three counseling programs operating independently of each other. Such fragmentation not only is costly in terms of redundancy and counterproductive competition, it works against developing cohesive approaches and maximizing results (Adelman & Taylor, 1997, 2000, 2002).

In short, various divisions and support staff usually must deal with the same common barriers to learning, such as poor instruction, lack of parent involvement, violence and unsafe schools, poor support for student transitions, and disabilities. And they tend to do so with little or no coordination and sparse attention to moving toward integrated efforts. Furthermore, in every facet of a district's operations, an unproductive separation often is manifested between staff focused directly on instruction and those concerned with student support. It is not surprising, then, how often efforts to address barriers to learning and teaching are planned, implemented, and evaluated in a fragmented, piecemeal manner.

Inadequate data are available on how much schools spend to address learning, behavior, and emotional problems. Figures most often gathered and reported focus on pupil service personnel. These data suggest that about 7% of a school district's budget goes to paying the salaries of such personnel. As to numbers employed, the *School Health Policies and Program Study 2000* conducted by the National Center for Chronic Disease Prevention and Health Promotion (2000) sampled 51 state departments of education, 560 school districts, and 950 schools. Findings indicate that 77% of schools have a part-time or full-time guidance counselor, 66% have a part-time or full-time school psychologist, and 44% have a part-time or full-time social worker.

While ratios change with economic conditions, professional-to-student ratios for school psychologists or school social workers have averaged 1 to 2,500 students; for school counselors, the ratio has been about 1 to 1,000 (Carlson, Paavola, & Talley, 1995). At the same time, estimates indicate that more than half the students in many schools are encountering major barriers that interfere with their functioning. Given existing ratios, it is obvious that more than narrow-band (individual and small-group-oriented) approaches must be used in such schools if the majority are to receive the help they need. Yet the prevailing orientation remains that of focusing on discrete problems and overrelying on specialized services provided to small numbers of students.

Because the need is so great, a variety of individuals often are called upon to address problems of youth and their families. As highlighted in Guide 1.1, these include other health professionals (such as school nurses and physicians), instructional professionals (health educators, other classroom teachers, special education staff, resource staff), administrative staff (principals, assistant principals), students (including trained peer counselors), family members, and almost everyone else involved with a school (aides, clerical and cafeteria staff, custodians, bus drivers, paraprofessionals, recreation personnel, volunteers, and professionals-in-training). In providing services to students, their families, and school staff, some schools also are using specialists employed by other public and private agencies, such as health departments, hospitals, social service agencies, and community-based organizations.

What Is Spent in Schools?

• Federal government figures indicate $5.2 million are spent on special education (U.S. Department of Education, 2001). Overall costs are about $43 billion (and rising), with the federal government funding only about $5.3 billion. Estimates in many school districts indicate that about 20% of the budget is consumed by special education. How much is used directly for efforts to address learning, behavior, and emotional problems is unknown, but remember that over 50% of those in special education are diagnosed as learning disabled and over 8% are labeled emotionally or behaviorally disturbed.

• Looking at total education budgets, one group of investigators reports that nationally, 6.7% of school spending (about $16 billion) is used for student support services, such as counseling, psychological services, speech therapy, health services, and diagnostic and related special services for students with disabilities (Monk, Pijanowski, & Hussain, 1997). Again, the amount specifically devoted to learning, behavior, and emotional problems is unclear. The figures do not include costs related to time spent on such matters by other school staff, such as teachers and administrators. Also not included are expenditures related to initiatives such as safe and drug-free schools programs and arrangements such as alternative and continuation schools and funding for school-based health, family, and parent centers.

Analyses that focus only on pupil service personnel salaries probably are misleading and a major underestimation of how much schools spend to address learning, behavior, and emotional problems. This is particularly so for schools receiving special funding. Studies are needed to clarify the entire gamut of resources that school sites devote to student problems. Budgets must be broken apart in ways that allow for tallying all resources allocated from general funds, support provided for compensatory and special education, and underwriting related to programs for dropout prevention and recovery, safe and drug-free schools, pregnancy prevention, teen parents, family literacy, homeless students, and more. In some schools, it has been suggested that as much as 30% of the budget is expended on problem prevention and correction.

WHY IT'S NOT ENOUGH

Whatever the expenditures, it is common knowledge that few schools come close to having enough resources to deal with a large number of students with learning, behavior, and emotional problems. Many schools offer only the bare essentials. Too many schools do not even meet basic needs. Thus it comes as no surprise to those who work in schools each day that most teachers do not have the supports they need when they identify students who are having problems.

Moreover, the contexts for intervention often are limited and makeshift because of how current resources are allocated and used. A relatively small proportion of space at schools is earmarked specifically for programs that address student problems. Many special programs and related efforts to promote health and positive behavior are assigned space on an ad hoc basis. Support service personnel often must rotate among schools as itinerant staff. These conditions contribute to the tendency for such personnel to operate in relative isolation from each other and other stakeholders. To make matters worse, little systematic inservice development is provided for new support staff when they arrive from their preservice programs. All this clearly is not conducive to effective practice and is wasteful of sparse resources.

Rather than address the deficiencies surrounding school-owned support programs and services, policy makers seem to have become enamored with the concept of school-linked services, as if adding a few community health and social services to a few schools is a sufficient solution. In part, this may be due to the social marketing that has gone on with respect to school-linked, integrated services. Whatever the reason, some policy makers have come to the mistaken impression that community resources alone can effectively meet the needs of schools in addressing learning, behavior, and emotional problems. In turn, this has led some legislators to view linking community services to schools as a way to free up dollars underwriting school-owned services. The reality is that even when one adds community and school assets together, the total set of services in impoverished locales is woefully inadequate. In situation after situation, it has become evident that as soon as the first few sites demonstrating school-community collaboration are in place, community agencies find their resources stretched to the limit.

Another problem is that overemphasis on school-linked services exacerbates tensions between school district service personnel and their counterparts in community-based organizations. As "outside" professionals offer services at schools, school specialists often view the trend as discounting their skills and threatening their jobs. At the same time, the outsiders often feel unappreciated and may be rather naive about the culture of schools. Conflicts arise over turf, use of space, confidentiality, and liability. Thus counterproductive competition rather than a substantive commitment to collaboration remains the norm.

Whether the emphasis is on school-based or school-linked student support or some combination of both, it is clear that there will never be enough services to meet the demand in many public schools. For the foregoing reasons and more, it is imperative to rethink how schools provide essential learning supports.

CONCLUDING COMMENTS

Early in the 21st century, the following state of affairs is evident:

- Too many kids are not doing well in schools.
- To change this, schools must play a major role in providing supports for students experiencing learning, behavior, and emotional problems.

- However, student support programs and services as they currently operate can't meet the needs of the many whose problems are affecting their learning at school.

Leaders at all levels need to understand the full implications of all this. Limited efficacy and cost-effectiveness seem inevitable as long as related interventions are fragmented and carried out in isolation from each other; limited systemic change is likely as long as the entire enterprise is marginalized in policy and practice. Clearly, school improvement and capacity-building efforts (including preservice and inservice staff development) have yet to deal effectively with the enterprise of providing supports for students and teachers. And the straightforward psychometric reality is that in schools where a large proportion of students encounter major barriers to learning, test score averages are unlikely to increase adequately until such supports are rethought and redesigned. Indeed, a major shift in thinking is long overdue.

The next decade must mark a turning point for the way schools and communities address the problems of children and youth. In particular, the focus must be on initiatives to reform and restructure the way schools work to prevent and ameliorate the many learning, behavior, and emotional problems experienced by students. And the end product must be schools where everyone—staff, students, families, and community stakeholders—feels supported. This means reshaping the functions of all school personnel who have a role to play in addressing barriers to learning and promoting healthy development. It means fully integrating their roles and functions into school improvement planning. There is much work to be done in addressing barriers to learning and teaching as public schools across the country strive to leave no child behind.

I failed every subject but algebra.   That's not too surprising since you didn't take algebra.

REFERENCES

Adelman, H. S., & Taylor, L. (1997). Addressing barriers to learning: Beyond school-linked services and full service schools. *American Journal of Orthopsychiatry, 67,* 408–421.

Adelman, H. S., & Taylor, L. (2000). Looking at school health and school reform policy through the lens of addressing barriers to learning. *Children's Services: Social Policy, Research, and Practice, 3,* 117–132.

Adelman, H. S., & Taylor, L. (2002). Building comprehensive, multifaceted, and integrated approaches to address barriers to student learning. *Childhood Education, 78,* 261–268.

Carlson, C., Paavola, J., & Talley, R. (1995). Historical, current, and future models of schools as health care delivery settings. *School Psychology Quarterly, 10,* 184–202.

Carnegie Council on Adolescent Development's Task Force on Education of Young Adolescents. (1989). *Turning points: Preparing American youth for the 21st century.* Washington, DC: Author.

Marx, E., & Wooley, S. F. (with Northrop, D.). (Eds.). (1998). *Health is academic: A guide to coordinated school health programs.* New York: Teachers College Press.

Monk, D. H., Pijanowski, J. C., & Hussain, S. (1997). How and where the education dollar is spent. *The Future of Children, 7,* 51–62.

National Center for Chronic Disease Prevention and Health Promotion. (2000). *School health policies and program study 2000.* Retrieved March 7, 2005, from www.cdc.gov/HealthyYouth/shpps/summaries/pdf/SH2000summ.pdf.

U.S. Department of Education. (2001). To assure the free appropriate public education of all children with disabilities. *Twenty-third annual report to Congress on the implementation of the Individuals with Disabilities Education Act.* Jessup, MD: Education Publications Center.

Which Students Need 2 Learning Supports?

In the last analysis, we see only what we are ready to see. We eliminate and ignore everything that is not part of our prejudices.

—Jean-Martin Charcot (1857)

Why do you say you're wasting your time by going to school?   Well, I can't read or write — and they won't let me talk!

ORIENTING QUESTIONS

? How do schools describe the range of learners when they say *all* students can learn?
? Why do so many students have learning and behavior problems?
? Why are so many students labeled as having a learning *disability*?
? What factors do learning supports address?

Consider the American penchant for ignoring the structural causes of problems. We prefer the simplicity and satisfaction of holding individuals responsible for whatever happens: crime, poverty, school failure, what have you. Thus, even when one high school crisis is followed by another, we concentrate on the particular people involved—their values, their character, their personal failings—rather than asking whether something about the system in which these students find themselves might also need to be addressed.

—Alfie Kohn (1999, p.1)

To answer questions such as, *Why are there so many problems? What can we do to make things better?* we need to understand factors that lead to learning and those that interfere. Although learning and behavior problems are not limited to any one time or place, they are recognized most often in classroom settings. And teaching, both in and out of schools, obviously encompasses one critical set of determinants. In understanding problems seen at school, then, it is important to

- Identify those caused by environmental factors, including the way schooling is conducted.
- Differentiate these from problems stemming from the type of central nervous system dysfunction believed to cause true learning *disabilities* (LD), attention-deficit/hyperactivity *disorders* (ADHD), and a host of other person-based pathologies.

By making such a differentiation, it becomes clearer that the prevention of some problems requires changes in school practices. Indeed, it becomes evident that quality teaching is a necessary context and provides the fundamentals for helping address learning and behavior problems.

And it also helps to clarify that those with true LD and ADHD require something more in the way of help.

In this chapter, we explore the factors that make it imperative for school improvement planning to account for the full range of learners who classroom teachers encounter regularly. The framework we use to outline causes emphasizes the importance of understanding fundamental differences in problem causality. Appreciation of such fundamentals provides a foundation for our subsequent discussion of what needs to be done.

MANY PROBLEMS: A RANGE OF LEARNERS

As Jerome Bruner (1966) has stated, "The single most characteristic thing about human beings is that they learn" (p. 13). Best estimates suggest that minimally, 95% of all children can be taught to read. This is not to say that all learning is the result of direct teaching. Indeed, some behavior problems clearly reflect something that was learned even though no one intended to teach it. And high quality teaching encourages learning that goes beyond specific instruction.

Learning and Behavior
Problems: Common Phenomena

Data from the National Center for Educational Statistics (NCES, 2000) indicate that 37% of fourth graders cannot read at a basic level. Best estimates suggest that at least 20% of elementary students in the United States have significant reading problems. Among those from poor families and those with limited English language skills, the percentage shoots up to 60% to 70%.

It surprises no one that certain groups have higher rates of problems or that one such group is composed of individuals living in poverty. For some time, official data have indicated that youngsters under age 18 were the age group with the greatest percentage (16.2%) living in poverty in the United States (U.S. Census Bureau, 2000). It is widely acknowledged that poverty is highly associated with school failure, high school dropout, delinquency, teenage pregnancy, and other problems.

Poverty, of course, is a correlate, not the cause. As Moos (2002) stresses,

We have progressed from a static model in which structural factors, such as poverty level, were linked to indices of community pathology, to a dynamic model of neighborhood processes and experiences, focusing on characteristics such as social integration, value consensus, and community resources and services. (p. 68)

It is important to understand the factors that lead many who grow up in poverty to manifest learning, behavior, and emotional problems. It is equally important to understand what enables those who overcome the negative impact of such conditions.

In comparison to students coming from middle or higher income families, many young children residing in poverty have less opportunity to develop the initial capabilities and attitudes most elementary school programs require for success. Most financially distressed families simply do not have the resources to provide the same preparatory experiences for their children as those who are better off financially. Moreover, many youngsters reside in decaying and violent neighborhoods and experience stress levels that make school adjustment and learning excessively difficult.

It is not surprising, then, that so many youngsters from poor families enter kindergarten and, over the years, come to school each day less than ready to meet the demands made of them. The mismatch may be particularly bad for individuals who have recently migrated from a different culture, do not speak English, or both.

There is a poignant irony in all this. Children of poverty and those from other countries often have developed a range of other cultural, subcultural, and language abilities that middle-class-oriented schools are unprepared to accommodate, never mind capitalize upon. As a result, many of these youngsters struggle to survive without access to their strengths. A high percentage of these youngsters soon are seen as having learning and behavior problems and may end up diagnosed as having learning disabilities, ADHD, and/or other disorders.

Of course, a youngster does not have to live in poverty to be deprived of the opportunity to develop the prerequisite capabilities and attitudes needed to succeed in elementary school programs. There are youngsters who in the preschool years develop a bit slower than their peers. Their learning potential in the long run need not be affected by this fact. However, if early school demands do not accommodate a wide range of differences, the youngsters are vulnerable. When a task demands a level of development they have not achieved, they cannot do it. For example, youngsters who have not yet developed to a level where they can visually discriminate between the letter *b* and *d* or make auditory discriminations between words such as *fan* and *man* are in trouble if the reading curriculum demands that they do so. Months later, when their development catches up to that curriculum demand, the reading program has moved on relentlessly, leaving them farther behind. Given what we know about the normal range of developmental variations, it is no surprise that many of these youngsters end up having problems and become candidates for an LD diagnosis.

By the late 1990s, about 50% of students designated as in need of special education were labeled LD. This translates into 2.8 million children. (The proportion of school-age children so labeled rose from 1.8% in 1976–1977 to

5.2% in 2001.) Reading and behavior problems were probably the largest source of the referrals that led to these students being so designated (Lyon, 2002). In testimony to Congress, federal officials have stressed that "of the children who will eventually drop out of school, over seventy-five percent will report difficulties in learning to read" (Pasternack, 2002, p. 1). The disproportionate number of students diagnosed as LD suggests that many of these youngsters actually are manifesting commonplace reading and related behavior problems.

A Continuum of Learners

Few youngsters start out with internal problems that interfere with learning what schools teach. Moreover, youngsters have protective buffers and areas of ability that help them develop, learn, and cope. One of the mantras of school reformers has been to declare that *all* students can learn. That, of course, is a truism. However, if our aim is to leave no child behind, then the need is to ensure that *all* youngsters have an *equal opportunity to succeed at school.* For this to happen, schools must recognize that they have a range of learners, and they must design learning support systems that really ensure equity of opportunity for the many—not just a few.

We offer the following continuum to highlight the range of learners that are likely to be in every school.

Students who are motivationally ready and able to learn what the teacher has prepared to teach	Students who are not very motivated; lack prerequisite knowledge and skills; have different learning rates and styles; and/or have minor vulnerabilities	Students who are avoidant; very deficient in current academic capabilities; have a disability; and/or have major health problems

A few comments should help clarify what we want to emphasize about this continuum. Every teacher we know would love to have a classroom full of youngsters who show up every day motivationally ready and able to learn what the lesson plan calls for that day. As noted in Chapter 1, in too many classrooms, teachers indicate that large numbers do not fit that category.

Proportions vary—for example, with the socioeconomic status of students' families. The majority of students in classrooms serving the economically disadvantaged fall into the middle group.

Note that the middle group includes the phrase "not very motivated." Be careful how you interpret this. Those who have had the good fortune to work with preschoolers and kindergartners report very few motivational problems. Once most little ones successfully negotiate the transition to a school setting, they manifest a high level of motivation to learn things in that environment. The picture changes dramatically, however, by the end of second grade. At that point, many students no longer display the same level of interest and commitment to classroom learning, and schools experience the first big wave of teacher referrals for learning, behavior, and emotional problems.

Something of considerable significance seems to happen in the first few years of schooling that learning support systems are not addressing well enough. And when problems are not appropriately corrected early after their onset, they tend to worsen. Students fall farther behind with each passing year and behavior and emotional problems become entrenched. As a result, teachers in the ensuing grades are confronted with growing numbers of students who do not have the prerequisite knowledge and skills to perform at grade level.

For example, fifth-grade teachers in too many schools are confronted with a continuum of learners whose reading skills range from virtual non-readers to a few who have reading skills at and maybe above grade level. On top of that, the students vary in terms of the rate at which they learn, the amount they learn in a given time period, the quality with which they perform, and their learning styles. Add to that students who have specific vulnerabilities that make it harder for them to function in the ways the classroom demands. And in underfunded schools, all this takes place in conditions that are far from satisfactory. In such a classroom, how can teachers rely on only the designated fifth-grade curriculum and expect all students to cope effectively?

Finally, the continuum ends with those youngsters who are school avoidant and those who are very behind academically, as well as those with major disabilities and health problems that interfere with learning. These are youngsters who need the most intensive special assistance and the most costly interventions. Service providers often refer to them as "deep end" problems.

Note from mother: Please excuse Jose for being absent from school. He had to go to the beach.

Follow-up call from teacher: Going to the beach instead of to school is unacceptable.

Mother: But it's the end of the month and we ran out of money, so all the kids and I had to go to the beach to collect recyclable aluminum cans to turn in for cash so we can eat and pay the rent.

Chronic truancy is perhaps the ultimate indicator of a strong motivational tendency to avoid school learning. And of course, schools can't teach a youngster who is not present. Moreover, the longer a student has not been engaged meaningfully in classroom learning, the more likely that the youngster has major deficits in academic capabilities and will manifest behavior and emotional problems.

Any school that means to ensure equity of opportunity for all students needs to evaluate what it is doing for youngsters at every point along the continuum. One key criterion for judging any school improvement plan is how well it incorporates ways to address the needs of the full range of learners.

UNDERSTANDING WHAT CAUSES STUDENTS' PROBLEMS IN TRANSACTIONAL TERMS

Accounting effectively for the range of learners requires a broad understanding of the causes of the learning, behavior, and emotional problems.

Many factors shape thinking about human behavior and learning and the problems individuals experience. It helps to begin with a broad transactional view such as currently prevails in theories of human behavior.

Before the 1920s, dominant thinking saw human behavior as determined primarily as a function of person variables, especially inborn characteristics. As behaviorism gained influence, a strong competitive view arose, and a paradigm shift emerged. Behavior was seen as primarily determined and shaped by environmental influences, particularly stimuli and reinforcers.

Times and views have changed. For some time now, the prevailing model for understanding human functioning has favored a transactional view that emphasizes the reciprocal interplay of person and environment. This view is sometimes referred to as *reciprocal determinism* (Bandura, 1978).

What Causes Problems?

Professionals focusing on learning and behavior problems often use models that view the cause of an individual's problems as either existing within the person or coming from the environment. Actually, two person-oriented models have been discussed widely: (1) the disordered or "ill" person medical model and (2) the slow-maturation model. In contrast, those favoring an environmental view have emphasized the notions of inadequate and pathological environments.

Based on these models, the current dominant approach to labeling and addressing human problems tends to create the impression that problems are determined by factors found in *either* the person or the environment. This is both unfortunate and unnecessary—unfortunate because such a view limits progress with respect to addressing problems and unnecessary because a transactional view encompasses the position that problems may be caused by person, environment, or both. This broader paradigm encourages a comprehensive perspective of cause and correction.

It has long seemed strange to us that the contemporary and prevailing view of learning and development reflects the transactional paradigm, while the view of problems remains dominated by person or environment models. We are not suggesting that these latter views always lead to wrong conclusions. Some individuals' problems certainly are due primarily to something wrong within them, and other people do have problems because of factors they encounter in their environment. But what about those whose problems stem from both sources?

It might seem reasonable to continue to use the person-based and environment-based models and *add* the transactional view, using it to cover those cases where problems stem from both person and environment. However, this is an unnecessarily fractured approach. *A transactional view actually encompasses the other models and provides the kind of comprehensive perspective needed to differentiate among learning and behavior problems.*

A transactional view acknowledges that there are cases in which an individual's disabilities predispose him or her to problems even in highly accommodating settings. At the same time, however, such a view accounts for instances in which the environment is so inadequate or hostile that individuals have problems despite having no disability. Finally, it recognizes problems caused by a combination of factors associated with the person and the environment. The value of a broad transactional perspective, then, is that it shifts the focus from asking whether there is a biological deficit causing the problem to asking whether the causes are to be found in one of the following as *primary* instigating factors:

- *The individual* (e.g., a neurological dysfunction; cognitive skill and/or strategy deficits; developmental and/or motivational differences)
- *The environment* (e.g., the primary environment, such as poor instructional programs or parental neglect; the secondary environment, such as racially isolated schools and neighborhoods; or the tertiary environment, such as broad social, economic, political, and cultural influences)
- The reciprocal *interplay of individual and environment*

To make all this less academic, let's apply a transactional view to a learning situation. In implementing a lesson, the teacher will find that some students learn easily and some do not. Even a good student may appear distracted on a given day.

Why the Differences?

A commonsense answer suggests that each student brings something different to the situation and therefore experiences it differently. That's a pretty good answer—as far as it goes. What gets lost in this simple explanation is the essence of the impact that student and situation have on each other, resulting in continuous change in both.

To amplify the point, for purposes of the present discussion, any student can be viewed as bringing to each situation *capacities, attitudes, and behaviors accumulated over time,* as well as *current states of being and behaving.* These "person" variables transact with each other and also with the environment.

At the same time, the situation in which students are expected to function consists not only of *instructional processes and content* but also the *physical and social context* in which instruction takes place. Each part of the environment also transacts with the others.

Obviously, the transactions can vary considerably and can lead to a variety of positive and/or negative outcomes. In general, the types of outcomes can be described as

- *Deviant functioning.* Capacities, attitudes, and behaviors change and expand but not in desirable ways.
- *Disrupted functioning.* There is interference with learning and performance, an increase in dysfunctional behaving, and possibly a decrease in capacities.
- *Delayed and arrested learning.* There is little change in capacities.
- *Enhancement of learning and positive behavior.* Capacities, attitudes, and behavior change and expand in desirable ways.

> Of course, there are limits to what different people are capable of achieving, but we should make no uninformed assumptions about what these limits are.
>
> —Harold Stevenson and
> James Stigler (1992, p. 223)

The Problem of Labeling Problems

The need to differentiate factors causing students to have problems leads to concerns about how to label different problems. This brings into play classification schemes, such as the ones used in special education and psychiatry. These sets of labels are used in differentially diagnosing individuals, and once a diagnostic label is assigned, the assumption is that an internal disorder has caused the problem. Too often, this conclusion is incorrect. Even when best practices are used, valid differential diagnosis is difficult and fraught with complex issues.[1] Added to these concerns is the pernicious tendency among the general public to use diagnostic labels in an offhand manner. For example, it is common to hear someone with a learning problem described as having learning *disabilities* and youngsters who are misbehaving referred to as having ADHD.

Strong images are associated with diagnostic labels, and people act upon these notions. Sometimes the images are useful generalizations, but often they are harmful stereotypes. Sometimes they guide practitioners toward good ways to help. But often they contribute to "blaming the victim," by making young people the focus of intervention rather than pursuing system deficiencies that are causing the problem. In all cases, diagnostic labels can profoundly shape a person's future.

For these and other reasons, there has been considerable criticism of some diagnostic labels, especially those applied to young children.

Nevertheless, there are sound reasons for wanting to differentially label problems. One reason is that, properly identified, some can be prevented; another is that proper identification can enhance correction.

However, the labeling process remains difficult. Severity has been the most common factor used to distinguish LD and ADHD from the many commonplace learning and behavior problems that permeate schools. Besides severity, there has been concern about how pervasive a problem is (e.g., how far behind an individual lags in academic and social skills). Specific criteria for judging severity and pervasiveness depend on prevailing age, gender, subculture, and social status expectations. Also important is how long the problem has persisted.

Because the number of misdiagnoses has increased dramatically over the past 20 years, greater attention is being paid to using *response to intervention* as a precursor and aid in differentiating commonplace problems from individual pathology. The core difficulty here is how to mobilize unmotivated students to function in ways that allow for a valid assessment of whether or not they have a true disability or disorder.

A Continuum of Problems

No simple typology can do justice to the complexities involved in classifying students' problems. In most cases, it is impossible to be certain what the cause of a specific individual's learning or behavior problem might be. Nevertheless, from a theoretical viewpoint, it makes sense to think of such problems as caused by different factors. And of course, a similar case can be made for a range of mental health and psychosocial concerns related to children and adolescents (Adelman, 1995; Adelman & Taylor, 1994). From this perspective, even a simple framework based on a transactional view can be helpful.

The following conceptual example illustrates how a broad framework can offer a useful *starting* place for classifying behavioral, emotional, and learning problems in ways that avoid overdiagnosing internal pathology. As indicated in Guide 2.1, such problems can be differentiated along a continuum that separates those caused by internal factors, environmental variables, or a combination of both.

Problems caused by the environment are placed at one end of the continuum and referred to as Type I problems. At the other end are problems caused primarily by pathology within the person; these are designated as Type III problems. In the middle are problems stemming from a relatively equal contribution from the environment and a person, labeled Type II problems.

In this scheme, diagnostic labels meant to identify *extremely* dysfunctional problems *caused by pathological conditions within a person* are reserved

Guide 2.1 A Continuum of Problems Based on a Broad Understanding of Cause

Problems primarily caused by factors in the environment (E)	Problems caused equally by environment and person	Problems primarily caused by factors in the person (P)
E (E ↔ p)	(E ↔ P)	(e ↔ P) P

Type I Problems	Type II Problems	Type III Problems (e.g., LD, ADHD, other disorders)
• Caused primarily by environments and systems that are deficient and/or hostile	• Caused primarily by a significant *mismatch* between individual differences and vulnerabilities and the nature of that person's environment (not by a person's pathology)	• Caused primarily by factors of a pathological nature located within the person
• Problems are mild to moderately severe and narrow to moderately pervasive.	• Problems are mild to moderately severe and pervasive.	• Problems are moderate to profoundly severe and moderate to broadly pervasive.

NOTE: Using a transactional view, the continuum emphasizes the *primary source* of the problem and, in each case, is concerned with problems that persist beyond the early stage of onset.

for individuals who fit the Type III category. Obviously, some problems caused by pathological conditions within a person are not manifested in severe, pervasive ways, and there are persons without such pathology whose problems do become severe and pervasive. The intent is not to ignore these individuals. As a first categorization step, however, it is essential that they not be confused with those seen as having Type III problems.

At the other end of the continuum are individuals with problems arising from factors outside themselves (i.e., Type I problems). Many people grow up in impoverished and hostile environmental circumstances. Such conditions should be considered first in hypothesizing what *initially* caused an individual's behavioral, emotional, and learning problems. After environmental causes are ruled out, hypotheses about internal pathology become more viable.

To provide a reference point in the middle of the continuum, a Type II category is used. This group consists of persons who do not function well in situations where their individual differences and minor vulnerabilities are poorly accommodated or are responded to hostilely. The problems of a person in this group are a product of individual characteristics and the failure of the environment to accommodate that individual, in relatively equal proportions.

There are, of course, variations along the continuum that do not precisely fit any of the three categories. At each point between the extreme ends, environment-person transactions are the cause, but the degree to which each contributes to the problem varies.

Clearly, a simple continuum cannot do justice to the complexities associated with labeling and differentiating problems. Furthermore, some problems are not easily assessed or do not fall readily into a group due to data limitations and individuals who have more than one problem (i.e., comorbidity). However, the foregoing scheme shows the value of starting with a broad model of cause. In particular, it helps counter the tendency to jump prematurely to the conclusion that a problem is caused by deficiencies or pathology within the individual and thus can help combat tendencies toward blaming the victim (Ryan, 1971). It also helps highlight the notion that improving the way the environment accommodates individual differences often may be a sufficient intervention strategy.

The Continuum and School
Learning and Behavior Problems

When students have trouble learning at school, they frequently manifest behavior problems. This is a common reaction to learning problems. And of course, behavior problems can get in the way of learning. Furthermore, both sets of problems may appear simultaneously and stem from the same or separate causes. It is important to remember that an individual can have more than one problem. That is, a student may manifest high levels of activity, lack of attention, and problems learning in class. This sometimes leads to a dual diagnosis of LD and ADHD.

A list of specific instigating factors that can cause learning and behavior problems based on a transactional view would fill the rest of this book. Guide 2.2 is offered as an alternative.

Given the foregoing, it is not surprising that it is difficult to differentiate commonplace learning, behavior, and emotional problems from disabilities and disorders. Yet it is essential to make every effort to do so. In using the Type I, II, and III continuum, only Type III problems should be considered in applying diagnostic terms, such as LD and ADHD (i.e., problems caused by factors within the person). The rest are common learning and behavior problems—some of which will have been caused by environmental factors and some will be the result of the interplay between minor student vulnerabilities and an unaccommodating learning situation.

Guide 2.2   Factors Instigating Learning, Behavior, and Emotional
Problems

Environment (E): Type I Problems

1. *Insufficient stimuli* (e.g., prolonged periods in impoverished environments; deprivation of learning opportunities at home or school, such as lack of play and practice situations and poor instruction; inadequate diet)

2. *Excessive stimuli* (e.g., overly demanding home, school, or work experiences, such as overwhelming pressure to achieve and contradictory expectations; overcrowding)

3. *Intrusive and hostile stimuli* (e.g., medical practices, especially at birth, leading to physiological impairment; contaminated environments; conflict in home, school, workplace; faulty child-rearing practices, such as long-standing abuse and rejection; dysfunctional family; migratory family; stress related to accommodating English language; social prejudices related to race, sex, age, physical characteristics, and behavior)

Person (P): Type III Problems

1. *Physiological insult* (e.g., cerebral trauma, such as accident or stroke, endocrine dysfunctions, and chemical imbalances; illness affecting brain or sensory functioning)

2. *Genetic anomaly* (e.g., genes which limit, slow down, or lead to any atypical development)

3. *Cognitive activity and affective states experienced by self as deviant* (e.g., lack of knowledge or skills such as basic cognitive strategies; lack of ability to cope effectively with emotions, such as low self-esteem)

4. *Physical characteristics shaping contact with environment and/or experienced by self as deviant* (e.g., visual, auditory, or motor deficits; excessive or reduced sensitivity to stimuli; easily fatigued; factors such as race, sex, age, or unusual appearance that produce stereotypical responses)

5. *Deviant actions of the individual* (e.g., performance problems, such as excessive performance errors; high or low levels of activity)

Interactions and Transactions Between E and P: Type II Problems*

1. *Severe to moderate personal vulnerabilities and environmental defects and differences* (e.g., person with extremely slow development in a highly demanding environment, all of which simultaneously and equally instigate the problem)

2. *Minor personal vulnerabilities not accommodated by the situation* (e.g., person with minimal CNS disorders resulting in auditory perceptual disability trying to do auditorily loaded tasks; very active person forced into situations at home, school, or work that do not tolerate this level of activity)

3. *Minor environmental defects and differences not accommodated by the individual* (e.g., person in the minority racially or culturally and not participating in many social activities because he or she thinks others may be unreceptive)

---

*May involve only one (P) and one (E) variable or may involve multiple combinations.

> Many well-known adolescent difficulties are not intrinsic to the teenage years but are related to the mismatch between adolescents' developmental needs and the kinds of experiences most junior high and high schools provide.
>
> —Linda Darling-Hammond
> (1997, p. 122)

Why Worry About Cause?

Not all professionals are concerned about what originally instigated a learning, behavior, or emotional problem. Many practitioners have adopted the view that initial causes (primary instigating factors) usually cannot be assessed, and even if they could, little can be done about the cause once the problem exists. Such practitioners tend to see appropriate corrective procedures as focused on (a) helping the individual acquire skills and strategies that should have been learned previously and on (b) eliminating factors that *currently* are contributing to problems. Thus they see little point in looking for initial causes.

In stressing the tendency of some practitioners to put aside the matter of the initial causes of learning and behavior problems, we do not mean to imply that their thinking ignores the causes of human behavior. All interveners are concerned about *current* factors (e.g., secondary instigating factors) that interfere with effective learning and performance. For example, a student may be a rather passive learner at school (e.g., not paying adequate attention) because of physical and emotional stress caused by inappropriate child-rearing practices, illness, poor nutrition, and so forth. Obviously, few will disagree that such factors should be assessed and corrected whenever feasible. Any of the factors indicated in Guide 2.2 may be secondary instigating factors that negatively affect current functioning.

Appropriate and effective application of learning supports depends on where students fit on the continuum. At this time, sophisticated responses to intervention strategies that address the problems of engaging and reengaging students in learning offer the greatest promise for such differentiation.

BARRIERS TO LEARNING AND RISK FACTORS

Sometimes when we use terms such as *barriers to learning* and *risk factors*, someone will worry that we are perpetuating the old "deficit" view that was so hurtful to some groups of students. They are worried about teachers and others having low expectations for what a student can do. They are worried about self-fulfilling prophecies and blaming the victim. We also worry about those things.

But we also worry about throwing the baby out with the bath water. As noted earlier, for a great many students, *external*, not *internal*, factors are the causal agents. That is, for the many students experiencing Type I and II problems, the barriers that must be addressed first and foremost are related to factors in their environments, and many of these factors reflect societal deficits.

If all students came ready and able to profit from "high standards" curricula, then there would be little to worry about. But *all* encompasses those who are experiencing external and/or internal barriers that interfere with benefiting from what the teacher is offering. Thus, providing all students an equal opportunity to succeed requires more than higher standards and greater accountability for instruction, better teaching, increased discipline, and an end to social promotion. It also requires addressing barriers to development, learning, and teaching. The intent of ensuring that *all* students succeed at school can only be achieved by actively addressing the full range of barriers and risk factors currently causing so many children to be left behind (see Guide 2.3).

The terrible fact is that too many youngsters are growing up and going to school in situations that not only fail to promote healthy development but are antithetical to the process. Some also bring with them intrinsic conditions that make learning and performing difficult. At one time or another, most students bring problems with them to school that affect their learning and perhaps interfere with the teacher's efforts to teach. As a result, some youngsters at every grade level come to school unready to effectively meet the setting's demands. As long as school reforms fail to address such barriers in comprehensive and multifaceted ways, especially in schools where large proportions of students are not doing well, it is unlikely that achievement test score averages can be meaningfully raised.

In some geographic areas, many youngsters bring a wide range of problems stemming from restricted opportunities associated with poverty and low income, difficult and diverse family circumstances, high rates of mobility, lack of English language skills, violent neighborhoods, problems related to substance abuse, inade-

At the most fundamental level, the answer to *Why worry about cause?* is best understood with reference to the term *etiology*. Etiology refers to the study of cause. From a scientific perspective, the study of cause needs no justification. From a learning supports viewpoint, etiological findings can be the key to prevention and in some cases are the best guide to appropriate corrective strategies and provide a useful perspective in avoiding misprescriptions.

Again, LD and ADHD provide useful illustrations. Partly because current assessment practices are so limited, there has been widespread failure to differentiate LD and ADHD from other types of learning and behavior problems, particularly with respect to cause. Failure to differentiate learning and behavior problems in terms of cause contributes to widespread misdiagnosis and unneeded specialized treatments (i.e., individuals without disabilities treated as if they were disabled). A result of this is that most programs designated for LD and ADHD have included individuals ranging from those whose problems were caused primarily by environmental deficiencies to those whose problems stem from internal disabilities. All this has contributed to profound misunderstanding of what interventions do and do not have unique promise for learning disabilities and ADHD. More generally, the scope of misdiagnoses and misprescriptions in these fields has undermined prevention, correction, research, and training and the policy decisions shaping such activities.

See Chapter 11 for more on the topic of understanding and labeling student problems.

quate health care, and lack of enrichment opportunities. Such problems are exacerbated as youngsters internalize the frustrations of confronting barriers and the debilitating effects of performing poorly at school. In some locales, the reality often is that more than 50% of students manifest forms of learning, behavior, and emotional problems. And in most schools in these locales, teachers are ill-prepared to address the problems in a potent manner.

Guide 2.3   Barriers to Development and Learning

Based on a review of more than 30 years of research, Hawkins and Catalano (1992) identify common risk factors that reliably predict such problems as youth delinquency, violence, substance abuse, teen pregnancy, and school dropout. These factors also are associated with such mental health concerns as school adjustment problems, relationship difficulties, physical and sexual abuse, neglect, and severe emotional disturbance. The majority of the factors identified by Hawkins and Catalano are external barriers to healthy development and learning. Such factors are not excuses for anyone not doing their best; they are, however, rather obvious impediments and ones to which no good parent would willingly submit his or her child. Our effort to synthesize various analyses of external and internal barriers follows.

External Factors*

Community

- Availability of drugs
- Availability of firearms
- Community laws and norms favorable to drug use, firearms, and crime
- Media portrayals of violence
- Transitions and mobility
- Low neighborhood attachment and community disorganization
- Extreme economic deprivation

Family

- Family history of the problem behavior
- Family management problems
- Family conflict
- Favorable parental attitudes and involvement in the problem behavior

School

- Academic failure beginning in late elementary school

Peers

- Friends who engage in the problem behavior
- Favorable attitudes toward the problem behavior

Internal Factors (Biological and Psychological)

- *Differences* (e.g., being farther along toward one end or the other of a normal developmental curve; not fitting local norms in terms of looks and behavior)
- *Vulnerabilities* (e.g., minor health, vision, or hearing problems and other deficiencies/deficits that result in school absences and other needs for special accommodations; being the focus of racial, ethnic, or gender bias; economical disadvantage; youngster or parent lacking interest in youngster's schooling, alienation, or rebelliousness; early manifestation of severe and pervasive problem/antisocial behavior)
- *Disabilities* (e.g., true learning, behavior, and emotional disorders)

---

*Other examples of external factors include exposure to crisis events in the community, home, and school; lack of availability and access to good school readiness programs; lack of home involvement in schooling; lack of peer support, positive role models, and mentoring; lack of access and availability of good recreational opportunities; lack of access and availability to good community housing, health and social services, transportation, law enforcement, sanitation; lack of access and availability to good school support programs; scarcity of high quality schools.

Schools tend to address barriers to learning as a last resort. This is not surprising since their assigned mission is to educate, and school staff are under increasing pressure both to quickly raise test scores and avoid discussing anything that sounds like excuses for not doing so. The irony, of course, is that most school staff are painfully aware of barriers that must be addressed. Moreover, the widespread emphasis on high stakes testing underscores not only how many students are not performing well but also the degree to which such testing adds another barrier that keeps some students from having an equal opportunity to succeed at school.

All this leads to concerns about what the role of schools is and should be in handling many barriers. Critics point out that the tendency is for schools to deal with risk factors only in a reactive way—waiting until problems become rather severe and pervasive. Moreover, because schools have been accused of having a *deficit orientation* toward many youngsters, they often have steered clear of terms denoting risks, barriers, and remediation.

It is well that schools realize that a focus solely on fixing problems is too limited and may be counterproductive. Overemphasis on remediation can diminish efforts to promote healthy development, limit opportunity, and be motivationally debilitating to all involved.

At the same time, it is essential not to lose sight of the research findings indicating that the primary causes for most youngsters' learning, behavior, and emotional problems are external factors (related to neighborhood, family, school, and/or peers). Problems stem from individual disorders and differences for only a few. An appreciation of the research on the role played by external and internal factors makes a focus on such matters a major part of any comprehensive, multifaceted approach for addressing barriers to learning, development, and teaching. (See additional examples highlighted in Guide 2.4.)

PROTECTIVE BUFFERS AND PROMOTING FULL DEVELOPMENT

One important outcome of the reaction to overemphasizing risks and problems is that increasing attention is being given to strengths, assets, resilience, and protective factors. Protective factors are conditions that *buffer* against the impact of barriers. Such conditions may prevent or counter risk-producing conditions by promoting development of neighborhood, family, school, peer, and individual strengths, assets, and coping mechanisms through special assistance and accommodations. The term *resilience* usually refers to an individual's ability to cope in ways that buffer negative conditions. Research on protective buffers also guides efforts to address barriers. Guide 2.5 provides examples.

It is essential, however, to remember that focusing just on enhancing assets is insufficient. As Scales and Leffert (1999) indicate in their work on developmental assets,

Guide 2.4   Examples of Risk-producing Conditions That Can Be Barriers to Development and Learning

Environmental Conditions*			Person-based Factors*
Neighborhood	Family	School and Peers	Individual
• Extreme economic deprivation • Community disorganization, including high levels of mobility • Violence, drugs, etc. • Minority and/or immigrant status	• Chronic poverty • Conflict/ disruptions/ violence • Substance abuse • Problem behavior modeled • Abusive caretaking • Inadequate provision for quality child care	• Poor quality school • Negative encounters with teachers • Negative encounters with peers and/or inappropriate peer models	• Medical problems • Low birth weight/ neurodevelopmental delay • Psychophysiological problems • Difficult temperament and adjustment problems • Inadequate nutrition

*A reciprocal determinist view of behavior recognizes the interplay of environment and person.

Young people also need adequate food, shelter, clothing, caregivers who at the minimum are not abusive or neglectful, families with adequate incomes, schools where both children and teachers feel safe, and economically and culturally vibrant neighborhoods—not ones beset with drugs, violent crime, and infrastructural decay. For example, young people who are disadvantaged by living in poor neighborhoods are consistently more likely to engage in risky behavior at higher rates than their affluent peers, and they show consistently lower rates of positive outcomes (Brooks-Gunn & Duncan, 1997). Moreover, young people who live in abusive homes or in neighborhoods with high levels of violence are more likely to become both victims and perpetrators of violence (Garbarino, 1995). (p. 10)

Finally, as often is stressed, being problem-free is not the same as promoting positive development. Efforts to reduce risks and enhance protection can help minimize problems but are insufficient for fostering full development, well-being, and a value-based life. Those concerned with establishing systems for promoting healthy development recognize the need for direct efforts to facilitate development and empowerment,

Guide 2.5   Examples of Protective Buffers

Conditions that prevent or counter risk-producing conditions—strengths, assets, corrective interventions, coping mechanisms, special assistance, and accommodations:

Environmental Conditions*			Person-based Factors*
Neighborhood	Family	School and Peers	Individual
• Strong economic conditions/ emerging economic opportunities • Safe and stable communities • Available and accessible services • Strong bond with positive other(s) • Appropriate expectations and standards • Opportunities to successfully participate, contribute, and be recognized	• Adequate financial resources • Nurturing, supportive family members who are positive models • Safe and stable (organized and predictable) home environment • Family literacy • Provision of high quality child care • Secure attachments, early and ongoing	• Success at school • Safe, caring, supportive, and healthy school environment • Positive relationships with one or more teachers • Positive relationships with peers and appropriate peer models • Strong bonds with positive other(s)	• Higher cognitive functioning • Psychophysiological health • Easygoing temperament, outgoing personality, and positive behavior • Strong abilities for involvement and problem solving • Sense of purpose and future • Gender considerations (girls less apt to develop certain problems)

*A reciprocal determinist view of behavior recognizes the interplay of environment and person.

including the mobilization of individuals for self-direction. In many cases, interventions to create buffers and foster full development are identical, and the payoff is the cultivation of developmental strengths and assets. However, promoting healthy development is not limited to countering risks and engendering protective factors. Efforts to promote full development represent ends that are valued in and of themselves and to which most of us aspire. Examples are presented in Guide 2.6.

In sum, there are considerable bodies of research and theory that provide guidance for designing a system to address barriers to learning and teaching (Adelman & Taylor, 1994; Deci & Ryan, 1985; Huffman, Mehlinger, & Kerivan, 2000; Strader, Collins, & Noe, 2000). As the examples in Guides

Guide 2.6 Examples of Conditions for Promoting Full Development

Conditions, over and beyond those that create protective buffers, that enhance healthy development, well-being, and a value-based life:

Environmental Conditions*			Person-based Factors*
Neighborhood	Family	School and Peers	Individual
• Nurturing and supportive conditions • Policy and practice promoting healthy development and sense of community	• Conditions that foster positive physical and mental health among all family members	• Nurturing and supportive climate schoolwide and in classrooms • Conditions that foster feelings of competence, self-determination, and connectedness	• Opportunities to pursue personal development and empowerment • Intrinsic motivation to pursue full development, well-being, and a value-based life

*A reciprocal determinist view of behavior recognizes the interplay of environment and person.

2.5 and 2.6 illustrate, some risk factors and protective buffers are mirror images; others are distinct, and many protective buffers are natural by-products of efforts to engender full development. From this perspective, interventions to address barriers to learning and development and those to promote learning and healthy development complement each other.

CONCLUDING COMMENTS

As Nicholas Hobbs (1975) stresses, "Society defines what is exceptional or deviant, and appropriate treatments are designed quite as much to protect society as they are to help the child. . . . 'To take care of them' can and should be read with two meanings: to give children help and to exclude them from the community" (pp. 20–21).

Schools are a social invention. All societies design schools in the service of social, cultural, political, and economic aims. Society shapes the content and context of all that goes on in schools. Guidelines for defining and differentiating among students' problems, for planning what is done with students, and for evaluating results—all are established through political processes. Choices are made and controversies arise around when to educate and when to train, when to help and when to socialize, when to be democratic and when to be autocratic. There should be no choice, however, about whether to *enable* all students to learn and succeed at school.

The role of leaders is not only to understand society's current agenda and what it has produced but also to move the agenda in ways that truly ensure that everyone is accounted for as schools strive to achieve their mission. It is only through effectively addressing barriers to learning and promoting full development (including engendering protective factors) that we can hope to stem the tide of students who are not succeeding at school and who are leaving in droves. As we stress in Chapter 3, this means going beyond the limited agenda of today and leading the way toward establishment of comprehensive, multifaceted learning support systems in every school.

No more prizes
for predicting rain . . .

Prizes only
for building arks!

NOTE

1. Special education classification labels for learning, behavior, and emotional problems are notorious for having poor validity for differential diagnosis. An example of a formal classification scheme for differentiating pathology from commonplace problems is seen in the classification scheme developed by the American Academy of Pediatrics. In that system, behaviors are described in terms of normal variations or as common problems that do not warrant diagnosis as disorders (see Wolraich, Felice, & Drotar, 1996). The need for a comprehensive perspective in labeling problems also is illustrated by efforts to develop multifaceted classification systems, such as the multiaxial system used in the *Diagnostic and Statistical Manual of Mental Disorders* (DSM-IV TR) (American Psychiatric Association, 2000). This system represents the dominant approach used throughout the United States, and it illustrates the problem of making differential diagnoses using a nontransactional approach. It does include a dimension acknowledging "psychosocial stressors"; however, this dimension is used mostly to deal with the environment as a contributing factor rather than as a primary cause. As a result, individuals are classified primarily in terms of whether their symptoms reach criteria to qualify for one (or more) personal disorder categories. The result has been a person-based pathology bias that minimizes the role played by environmental factors as primary causes of many behavior, emotional, and learning problems.

REFERENCES

Adelman, H. S. (1995). Clinical psychology: Beyond psychopathology and clinical interventions. *Clinical Psychology: Science and Practice, 2,* 28–44.

Adelman, H. S., & Taylor, L. (1994). *On understanding intervention in psychology and education.* Westport, CT: Praeger.

American Psychiatric Association. (2000). *Diagnostic and statistical manual of mental disorders (DSM-IV TR).* Washington, DC: Author.

Bandura, A. (1978). The self system in reciprocal determinism. *American Psychologist, 33,* 344–358.

Brooks-Gunn, J., & Duncan, G. J. (1997). The effects of poverty on children. *The Future of Children, 7,* 55–71.

Bruner, J. S. (1966). *Toward a theory of instruction.* Cambridge, MA: Belknap.

Charcot, J.-M. (1857). De l'expectoration en medecine. Charcot-Leyden crystals. Retrieved March 12, 2005, from www.whonamedit.com.

Darling-Hammond, L. (1997). *The right to learn: A blueprint for creating schools that work.* San Francisco: Jossey-Bass.

Deci, E., & Ryan, R. (1985). *Intrinsic motivation and self-determination in human behavior.* New York: Plenum.

Garbarino, J. (1995). *Raising children in a socially toxic environment.* San Francisco: Jossey-Bass.

Hawkins, J. D., & Catalano, R. F. (1992). *Communities that care.* San Francisco: Jossey-Bass.

Hobbs, N. (1975). *The futures of children.* San Francisco: Jossey-Bass.

Huffman, L., Mehlinger, S., & Kerivan, A. (2000). *Research on the risk factors for early school problems and selected federal policies affecting children's social and emotional development and their readiness for school.* The Child and Mental Health Foundation and Agencies Network. Retrieved March 12, 2005, from http://www.nimh.nih.gov.

Kohn, A. (1999). Constant frustration and occasional violence: The legacy of American high schools. *American School Board Journal.* Retrieved March 12, 2005, from www.asbj.com/security/contents/0999kohn.html.

Lyon, G. R. (2002). *Testimony before the U.S. Senate Subcommittee for Educational Reform.* Retrieved March 12, 2005, from http://www.nih.gov.

Moos, R. H. (2002). The mystery of human context and coping: An unraveling of clues. *American Journal of Community Psychology, 30,* 67–88.

National Center for Educational Statistics. (2000). *The digest of educational statistics.* Washington, DC: Institute of Education Sciences, U.S. Department of Education. Retrieved March 12, 2005, from www.nces.ed.gov/programs/digest.

Pasternack, R. (2002). *Testimony before the U.S. Senate Subcommittee for Educational Reform by the Assistant Secretary for Special Education and Rehabilitative Services in the U.S. Dept. of Education.* Retrieved March 12, 2005, from www.ed.gov/Speeches/04–2002/20020425a.

Ryan, W. (1971). *Blaming the victim.* New York: Random House.

Scales P. C., & Leffert, N. (1999). *Developmental assets.* Minneapolis, MN: Search Institute.

Stevenson, H. W., & Stigler, J. W. (1992). *The learning gap: Why our schools are failing and what we can learn from Japanese and Chinese education.* New York: Summit.

Strader, T. N., Collins, D. A., & Noe, T. D. (2000). *Building healthy individuals, families, and communities: Creating lasting connections.* New York: Kluwer Academic/ Plenum.

U.S. Census Bureau. (2000). *Households and families: Census 2000 brief.* Washington, DC: U.S. Department of Commerce. Retrieved March 12, 2005, from www.census.gov.

Wolraich, M. L., Felice, M. E., & Drotar, D. (Eds.). (1996). *The classification of child and adolescent mental diagnosis in primary care: Diagnostic and statistical manual for primary care (DSM-PC; child and adolescent version).* Elk Grove Village, IL: American Academy of Pediatrics.

Complex Problems, Limited Solutions **3**

It is either naive or irresponsible to ignore the connection between children's performance in school and their experiences with malnutrition, homelessness, lack of medical care, inadequate housing, racial and cultural discrimination, and other burdens.

—Harold Howe II

What's easy to get into
but hard to get out of?   Trouble!

ORIENTING QUESTIONS

? What constitutes a full continuum of interventions in providing learning supports?
? Why don't most schools have a comprehensive learning supports component?
? What type of policy shift is needed to promote the development of a comprehensive approach to providing learning supports in schools?

Teachers and student support staff know that a student who has a learning problem is likely to have behavior problems and vice versa. Moreover, students with learning and behavior problems tend to develop an overlay of emotional problems. And of course, emotional problems can lead to and exacerbate behavior and/or learning problems. Schools find that students who are abusing drugs often also have poor grades, are truant, are at risk of dropping out, and more. The term *co-morbidity* is used to account for the fact that individuals frequently have several problems at the same time; clinicians use this term to indicate that an individual has more than one diagnosable problem. All this underscores the reality that the problems students bring to school tend to be multifaceted and complex.

In many schools, when students are not doing well, the trend is to refer them directly for assessment in hopes of referral for special assistance, perhaps even assignment to special education. In some schools and classrooms, the numbers of referrals are dramatic. Where special teams exist to review students for whom teachers request help, the list grows as the year proceeds. The longer the list, the longer the lag time for review—often to the point that by the end of the school year, the team has reviewed just a small percentage of those referred. *And no matter how many are reviewed, there are always more referrals than can be served.* In many schools, the numbers of students experiencing problems are staggering.

So how do schools respond? As we have discussed, school interventions to address student problems usually are developed and function in relative isolation from each other. Organizationally, the tendency is for policymakers to mandate and planners and developers to focus on specific programs. Functionally, most practitioners spend their time working directly with specific interventions and targeted problems and give little thought or time to developing comprehensive and cohesive approaches. Furthermore, the need to label students in order to obtain special, categorical funding often skews practices toward narrow and unintegrated intervention approaches. One result is that a student identified as having multiple problems may be involved in programs with several professionals working independently of each other. Similarly, a youngster identified and helped in preschool or elementary school who later still requires special support may cease to receive appropriate help upon entering kindergarten or middle school. Pursuit of grant money often further diverts attention from one concern to another. And so forth.

What should be clear, then, is that the problems addressed are complex and multifaceted and the response is piecemeal. The result is fragmented intervention that does not and cannot meet the needs in any school where large numbers of students are experiencing problems.

The solution is not to be found in efforts to convince policymakers to fund more special programs and services at schools. Even if the policy climate favored more special programs, such interventions alone are insufficient. More services to treat problems certainly are needed. But so are programs for prevention and for early-after-problem onset that can reduce the number of students teachers send to review teams. It is time to face the fact that *multifaceted problems usually require comprehensive, integrated solutions applied concurrently and over time.*

HOW CLOSE ARE WE TO HAVING A COMPREHENSIVE APPROACH?

We use the framework presented in Guide 3.1 and the outline in Guide 3.2 to analyze what a school and community already have and where the gaps are. We emphasize both school and community because developing a comprehensive approach takes the efforts of both working together with a shared commitment to establish a *comprehensive, multifaceted,* and *cohesive* approach.

Frameworks for Mapping and Analysis

The continuum in Guide 3.1 is conceived in terms of three overlapping *systems:*

- Systems for positive development and prevention of problems
- Systems of early intervention to address problems as soon after their onset as feasible
- Systems of care for those with chronic and severe problems

Anticipating the discussion later in this chapter, we note that to date, society's policymakers have not committed to establishing such a continuum of interconnected systems.

As can be seen, the array of programmatic examples in Guide 3.2 amplifies the nature and scope of the continuum. It illustrates (a) public health

Guide 3.1 Interconnected Systems for Meeting the Needs of
All Children

- Providing a *Continuum of School-Community Programs and Services*
- Ensuring Use of the *Least Intervention Needed*

School Resources
(facilities, stakeholders,
programs, services)

Community Resources
(facilities, stakeholders,
programs, services)

Examples:

Examples:

*Systems for Promoting
Healthy Development &
Preventing Problems*
Primary prevention–includes
universal interventions
(low end need/low cost
per individual programs)

- General health education
- Drug and alcohol education
- Enrichment programs
- Support for transitions
- Conflict resolution
- Home involvement

- Public health & safety
  programs
- Prenatal care
- Immunizations
- Preschool programs
- Recreation & enrichment
- Child abuse education

Systems of Early Intervention
Early-after-onset–includes
selective & indicated interventions
(moderate need, moderate
cost per individual)

- Drug counseling
- Pregnancy prevention
- Violence prevention
- Dropout prevention
- Suicide prevention
- Learning/behavior
  accomodations and
  response to intervention
- Work programs

- Early identification to treat
  health problems
- Monitoring health problems
- Short-term counseling
- Foster placement/group
  homes
- Family support
- Shelter, food, clothing
- Job programs

Systems of Care
Treatment/indicated
interventions for severe and
chronic problems
(high end need/high cost
per individual programs)

- Special education for
  learning disabilities,
  emotional disturbance,
  and other health
  impairments

- Emergency/crisis treatment
- Family preservation
- Long-term therapy
- Probation/incarceration
- Disabilities programs
- Hospitalization
- Drug treatment

Systemic collaboration* is essential to establish interprogram connections on a daily basis and over time
to ensure seamless intervention within each system and among *systems of prevention, systems of
early intervention*, and *systems of care*.

*Such collaboration involves horizontal and vertical restructuring of programs and services (a) within
jurisdictions, school districts, and community agencies (e.g., among departments, divisions, units, schools,
clusters of schools) or (b) between jurisdictions, school and community agencies, public and private sectors;
among schools; among community agencies.

protection, promotion, and maintenance that foster positive development
and wellness, (b) pre-school-age support and assistance to enhance health
and psychosocial development, (c) interventions targeted for early schooling, (d) improvement and augmentation of ongoing regular support, (e)
other interventions prior to referral for intensive and ongoing targeted
treatments, and (f) intensive treatments.

It should be noted that we conceive the continuum framed in Guides
3.1 and 3.2 as encompassing a holistic and developmental emphasis. The
focus is on individuals, families, and the contexts in which they live, learn,

Guide 3.2   From Primary Prevention to Treatment of Serious Problems: A
Continuum of Community-School Programs to Address Barriers to
Learning and Enhance Healthy Development

Intervention Continuum	*Examples of Focus and Types of Intervention* (Programs and services aimed at system changes and individual needs)
Systems for health promotion and primary prevention	1. *Public health protection, promotion, and maintenance to foster opportunities, positive development, and wellness* • Economic enhancement of those living in poverty (e.g., work/welfare programs) • Safety (e.g., instruction, regulations, lead abatement programs) • Physical and mental health (including healthy start initiatives, immunizations, dental care, substance abuse prevention, violence prevention, health/mental health education, sex education and family planning, recreation, social services to access basic living resources, and so forth)
	2. *Pre-school-age support and assistance to enhance health and psychosocial development* • Systems enhancement through multidisciplinary team work, consultation, and staff development • Education and social support for parents of preschoolers • Equality day care • Quality early education • Appropriate screening and amelioration of physical and mental health and psychosocial problems
Systems for early-after-problem onset intervention	3. *Interventions targeted for early schooling* • Orientations, welcoming and transition support into school and community life for students and their families (especially immigrants) • Support and guidance to ameliorate school adjustment problems • Personalized instruction in the primary grades • Additional support to address specific learning and behavior problems • Home involvement in problem solving • Comprehensive and accessible psychosocial and physical and mental health programs (including a focus on community and home violence and other problems identified through community needs assessment)
	4. *Improvement and augmentation of ongoing regular support* • Systems enhancement through multidisciplinary team work, consultation, and staff development • Preparation and support for school and life transitions • Teaching "basics" of support and remediation to regular teachers (including use of available resource personnel, peer and volunteer support) • Parent involvement in problem solving • Resource support for parents-in-need (including assistance in finding work, legal aid, ESL and citizenship classes, and so forth) • Comprehensive and accessible psychosocial and physical and mental health interventions (including health and physical education, recreation, violence reduction programs, medical help, and so forth) • Academic guidance and assistance • Emergency and crisis prevention and response mechanisms
	5. *Other interventions prior to referral for intensive, ongoing targeted treatments* • Systems enhancement through multidisciplinary team work, consultation, and staff development • Short-term specialized interventions (including resource teacher instruction and family mobilization; programs for suicide prevention, pregnant minors, substance abusers, gang members, and other potential dropouts)
Systems for treatment for severe/chronic problems	6. *Intensive treatments* • Referral, triage, placement guidance and assistance, case management, and resource coordination • Family preservation programs and services • Special education and rehabilitation • Dropout recovery and follow-up support • Services for severe, chronic psychosocial/mental/physical health problems

work, and play. And a basic assumption underlying the application of any of the interventions is that the least restrictive and intrusive forms of intervention required to address problems and accommodate diversity would be used initially. Another assumption is that problems are not discrete, and therefore, interventions that address root causes should be used.

In support of specific types of programs exemplified, a little bit of data can be gleaned from various facets of the research literature—most often, project evaluations and dissertations. For obvious reasons, no study has ever looked at the impact of implementing the full continuum in any one geographic catchment area. However, we can make inferences from naturalistic "experiments" taking place in every wealthy and most upper-middle-income communities. Across the country, concerned parents who have the financial resources, or who can avail themselves of such resources when necessary, will purchase any of the interventions listed in order to ensure their children's well-being. This represents a body of empirical support for the value of such interventions that cannot be ignored. (As one wag put it, *The range of interventions is supported by a new form of validation—market validity!*)

Although schools cannot do everything, the foregoing conceptualization provides a reasonable basis for mapping what is currently being done by schools and then conducting a variety of analyses. Our focus here is on how well the current state of the art approximates the ideal of having a comprehensive, multifaceted, and cohesive approach for addressing barriers to learning.

Analyzing Learning Supports in Schools

Our analyses have highlighted major gaps and the high degree of fragmentation and marginalization that characterizes efforts to address barriers to development and learning (Adelman, 1995; Adelman & Taylor, 1997). Most collaborative initiatives are not braiding resources and establishing effective mechanisms for sustaining regular and long-term interprogram planning, implementation, and evaluation. There is a need for horizontal and vertical restructuring of programs and services within and between jurisdictions (e.g., among departments, divisions, units, schools, clusters of schools, districts, community agencies, and public and private sectors). Such connections are essential to counter tendencies to develop separate programs for every observed problem.

For the most part, schools are not playing much of a role in establishing the type of student supports and developing the support systems that are essential to enabling all students to benefit from higher standards and improved instruction. In particular, they do relatively little to prevent or intervene early after the onset of a student's learning, behavior, or emotional problem. Indeed, as budgets have tightened, they are doing less to provide students with social supports and recreational and enrichment opportunities. And even as educators call for greater home involvement, schools do little proactive outreach to help family members overcome barriers to such involvement, including improving their literacy, learning English, and facilitating social support networks.

WHAT'S HOLDING US BACK?

Keeping the full continuum in mind, let's look at school reform and improvement through the lens of learning, behavior, and emotional problems. Doing so, we find that school improvement policies and planning mostly give short shrift to such problems. The exceptions proving the point are a few pioneering initiatives around the country demonstrating how schools and communities can meet the challenge by addressing persistent barriers to student learning.

Our analysis of prevailing policies for improving schools indicates that the primary focus is on two major components: (1) enhancing instruction and curriculum and (2) restructuring school governance/management. The implementation of such efforts is shaped by demands for every school to adopt high standards and expectations and be accountable for results, as measured by standardized achievement tests. Toward these ends, the calls have been to enhance direct academic support and move away from a "deficit" model by adopting a strengths-oriented or resilience-oriented paradigm. All this is reflected in federal legislation and guidelines. It is particularly ironic that the federal agenda provides for "supplemental services," but the emphasis is on tutoring. This underscores the fragmented and marginalized ways in which policymakers are attending to the multi-faceted barriers that interfere with students' learning and performing well at school.

Barriers that cannot be ignored also are addressed in a piecemeal manner—school violence, drugs on campus, dropouts, teen pregnancy, delinquency, and so forth. We already have noted the variety of "categorical" initiatives that generate auxiliary programs, some supported by school district general funds and some underwritten by federal and private-sector money.

Policymakers have come to appreciate that limited intervention efficacy is related to the widespread tendency for such programs to operate in isolation. As a result, some initiatives have been designed to reduce the *fragmentation.* However, policymakers have failed to deal with the overriding issue, namely, that addressing such problems, and indeed all barriers to development and

> The marginalization of efforts to address barriers to learning and teaching is seen in the lack of attention to such matters in school improvement plans and certification reviews. It is also seen in the lack of attention to mapping, analyzing, and rethinking how the resources used to address barriers are allocated: educational reformers virtually have ignored the need to reframe the work of pupil services professionals and other student support staff. All this seriously hampers efforts to provide the help teachers and their students so desperately need.

learning, remains a *marginalized* aspect of school policy and practice. The whole enterprise is treated as supplementary (often referred to as "auxiliary services").

Needed: A Policy Shift

Current policies designed to enhance support for teachers, students, and families are seriously flawed. It is unlikely that an agenda to enhance academics can succeed in the absence of concerted attention to ending the marginalized status of efforts to address barriers to learning and teaching.

Increased awareness of policy deficiencies has stimulated analyses that indicate that current policy is dominated by a two-component model of school improvement. That is, the primary thrust is on improving instruction and school management. While these two facets obviously are essential, our analyses emphasize that a third essential component—a component to enable students to learn and teachers to teach—is missing (see the top part of Guide 3.3).

Used as proxies for the missing component are all the marginalized and fragmented activities, illustrated in Chapter 1, that go on as school after school struggles to address the many factors interfering with student learning and performance (see the bottom section of Guide 3.3). Various states and localities are moving in the direction of pulling all these resources together into a primary and essential third component for school improvement. We highlight some of these in Part II. In each case, there is recognition at a policy level that schools must do much more to enable *all* students to learn and *all* teachers to teach effectively. In effect, the intent, over time, is for schools to play a major role in establishing a school-community continuum of interventions.

Overlapping the efforts of schools are initiatives from the community to link their resources to schools. Terms used in conjunction with these initiatives include *school-linked services* (especially health and social services), *full-service schools, school-community partnerships,* and *community schools.* Some of these initiatives have shown the potential of braiding resources together; others have contributed to additional fragmentation, counterproductive competition, and further marginalization of student support.

A third and narrower set of initiatives is designed to promote coordination and collaboration among *governmental* departments and their service agencies. The intent is to foster integrated services, with an emphasis on greater local control, increased involvement of parents, and locating services at schools when feasible. Although the federal government has offered various forms of support to promote this policy direction, few school districts have pursued the opportunity in ways that have resulted in comprehensive approaches to addressing barriers to learning.[1] To facilitate coordinated planning and organizational change, local, state, and federal intra-agency and interagency councils have been established. Also,

Guide 3.3   Current Two-component Model for Reform and Restructuring

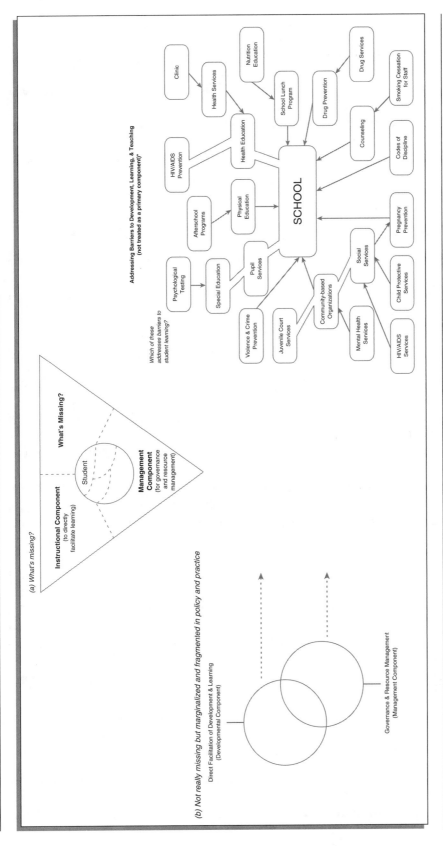

*While not treated as a primary and essential component, every school offers a relatively small amount of school-owned student "support" services—some of which link with community-owned resources. Many schools have been reaching out to community agencies to add a few more services. All of this, however, remains marginalized and fragmented in policy and practice.

legislative bodies have been rethinking their committee structures, and some states have gone so far as to create new executive branch structures (e.g., combining education and all agencies and services for children and families under one cabinet-level department).

The various initiatives do help *some* students who are not succeeding at school. However, they come nowhere near addressing the scope of need. Indeed, their limited potency further highlights the degree to which efforts to address barriers to learning and development are marginalized in policy and practice.

Needed: A Three-component Model for School Improvement

The limited impact of current policy points to the need to rethink school reform and improvement. Our analyses indicate that the two-component model on which current reforms are based is inadequate for improving schools in ways that will be effective in preventing and correcting learning and behavior problems. Movement to a three-component model is necessary if schools are to enable all young people to have an equal opportunity to succeed at school.

Stated directly, the prevailing approaches to school reform do not address barriers to learning, development, and teaching in comprehensive and multifaceted ways, especially in schools where large proportions of students are not doing well. Rather, in their efforts to raise test scores, school leaders usually have pursued instruction as the primary route. The emphasis is on intensifying and narrowing attention to focus on curriculum, instruction, and classroom discipline. This ignores the need for fundamental restructuring of school and community resources for enabling learning and continues to *marginalize* such efforts. The irony is that proceeding in this way undermines providing equity of opportunity for many students.

While improved instruction is necessary, for too many youngsters, it is not sufficient. Students who arrive at school on any given day lacking motivational readiness and/or certain abilities need something more. That something more is found in comprehensive, multifaceted, and integrated approaches to addressing barriers to learning and teaching. A three-component model calls for elevating such approaches to the level of one of three fundamental facets of education reform and school improvement. Part II discusses this in detail.

CONCLUDING COMMENTS

How often have you been asked, *Why don't schools do a better job in addressing learning, behavior, and emotional problems?* In answering the question, leaders must draw attention to the root of the problem: *efforts to address such problems are marginalized in school policy and daily practice.* That is, most programs, services, and special projects providing learning supports at a school and districtwide are treated as supplementary. We all need to stress that the results of marginalization are that

- Planning and implementation often are done on an ad hoc basis.
- Staff tend to function in relative isolation from each other and other stakeholders, with a great deal of the work oriented to discrete problems and with an overreliance on specialized services for individuals and small groups.
- In some schools, the deficiencies of current policies give rise to such aberrant practices as assigning a student identified as at risk for grade retention, dropout, and substance abuse to three counseling programs operating independently of each other. Such fragmentation not only is costly, it works against cohesiveness and maximizing results.

It also should be stressed that the tendency among reformers has been to focus mainly on the symptom: fragmentation. As a result, the main prescription for improvement has been strategies to improve coordination. Better coordination is a good idea. But it doesn't really address the problem that school-owned student supports are marginalized in policy and practice.

And it should be noted that for the most part, community involvement at schools also remains a token and marginal concern. Moreover, the trend toward fragmentation is compounded by most school-linked services' initiatives. This happens because such initiatives focus primarily on coordinating *community* services and *linking* them to schools using a collocation model, rather than integrating such services with the ongoing efforts of school staff.

The marginalized status and the associated fragmentation of efforts to address student problems are long-standing and ongoing. The situation is likely to go unchanged as long as educational reformers continue to ignore the need to restructure the work of student support professionals. Currently, most school improvement plans do not focus on using such staff to develop the type of comprehensive, multifaceted, and integrated approaches necessary to address the many overlapping barriers to learning and development. At best, most reformers have offered the notions of *family resource centers* and *full-service schools* to link community resources to schools (e.g., school-linked services) and enhance coordination of services. Much more fundamental changes are needed.

Also mediating against developing schoolwide approaches to address factors interfering with learning and teaching is the marginalized, fragmented, and flawed way in which these matters are handled in providing on-the-job education. Little or none of a teacher's inservice training focuses on improving classroom and schoolwide approaches for dealing effectively with mild to moderate behavior, learning, and emotional problems. Paraprofessionals, aides, and volunteers working in classrooms or with special school projects and services receive little or no formal training or supervision before or after they are assigned duties. And little or no attention is paid to inservice for student support staff.

The time has come to change all this. New directions for learning supports must be made an essential agenda item in ensuring that no child is left behind. Or, as a colleague of ours often says, *All children want to be successful—let's give them a fighting chance.*

NOTE

1. For example, Title XI of the Improving America's Schools Act of 1994, administered by the U.S. Department of Education, was intended to foster service coordination for students and their families. Title I of the No Child Left Behind Act (2002) can be used in a similar way. A comparable provision was introduced in the 1997 reauthorization of the Individuals with Disabilities Education Act. And the Center for Disease Control and Prevention's grants to foster coordinated school health programs pursue this direction by establishing an infrastructure between state departments of health and education.

Do you have a solution for the problem?

No, but I'm sure good at admiring it.

REFERENCES

Adelman, H. S. (1995). Education reform: Broadening the focus. *Psychological Science, 6*, 61–62.

Adelman, H. S., & Taylor, L. (1997). Addressing barriers to learning: Beyond school-linked services and full service schools. *American Journal of Orthopsychiatry, 67*, 408–421.

Marx, E., & Wooley, S. F. (with Northrop, D.). (Eds.). (1998). *Health is academic: A guide to coordinated school health programs.* New York: Teachers College Press.

No Child Left Behind Act of 2001, Pub. L. No. 107–110, § 2, 115 Stat.1425 (2002).

Controlling Behavior at the Expense of Motivating Learning

4

Many students say that . . . they feel their classes are irrelevant and boring, that they are just passing time . . . [and] are not able to connect what they are being taught with what they feel they need for success in their later life. This disengagement from the learning process is manifested in many ways.

—American Youth Policy Forum (2000)

ORIENTING QUESTIONS

? What are optimal ways to address behavior problems at school?
? Why is an understanding of how to reengage students in classroom learning essential in developing learning supports?
? What is intrinsic motivation and what are the implications for addressing barriers to student learning?

External reinforcement may indeed get a particular act going and may lead to its repetition, but it does not nourish, reliably, the long course of learning by which [one] slowly builds in [one's] own way a serviceable model of what the world is and what it can be.

—Jerome Bruner (1966, p. 128)

As we have stressed, curriculum content is learned as a result of transactions between the learner and environment. The essence of the teaching process is to create an environment that first can mobilize the learner to pursue the curriculum and then can maintain that mobilization, while facilitating learning. Behavior problems clearly get in the way of all this.

Misbehavior disrupts. In some forms, such as bullying and intimidating others, it is hurtful. And observing such behavior may disinhibit others.

When a student misbehaves, a natural reaction is to want that youngster to experience and other students to see the consequences of misbehaving. One hope is that public awareness of consequences will deter subsequent problems. As a result, a considerable amount of time at schools is devoted to discipline; a common concern for teachers is "classroom management." In their efforts to deal with deviant and devious behavior and to create safe environments, unfortunately, schools increasingly over-

> I suspect that many children would learn arithmetic, and learn it better, if it were illegal.
>
> —John Holt (1989, p. 12)

rely on negative consequences and control techniques. Such practices model behavior that can foster rather than counter development of negative values and often produce other forms of undesired behavior. Moreover, the tactics often make schools look and feel more like prisons than community treasures.

To move schools beyond overreliance on punishment and control strategies, there is ongoing advocacy for social skills training, positive behavior support, and new agendas for emotional intelligence training, asset development, and character education. Relatedly, there are calls for greater home involvement, with emphasis on enhanced parent responsibility for their children's behavior and learning. More comprehensively, some reformers want to transform schools in ways that create an atmosphere of caring, cooperative learning, and a sense of community. Such advocates usually argue for schools that are holistically oriented and family centered. They want curricula to enhance values and character, including responsibility (social and moral), integrity, self-regulation (self-discipline), and a work ethic, and also want schools to foster self-esteem, diverse talents, and emotional well-being. These trends are important. When paired with a contemporary understanding of human motivation, they recognize that the major intent in dealing with behavior problems at school must be the engagement and reengagement of students in classroom learning (Adelman & Taylor, 1993; Center for Mental Health in Schools, 2001).

Fredricks, Blumenfeld, and Paris (2004) note that

Engagement is defined in three ways in the research literature:

- *Behavioral engagement* draws on the idea of participation; it includes involvement in academic and social or extracurricular activities and is considered crucial for achieving positive academic outcomes and preventing dropping out.
- *Emotional engagement* encompasses positive and negative reactions to teachers, classmates, academics, and school and is presumed to create ties to an institution and influences willingness to do the work.
- *Cognitive engagement* draws on the idea of investment; it incorporates thoughtfulness and willingness to exert the effort necessary to comprehend complex ideas and master difficult skills.

DISENGAGED STUDENTS AND SOCIAL CONTROL

After an extensive review of the literature, Fredricks, Blumenfeld, and Paris

Antecedents of engagement can be organized into

- *School-level Factors:* Voluntary choice, clear and consistent goals, small class size, student participation in school policy and management, opportunities for staff and students to be involved in cooperative endeavors, and academic work that allows for the development of products
- *Classroom Context:* Teacher support, peers, classroom structure, autonomy support, task characteristics
- *Individual Needs:* Need for relatedness, autonomy, competence

Engagement can be measured by

- *Behavioral Engagement:* Conduct, work involvement, participation, persistence (e.g., completing homework, complying with school rules, absent/tardy, off task)
- *Emotional Engagement:* Self-report related to feelings of frustration, boredom, interest, anger, satisfaction; student-teacher relations; work orientation
- *Cognitive Engagement:* Investment in learning, flexible problem solving, independent work styles, coping with perceived failure, preference for challenge and independent mastery, commitment to understanding the work

(2004) conclude that *engagement is associated with positive academic outcomes, including achievement and persistence in school; and it is higher in classrooms with supportive teachers and peers, challenging and authentic tasks, opportunities for choice, and sufficient structure.* Conversely, for many students, disengagement is associated with behavior problems, and behavior and learning problems may eventually lead to dropout. The degree of concern about student engagement varies, depending on school population.

In general, teaching involves being able to apply strategies focused on the content to be taught and knowledge and skills to be acquired—with some degree of attention given to the process of engaging students. All this works fine in schools where most students come each day ready and able to deal with what the teacher is ready and able to teach. Indeed, teachers are fortunate when they have a classroom where the majority of students show up and are receptive to the planned lessons. In schools that are the greatest focus of public criticism, this certainly is not the case. What most of us realize, at least at some level, is that teachers in such settings are confronted with an entirely different teaching situation. Among the various supports they absolutely must have are ways to reengage students who have become disengaged and often resistant to broadband (nonpersonalized) teaching approaches (see Guide 4.1). To the dismay of most teachers, however, strategies for reengaging students in *learning* rarely are a prominent part of preservice or inservice preparation and seldom are the focus of interventions pursued by professionals whose role is to support teachers and students (National Research Council and the Institute of Medicine, 2004).

It is commonplace to find that when students are not engaged in the lessons at hand, they tend to pursue other activity. As teachers and other staff try to cope with those who are disruptive, the main concern usually is classroom management. At one time, a heavy dose of punishment was the dominant approach. Currently, the stress is on more positive practices designed to provide behavior support in and out of the classroom. For the most part, however, the strategies are applied as a form of *social control* aimed directly at stopping disruptive behavior.

An often stated assumption is that stopping the behavior will make the student amenable to teaching. In a few cases, this may be so. However, the assumption ignores all the work that has led to understanding *psychological reactance* and the need for individuals to restore their sense of self-determination (Deci, 1995). Moreover, it belies two painful realities: the number of students who continue to manifest poor academic achievement and the staggering dropout rate in too many schools.

Guide 4.1   Broadband (Nonpersonalized) Teaching

Once upon a time, the animals decided that their lives and their society would be improved by setting up a school. The basics identified as necessary for survival in the animal world were swimming, running, climbing, jumping, and flying. Instructors were hired to teach these activities, and it was agreed that all the animals would take all the courses. This worked out well for the administrators, but it caused some problems for the students.

The squirrel, for example, was an A student in running, jumping, and climbing but had trouble in flying class, not because of an inability to fly, for she could sail from the top of one tree to another with ease, but because the flying curriculum called for taking off from the ground. The squirrel was drilled in ground-to-air takeoffs until she was exhausted and developed charley horses from overexertion. This caused her to perform poorly in her other classes, and her grades dropped to D's.

The duck was outstanding in swimming class—even better than the teacher. But she did so poorly in running that she was transferred to a remedial class. There she practiced running until her webbed feet were so badly damaged that she was only an average swimmer. But since average was acceptable, nobody saw this as a problem—except the duck.

In contrast, the rabbit was excellent in running, but being terrified of water, he was an extremely poor swimmer. Despite a lot of makeup work in swimming class, he never could stay afloat. He soon became frustrated and uncooperative and was eventually expelled because of behavior problems.

The eagle naturally enough was a brilliant student in flying class and even did well in running and jumping. He had to be severely disciplined in climbing class, however, because he insisted that his way of getting to the top of the tree was faster and easier.

It should be noted that the parents of the groundhog pulled him out of school because the administration would not add classes in digging and burrowing. The groundhogs, along with the gophers and badgers, got a prairie dog to start a private school. They all have become strong opponents of school taxes and proponents of voucher systems.

By graduation time, the student with the best grades in the animal school was a compulsive ostrich who could run superbly and also could swim, fly, and climb a little. She, of course, was made class valedictorian and received scholarship offers from all the best universities.

SOURCE: George H. Reeves is credited with giving this parable to American educators.

The argument sometimes is made that the reason students continue to misbehave is because the wrong socialization practices have been used or have been implemented incorrectly. In particular, schools have been criticized for overemphasizing punishment. There is ongoing advocacy for moving to positive behavior support. The move from punishment to positive approaches is a welcome one. However, most of the new initiatives have not focused enough on a basic system failure that must be addressed if improved behavior is to be maintained. That is, strategies that focus on positive behavior have paid too little attention to helping teachers deal with student engagement in classroom learning.

Student engagement encompasses not only engaging and maintaining engagement but also *reengaging* those who have disengaged. Of particular concern is what teachers do when they encounter a student who has disengaged and is misbehaving. In most cases, the emphasis shouldn't be first and foremost on implementing social control techniques. (See Chapter 12 for more on the topic of addressing behavior problems.)

What teachers need even more are ways to reengage students who have become disengaged and resistant to standard instruction. Despite this need, strategies that have the greatest likelihood of reengaging students in *learning* rarely are a prominent part of preservice or inservice preparation. And such strategies seldom are the focus of interventions applied by professionals whose role is to support teachers and students. To correct these deficiencies, the developmental trend in intervention thinking must be toward practices that embrace an expanded view of engagement and human motivation (see Guide 4.2).

INTRINSIC MOTIVATION IS FUNDAMENTAL

Engaging and reengaging students in learning is the facet of teaching that draws on what is known about human motivation (e.g., see Brophy, 2004; Deci, 1995; Deci & Ryan, 1985, 2002; Fredricks et al., 2004; Ryan & Deci, 2000; Stipek, 1998). What many of us have been taught about dealing with student misbehavior and learning problems runs counter to what we intuitively understand about human motivation. Teachers and parents, in particular, often learn to overdepend on reinforcement theory, despite the appreciation they have about the importance of intrinsic motivation. Those who argue that we must focus on "basics" are right. But the basics that need attention have to do with motivation.

Maria doesn't want to work on improving her reading. Not only is her *motivational readiness* for learning in this area low, but she also has a fairly high level of *avoidance motivation* for reading. Most of the time during reading instruction, she is disengaged and acting out.

In contrast, David is motivationally ready to improve reading skills, but he has very little motivation to do so in the ways his teacher proposes.

Guide 4.2   Developmental Trend in Intervention Thinking: Behavioral
Initiatives and Beyond

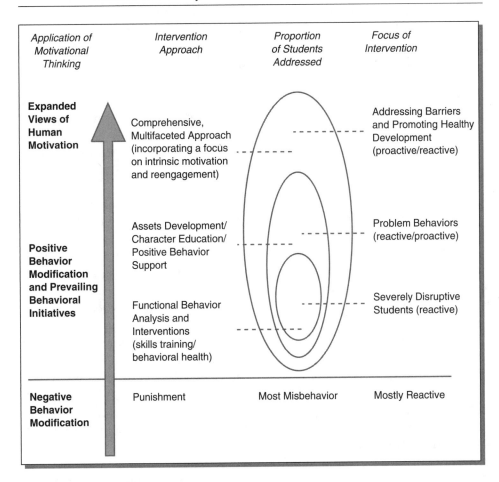

He has high motivation for the *outcome* but low motivation for the *processes*
prescribed for getting there.

Matt was highly motivated to do whatever was prescribed to help him
learn to read better, but his motivation started to disappear after a few
weeks of hard work. He has trouble maintaining a sufficient amount of
ongoing or *continuing motivation,* and this affects his attention and behavior.

Helena appeared motivated to learn and did learn many new vocabulary words and improved her reading comprehension on several occasions
over the years she was in special school programs. Her motivation to read
after school, however, has never increased. It was assumed that as her
skills improved, her attitude toward reading would, too. But it never has.

No one expected James to become a good reader because of low scores
on tests related to phonics ability and reading comprehension in second
grade. However, his teacher found some beginning-level books on his

favorite sport (baseball) and found that he really wanted to read them. He asked her and other students to help him with words and took the books home to read (where he also asked an older sister for some help). His skills started to improve rapidly, and he was soon reading on a par with his peers.

What the preceding examples illustrate is that

- Motivation is a learning prerequisite, and its absence may be a cause of learning and behavior problems, a factor maintaining such problems, or both.
- Individuals may be motivated toward the idea of obtaining a certain learning outcome but may not be motivated to pursue certain learning processes.
- Individuals may be motivated to start to work on overcoming their learning and behavior problems but may not maintain their motivation.
- Individuals may be motivated to learn basic skills but maintain negative attitudes about the area of functioning and thus never use the skills except when they must.
- Motivated learners can do more than others might expect.

Obviously, intrinsic motivation is a fundamental consideration in designing learning supports. An increased understanding of motivation clarifies how essential it is to avoid processes that limit options, make students feel controlled and coerced, and focus mostly on remedying problems. From a motivational perspective, such processes are seen as likely to produce avoidance reactions in the classroom and to school in general and thus reduce opportunities for positive learning and for development of positive attitudes.

Eventually, these students disengage from classroom learning. Reengagement depends on the use of interventions that help minimize conditions that negatively affect motivation and maximize conditions that have a positive motivational effect.

Of course, teachers, parents, and support staff cannot control all factors affecting motivation. Indeed, when any of us address learning and behavior concerns, we have direct control over a relatively small segment of the physical and social environment. We try to maximize the likelihood that opportunities to learn are a good fit with the current *capabilities* of a given youngster. And with learning engagement in mind, we try to match individual differences in *motivation*.

Matching individual differences in *motivation* means attending to such matters as

- *Motivation as a readiness concern:* Optimal performance and learning require motivational readiness. The absence of such readiness can cause or maintain problems. If a learner does not have enough motivational readiness, strategies must be implemented to develop it (including ways to reduce avoidance motivation). Readiness should not be viewed in the old sense of waiting until an individual is interested. Rather, it should be understood in the contemporary sense of establishing environments that are perceived by students as caring, supportive places and as offering stimulating activities that are valued, challenging, and doable.

• *Motivation as a key ongoing process concern:* Many learners are caught up in the novelty of a new subject, but after a few lessons, interest often wanes. Some students are motivated by the idea of obtaining a given outcome but may not be motivated to pursue certain processes and thus may not pay attention or may try to avoid them. For example, some are motivated to start work on overcoming their problems but may not maintain that motivation. Strategies must be designed to elicit, enhance, and maintain motivation so that a youngster stays mobilized.

• *Minimizing negative motivation and avoidance reactions as process and outcome concerns:* Teachers and others at a school and at home not only must try to increase motivation—especially intrinsic motivation—but also take care to avoid or at least minimize conditions that decrease motivation or produce negative motivation. For example, care must be taken not to overrely on extrinsics to entice and reward, because to do so may decrease intrinsic motivation. At times, school is seen as unchallenging, uninteresting, overdemanding, overwhelming, overcontrolling, nonsupportive, or even hostile. When this happens, a student may develop negative attitudes and avoidance related to a given situation, and over time, to school and all it represents.

• *Enhancing intrinsic motivation as a basic outcome concern:* It is essential to enhance motivation as an outcome so that the desire to pursue a given area (e.g., reading, good behavior) increasingly is a positive intrinsic attitude that mobilizes learning and behaving outside the teaching situation. Achieving such an outcome involves use of strategies that do not overrely on extrinsic rewards and that do enable youngsters to play a meaningful role in making decisions related to valued options. In effect, enhancing intrinsic motivation is a fundamental *protective factor* and is the key to developing *resiliency*.

Students who are intrinsically motivated to learn at school seek out opportunities and challenges and go beyond requirements. In doing so, they learn more and learn more deeply than do classmates who are extrinsically motivated. Facilitating the learning of such students is a fairly straightforward matter and fits well with school improvements that primarily emphasize enhancing instructional practices. The focus is on helping establish ways for students who are motivationally ready and able to achieve and, of course, to maintain and enhance their motivation. The process involves knowing when, how, and what to teach and also knowing when and how to structure the situation so they can learn on their own.

In contrast, students who manifest learning, behavior, and/or emotional problems may have developed extremely negative perceptions of teachers and programs. In such cases, they are not likely to be open to people and activities that look like the same old thing. Major changes in approach are required if the youngsters are even to perceive that something has changed in the situation. Minimally, exceptional efforts must be made to have them (a) view the teacher and other interveners as supportive (rather than controlling and indifferent) and (b) perceive content, outcomes, and activity options as personally valuable and obtainable. Thus any effort to reengage disengaged students must begin by addressing negative perceptions. School support staff and teachers must work together to reverse conditions that led to such perceptions.

> Increasing intrinsic motivation involves affecting a student's thoughts, feelings, and decisions. In general, the intent is to use procedures that can potentially reduce negative and increase positive feelings, thoughts, and coping strategies with respect to learning. For learning and behavior problems, in particular, this means identifying and minimizing experiences that maintain or may increase avoidance motivation.

TWO KEY COMPONENTS OF MOTIVATION: VALUING AND EXPECTATIONS

Two common reasons people give for not bothering to learn something are "It's not worth it" and "I know I won't be able to do it." In general, the amount of time and energy spent on an activity seems dependent on how much the activity is valued by the person and on the person's expectation that what is valued will be attained without too great a cost.

About Valuing

What makes something worth doing? Prizes? Money? Merit awards? Praise? Certainly!

We all do a great many things, some of which we don't even like to do, because the activity leads to a desired reward. Similarly, we often do things to escape punishment or other negative consequences that we prefer to avoid.

Rewards and punishments may be material or social. For those with learning, behavior, and emotional problems, there has been widespread use of such incentives (e.g., systematically giving points or tokens that can be exchanged for candy, prizes, praise, free time, or social interactions). Punishments have included loss of free time and other privileges, added

Guide 4.3   Is It Worth It?

In a small town, there were a few youngsters who were labeled as handicapped. Over the years, a local bully had taken it upon himself to persecute them. In one recent incident, he sent a gang of young ragamuffins to harass one of his classmates who had just been diagnosed as having learning disabilities. He told the youngsters that the boy was retarded, and they could have some fun calling him a "retard."

Day after day in the schoolyard, the gang sought the boy out. "Retard! Retard!" they hooted at him.

The situation became serious. The boy took the matter so much to heart that he began to brood and spent sleepless nights over it. Finally, out of desperation, he told his teacher about the problem, and together they evolved a plan.

The following day, when the little ones came to jeer at him, he confronted them saying, "From today on, I'll give any of you who calls me a 'retard' a quarter."

Then he put his hand in his pocket and, indeed, gave each boy a quarter.

Well, delighted with their booty, the youngsters, of course, sought him out the following day and began to shrill, "Retard! Retard!"

The boy looked at them—smiling. He put his hand in his pocket and gave each of them a dime, saying, "A quarter is too much—I can only afford a dime today."

Well, the boys went away satisfied because, after all, a dime was money too.

However, when they came the next day to hoot, the boy gave them only a penny each.

"Why do we get only a penny today?" they yelled.

"That's all I can afford."

"But two days ago you gave us a quarter, and yesterday we got a dime. It's not fair!"

"Take it or leave it. That's all you're going to get."

"Do you think we're going to call you a 'retard' for one lousy penny?"

"So don't."

And they didn't.

SOURCE: Adapted from a fable presented by Ausubel, 1948.

work, fines, isolation, censure, and suspension. Grades have been used both as rewards and punishments. Because people will do things to obtain rewards or avoid punishment, rewards and punishment often are called *reinforcers*. Because they generally come from sources outside the person, they often are called *extrinsics*.

Extrinsic reinforcers are easy to use and can immediately affect behavior. Therefore, they have been widely adopted in the fields of special education and psychology. Unfortunately, the immediate effects are usually limited to very specific behaviors and often are short-term. Moreover, extensive use of extrinsics can have some undesired effects. And sometimes the available extrinsics simply aren't powerful enough to get the desired results (see Guide 4.3).

It is important to remember that what makes an extrinsic factor rewarding is the fact that it is experienced by the recipient as a reward. What makes it a highly valued reward is that the recipient highly values it. If someone doesn't like candy, there is not much point in offering it as a reward. Furthermore, because the use of extrinsics has limits, it's fortunate that people often do things even without apparent extrinsic reasons. In fact, a lot of what people learn and spend time doing is done for intrinsic reasons. *Curiosity* is a good example. Curiosity seems to be an innate quality that leads us to seek stimulation, avoid boredom, and learn a great deal.

People also pursue some things because of what has been described as an innate *striving for competence.* Most of us value feeling competent. We try to conquer some challenges, and if none are around, we usually seek one out. Of course, if the challenges confronting us seem unconquerable or make us too uncomfortable (e.g., too anxious or exhausted), we try to put them aside and move on to something more promising.

Another important intrinsic motivator appears to be an internal push toward *self-determination.* People seem to value feeling and thinking that they have some degree of choice and freedom in deciding what to do. And human beings also seem intrinsically moved toward establishing and maintaining relationships. That is, we value the feeling of *interpersonal connection.*

About Expectations

We may value something a great deal, but if we believe we can't do it or can't obtain it without paying too great a personal price, we are likely to look for other valued activities and outcomes to pursue. Expectations about these matters are influenced by past experiences.

Previously unsuccessful arenas usually are seen as unlikely paths to valued extrinsic rewards or intrinsic satisfactions. We may perceive past failure as the result of our lack of ability, or we may believe that more effort was required than we were willing to give. We may also feel that the help we needed to succeed was not available. If our perception is that very little has changed with regard to these factors, our expectation of succeeding now will be rather low. *In general, then, what we value interacts with our expectations, and motivation is one product of this interaction* (see Guide 4.4).

There are many intervention implications to derive from understanding intrinsic motivation. For example, mobilizing and maintaining a youngster's motivation depend on how a classroom program addresses concerns about valuing and expectations. Schools and classrooms that offer a broad range of opportunities (e.g., content, outcomes, procedural options) and involve students in decision making are best equipped to meet the challenge.

OVERRELIANCE ON EXTRINSICS: A BAD MATCH

Throughout this discussion of valuing and expectations, the emphasis has been on the fact that motivation is not something that can be determined solely by forces outside the individual. Others can plan activities and outcomes to influence motivation and learning; however, how the activities and outcomes are experienced determines whether they are pursued (or avoided) with a little or a lot of effort and ability. Understanding that an

Guide 4.4   A Bit of Theory

Motivation theory has many facets. At the risk of oversimplifying things, the following discussion is designed to make a few big points.

$$E \times V$$

Can you decipher this? (Don't go on until you've tried.)

Hint: the "×" is a multiplication sign.

In case the equation stumped you, don't be surprised. The main introduction to motivational thinking that many people have been given in the past involves some form of reinforcement theory (which essentially deals with extrinsic motivation). Thus all this may be new to you, even though motivational theorists have been wrestling with it for a long time, and intuitively, you probably understand much of what they are talking about.

E represents an individual's *expectations* about outcome; in school this often means expectations of success or failure. *V* represents *valuing,* with valuing influenced by what is valued both intrinsically and extrinsically. Thus in a general sense, motivation can be thought of in terms of expectancy times valuing. *Such theory recognizes that human beings are thinking and feeling organisms and intrinsic factors can be powerful motivators. This understanding of human motivation has major implications for learning, teaching, parenting, and mental health interventions.*

Within some limits (which we need not discuss here), high expectations and high valuing produce high motivation, while low expectations and high valuing produce relatively weak motivation.

Youngsters may greatly value the idea of improving their reading. They usually are not happy with limited skills and know they would feel a lot better about school and themselves if they could read. But often, they experience everything the teacher asks them to do as a waste of time. They have done it all before, and they *still* have a reading problem. Sometimes they will do the exercises but just to earn points to go on a field trip and to avoid the consequences of not cooperating. Often, however, they try to get out of doing the work by distracting the teacher. After all, why should they do things they are certain won't help them read any better?

(Expectancy × Valuing = Motivation)

$$0 \times 1.0 = 0$$

High expectations paired with low valuing also yield low approach motivation. Thus the often-cited remedial strategy of guaranteeing success by designing tasks to be very easy is not as simple a recipe as it sounds. Indeed, the approach is likely to fail if the outcome (e.g., improved reading, learning math fundamentals, applying social skills) is not valued or if the tasks are experienced as too boring or if doing them is seen as too embarrassing. In such cases, a strong negative value is attached to the activities, and this contributes to avoidance motivation.

(Expectancy × Valuing = Motivation)

$$1.0 \times 0 = 0$$

Appropriate appreciation of all this is necessary in designing a match for optimal learning and performance.

individual's perceptions can affect motivation has led researchers to important findings about some undesired effects resulting from over-reliance on extrinsics.

Because of the prominent role they play in school programs, grading, testing, and other performance evaluations are a special concern in any

Guide 4.5   Rewards: To Control or Inform?

As Ed Deci (1975) has cogently stressed:

Rewards are generally used to control behavior. Children are sometimes rewarded with candy when they do what adults expect of them. Workers are rewarded with pay for doing what their supervisors want. People are rewarded with social approval or positive feedback for fitting into their social reference group. In all these situations, the aim of the reward is to control the person's behavior—to make [the person] continue to engage in acceptable behaviors. And rewards often do work quite effectively as controllers. Further, whether it works or not, each reward has a controlling aspect. Therefore, the first aspect to every reward (including feedback) is a controlling aspect. However, rewards also provide information to the person about his effectiveness in various situations. When David did well at school, his mother told him she was proud of him, and when Amanda learned to ride a bike, she was given a brand new two-wheeler. David and Amanda knew from the praise and bicycle that they were competent and self-determining in relation to school and bicycling. The second aspect of every reward is the information it provides a person about his competence and self-determination.

When the controlling aspect of the reward is very salient, such as in the case of money or the avoidance of punishment, [a] change in perceived locus of causality . . . will occur. The person is "controlled" by the reward and s/he perceives that the locus of causality is external. (pp. 141–142)

discussion of the overreliance on extrinsics as a way to reinforce positive learning. Although grades often are discussed as simply providing information about how well a student is doing, many, if not most, students perceive each grade as a reward or a punishment. Certainly, many teachers use grades to try to control behavior—to reward those who do assignments well and to punish those who don't (see Guide 4.5). Sometimes parents add to a student's perception of grades as extrinsic reinforcers by giving a reward for good report cards.

We all have our own horror stories about the negative impact of grades on ourselves and others. In general, grades have a way of reshaping what students do with their learning opportunities. In choosing what to study, students strongly consider what grades they are likely to receive. As deadlines for assignments and tests get closer, interest in the topic gives way to interest in maximizing one's grade. Discussion of interesting issues and problems related to the area of study gives way to questions about how long a paper should be and what will be on the test. None of this is surprising given that poor grades can result in having to repeat a course or being denied certain immediate and long-range opportunities. It is simply a good example of how systems that overemphasize extrinsics may have a serious negative impact on intrinsic motivation for learning. *And if the impact of current practices is harmful to those who are able learners, imagine the impact on students with learning and behavior problems!*

The point is that extrinsic rewards can undermine intrinsic reasons for doing things. Although this is not always the case and may not always be a bad thing, it is an important consideration in deciding to rely on extrinsic reinforcers in addressing learning, behavior, and emotional problems.

THE PROBLEM OF REENGAGING STUDENTS IN SCHOOL LEARNING

Many individuals with learning problems also are described as hyperactive, distractable, impulsive, behavior disordered, and so forth. Their behavior patterns are seen as interfering with efforts to remedy their learning problems. Although motivation has always been a concern to those who work with learning and behavior problems, the emphasis in handling these interfering behaviors usually is on using extrinsics as part of efforts to directly control and/or in conjunction with direct skill instruction. For example, interventions are designed to improve impulse control, perseverance, selective attention, frustration tolerance, sustained attention and follow-through, and social awareness and skills. In all cases, the emphasis is on reducing or eliminating interfering behaviors, usually with the presumption that then the student will reengage in learning. However, there is little evidence that these strategies enhance a student's motivation toward classroom learning (National Research Council, 2004).

Psychological scholarship over the past 50 years has brought renewed attention to motivation as a central concept in understanding learning and attention problems. This work is just beginning to find its way into applied fields and programs. One line of work has emphasized the relationship of learning and behavior problems to deficiencies in intrinsic motivation. This work clarifies the value of interventions designed to increase

- Feelings of self-determination
- Feelings of competence and expectations of success
- Feelings of interpersonal relatedness
- The range of interests and satisfactions related to learning

Activities to correct deficiencies in intrinsic motivation are directed at improving awareness of personal motives and true capabilities, learning to set valued and appropriate goals, learning to value and to make appropriate and satisfying choices, and learning to value and accept responsibility for choice.

The point for emphasis here is that engaging and reengaging students in learning involve matching motivation. Matching motivation requires an appreciation of the importance of a student's perceptions in determining the right mix of intrinsic and extrinsic reasons. It also

> You have to get up and go to school!
>
> I don't want to. It's too hard and the kids don't like me.
>
> But you have to go. You're the principal.

requires understanding the key role played by expectations related to outcome. Without a good match, social control strategies can suppress negative attitudes and behaviors, but reengagement in classroom learning is unlikely.

General Strategic Considerations

To clarify matters with respect to designing new directions for student support for disengaged students, following are four general strategies to think about in planning ways to work with such students:

Clarifying Student Perceptions of the Problem: It is desirable to create a situation where it is feasible to talk openly with students about why they have become disengaged. This provides an invaluable basis for formulating a personalized plan for helping to alter their negative perceptions and for planning ways to prevent others from developing such perceptions.

Reframing School Learning: As noted earlier, in the case of those who have disengaged, major reframing in teaching approaches is required so that these students (a) view the teacher as supportive (rather than controlling and indifferent) and (b) perceive content, outcomes, and activity options as personally valuable and obtainable. It is important, for example, to eliminate threatening evaluative measures, reframe content and processes to clarify purpose in terms of real-life needs and experiences and underscore how it all builds on previous learning, and clarify why the procedures are expected to be effective—especially those designed to help correct specific problems.

Renegotiating Involvement in School Learning: New and mutual agreements must be developed and evolved over time through conferences with the student and, where appropriate, including parents. The intent is to affect perceptions of choice, value, and probable outcome. The focus throughout is on clarifying awareness of valued options, enhancing expectations of positive outcomes, and engaging the student in meaningful, ongoing decision making. For the process to be most effective, students should be assisted in sampling new processes and content, options should include valued enrichment opportunities, and there must be provision for reevaluating and modifying decisions as perceptions shift.

Reestablishing and Maintaining an Appropriate Working Relationship: This requires the type of ongoing interactions that creates a sense of trust and open communication and provides personalized support and direction.

To maintain reengagement and prevent disengagement, the foregoing strategies must be pursued using processes and content that

- Minimize threats to feelings of competence, self-determination, and relatedness to valued others.
- Maximize such feelings (included here is an emphasis on a school's taking steps to enhance public perception that it is a welcoming, caring, safe, and just institution).
- Guide motivated practice (e.g., provide opportunities for meaningful applications and clarifying ways to organize practice).
- Provide continuous information on learning and performance in ways that highlight accomplishments.

- Provide opportunities for continued application and generalization (e.g., offer ways in which students can pursue additional, self-directed learning or can arrange for additional support and direction).

Obviously, it is no easy task to decrease well-assimilated negative attitudes and behaviors. And the task is likely to become even harder with the escalation toward high stakes testing policies (no matter how well-intentioned). It also seems obvious that *for many schools, enhanced achievement test scores will be feasible only when the large number of disengaged students are reengaged in learning at school.*

All this argues for (a) minimizing student disengagement and maximizing reengagement by moving school culture toward a greater focus on intrinsic motivation and (b) minimizing psychological reactance and enhancing perceptions that lead to reengagement in learning at school by rethinking social control practices. From a motivational perspective, key facets of accomplishing this involve enhancing student options and decision making.

Options and Student Decision Making as Key Facets

A greater proportion of individuals with avoidance or low motivation for learning at school are found among those with learning, behavior, and/or emotional problems. For these individuals, few currently available options may be appealing. How much greater the range of options needs to be depends primarily on how strong avoidance tendencies are. In general, however, the initial strategies for working with such students involve

- Further expansion of the range of options for learning (if necessary, this includes avoiding established curriculum content and processes)
- Primarily emphasizing areas in which the student has made personal and active decisions
- Accommodation of a wider range of behavior than usually is tolerated (e.g., a widening of limits on the amount and types of "differences" tolerated)

From a motivational perspective, one of the most basic concerns is the way in which students are involved in making decisions about options. Critically, decision-making processes can lead to perceptions of coercion and control or to perceptions of real choice (e.g., being in control of one's destiny, being self-determining). Such differences in perception can affect whether a student is mobilized to pursue or avoid planned learning activities and outcomes.

People who have the opportunity to make decisions among valued and feasible options tend to be committed to following through. In contrast, people who are not involved in decisions often have little commitment to what is decided. And if individuals disagree with a decision that affects them, besides not following through, they may react with hostility.

Thus essential to programs focusing on motivation are decision-making processes that affect perceptions of choice, value, and probable outcome. Three special points should be noted about decision making:

- Decisions are based on current perceptions. As perceptions shift, it is necessary to reevaluate decisions and modify them in ways that maintain a mobilized learner.
- Effective and efficient decision making is a basic skill and one that is as fundamental as the three R's. Thus if an individual does not do it well initially, this is not a reason to move away from learner involvement in decision making. Rather, it is an assessment of a need and a reason to use the process not only for motivational purposes but also to improve this basic skill.
- Among students manifesting learning, behavior, and emotional problems, it is well to remember that the most fundamental decision some of these individuals have to make is whether they want to participate or not. That is why it may be necessary in specific cases temporarily to put aside established options and standards. As we have stressed, before some students will decide to participate in a proactive way, they have to perceive the learning environment as positively different—and quite a bit so—from the one in which they had so much failure.

Reviews of the literature on human motivation suggest that providing students with options and involving them in decision making are key facets of addressing the problem of engagement in the classroom and at school (Deci, 1995; Deci & Ryan, 1985, 2002; Ryan & Deci, 2000; Stipek, 1998). For example, numerous studies have shown that opportunities to express preferences and make choices lead to greater motivation, academic gains, increases in productivity, and on-task behavior and decreases in aggressive behavior. Similarly, researchers report that student participation in goal setting leads to more positive outcomes (e.g., higher commitment to goals and increased performance).

I KNOW YOU LIKE LUNCH TIME BEST, BUT THERE MUST BE SOMETHING ELSE YOU'D LIKE TO DO AT SCHOOL!

CONCLUDING COMMENTS

Getting students involved in their education programs is more than having them participate; it is connecting students with their education, enabling them to influence and affect the program and, indeed, enabling them to become enwrapped and engrossed in their educational experiences.

—Wehrmeyer (1998, p. 2)

Whatever the initial cause of individuals' learning and behavior problems, the longer they have lived with such problems, the more likely that they will have negative feelings and thoughts about instruction, teachers, and schools. The feelings include anxiety, fear, frustration, and anger. The thoughts may include strong expectations of failure and vulnerability and low valuing of many learning "opportunities." Such thoughts and feelings can result in avoidance motivation or low motivation for learning and performing in many areas of schooling.

Low motivation leads to halfhearted effort. Avoidance motivation leads to avoidance behaviors. Individuals with avoidance and low motivation often also are attracted to socially disapproved activity. Poor effort, avoidance behavior, and active pursuit of disapproved behavior on the part of students are surefire recipes for failure and worse.

It remains tempting to focus directly on student misbehavior. And it also is tempting to think that behavior problems can be exorcized by laying down the law. We have seen many administrators pursue this line of thinking. For every student who shapes up, ten others experience a Greek tragedy that inevitably ends in the student being pushed out of school through a progression of suspensions, "opportunity" transfers, and expulsions. Official dropout figures don't tell the tale. What we see in most high schools in cities such as Los Angeles; Baltimore; Washington, DC; Miami; and Detroit is that only about half those who were enrolled in the ninth grade are still around to graduate from twelfth grade.

Most of these students entered kindergarten with a healthy curiosity and a desire to learn to read and write. By the end of second grade, the first referrals started being made by classroom teachers because of learning and behavior problems. From that point on, increasing numbers of students became disengaged from classroom learning, and most of these manifested some form of behavioral and emotional problems.

It is not surprising, then, that many people are heartened to see the shift from punishment to positive behavior support in addressing unwanted behavior. However, as long as factors that lead to disengagement are left unaddressed, we risk perpetuating the phenomenon that William Ryan (1971) identified as *blaming the victim.*

From an intervention perspective, the point for emphasis is that engaging and reengaging students in classroom learning involves matching motivation. Matching motivation requires factoring in students' perceptions in determining the right mix of intrinsic and extrinsic reasons. It also requires understanding the key role played by expectations related to outcome. Without a good match, social control strategies can temporarily suppress negative attitudes and behaviors, but reengagement in classroom learning is unlikely. And without reengagement in classroom learning, unwanted behavior is very likely to reappear.

The remainder of this book is concerned with new directions for learning support that can help reverse negative trends related to student attendance, participation, and achievement. We explore what leaders need to change in classrooms, schoolwide, and in collaboration with families and the community at large.

Let the main object . . . be as follows: To seek and to find a method of instruction by which teachers may teach less but learners learn more; by which schools may be the scene of less noise, aversion, and useless labour, but of more leisure, enjoyment, and solid progress.

—Comenius (1632)

REFERENCES

Adelman, H. S., & Taylor, L. (1993). *Learning problems and learning disabilities: Moving forward.* Pacific Grove, CA: Brooks/Cole.

American Youth Policy Forum. (2000). *High schools of the millennium report,* Washington, DC: Author.

Ausubel, N. (Ed.). (1948). *A treasury of Jewish folklore.* New York: Crown.

Brophy, J. (2004). *Motivating students to learn* (2nd ed.). Mahwah, NJ: Erlbaum.

Bruner, J. S. (1966). *Toward a theory of instruction.* Cambridge, MA: Belknap.

Center for Mental Health in Schools at UCLA. (2001). *Enhancing classroom approaches for addressing barriers to learning: Classroom focused enabling.* Los Angeles: Author.

Deci, E. L. (1975). *Intrinsic motivation.* New York: Plenum.

Deci, E. L. (with Flaste, R.). (1995). *Why we do what we do.* New York: Penguin.

Deci, E. L., & Ryan, R. M. (1985). *Intrinsic motivation and self-determination in human behavior.* New York: Plenum.

Deci, E. L., & Ryan, R. M. (2002). The paradox of achievement: The harder you push, the worse it gets. In J. Aronson (Ed.), *Improving academic achievement: Contributions of social psychology* (pp. 59–85). New York: Academic Press.

Fredricks, J. A., Blumenfeld, P. C., & Paris, A. H. (2004). School engagement: Potential of the concept, state of the evidence. *Review of Educational Research, 74,* 59–109.

Holt, J. (1989). *Learning all the time.* Reading, MA: Addison-Wesley.

National Research Council and the Institute of Medicine. (2004). *Engaging schools: Fostering high school students' motivation to learn.* Washington, DC: National Academies Press.

Ryan, R. M., & Deci, E. L. (2000). Intrinsic and extrinsic motivations: Classic definitions and new directions. *Contemporary Educational Psychology, 25,* 54–67.

Ryan, W. (1971). *Blaming the victim.* New York: Random House.

Stipek, D. J. (1998). *Motivation to learn: From theory to practice* (3rd ed.). Boston: Allyn & Bacon.

Wehrmeyer, M. L. (1998). Student involvement in education planning, decision making, and instruction: An idea whose time has arrived. In M. L. Wehrmeyer & D. J. Sands (Eds.), *Making it happen: Student involvement in education planning, decision making, and instruction.* Baltimore: Brookes.

PART II

New Directions for Learning Support at a School Site

I find the great thing in this world is not so much where we stand, as in which direction we are moving.

—Oliver W. Holmes

S chools are getting better and better at building triage and referral systems for students who manifest learning, behavior, and emotional problems. Not surprisingly, this leads to the "field of dreams" effect (*build it and they will come*). In some schools, the number of requests is so large that these systems are overwhelmed and unable to handle more than a small percentage of students. As stressed in Part I, schools committed to the success of all children must be redesigned so that teachers and support staff are better equipped to help many more of these students. In this respect, we stressed that schools need a major component for addressing barriers to learning that is fully integrated with the school's efforts to facilitate learning and promote healthy development. Such a component is key to appropriately stemming the tide of referrals out of the classroom.

Good schools want to do their best for *all* students. This, of course, reflects our society's commitment to equity, fairness, and justice. But if this commitment is to be meaningful, it cannot be approached simplistically. (It was said of the legendary coach Vince Lombardi that he was always fair because he treated all his players the same—like dogs!) In schools, equity, fairness, and justice start with designing instruction in ways that account for a wide range of individual differences and circumstances. But the work can't stop there if we are to ensure that all students have an equal opportunity to succeed at school. Teachers and student support staff must be prepared to design a comprehensive approach that accommodates and assists the many learning, behavior, and emotional problems they encounter.

Good teachers and support staff are keenly interested in improving schools. In the process, they tend to look around at what others have found to work well. As a result, most end up being rather eclectic in their daily practice. Thoughtfully put together, an eclectic approach can be a healthy alternative to fads, fancies, and dogmatisms. But care must be taken to avoid grabbing hold of every new idea one learns about. (Too often, if it looks appealing, it is adopted—regardless of whether it is valid or consistent with other practices being used.) This is naive eclecticism and can result in more harm than good. No one should use a casual and undiscriminating approach in pursuing the mission of schools. Moreover, no one should think there is a "magic bullet" that will solve the many dilemmas school staff encounter every day.

The way to avoid naive eclecticism is to build one's intervention approaches on a coherent and consistent set of

- Underlying concepts
- Practice guidelines that reflect these concepts
- Best practices that fit the guidelines
- Valid scientific data as they become available

Each of these considerations guides the following discussion about developing a component to address barriers to learning and teaching.

New directions for learning supports must be a key facet of school improvement, especially where large numbers of students are not doing well and at any school that is not yet paying adequate attention to considerations related to equity and diversity. A schoolwide improvement plan that addresses learning and behavior problems must spell out a component that enables the entire school to ensure that *all* students have an equal opportunity to learn and *all* teachers have the capacity to teach effectively. In Part II, we discuss such an *Enabling* or *Learning Supports Component*.

Chapter 5 introduces what is involved in reframing policy and practice for the way schools address barriers to learning and teaching. Outlined is a comprehensive, multifaceted, and cohesive approach that is designed to end the marginalization, fragmentation, and counterproductive competition that characterizes existing student support programs and services. Chapter 6 highlights specific facets of an Enabling or Learning Supports Component, and Chapter 7 highlights the process of establishing such a component.

Development of a comprehensive approach also requires doing more to connect families and communities to schools. Fortunately, this can be done by appropriately capitalizing on the increasing interest in *school-community collaborations*. We discuss this in Chapter 8.

Then in Chapter 9, we look at matters related to accountability and evaluation. In doing so, we explore the available research base for developing comprehensive, multifaceted approaches and explore the question of what constitutes appropriate evaluation.

> Because kids need us most when they are at their worst, we must redesign schools and prepare school staff to meet the challenge.

Finally, we offer a coda to touch upon the problems of developing innovative approaches and taking them to scale across a school district.

Addressing Barriers   **5**
to Learning in Schools

It is not enough to say that all children can learn or that no child will be left behind; the work involves . . . achieving the vision of an American education system that enables all children to succeed in school, work, and life.

—Council of Chief State School Officers (2002)

Now that you've been
in school for a while,
how do you like it?   Closed!
    \   /

ORIENTING QUESTIONS

? What type of policy shift is needed to move in new directions for
  learning supports?
? What are some guidelines for a comprehensive Learning Supports
  Component?

In Chapter 2, we outlined the range of learners and the types of
problems found in every school. We noted that the proportions of each
type differ depending on such matters as the socioeconomic status of the
families who send their youngsters to the school. This is clear from any
analysis comparing the majority of suburban schools with most schools in
urban and rural areas serving poor families. We begin by exploring some
implications of this state of affairs for efforts to increase achievement test
scores and close the achievement gap.

As portrayed in Guide 5.1, those students who come to school each day
motivationally ready and able to learn what the teacher will be teaching can

Guide 5.1   Barriers to Learning Interfere With Enhancing Achievement

---

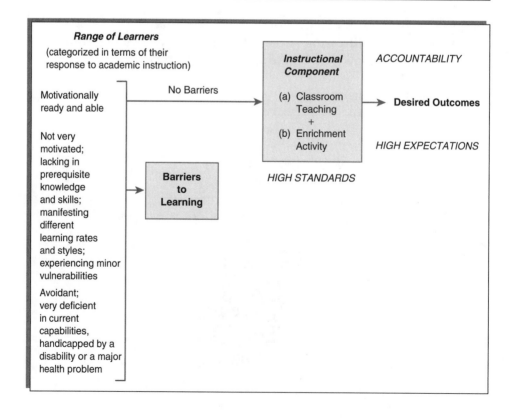

be viewed as a group that does not experience barriers to learning. For these students, a focus on making instruction better is sufficient to ensure that desired outcomes for academic achievement are reached. All others encounter barriers that interfere with benefiting from their teachers' efforts to provide good instruction. (Remember, for most students, the barriers are not the result of personal deficits.)

In some schools, particularly those in urban and rural areas serving poor families, a large proportion of students encounter barriers. Where this is the case, enhancing achievement test scores and closing the achievement gap over the long run require more than just improving instruction.

Available evidence suggests that many schools use a variety of short-term strategies to produce some quick achievement test gains. However, within a few years, most bump into what some researchers have called a "plateau" effect, whereby student scores improve the first few years and then stabilize or stagnate around year three or four (e.g., Elmore, 2003; Linn & Haug, 2002; National Center for Educational Statistics, 2003).

Picture a school where most of the students come from economically disadvantaged families. The overall reading test scores for the fourth graders are somewhere in the 20th percentile. The administrators pursue a number of strategies to improve the situation. Among other things, they adopt a new reading curriculum and provide teachers with inservice training and supervision as the new approaches are implemented; they take steps to be certain the teachers know what student achievement tests will cover; students are taught specific test-taking skills so that the test process won't throw them; and extra tutoring is provided, especially in the weeks before tests are administered. As a result, the next test scores indicate an average increase of 8 percentile points; the following test period yields a 3 percentile increase. After that, however, the scores level off. This state of affairs wouldn't be so bad for a suburban school with students scoring initially about the 75th percentile and moving up to the 86th percentile before plateauing. For a low performing school, however, moving students from the 25th to the 36th percentile and then hitting a ceiling is a disaster for the school and for the future of its students.

A simple psychometric reality exists for schools with a high proportion of learners who do not come to school motivationally ready and able to learn what the teacher is teaching each day. Test score averages in a school district and for big schools are unlikely to increase substantially over the long term unless schools enable a large number of these students to move around the barriers that interfere with their benefiting from a teacher's efforts to provide good instruction.

Thus, although schools aren't responsible for meeting every need of their students, as the Carnegie Council's Task Force on Education of Young Adolescents (1989) cogently states, *When the need directly affects learning, the school must meet the challenge.* And we would add that meeting the challenge requires reframing and restructuring student support programs, resources, and personnel roles and functions.

RETHINKING STUDENT AND LEARNING SUPPORTS

Rather than address the problems surrounding school-owned support programs and services, policymakers seem to have become enamored with the concept of school-linked services, as if adding a few community health and social services to a few schools is a sufficient solution. The social marketing around "school-linked, integrated services" has led some policymakers to the mistaken impression that community resources alone can effectively meet the needs of schools in addressing barriers to learning. In turn, this has led some legislators to view linking community services to schools as a way to free up dollars underwriting school-owned services. The reality is that even when one adds together community and school assets, the total set of services in impoverished locales is woefully inadequate. In situation after situation, it has become evident that as soon as the first few sites demonstrating school-community collaboration are in place, community agencies find their resources stretched to the limit.

Thus, while school-linked services might provide more referral resources for a few students in such locales, the number of students in need of support far outstrips what publicly supported community agencies can make available. Awareness is growing that there can never be enough school-based and school-linked support services to meet the demand in many public schools. Moreover, it is becoming more and more evident that efforts to address barriers to student learning will continue to be marginalized in policy and practice as long as the focus is narrowly on providing "services."

Another problem is that overemphasis on school-linked services exacerbates tensions between school district service personnel and their counterparts in community-based organizations. As "outside" professionals offer services at schools, school specialists often view the trend as discounting their skills and threatening their jobs. At the same time, the "outsiders" often feel unappreciated and may be rather naive about the culture of schools. Conflicts arise over turf, use of space, confidentiality, and liability. Thus competition rather than a substantive commitment to collaboration remains the norm.

As inadequate as school-owned student support services are at most schools, the resources invested in student support staff (e.g., school psychologists, counselors, social workers, nurses) usually exceeds to a considerable degree what local public agencies can afford to link to a school. Moreover, schools have other resources they can use to meet the challenge of ensuring that all students have an equal opportunity to succeed at school. Besides traditional pupil service personnel, student support is provided by compensatory education personnel (e.g., Title I staff), resource teachers who focus on prereferral interventions, and staff associated with a variety of schoolwide programs (e.g., afterschool and safe and drug-free school programs).

Rethinking how all these resources are used can lead to

- More effective deployment of existing resources (by minimizing fragmentation, redundancy, counterproductive competition, and policy marginalization)
- Reframing student supports as *learning supports* that address barriers to student learning and realigning support staff roles and functions to develop comprehensive, multifaceted, and cohesive approaches
- Fully integrating learning supports programs and staff into the school improvement agenda at every school
- Revamping infrastructures to weave resources together and provide mechanisms for enhancing and evolving how schools address barriers to student learning

All this calls for a significant shift in the policy currently driving school improvement.

A POLICY SHIFT

As indicated in Chapter 3, analyses of current policy indicate that school improvement initiatives are dominated by a two-component model. The main thrust is on improving instruction and how schools manage resources. While there are a variety of student support programs and services, they are marginalized in policy and practice, and they are pursued in piecemeal and fragmented ways. Throughout many years of school reform, little or no attention has been paid to rethinking these learning supports. As we stressed in Part I, this state of affairs must change if *all* students are to have an equal opportunity to succeed at school.

Guide 5.2 illustrates the notion that school improvement policy must shift from a two- to a three-component approach. This means taking all the resources currently expended for learning supports and creating a comprehensive and cohesive third component for addressing barriers to enable students to learn and teachers to teach. As with the other two components, such an Enabling or Learning Supports Component must be treated in policy and practice as primary and essential in order to combat marginalization and fragmentation of learning supports. Furthermore, to be effective, it must be fully integrated with the other two components. Properly conceived, it provides a focal point for developing a comprehensive framework to guide planning and implementation of learning supports at all levels.

Various states and localities are moving in the direction of a three-component approach for school improvement. In doing so, they are adopting different labels for their enabling component. For example, the state education agencies in California and Iowa and various districts across the

Guide 5.2 Moving From a Two-component to a Three-component Model for School Improvement

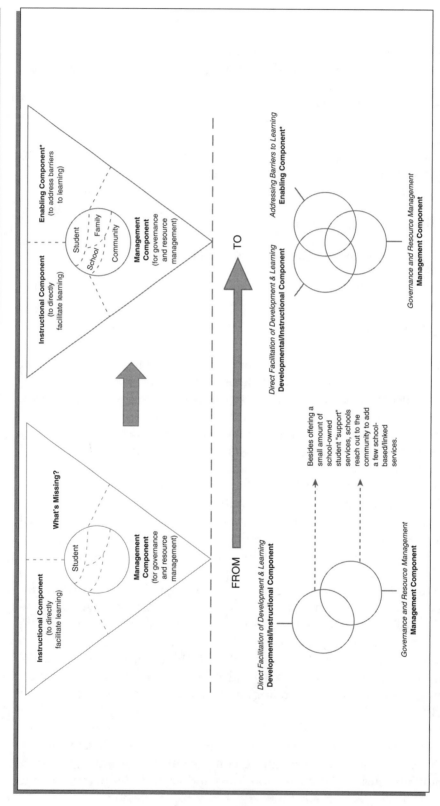

*The third component (an Enabling or Learning Supports Component) is established in policy and practice as primary and essential and is developed into a comprehensive approach by weaving together school and community resources.

country have adopted the term *learning supports.* So has the New American Schools' Urban Learning Center's comprehensive school reform model. Because the Urban Learning Center model is listed in legislation for comprehensive school reform, the concept of a Learning Supports Component is being adopted in schools in California, Oregon, Utah, and other locales. Some states use the term *supportive learning environment.* The Hawaii Department of Education calls it a *Comprehensive Student Support System.* Building on this, proposed legislation in California calls it a *Comprehensive Pupil Learning Supports System.* Whatever the component is called, the important points are that (a) all three components are seen as necessary, complementary, and overlapping and (b) efforts to address barriers to development, learning, and teaching can no longer be marginalized in policy and practice.

Each pioneering initiative recognizes *at a policy level* that schools must do much more to *enable* all students to learn and all teachers to teach effectively. This translates not only into improvement of instruction and school management but also into development of a comprehensive way to address barriers to learning. In effect, the intent, over time, is for schools to play a major role in establishing the type of widely advocated framework for a full school-community continuum of interventions, consisting of

- Systems for promoting healthy development and preventing problems
- Systems for intervening early to address problems as soon after onset as is feasible
- Systems for assisting those with chronic and severe problems (again see Guide 3.1)

Such a continuum encompasses efforts to enable academic, social, emotional, and physical development and address learning, behavior, and emotional problems at every school. As noted, most schools have some programs and services that fit along the entire continuum. However, the tendency to focus mostly on the most severe problems has skewed things so that too little is done to prevent and intervene early after the onset of a problem. As a result, the whole enterprise has been characterized as a "waiting for failure" approach.

SOME CHARACTERISTICS OF A COMPREHENSIVE, MULTIFACETED APPROACH TO ADDRESSING BARRIERS TO DEVELOPMENT AND LEARNING

The concept of an Enabling or Learning Supports Component is formulated around the proposition that a comprehensive, multifaceted, integrated continuum of enabling activity is essential in addressing the needs of youngsters who encounter barriers that interfere with their learning.

The concept of an Enabling or Learning Supports Component embraces healthy development, prevention, and addressing barriers. It stresses the value of establishing high standards and appropriately high expectations. Thus it is not a case of a negative versus a positive emphasis (or excusing or blaming anyone). It's not about what's wrong versus what's right with kids. It is about continuing to face up to the reality of major extrinsic barriers as well as personal vulnerabilities and real disorders and disabilities— all factors that can interfere with a youngster's reaching full potential.

The focus begins in the classroom, with differentiated classroom practices as the base of support for each youngster. This includes

- Addressing barriers through a broader view of "basics" and through effective accommodation of learner differences
- Enhancing the focus on motivational considerations with a special emphasis on intrinsic motivation as it relates to learner readiness and ongoing involvement, with the intent of fostering intrinsic motivation as a basic outcome
- Adding remediation as necessary but only as necessary

Note that remedial procedures are added to instructional programs for certain individuals but only after appropriate nonremedial procedures for facilitating learning have been tried. Moreover, such procedures are designed to build on strengths and are not allowed to supplant a continuing emphasis on promoting healthy development.

Beyond the classroom, the focus is on policy, leadership, and various organizational and operational mechanisms to ensure development of a full array of learning supports. The emphasis is on ensuring that such supports effectively address a wide range of barriers to development, learning, parenting, and teaching. Some of this activity requires partnering among schools; some requires weaving school and community resources and programs together. The intent is to have youngsters, families, and staff feel that they are truly welcome at school and throughout the community, to provide them with a range of supports, and to ensure emergence of a healthy and caring environment and a sense of community.

In sum, for students, the intent of an Enabling or Learning Supports Component is to prevent and minimize the impact of as many problems as feasible and to do so in ways that maximize engagement in productive learning and positive development. For the school and community as a whole, the intent is to produce a safe, healthy, nurturing environment and culture characterized by respect for differences, trust, caring, and support.

Reframing How Schools Address Barriers to Learning

In restructuring learning supports and braiding school, community, and home resources, it is important to design the process from the school outward. That is, the initial emphasis is on what the classroom and school must do to reach and teach all students effectively. Then the focus expands to include planning how the feeder pattern of schools and the surrounding community can complement each other's efforts and achieve economies of scale. Central district and community agency staff then restructure in ways that best support these efforts.

Pioneering efforts have operationalized the continuum of interventions into a framework consisting of six programmatic arenas. In effect, they have moved from a "laundry list" of programs, services, and activities to a defined content or "curriculum" framework that categorizes and captures the essence of the multifaceted ways that schools need to address barriers to learning (see Guide 5.3).

As illustrated in Guide 5.3, the six content arenas organize learning supports into programs for

- *Enhancing regular classroom strategies to enable learning* (e.g., improving instruction for students with mild to moderate learning and behavior problems and reengaging those who have become disengaged from learning at school)
- *Supporting transitions* (e.g., assisting students and families as they negotiate school and grade changes, daily transitions)
- *Increasing home and school connections*
- *Responding to and, where feasible, preventing school and personal crises*
- *Increasing community involvement and support* (e.g., outreach to develop greater community involvement and support, including enhanced use of volunteers)
- *Facilitating student and family access to effective services and special assistance as needed*

Combining these six content arenas with the continuum of interventions illustrated in Guide 3.1 provides a "big picture" of what we mean by the phrase *a comprehensive, multifaceted, and integrated approach*. The resulting matrix creates a unifying umbrella framework to guide the rethinking and restructuring of the daily work of all staff who provide learning supports at a school (see Guide 5.4). The matrix can be used to guide the mapping and analysis of the current scope and content of the way one school, a family of schools, and a school district address barriers to learning, development, and teaching.

Most *formal* studies have focused on specific interventions. This literature reports positive outcomes (for school and society) associated with a wide range of interventions. Because of the fragmented nature of available research, the findings are best appreciated in terms of the whole being greater than the sum of the parts, and implications are best derived from the total theoretical and empirical picture. When such a broad perspective is adopted, schools have a large research base to draw upon in addressing barriers to learning and enhancing healthy development. Examples of this research base have been organized into the earlier mentioned six arenas and are highlighted in Chapter 9.

Guide 5.3   A School Site Component to Address Barriers to Learning and Enhance Healthy Development

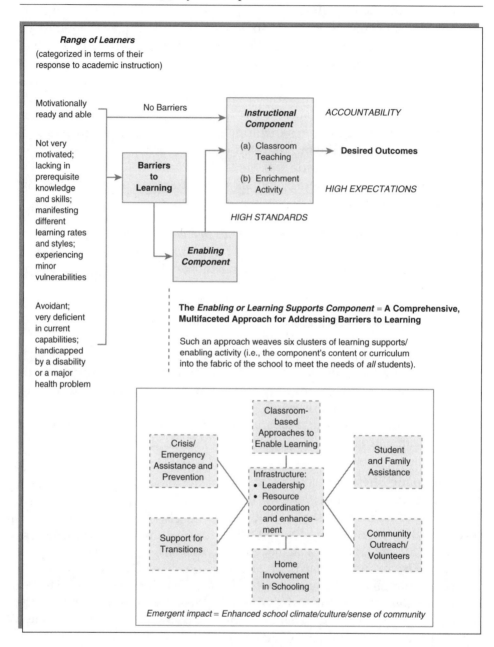

Guide 5.5 captures the essence of the matrix but is intended to convey another message. The aim in developing such a comprehensive approach is to prevent the majority of problems, deal with another significant segment as soon after problem onset as is feasible, and end up with relatively few needing specialized assistance and other intensive and costly interventions. Research on this type of comprehensive approach is still in

Guide 5.4   A Unifying Umbrella Framework to Guide Rethinking of Learning Supports*

| | | Scope of Intervention | | |
		Systems for Promoting Healthy Development & Preventing Problems	Systems for Early Intervention (early after problem onset)	Systems of Care
Organizing around the **Content/ "Curriculum"** for addressing barriers to learning & promoting healthy development	Classroom-focused Enabling			
	Crisis/ Emergency Assistance & Prevention			
	Support for Transitions			
	Home Involvement in Schooling			
	Community Outreach/ Volunteers			
	Student and Family Assistance			

Accommodations for Differences & Disabilities   Specialized Assistance & Other Intensified Interventions (e.g., Special Education & School-based Behavioral Health)

*Note that specific schoolwide and classroom-based activities related to positive behavior support, prereferral interventions, and the eight components of the Center for Prevention and Disease Control's Coordinated School Health Program are embedded into the six content areas.

its infancy. There are, of course, many "natural" experiments underscoring the promise of ensuring all youngsters access to a comprehensive set of interventions. These natural experiments are playing out in every school and neighborhood where families are affluent enough to purchase the additional programs and services that they feel will maximize their youngsters' well-being. It is obvious that those who can afford such interventions understand their value.

Guide 5.5   A Comprehensive Approach to Reduce Learning, Behavior, and Emotional Problems

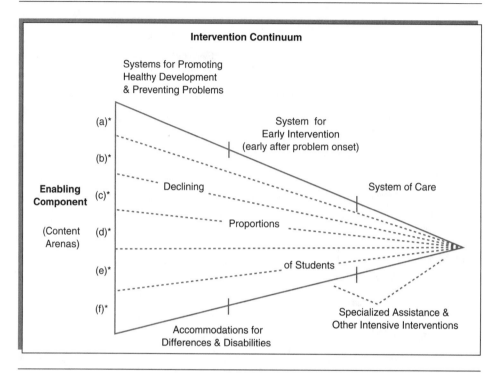

^a Classroom-based approaches to enable and reengage students in classroom learning
^b Support for transitions
^c Home involvement in schooling
^d Community outreach
^e Crisis and emergency assistance and prevention
^f Student and family assistance

WHAT NEXT?

Policy action is needed to guide and facilitate the development of a potent component to address barriers to learning and support the promotion of healthy development at every school. As recommended by participants in the *Summits Initiative: New Directions for Student Support* (Center for Mental Health in Schools, 2002), the policy should specify that such an Enabling or Learning Supports Component is to be pursued as a primary and essential facet of school improvement in ways that complement, overlap, and fully integrate with the instructional component.

The outline in Guide 5.6 provides a set of guidelines for a school's Learning Supports Component. Clearly, no school currently offers the nature and scope of what is embodied in the outline. In a real sense, the guidelines define a vision for such a component. They also provide the basis for delineating standards and quality and accountability indicators for such a component.

[a] Classroom-based approaches to enable and reengage students in classroom learning
[b] Support for transitions
[c] Home involvement in schooling
[d] Community outreach
[e] Crisis and emergency assistance and prevention
[f] Student and family assistance

Guide 5.6   Guidelines for an Enabling or Learning Supports
Component

1. Major Areas of Concern Related to Barriers to Student Learning

1.1. Addressing common educational and psychosocial problems (e.g., learning problems; language difficulties; attention problems; school adjustment and other life transition problems; attendance problems and dropouts; social, interpersonal, and familial problems; conduct and behavior problems; delinquency and gang-related problems; anxiety problems; affect and mood problems; sexual and/or physical abuse; neglect; substance abuse; psychological reactions to physical status and sexual activity; physical health problems)

1.2. Countering external stressors (e.g., reactions to objective or perceived stress, demands, crises, or deficits at home, school, and in the neighborhood; inadequate basic resources, such as food, clothing, and a sense of security; inadequate support systems; hostile and violent conditions)

1.3. Teaching, serving, and accommodating disorders and disabilities (e.g., learning disabilities; attention-deficit/hyperactivity disorder; school phobia; conduct disorder; depression; suicidal or homicidal ideation and behavior; posttraumatic stress disorder; anorexia and bulimia; special education designated disorders such as emotional disturbance and developmental disabilities)

2. Timing and Nature of Problem-oriented Interventions

2.1. Primary prevention

2.2. Intervening early after the onset of problems

2.3. Interventions for severe, pervasive, or chronic problems

3. General Domains for Intervention in Addressing Students' Needs and Problems

3.1. Ensuring academic success and also promoting healthy cognitive, social, emotional, and physical development and resilience (including promoting opportunities to enhance school performance and protective factors; fostering development of assets and general wellness; enhancing responsibility and integrity, self-efficacy, social and working relationships, self-evaluation and self-direction, personal safety and safe behavior, health maintenance, effective physical functioning, careers and life roles, creativity)

3.2. Addressing external and internal barriers to student learning and performance

3.3. Providing social and emotional support for students, families, and staff

4. Specialized Student and Family Assistance (Individual and Group)

4.1. Assessment for initial (first level) screening of problems, as well as for diagnosis and intervention planning (including a focus on needs and assets)

4.2. Referral, triage, and monitoring and management of care

4.3. Direct services and instruction (e.g., primary prevention programs, including enhancement of wellness through instruction, skills development, guidance counseling, advocacy, schoolwide programs to foster safe and caring climates, and liaison connections between school and home; crisis intervention and assistance, including psychological and physical first aid; prereferral interventions; accommodations to allow for differences and disabilities; transition and follow-up programs; short- and longer-term treatment, remediation, and rehabilitation)

4.4. Coordination, development, and leadership related to school-owned programs, services, resources, and systems—toward evolving a comprehensive, multifaceted, and integrated continuum of programs and services

4.5. Consultation, supervision, and inservice instruction with a transdisciplinary focus

4.6. Enhancing connections with and involvement of home and community resources (including but not limited to community agencies)

5. Assuring Quality of Intervention

5.1. Systems and interventions are monitored and improved as necessary.

5.2. Programs and services constitute a comprehensive, multifaceted continuum.

5.3. Interveners have appropriate knowledge and skills for their roles and functions and provide guidance for continuing professional development.

5.4. School-owned programs and services are coordinated and integrated.

5.5. School-owned programs and services are connected to home and community resources.

5.6. Programs and services are integrated with instructional and governance/management components at schools.

5.7. Programs and services are available, accessible, and attractive.

5.8. Empirically supported interventions are used when applicable.

5.9. Differences among students or families are appropriately accounted for (e.g., diversity, disability, developmental levels, motivational levels, strengths, weaknesses).

5.10. Legal considerations are appropriately accounted for (e.g., mandated services; mandated reporting and its consequences).

5.11. Ethical issues are appropriately accounted for (e.g., privacy & confidentiality; coercion).

5.12. Contexts for intervention are appropriate (e.g., office; clinic; classroom; home).

6. Outcome Evaluation and Accountability

6.1. Short-term outcome data

6.2. Long-term outcome data

6.3. Reporting to key stakeholders and using outcome data to enhance intervention quality

SOURCE: Adapted from *Mental Health in Schools: Guidelines, Models, Resources, and Policy Considerations,* a document developed by the Policy Leadership Cadre for Mental Health in Schools (2002). This document is available from the Center for Mental Health in Schools at UCLA; downloadable from the center's Web site at: http://smhp.psych.ucla.edu/pdf docs/policymakers/guidelinesexecsumm.pdf. A separate document providing the rationale and science base for the version of the guidelines adapted for learning supports is available at http://smhp.psych.ucla.edu/summit2002/guidelinessupportdoc.pdf.

Beyond component guidelines, it is clear that the systemic changes necessary to move toward a comprehensive component will require support and direction related to

1. *Phasing in* development of the component's six content arenas at every school

2. *Expanding standards and accountability indicators* for schools to ensure that this component is fully integrated with the instructional component and pursued with equal effort in policy and practice

3. *Restructuring* at every school and at the district level with respect to
   - Redefining administrative roles and functions to ensure dedicated administrative leadership that is authorized and has the capability to facilitate, guide, and support the systemic changes for ongoing development of such a component at every school
   - Reframing the roles and functions of pupil services personnel and other student support staff to ensure development of the component (see Chapter 13)
   - Redesigning the infrastructure to establish a team at every school and at the district level that plans, implements, and evaluates how resources are used to build the component's capacity[1]

4. *Weaving resources* into a cohesive and integrated continuum of interventions over time

   In addition, action steps should focus on

   - *Boards of Education:* To move each toward establishing a standing subcommittee focused specifically on ensuring effective implementation of policy for developing a component to address barriers to student learning at each school
   - *Preservice and Inservice Programs for School Personnel:* To move them toward the inclusion of a substantial focus on the concept of an Enabling or Learning Supports Component and how to operationalize it at a school in ways that fully integrate with instruction

All this will require effective collaboration among a wide range of stakeholders.

CONCLUDING COMMENTS

Limited efficacy seems inevitable as long as the full continuum of necessary programs is unavailable and staff development remains deficient; limited cost-effectiveness seems inevitable as long as related interventions are carried out in isolation of each other; limited systemic change is likely as long as the entire enterprise is marginalized in policy and practice. Given all this, it is not surprising that many in the field doubt that major breakthroughs can occur without major commitment to a comprehensive, multifaceted, and integrated continuum of interventions. Such views add impetus to trailblazing initiatives that are under way, designed to restructure the way schools operate in addressing learning and behavior problems.

A fundamental shift in policy thinking is long overdue. The next decade must mark a turning point in how schools and communities address the problems of children and youth and promote healthy development. Policymakers must establish better ways for schools, families, and communities to work together in meeting the challenge. Particularly needed are initiatives to reform and restructure the ways schools work to prevent and ameliorate the learning, behavior, and emotional problems experienced by many students. In the process, the roles and functions of all school personnel who have a role to play in this will have to be reshaped. At this stage in the ongoing development of our schools, it is essential to take the next steps toward ensuring that such approaches are in place. There is much work to be done as public schools across the country are called upon to leave no child behind.

NOTE

1. The Center for Mental Health in Schools at UCLA has a variety of resources related to all these matters. For example, see

- *Developing Resource-oriented Mechanisms to Enhance Learning Supports.* (2003). http://smhp.psych.ucla.edu/pdfdocs/contedu/developing_resource_oriented-mechanisms.pdf.
- *Resource-oriented Teams: Key Infrastructure Mechanisms for Enhancing Education Supports.* (2001). http://smhp.psych.ucla.edu/qf/infrastructure_tt/excerpt fromresource_oriented_teams.pdf.

- *New Directions in Enhancing Educational Results: Policymakers' Guide to Restructuring Student Support Resources to Address Barriers to Learning.* (1999). http://smhp.psych.ucla.edu/pdfdocs/policymakers/restrucguide.pdf.
- *Framing New Directions for School Counselors, Psychologists, & Social Workers.* (2001). http://smhp.psych.ucla.edu/pdfdocs/Report/framingnewdir.pdf.

All also are available in hard copy.

REFERENCES

Carnegie Council on Adolescent Development's Task Force on Education of Young Adolescents. (1989). *Turning points: Preparing American youth for the 21st century.* Washington, DC: Author.

Center for Mental Health in Schools. (2002). *Summits initiative: New directions for student support.* Los Angeles: Author, UCLA. Retrieved March 21, 2005, from www. smhp.psych.ucla.edu.

Council of Chief State School Officers. (2002). Council of Chief State School Officers unveils new strategic direction. News release. Washington, DC: CCSSO. Retrieved March 23, 2005, from www.ccsso.org/Whats_New/press_releases/148.cfm.

Elmore, R. F. (2003). *Knowing the right thing to do: School improvement and performance-based accountability.* Washington, DC: NGA Center for Best Practices. Retrieved March 21, 2005, from www.nga.org.

Linn, R. L., & Haug, C. (2002). Stability of school building accountability scores and gains. *Educational Evaluation and Policy Analysis, 24,* 29–36.

National Center for Educational Statistics. (2003). *National trends in reading, mathematics, and science.* Retrieved March 21, 2005, from www.nces.ed.gov/ssbr/pages/trends.asp.

Policy Leadership Cadre for Mental Health in Schools. (2002). *Mental health in schools: Guidelines, models, resources, and policy considerations.* Los Angeles: Center for Mental Health in Schools at UCLA. Retrieved March 23, 2005, from www.smhp.psych.ucla.edu/pdfdocs/policymakers/guidelinesexecsumm.pdf.

A Schoolwide Component for Learning Support

6

As for the future, our task is not to foresee, but to enable it.

—Antoine de Saint-Exupery

Education reform is a paradox.

That's right. Everyone is going down the same road in different directions.

ORIENTING QUESTIONS

? What is a promising framework for a schoolwide component for learning supports?
? What might such a component be called?
? In providing learning supports, why is it important to keep mutual support, caring, and a sense of community in mind?

If we replace anonymity with community, sorting with support, and bureaucracy with autonomy, we can create systems of schools that truly help all students achieve.

—Tom Vander Ark (2002)

Adoption of a three-component model is intended to end the marginalization and fragmentation of education support programs and services at school sites. Moreover, the notion of a third component can be operationalized in ways that unify a school's efforts in developing a comprehensive, multifaceted, and cohesive approach.

Based on an extensive analysis of activities used to address barriers to learning, a delimited framework has been formulated as a guide for initiatives implementing an enabling component. In this chapter, we elaborate on all this.

THE CONCEPT OF AN ENABLING COMPONENT

Enabling is defined as providing with the means or opportunity; making possible, practical, or easy; giving power, capacity, or sanction to (World Health Organization, 1998). The concept of an enabling component is formulated on the proposition that a comprehensive, multifaceted, integrated continuum of enabling activity *is essential* for addressing the needs of youngsters who encounter barriers that interfere with their learning at school. From this perspective, schools committed to the success of all children should be redesigned to *enable learning* by addressing interfering barriers. This entails a focus not only on improving instruction but also on ways to improve how schools support learning and teaching.

The concept of an enabling component is meant to expand the focus of school improvement and provide a unifying framework to guide new directions for learning supports. It underscores the need to weave together school and community resources to address a wide range of factors interfering with young people's learning, performance, and well-being. It embraces efforts to promote healthy development and foster positive functioning as the best way to prevent many learning, behavior, emotional, and health problems and as a necessary adjunct to correcting problems experienced by teachers, students, and families.

As noted in Chapter 5, schools, districts, and states across the country are beginning to explore the value of enhancing efforts to develop a comprehensive, multifaceted, and integrated approach to addressing barriers to student learning. In doing so, they are adopting different names. Many feel comfortable with calling it an Enabling Component. Others have a negative association with the term because in the substance abuse literature on codependency, "enablers" are seen as a problem. While it is too bad that some have a negative association with the term, we think "to enable" is a fine verb. We were particularly pleased to see the Council of Chief State School Officers (2002) revamp their mission statement in 2002 to clarify that the aim is to achieve the vision of "an American education system that *enables* all children to succeed in school, work, and life" (italics are ours). Our preferences aside, others are adopting terms such as a "Learning Supports Component" and a component for a "Supportive Learning Environment." In the state of Hawaii, the component is called a Comprehensive Student Support System, and efforts are under way to create such a component in every school. As a terminology compromise, we use both Enabling and Learning Supports throughout this book.

Building on our work, many places are grouping all enabling or learning supports activity into a delimited set of programmatic arenas. With some modifications, the six arenas highlighted in Chapter 5 and illustrated in Guides 5.3 through 5.5 have provided a broad unifying framework around which learning supports can be restructured. The six arenas are illustrated again in Guide 6.1 as a focus for the ensuing discussion.

To reiterate, the six arenas are

- Enhancing the classroom teacher's capacity to address problems; reengage students in classroom learning; and foster social, emotional, intellectual, and behavioral development
- Enhancing the capacity of schools to handle the many transition concerns confronting students and their families
- Responding to, minimizing the impact of, and preventing crises
- Enhancing home involvement
- Reaching out to the surrounding community to build linkages and develop greater community involvement and support
- Providing special assistance for students and families

Note that a key element of the component involves building the capacity of classrooms to enhance instructional effectiveness. Such classroom-focused enabling involves personalized instruction that

Guide 6.1   Six Arenas of an Enabling Component

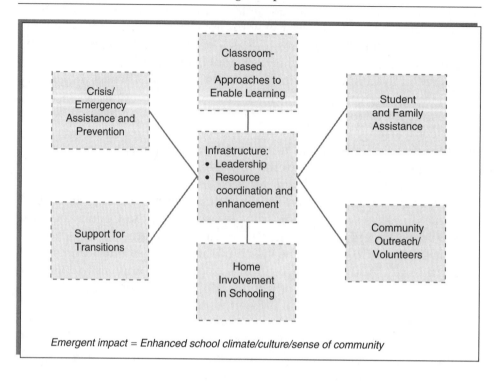

accounts for motivational and developmental differences and special assistance in the classroom as needed. Beyond the classroom, the other five arenas encompass a range of programs and services that enable teaching and learning.

Unfortunately, most school reformers seem unaware that for all students to benefit from higher standards and improved instruction, schools must play a major role in developing such an enabling curriculum. Without it, the resolution of learning and behavior problems is left to current strategies for improving instruction and controlling behavior. And clearly, this has been tried and found wanting.

AN ENABLING OR LEARNING SUPPORTS COMPONENT AT A SCHOOL SITE

A first task in operationalizing an enabling or learning supports component involves delineating each content arena. Each arena is described briefly in the discussion to follow and outlined more fully in the series of self-study surveys in Chapter 14.

Classroom-based Approaches to Enable and Reengage Students in Classroom Learning

This arena provides a fundamental example not only of how an enabling component overlaps the instructional component but also of how it adds value to prevailing efforts to improve instruction. Classroom-based efforts to enable learning can (a) prevent problems, (b) facilitate intervening as soon as problems are noted, (c) enhance intrinsic motivation for learning, and (d) reengage students who have become disengaged from classroom learning.

When a teacher has difficulty with students, the first step is to address the problem within the regular classroom and involve the home to a greater extent. Through programmatic activity, classroom-based efforts that enable learning are enhanced. This is accomplished by increasing teachers' effectiveness so they can account for a wider range of individual differences, foster a caring context for learning, and prevent or handle a wider range of problems when they arise. Effectiveness is enhanced through personalized staff development and opening the classroom door to others who can help. One objective is to provide teachers with the knowledge and skills to develop a classroom infrastructure that transforms a big class into a set of smaller ones. Such a focus is essential for increasing the effectiveness of regular classroom instruction, supporting inclusionary policies, and reducing the need for specialized services.

Guide 6.2   Classroom-based Approaches

Classroom-based Approaches encompass

- *Opening the classroom door to bring available supports in* (e.g., peer tutors, volunteers, aides trained to work with students in need; resource teachers and student support staff to work in the classroom as part of the teaching team)
- *Redesigning classroom approaches* to enhance teacher capability to prevent and handle problems and reduce the need for out-of-class referrals (e.g. personalized instruction, special assistance as necessary, developing small-group and independent learning options, reducing negative interactions and overreliance on social control, expanding the range of curricular and instructional options and choices, systematic use of prereferral interventions)
- *Enhancing and personalizing professional development* (e.g., creating a learning community for teachers; ensuring opportunities to learn through coteaching, team teaching, and mentoring; teaching intrinsic motivation concepts and their application to schooling)
- *Curricular enrichment and adjunct programs* (e.g., varied enrichment activities not tied to reinforcement schedules; visiting scholars from the community)
- *Classroom and schoolwide approaches used to create and maintain a caring and supportive climate*

Emphasis at all times is on enhancing feelings of competence, self-determination, and relatedness to others at school and reducing threats to such feelings.

Work in this arena requires programmatic approaches and systems designed to personalize professional development of teachers and support staff, develop the capabilities of paraeducators and other paid assistants and volunteers, provide temporary out-of-class assistance for students, and enhance resources. For example, personalized help is provided to increase a teacher's array of strategies for accommodating, as well as teaching students to compensate for, differences, vulnerabilities, and disabilities. Teachers learn to use paid assistants, peer tutors, and volunteers in targeted ways to enhance social and academic support.

As appropriate, support *in the classroom* also is provided by resource and itinerant teachers and counselors. This involves restructuring and redesigning the roles, functions, and staff development of resource and itinerant teachers, counselors, and other pupil service personnel so they are able to work closely with teachers and students in the classroom and on regular activities. See Guide 6.2.

Crisis Assistance and Prevention

Schools must respond to, minimize the impact of, and prevent school and personal crises. This requires schoolwide and classroom-based systems and programmatic approaches. Such activity focuses on (a) emergency or crisis response at a site, throughout a school complex, and communitywide (including a focus on ensuring follow-up care), (b) minimizing the impact of crises, and (c) prevention at school and in the community to address school safety and violence reduction, suicide prevention, child abuse prevention, and so forth.

Guide 6.3   Crisis Assistance and Prevention

Crisis Assistance and Prevention encompasses

- *Ensuring immediate assistance in emergencies so students can resume learning*
- *Providing follow-up care as necessary* (e.g., brief and longer-term monitoring)
- *Forming a school-based crisis team to formulate a response plan and take leadership for developing prevention programs*
- *Mobilizing staff, students, and families to anticipate response plans and recovery efforts*
- *Creating a caring and safe learning environment* (e.g., developing systems to promote healthy development and prevent problems; bullying and harassment abatement programs)
- *Working with neighborhood schools and the community to integrate planning for response and prevention*
- *Capacity building to enhance crisis response and prevention* (e.g., staff and stakeholder development, enhancing a caring and safe learning environment)

Desired outcomes of crisis assistance include ensuring immediate emergency and follow-up care so that students are able to resume learning without too much delay. Prevention outcome indices point to a safe and productive environment where students and their families display the types of attitudes and capacities needed to deal with violence and other threats to safety.

A key mechanism in this arena often is the development of a crisis team. Such a team is trained in emergency response procedures, physical and psychological first aid, aftermath interventions, and so forth. The team also can take the lead in planning ways to prevent some crises by facilitating development of programs to mediate and resolve conflicts, enhance human relations, and promote a caring school culture (see Guide 6.3).

Support for Transitions

Students and their families are regularly confronted with a variety of transitions—changing schools, changing grades, encountering a range of other daily hassles and major life demands. Many of these can interfere with productive school involvement. A comprehensive focus on transitions requires schoolwide and classroom-based systems and programs designed to (a) enhance successful transitions, (b) prevent transition problems, and (c) use transition periods to reduce alienation and increase positive attitudes toward school and learning. Examples of such programs include schoolwide and classroom-specific activities for welcoming new arrivals (students, their families, staff) and rendering ongoing social support; counseling and articulation strategies to support grade-to-grade and school-to-school transitions and moves to and from special education, college, and postschool living and work; and beforeschool, afterschool, and intersession activities to enrich learning and provide recreation in a safe environment.

Guide 6.4 Support for Transitions

Support for Transitions encompasses

- *Welcoming and social support programs for newcomers* (e.g., welcoming signs, materials, and initial receptions; peer buddy programs for students, families, staff, volunteers)
- *Daily transition programs* (e.g., for before school, breaks, lunch, after school)
- *Articulation programs* (e.g., grade to grade: new classrooms, new teachers; elementary to middle school; middle to high school; in and out of special education programs)
- *Summer or intersession programs* (e.g., catch-up, recreation, and enrichment programs)
- *School to career or higher education* (e.g., counseling, pathway, and mentor programs)
- *Broad involvement of stakeholders in planning for transitions* (e.g., students, staff, home, police, faith groups, recreation, business, higher education)
- *Capacity building to enhance transition programs and activities*

Anticipated overall outcomes are reduced alienation and enhanced motivation and increased involvement in school and learning activities. Examples of early outcomes include reduced tardies resulting from participation in beforeschool programs and reduced vandalism, violence, and crime at school and in the neighborhood resulting from involvement in afterschool activities. Over time, articulation programs can reduce school avoidance and dropouts as well as enhance the number who make successful transitions to higher education and postschool living and work. It is also likely that a caring school climate can play a significant role in reducing student transience (see Guide 6.4).

Home Involvement in Schooling

This arena expands concern for parent involvement to encompass anyone in the home who influences the student's life. In some cases, grandparents, aunts, or older siblings have assumed the parenting role. Older brothers and sisters often are the most significant influences on a youngster's life choices. Thus schools and communities must go beyond focusing on parents in their efforts to enhance home involvement.

This arena includes schoolwide and classroom-based efforts designed to strengthen the home situation, enhance family problem-solving capabilities, and increase support for student well-being. Accomplishing all this requires schoolwide and classroom-based systems and programs to (a) address the specific learning and support needs of adults in the home, such as offering them ESL, literacy, vocational and citizenship classes,

Guide 6.5   Home Involvement in Schooling

Home Involvement in Schooling encompasses

- *Addressing specific support and learning needs of families* (e.g., support services for those in the home to assist in addressing basic survival needs and obligations to the children; adult education classes to enhance literacy, job skills, English as a second language, citizenship preparation)
- *Improving mechanisms for communication and connecting school and home* (e.g., opportunities at school for family networking and mutual support, learning, recreation, and enrichment and for family members to receive special assistance and to volunteer to help; phone calls or e-mail from teacher and other staff with good news; frequent and balanced conferences (student-led when feasible); outreach to attract hard-to-reach families—including student dropouts)
- *Involving homes in student decision making* (e.g., families prepared for involvement in program planning and problem solving)
- *Enhancing home support for learning and development* (e.g., family literacy; family homework projects; family field trips)
- *Recruiting families to strengthen school and community* (e.g., volunteers to welcome and support new families and help in various capacities; families prepared for involvement in school governance)
- *Capacity building to enhance home involvement*

enrichment and recreational opportunities, and mutual support groups, (b) help those in the home improve how basic student obligations are met, such as providing guidance related to parenting and how to help with schoolwork, (c) improve forms of basic communication that promote the well-being of student, family, and school, (d) enhance the home-school connection and sense of community, (e) foster participation in making decisions essential to a student's well-being, (f) facilitate home support of student learning and development, (g) mobilize those at home to problem solve related to student needs, and (h) elicit help (support, collaborations, and partnerships) from those at home with respect to meeting classroom, school, and community needs. The context for some of this activity may be a *parent or family center* if one has been established at the site. Outcomes include indices of parent learning, student progress, and community enhancement specifically related to home involvement (see Guide 6.5).

Community Outreach for Involvement and Support (Including Volunteers)

Most schools do their job better when they are an integral and positive part of the community. Unfortunately, schools and classrooms often are seen as separate from the community in which they reside. This contributes to a lack of connection between school staff, parents, students, and other community residents and resources. And it undercuts the contributions community resources can make to the school's mission. For example, it is a truism that learning is neither limited to what is formally taught nor to time spent in classrooms. It occurs whenever and wherever the learner interacts with the surrounding environment. All facets of the community (not just the school) provide learning opportunities. *Anyone in the community who*

Guide 6.6   Community Outreach for Involvement and Support

Community Outreach for Involvement and Support encompasses

- *Planning and implementing outreach to recruit a wide range of community resources* (e.g., public and private agencies; colleges and universities; local residents; artists and cultural institutions; businesses and professional organizations; service, volunteer, and faith-based organizations; community policymakers and decision makers)
- *Systems to recruit, screen, prepare, and maintain community resource involvement* (e.g., mechanisms to orient and welcome, enhance the volunteer pool, maintain current involvements, enhance a sense of community)
- *Reaching out to students and families who don't come to school regularly—including truants and dropouts*
- *Connecting school and community efforts to promote child and youth development and a sense of community*
- *Capacity building to enhance community involvement and support* (e.g., policies and mechanisms to enhance and sustain school-community involvement, staff and stakeholder development on the value of community involvement, "social marketing")

wants to facilitate learning might be a contributing teacher. This includes aides, volunteers, parents, siblings, peers, mentors in the community, librarians, recreation staff, college students, and so on. They all constitute what can be called *the teaching community.* When a school successfully joins with its surrounding community, everyone has the opportunity to learn and to teach.

For schools to be seen as an integral part of the community, outreach steps must be taken to create and maintain linkages and collaborations. The intent is to maximize mutual benefits, including better student progress, an enhanced sense of community, community development, and more. In the long run, the aims are to strengthen students, schools, families, and neighborhoods.

Outreach focuses on public and private agencies, organizations, universities, colleges, and facilities; businesses and professional organizations and groups; and volunteer service programs, organizations, and clubs. Greater volunteerism on the part of parents, peers, and others from the community can break down barriers and increase home and community involvement in schools and schooling. Thus enhanced use of community volunteers is a good place to start. This requires development of a system that effectively recruits, screens, trains, and nurtures volunteers. Another key facet is opening up school sites as places where parents, families, and other community residents can engage in learning, recreation, and enrichment and find services they need.

Over time, this area can include systems and programs designed to

- Recruit a wide range of community involvement and support (e.g., linkages and integration with community health and social services; cadres of volunteers, mentors, and individuals with special expertise and resources; local businesses to provide resources, awards, incentives, job-shadowing opportunities, and jobs; formal partnership arrangements).
- Train, screen, and maintain volunteers (e.g., parents, college students, senior citizens, peer and cross-age tutors and counselors, and professionals-in-training to provide direct help for staff and students—especially with targeted students).
- Reach out to students and families who don't come to school regularly—including truants and dropouts.
- Enhance community-school connections and sense of community (e.g., orientations, open houses, performances, cultural and sports events, festivals, celebrations, fairs, workshops).

For more details, see Guide 6.6.

Student and Family Assistance

Specialized assistance for students and their families should be reserved for the relatively few problems that cannot be handled without adding special interventions. In effect, this arena encompasses most of the services and related systems that are the focus of integrated service models (see Chapter 16).

Guide 6.7 Student and Family Assistance

Student and Family Assistance encompasses

- *Providing extra support as soon as a need is recognized and doing so in the least disruptive ways* (e.g., prereferral interventions in classrooms; problem-solving conferences with parents; open access to school, district, and community support programs)
- *Timely referral interventions for students and families with problems based on response to extra support* (e.g., identification and screening processes, assessment, referrals, and follow-up—school-based, school-linked)
- *Enhancing access to direct interventions for health, mental health, and economic assistance* (e.g., school-based, school-linked, and community-based programs and services)
- *Care monitoring, management, information sharing, and follow-up assessment to coordinate individual interventions and check whether referrals and services are adequate and effective*
- *Mechanisms for resource coordination and integration to avoid duplication, fill gaps, garner economies of scale, and enhance effectiveness* (e.g., braiding resources from school-based and school-linked interveners, feeder pattern or family of schools, community-based programs; linking with community providers to fill gaps)
- *Enhancing stakeholder awareness of programs and services*
- *Capacity building to enhance student and family assistance systems, programs, and services*

The emphasis is on providing special services in a personalized way to assist with a broad range of needs. To begin with, social, physical, and mental health assistance available in the school and community is used. As community outreach brings in other resources, these are linked to existing activities in an integrated manner. Additional attention is paid to enhancing systems for triage, case and resource management, direct services for immediate needs, and referral for special services and special education as appropriate. Ongoing efforts are made to expand and enhance resources. While any office or room can be used, a valuable context for providing such services is a center facility, such as a family, community, health, or parent resource center.

A programmatic approach in this arena requires systems designed to provide special assistance in ways that increase the likelihood that a student will be more successful at school, while also reducing the need for teachers to seek special programs and services. The work encompasses providing all stakeholders with information clarifying available assistance and how to access help, facilitating requests for assistance, handling referrals, providing direct service, implementing case and resource management, and interfacing with community outreach to assimilate additional resources into current service delivery. It also involves ongoing analyses of requests for services as a basis for working with school colleagues to design strategies that can reduce inappropriate reliance on special assistance. Thus major outcomes are enhanced access to special assistance as needed, indices of effectiveness, *and* the reduction of inappropriate referrals for such assistance (see Guide 6.7).

A well-designed and supported *infrastructure* is needed to establish, maintain, and evolve the type of comprehensive approach to addressing barriers to student learning that has been outlined. Such an infrastructure includes mechanisms for coordinating among learning supports, enhancing resources by developing direct linkages between school and community programs, moving toward increased integration of school and community resources, and integrating the instructional and developmental, enabling, and management components. We discuss infrastructure considerations in Chapters 7 and 8.

KEEPING MUTUAL SUPPORT, CARING, AND A SENSE OF COMMUNITY IN MIND

In clarifying each element of an enabling component, there is danger of losing sight of the "big picture." Ultimately, within the school context, such a component must blend with the instructional and management components in ways that create a schoolwide atmosphere encouraging mutual support, caring, and a sense of community. The degree to which a school can create such an atmosphere seems highly related to its capacity to prevent and ameliorate learning, behavior, and emotional problems. And there is an obvious connection between all this and sustaining morale and minimizing burnout. Thus, in developing an enabling or learning supports component, a constant concern is to ensure an increasingly supportive and caring context for learning and enhance a psychological sense of community among students, staff, families, and community stakeholders.

Throughout a school and in each classroom, a psychological sense of community exists when a critical mass of stakeholders are committed to each other *and* to the setting's goals and values, *and* they exert effort to achieve the goals and maintain positive relationships with each other. Being together is no guarantee of feeling a sense of belonging or feeling responsible for a collective vision or mission. A perception of community is shaped by daily experiences. Initially, it probably is engendered when a person feels welcomed, supported, nurtured, respected, liked, and connected in reciprocal relationships with others. Maintaining a sense of community over time requires that a critical mass of participants feel like valued members who are contributing to the collective identity, destiny, and vision and also are committed to being and working together in supportive and efficacious ways. All this takes conscientious effort and mechanisms that effectively provide support, promote self-efficacy, and foster positive relationships.

Welcoming and Ongoing Social Support

Building a sense of community and caring begins when students first arrive at a school or move from grade to grade. Classrooms and schools can do their job better if students feel that they are truly welcome and have a range of social supports. A key facet of welcoming encompasses effectively connecting new students with peers and adults who can provide social support and advocacy. A need for peer support also applies to new families and staff. After successful induction into a new setting, caring is best maintained through the use of strategies that promote feelings of competence, self-determination, and connectedness.

Efforts to create a caring classroom climate are facilitated through use of personalized instruction and providing special assistance as necessary. The emphasis is on using each opportunity to nurture and support, including regular student conferences, cooperative learning, peer tutoring, and any activity designed to foster social and emotional development.

Schoolwide, a caring culture pays special attention to assisting and advocating for students who have difficulty making friends or who get into trouble. Some of these students need just a bit of support to overcome a problem (e.g., a few suggestions, a couple of special opportunities). Some, however, need much more help. They may be overly shy or lacking in social skills, or they may act in negative ways. Efforts to assist these youngsters include strategies that facilitate establishing friendships, mentoring, counseling, mediation, conflict resolution, and programs to enhance human relations. A range of school staff, including teachers, classroom or yard aides, counselors and other support and resource staff, and parents can work together to address the problems. For example, a "peer buddy" may be brought into the picture. This can be any student with similar interests and temperament or a student who can be understanding and is willing to reach out to the one who needs a friend. Regular and natural opportunities may be created for the student to work with others on shared activities or projects at and away from school (more about this in Chapter 15). A special relationship may be established with almost anyone on the staff who is willing to help the student feel positively connected at school. For youngsters who really don't know how to act like a friend, specific guidelines and social skills also can be taught.

Given the importance of home involvement in schooling, attention also must be paid to creating a caring atmosphere for family members. Increased home involvement is more likely if families feel welcome and have access to social support at school. Thus teachers and other school staff need to establish programs that effectively welcome and connect families with school staff and other families to generate ongoing social support and greater participation in home involvement efforts.

And don't forget that school staff also need to feel truly welcome and socially supported. Rather than leaving this to chance, a caring school develops and institutionalizes a program to welcome and connect new staff with those with whom they will be working. Moreover, it does so in ways that effectively incorporate newcomers into the organization and build their capacity to function effectively.

Collaboration and Teaming

In discussing burnout, many writers have emphasized that too often, teaching is carried out under highly stressful working conditions and without much collegial and social support. Teachers must feel good about themselves if classrooms and schools are to be caring environments. Teaching is one of society's most psychologically demanding jobs, yet few schools have programs designed specifically to counter job stress and enhance staff feelings of well-being. Recommendations to redress this deficiency usually factor down to strategies that reduce environmental stressors, increase personal capabilities, and enhance job and social supports. However, most schools simply do not have adequate mechanisms in place to plan for and implement such recommendations.

Fundamental to dealing with these concerns and to improving instruction are approaches that enable teachers to work closely with other teachers and school personnel as well as with parents, professionals-in-training, volunteers, and so forth. In particular, systemic promotion of collaboration and teaming are key facets of addressing barriers to learning. Such approaches allow teachers to broaden the resources and strategies available in and out of the classroom to enhance learning and performance. As Hargreaves (1994) cogently notes, the way to relieve the uncertainty and open-endedness that characterize classroom teaching is to create "communities of colleagues who work collaboratively [in cultures of shared learning and positive risk taking] to set their own professional limits and standards, while still remaining committed to continuous improvement. Such communities can also bring together the professional and personal lives of teachers in a way that supports growth and allows problems to be discussed without fear of disapproval or punishment" (p. 156).

Collaboration and collegiality are basic to enhancing morale and work satisfaction and to transforming classrooms into caring contexts for learning. Collegiality, however, cannot be demanded. As Hargreaves (1994) stresses, when collegiality is *mandated*, it can produce what is called *contrived collegiality*, which tends to breed inflexibility and inefficiency. Contrived collegiality is compulsory, implementation-oriented, regulated administratively, fixed in time and space, and predictable. In contrast, *collaborative cultures* foster working relationships that are voluntary, development-oriented, spontaneous, pervasive across time and space, and unpredictable.

Collaborative cultures also can foster a school's efforts to organize itself into a learning community that personalizes inservice teacher education. Such "organizational learning" requires an organizational structure "'where people continually expand their capabilities to understand complexity, clarify vision and improve shared mental models' [Senge, 1990] by engaging in different tasks, acquiring different kinds of expertise, experiencing and expressing different forms of leadership, confronting uncomfortable organizational truths, and searching together for shared solutions" (Hargreaves, 1994, p. 66).

Finally, collaborative cultures recognize the need to build capacity for dealing with problems in working relationships. Despite the best of intentions, relationships often go astray—especially when staff become frustrated and angry because students don't respond in desired ways or seem not to be trying. To minimize relationship problems, inservice education must foster understanding of interpersonal dynamics and barriers to working together, and sites must establish problem-solving mechanisms to eliminate or at least minimize such problems.

CONCLUDING COMMENTS

Given the tremendous pressure on schools to improve academic indicators, it is not surprising that so much attention centers on direct instructional strategies. For too many students, however, teachers are finding the educational mission is thwarted because of multifaceted factors that interfere with youngsters' learning and performance. Schoolwide approaches to address barriers to learning and teaching are essential for teachers and students to succeed.

Policymakers do understand that they must invest in learning supports, and they do so. But they give little thought to this component of school improvement. Indeed, with the increasing focus on test scores and decreasing budgets, the tendency is to lay off student support staff, rather than understanding that such personnel could be used in ways that are essential to the aim of leaving no child behind. In this chapter, we have tried to lay a foundation for understanding new directions for such support staff.

Clearly, establishing any new direction for schools requires policy and leadership. Policy should specify that an Enabling or Learning Supports Component is to be pursued as a primary and essential facet of school improvement and in ways that complement, overlap, and fully integrate

Guide 6.8   What Might a Fully Functioning Enabling or Learning Supports Component Look Like at a School?

The following is adapted from a description developed for use by Hawaii's *Comprehensive Student Support System* (CSSS). CSSS is designed to ensure that every school develops a comprehensive, multifaceted, and integrated component to address barriers to learning and promote healthy development as primary and essential facets of school improvement.

A school with an Enabling or Learning Supports Component integrates the component as a primary and essential facet of school improvement. The aim is to ensure the school develops a comprehensive, multifaceted, and cohesive approach to address barriers to learning and promote healthy development. Given limited resources, such a component is established by deploying, redeploying, and weaving all existing learning support resources together.

The school has redesigned its infrastructure to establish an administrative leader who guides the component's development and is accountable for daily implementation, monitoring, and problem solving. There is a team (e.g., a Learning Supports Resource Team) focused on ensuring that all relevant resources are woven together to install a comprehensive, multifaceted, and integrated continuum of interventions over a period of years. The team maps and analyzes available resources, sets priorities, and organizes work groups to plan program development. As illustrated in Guide 3.1, the goal is to establish effective

- Systems for promoting healthy development and preventing problems
- Systems for responding to problems as soon after onset as is feasible
- Systems for providing specialized assistance and care

And the work involves creating the continuum in keeping with the content or curriculum framework the school has adopted for its Enabling or Learning Supports Component (e.g., see the six areas illustrated in Guide 5.2).

While the focus of the team is on resource use and program development, it also ensures that effective mechanisms are in operation for responding rapidly when specific students are identified as having mild to moderate learning, behavior, and emotional problems. For most students, the problems are resolved through relatively straightforward situational and program changes and problem-solving strategies. Based on analyses of their response to such interventions, additional assistance *in the classroom* is provided to those for whom these first methods are insufficient. Those whose problems persist are referred for additional and sometimes specialized assistance. Before such interventions are set in motion, in-depth analyses are made of the reasons for their problems in order to ensure that appropriate assistance is planned. All special interventions are carefully monitored and coordinated. Through a sequential strategy that begins with the least intervention needed and gauges students' responses to intervention at every stage, there is a significant reduction in the number requiring intensive help and referral for specialized assistance.

Because there is an emphasis on programs and activities that create a schoolwide culture of caring and nurturing, students, families, staff, and the community feel that the school is a welcoming and supportive place, accommodating of diversity, and committed to promoting equal opportunities for all students to succeed at school. When problems arise, they are responded to positively, quickly, and effectively. Morale is high.

The following should be understood as examples of the types of interventions that might be used with any student who experiences barriers to learning. Remember, the point is to ensure that a full continuum is available at schools so that strategies for the least intervention needed are implemented and students' responses to intervention can be used to gauge whether more intensive help and referrals for specialized assistance are required. When such a sequential approach is followed, schools can expect a significant reduction in the flow of referrals for specialized assistance.

Example 1: Focusing on Helping the Teacher With Student Reengagement Rather Than Overemphasizing Discipline and Referral for Services

Matt, a third grader, has not been doing well at school. He often is in trouble on the school playground before school and during lunch. Before the Learning Supports Component was established, his teacher constantly had to discipline him and send him to the principal's office. He had been referred to the Student Success Team but just was one of a long list in line to be reviewed. Now, the focus is on how to enhance what goes on in the classroom and on schoolwide changes that minimize negative encounters; this minimizes the need for classroom management, discipline, and referral out for expensive special services.

The focus on enhancing teacher capacity to reengage students in daily learning activities is helping Matt's teacher learn more about matching his individual interests and skills and how to design the instructional day to provide additional supports from peers and community volunteers. Rather than seeing the solution in terms of discipline, she learns how to understand what is motivating Matt's problem and is able to provide a more personalized approach to instruction and extra in-classroom support that will reengage Matt in learning. Over time, all student support staff (all professional staff who are not involved in classroom instruction) will be trained to go into the classroom to help the teacher learn and implement new approaches designed not just for Matt but for all students who are not well-engaged in classroom learning.

At the same time, the focus on enhancing support for transition times (such as before school and lunch) increases the recreational and enrichment opportunities available for all students so that they have positive options for interaction. Staff involved in playground supervision are specifically asked to work with Matt to help him engage in an activity that interests him (e.g., a sports tournament, an extramural club activity). They will monitor his involvement to ensure that he is truly engaged, and they, along with one of the student support staff (e.g., school psychologist, counselor, social worker, nurse), will use the opportunity to help him and other students learn any interpersonal skills needed to interact well with peers.

Example 2: What a Family Might Experience When Their Children Have a Problem

Clara, a third grader, finds reading difficult. Her teacher asks one of the many community volunteers to work with Clara to improve her skills, motivation, and confidence. Clara goes to the school library with a volunteer, a local college student, where she is encouraged to choose books on subjects that interest her, and they read together. Clara also writes stories on topics she likes. To further improve her skills, her family is encouraged to have her read the stories to them at home.

As Clara's skills improve, she also begins reading to her younger sister, Emma, who needs help in getting ready for kindergarten. She is enrolled in Head Start. Her family, including her grandmother who lives with them, comes to parent meetings to learn ways to enrich Emma's readiness skills.

When the family's oldest child, Tommy, got into trouble for fighting at school, his behavior was reviewed by a student support staff member and the youngster's teacher who then met with the family and Tommy to explore the causes of his behavior problems and planned some solutions. At subsequent meetings, they reviewed the plan's effectiveness. One of the strategies called for Tommy's becoming a peer buddy to help provide social support for new students. When the next new family enrolled, Tommy spent several days showing the new student around the school, and they both got involved in some extracurricular activities. Tommy's behavior problems quickly turned around, and he soon was able to assume a leadership role during various school events.

In the middle of the year, the grandmother got sick and went to the hospital. Support staff at each of the children's schools were sensitive to the disruption in the home. When in the middle of the year, the grandmother got sick and went to the hospital, support staff at each of the children's schools were sensitive to the disruption in the home. When Tommy and Clara regressed a bit, some extra support was arranged and ways to assist the family's efforts to cope were explored. The work with the family and the two schools involved was coordinated through a care-monitoring mechanism developed by a multisite council that focuses regularly on common concerns of all schools in the neighborhood.

Newcomers: One Example of Support for Transitions and Home Involvement

To increase family involvement in schooling, special attention is placed on enhancing welcoming and social support strategies for new students and families. Student support staff work with office staff to develop welcoming programs and establish social support networks (e.g., peer buddy systems for students; parent-parent connections). As a result, newcomers (and all others) are greeted promptly and with an inviting attitude when they come into the school. Those without correct enrollment records are helped to access what they need. Parents are connected with other parents who help them learn about school and neighborhood resources. Upon entering the new classroom, a newcomer is connected, by the teacher, with a trained peer buddy who will stick with the newcomer for a few weeks while he or she learns the ropes.

Support staff work with each teacher to identify any student who hasn't made a good transition. Together they will determine why and work with the family to turn things around.

Crisis Prevention

To reduce the number of crises, student support staff analyze what is preventable (usually related to human relations problems) and then design a range of schoolwide prevention approaches. Among these are strategies for involving all school personnel (credentialed and classified) in activities that promote positive interactions and natural opportunities for learning prosocial behavior and mutual respect.

Fewer Referrals, Better Response

As the in-classroom and schoolwide approaches emerge, the need for out-of-classroom referrals declines. This allows for rapid and early response when a student is having problems, and it enables student support staff to work more effectively in linking students up with community services when necessary.

with the instructional component. However, even before policy is enacted, leaders can begin the work.

We turn now to processes leaders can pursue in establishing a school-wide component for learning supports.

I can never answer the teacher's questions.

Perhaps if you went to class, you could.

Nah, I never pay attention anyway!

REFERENCES

Council of Chief State School Officers. (2002). *Council of Chief State School Officers unveils new strategic direction*. News release. Washington, DC: CCSSO. Retrieved February, 2002, from www.ccsso.org/Whats_New/press_releases/148.cfm.

Hargreaves, A. (1994). *Changing teachers, changing times: Teachers' work and culture in the postmodern age.* New York: Teachers College Press.

Senge, P. M. (1990). *The fifth discipline: The art and practice of the learning organization.* New York: Currency/Doubleday.

Vander Ark, T. (2002). The case for small schools. *Educational Leadership, 59,* 55–59.

World Health Organization. (1998). *Health promotion glossary.* Geneva: Author.

Rethinking Infrastructure

7

Starting at the School Level

Do not follow where the path may lead. Go instead where there is no path and leave a trail.

Have you ever heard of Stenderup's Law?

Sure, it states:
The sooner you fall behind, the more time you will have to catch up.

ORIENTING QUESTIONS

? Why is it important to rethink infrastructure from the school level outward?

? How does a learning supports resource-oriented mechanism differ from a case-oriented team?

? What are the benefits of linking school resource-oriented mechanisms across a "family" of schools?

The Parable of the Policy-Making Owl

 A field mouse was lost in a dense wood, unable to find his way out. He came upon a wise old owl sitting in a tree. "Please help me, wise old owl, how can I get out of this wood?" said the field mouse.

"Easy," said the owl, "Fly out, as I do."

"But how can I fly?" asked the mouse.

The owl looked at him haughtily, sniffed disdainfully, and said, "Don't bother me with the details, I only decide the policy."

Moral: Leadership involves providing details.

Development of a comprehensive schoolwide approach is easy to call for and hard to accomplish. Anyone who has been involved in systemic reform can describe the difficulties in terms of lack of time, insufficient budget, lack of space, disgruntled stakeholders, inadequate capacity building, and on and on. Such difficulties and various strategies for dealing with them are well discussed in the literature on systemic change. At this point, we simply want to highlight a few fundamentals, with the caveat that each facet described carries with it myriad implementation difficulties.

SYSTEMIC CHANGES AT THE SCHOOL LEVEL

As noted, the *development* of comprehensive schoolwide approaches requires shifts in prevailing policy and new frameworks for practice. In addition, for significant systemic change to occur, policy and program commitments must be demonstrated through effective allocation and redeployment of resources. That is, finances, personnel, time, space, equipment, and other essential resources must be made available, organized, and used in ways that adequately operationalize policy and promising practices. This includes ensuring sufficient resources to develop an effective structural foundation for systemic changes, sustainability, and ongoing capacity building.

To these ends, existing infrastructure mechanisms must be modified in ways that guarantee that new policy directions are translated into appropriate daily operations. Well-designed infrastructure mechanisms ensure local ownership, a critical mass of committed stakeholders, processes that overcome barriers to stakeholders' effectively working together, and strategies that mobilize and maintain proactive efforts so that changes are implemented and there is renewal over time. From this perspective, the importance of creating an atmosphere that encourages mutual support, caring, and a sense of community takes on another dimension.

Institutionalization of a comprehensive component for learning supports that is fully integrated into school improvement efforts necessitates restructuring the mechanisms associated with at least seven infrastructure concerns. These encompass processes for daily (1) governance, (2) leadership, (3) planning and implementation of specific organizational and program objectives, (4) coordination and integration for cohesion, (5) management of communication and information, (6) capacity building, and (7) quality improvement and accountability. For example, infrastructure changes must be redesigned to ensure the integration, quality improvement, accountability, and self-renewal related to *all three* components illustrated in Chapter 5's Guide 5.2.

In redesigning mechanisms to address these matters, new collaborative arrangements must be established and authority (power) redistributed—again easy to say, extremely hard to accomplish. Reform obviously requires ensuring that those who operate essential mechanisms have adequate resources and support, both initially and over time. Moreover, there must be appropriate incentives and safeguards for individuals as they become enmeshed in the complexities of systemic change.

And let's not forget about linking schools together to maximize use of limited resources. When a family of schools in a geographic area collaborates to address barriers, the schools can share programs and personnel in many cost-effective ways. This includes achieving economies of scale by assigning learning support staff and implementing staff development across a feeder pattern of schools. It encompasses streamlined processes to coordinate and integrate assistance to a family that has children at several of the schools. For example, the same family may have youngsters in the elementary and middle schools, and both students may need special counseling. This might be accomplished by assigning one counselor or case manager to work with the family. Also, in connecting with community resources, a group of schools can maximize distribution of limited resources in ways that are efficient, effective, and equitable.

All of the foregoing requires substantive organizational and programmatic transformation. Thus key stakeholders and their leadership must understand and commit to the changes. And the commitment must be reflected in policy statements and creation of an organizational structure at all levels that ensure effective leadership and resources. This leaders' guide lays out the rationale for moving forward, and to provide specifics for administrators, teachers, support staff, and other stakeholders, we have prepared a companion work titled *The Implementation Guide to Student Learning Supports in the Classroom and Schoolwide.*

Any move toward substantive systemic change should begin with activity designed to create readiness by enhancing a climate and culture for change. With respect to new directions for learning supports, steps include

1. Building interest and consensus for establishing a comprehensive, multifaceted component to address barriers to learning and teaching

2. Introducing basic concepts to relevant groups of stakeholders

3. Establishing a policy framework that recognizes that such a component is a primary and essential facet of the institution's activity

4. Appointing leaders for the component, who are of equivalent status to the leaders for the instructional and management facets, to ensure that commitments are carried out

Overlapping the efforts to create readiness are processes to develop an organizational structure for start-up and phase-in. This involves establishing mechanisms and procedures to guide reforms, such as a steering group and leadership training, formulation of specific start-up and phase-in plans, and so forth.

Although many of the foregoing points about systemic change seem self-evident, their profound implications are widely ignored. Relatively little work has been done to build conceptual models and develop specific interventions for dealing with the processes and problems associated with introducing, sustaining, and scaling up new initiatives and reforms. As a result, it is not surprising that so many efforts to improve schools fail. We discuss all this further in Chapter 10, the Coda.

SCHOOL INFRASTRUCTURE FOR A LEARNING SUPPORTS COMPONENT

At schools, obviously the administrative leadership is key to ending the marginalization of efforts to address learning, behavior, and emotional problems. Another key is establishment of a mechanism that focuses specifically on how resources for learning supports are used at the school.

For those concerned with school improvement, resource-oriented mechanisms are a major facet of efforts to transform and restructure daily operations. As noted in Chapter 2, in some schools as much as 30% of the budget may be going to problem prevention and correction. Every school is expending resources to enable learning; few have a mechanism to ensure appropriate use of existing resources and enhance current efforts related to learning supports. Such a mechanism contributes to cost-efficacy of learner supports by ensuring that all such activity is planned, implemented, and evaluated in a coordinated and increasingly integrated manner. It also provides another means for reducing marginalization. Creation of such a mechanism is essential for braiding together existing school and community resources and encouraging services and programs to function in an increasingly cohesive way. When this mechanism is created in the form of a team, it also is a vehicle for building working relationships and can play an expanded role in solving turf and operational problems.

One of the primary and essential tasks a learning supports resource-oriented mechanism undertakes is that of enumerating school and community programs and services that are in place to support students, families, and staff. A comprehensive gap assessment is generated as resources are mapped and compared with surveys of the unmet needs of and desired outcomes for students, their families, and school staff. Analyses of what is available, effective, and needed provide a sound basis for formulating priorities and developing strategies to link with additional resources at other schools, district sites, and in the community; they also enhance resource use. Such analyses also can guide efforts to improve cost-effectiveness.

In a similar fashion, a resource-oriented mechanism for a complex or family of schools (e.g., a high school and its feeder schools) and one at the district level provide mechanisms for analyses of learning supports on a larger scale. This can lead to strategies for cross-school, communitywide, and districtwide cooperation and integration to enhance intervention effectiveness and garner economies of scale.

A Learning Supports Resource Team

Early in our work, we called the school-level resource-oriented mechanism a Resource Coordinating Team. However, coordination is too limited a descriptor of the team's role and functions. So we now use the term *Learning Supports Resource Team*. Properly constituted, such a team works with the school's administrators to expand on-site leadership for efforts to address barriers comprehensively, and it ensures the maintenance and improvement of a multifaceted and integrated approach.

When we mention a Learning Supports Resource Team, some school staff quickly respond, *We already have one!* When we explore this with them, we usually find that what they have is a *case-oriented team*—a team that focuses on individual students who are having problems. Such a team may be called a student study team, student success team, student assistance team, teacher assistance team, and so forth.

To help clarify the difference between resource and case-oriented teams, we contrast the functions of each as outlined in Guide 7.1.

Two parables help differentiate the two types of mechanisms and the importance of both sets of functions. A *case orientation* fits the *starfish* metaphor:

Guide 7.1   Contrasting Team Functions

A Case-oriented Team	A Resource-oriented Team
Focuses on specific *individuals* and discrete *services* to address barriers to learning	Focuses on *all* students and the *resources, programs, and systems* to address barriers to learning and promote healthy development
Sometimes called • Child Study Team • Student Study Team • Student Success Team • Student Assistance Team • Teacher Assistance Team • IEP Team	Possibly called • Learning Supports Resource Team • Resource Coordinating Team • Resource Coordinating Council • School Support Team
Examples of Functions • Triage • Referral • Case monitoring and management • Case progress review • Case reassessment	*Examples of Functions* • Aggregating data across students and from teachers to analyze school needs • Mapping resources in school and community • Analyzing resources • Identifying the most pressing program development needs at the school • Coordinating and integrating school resources and connecting with community resources • Establishing priorities for strengthening programs and developing new ones • Planning and facilitating ways to strengthen and develop new programs and systems • Recommending how resources should be deployed and redeployed • Developing strategies for enhancing resources • Social marketing

The day after a great storm had washed all sorts of sea life far up onto the beach, a youngster set out to throw back as many of the still-living starfish as he could. After watching him toss one after the other into the ocean, an old man approached him and said, *It's no use your doing that, there are too many. You're not going to make any difference.*

The boy looked at him in surprise, bent over, picked up another starfish, threw it in, and then replied, *It made a difference to that one!*

This parable, of course, reflects all the important clinical efforts undertaken by staff alone and when they meet together to work on specific cases.

The *resource-oriented* focus is captured by what can be called the *bridge* parable:

In a small town one weekend, a group of school staff went to the river to go fishing. Not long after they got there, a child came floating down the rapids calling for help. One of the group on the shore quickly dived in and pulled the child out. Minutes later another, then another, and then many more children were coming down the river. Soon everyone was diving in and dragging children to the shore and then jumping back in to save as many as they could.

In the midst of all this frenzy, one of the group was seen walking away. Her colleagues were irate. How could she leave when there were so many children to save? After long hours, to everyone's relief, the flow of children stopped, and the group could finally catch their breath.

At that moment, their colleague came back. They turned on her and angrily shouted, "How could you walk off when we needed everyone here to save the children?"

She replied, "It occurred to me that someone ought to go upstream and find out why so many kids were falling into the river. What I found is that the old wooden bridge had several planks missing, and when some children tried to jump over the gap, they couldn't make it and fell through into the river. So I got someone to fix the bridge."

Fixing and building better bridges is a good way to think about prevention, and it helps underscore the importance of taking time to improve and enhance resources, programs, and systems.

A resource-oriented team exemplifies the type of mechanism needed for overall cohesion and ongoing development of school learning supports programs and systems. As indicated, its focus is not on specific individuals but on how resources are used.

In pursuing its functions, the team provides what often is a missing link for managing and enhancing programs and systems in ways that integrate, strengthen, and stimulate new and improved interventions. For example, such a mechanism can be used to (a) map and analyze activities and resources to improve their use in preventing and ameliorating problems, (b) build effective referral, case management, and quality assurance systems, (c) enhance procedures for management of programs and information and for communication among school staff and with the home, and (d) explore ways to redeploy and enhance resources—such as clarifying which activities are nonproductive, suggesting better uses for resources, and establishing priorities for developing new interventions, as well as reaching out to connect with additional resources in the school district and community.

At a minimum, a resource-oriented team can reduce fragmentation and enhance cost-efficacy by assisting in ways that encourage programs to function in a coordinated and increasingly integrated way. For example, the team can coordinate resources, enhance communication among school staff and with the home about available assistance and referral processes, and monitor programs to be certain they are functioning effectively and efficiently. More generally, this group can provide leadership in guiding school personnel and clientele in evolving the school's vision, priorities, and practices for learning supports and enhancing resources.

Although a resource-oriented mechanism might be created solely around psychosocial programs, it is meant to focus on resources related to all major learning supports programs and services. Thus it tries to bring together representatives of all these programs and services. This might include, for example, school counselors, psychologists, nurses, social workers, attendance and dropout counselors, special education staff, physical educators and afterschool program staff, bilingual and Title I program coordinators, health educators, safe-school and drug-free-school staff, and union reps. It also should include representatives of any community agency that is significantly involved with the school. Beyond these service providers, such a team needs a leader from the school's administration, and it would be well advised to add the energies and expertise of regular classroom teachers, noncertificated staff (e.g., front office, food service, custodian, bus driver), parents, and older students.

Properly constituted, trained, and supported, a resource-oriented team complements the work of the site's governance body through providing on-site overview, leadership, and advocacy for all activity aimed at addressing barriers to learning and teaching. Having at least one representative from the resource team on the school's governing and planning bodies ensures infrastructure connections for maintaining, improving, and increasingly integrating learning supports and classroom instruction. And of course, having an administrator on the team provides the necessary link with the school's administrative decision making about allocation of budget, space, staff development time, and other resources.

It is conceivable that one person could start the process of understanding the fundamental resource-oriented functions and delineating an infrastructure to carry them out. It is better, however, if several stakeholders put their heads together. Where creation of another team is seen as a burden, existing teams, such as student or teacher assistance teams, school crisis teams, and healthy school teams, have demonstrated the ability to do resource-oriented functions. In adding the resource-oriented functions to another team's work, great care must be taken to structure the agenda so that sufficient time is devoted to the additional tasks. For small schools, a large team often is not feasible, but a two-person team can still do the job.

A School Steering Body for a Learning Supports Component

All initiatives need a team of "champions" who agree to steer the process. Thus, at the school level, initially it helps not only to have a resource-oriented team but also to establish an advisory or steering group. This leadership body ensures overall development of the component to address barriers to learning and guides and monitors the resource team. These advocates must be competent with respect to the work to be done and highly motivated not just to help get things under way but to ensure that the changes are sustained over time.

The group's first focus is on assuring that capacity is built to accomplish the desired systemic changes. This includes ensuring an adequate policy and leadership base. If such a base is not already in place, the group needs to focus on getting one established. Capacity building, of course, also includes special training for change agents. Over time, the main functions of a steering group are to ensure that staff assigned to facilitate changes (a) maintain a big-picture perspective and appropriate movement toward long-term goals and (b) have sufficient support and guidance.

The steering group should be fully connected with teams guiding the instructional and management components at the school. Each school's steering body needs to be linked formally to the district mechanism designed to guide development of learning supports components at schools.

Steering groups should not be too large. For example, at a school level, membership might include key change agents, one or two other key school leaders, perhaps someone from a local institution of higher education, perhaps a key agency person or two, and a few well-connected champions. Such a group can meet monthly (or more often if major problems arise) to review progress, problem solve, and decide on midcourse corrections. To work against the perception that it is a closed, elite group, it can host focus groups to elicit input and feedback and provide information.

Ad Hoc and Standing Work Groups for a Resource Team

Work groups are formed as needed by a Learning Supports Resource Team to address specific concerns (e.g., mapping resources, planning for capacity building and social marketing, addressing problems related to case-oriented systems), develop new programs (e.g., welcoming and social support strategies for newcomers to the school), implement special initiatives (e.g., positive behavior support), and so forth. Such groups usually are facilitated by a member of the resource team who recruits a small group of others from the school and community who are willing and able to help. The group facilitator provides regular updates to the resource team on work group progress and brings back feedback from the team.

Ad hoc work groups take on tasks that can be done over a relatively short time period, and the group disbands once the work is accomplished. *Standing* work groups focus on defined program arenas and pursue current priorities for enhancing intervention in a given arenas. For example, a standing work group might be established for any of the six intervention arenas outlined in Chapter 6.

Integrating the Component Into the School Infrastructure

Guide 7.2 illustrates the type of infrastructure that needs to emerge at a school if it is to effectively develop a comprehensive component to address barriers to learning. Note especially the links among the three components and the connection within the various groups involved in planning, implementing, evaluating, and sustaining learning supports.

A LEARNING SUPPORTS RESOURCE MECHANISM FOR A FAMILY OF SCHOOLS

Schools in the same geographic or catchment area have a number of shared concerns, and schools in the feeder pattern often interact with students from the same family. Furthermore, some programs and personnel already are or can be shared in strategic ways by several neighboring schools, thereby reducing costs by minimizing redundancy and opening up ways to achieve economies of scale.

A multisite council can provide a mechanism to help ensure cohesive and equitable deployment of resources and also can enhance the pooling of resources. Such a mechanism can be particularly useful for integrating the efforts of high schools and their feeder middle and elementary schools and connecting with neighborhood resources. This clearly is important in addressing barriers with those families who have youngsters attending more than one level of schooling in the same cluster. It is neither cost-effective nor good intervention for each school to contact a family separately in instances where several children from a family are in need of special attention. With respect to linking with community resources, multischool

Guide 7.2   Example of an Integrated Infrastructure at a School Site

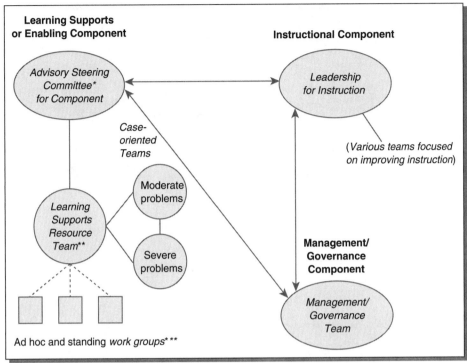

*A Learning Supports or Enabling Component Advisory/Steering Committee at a school site consists of a leadership group whose responsibility is to ensure that the vision for the component is not lost. It meets as needed to monitor and provide input to the Learning Supports Resource Team.

**A Learning Supports Resource Team is the key to ensuring component cohesion, integrated implementation, and ongoing development. It meets weekly to guide and monitor daily implementation and development of all programs, services, initiatives, and systems at a school that are concerned with providing learning supports and specialized assistance.

***Ad hoc and standing work groups are formed as needed by the Learning Supports Resource Team to address specific concerns. These groups are essential for accomplishing the many tasks associated with such a team's functions.

teams are especially attractive to community agencies that often don't have the time or personnel to make independent arrangements with every school.

In general, a group of schools can benefit from a multisite resource mechanism designed to provide leadership, facilitate communication and connection, and ensure quality improvement across sites. For example, a multisite body, or what we call a *Learning Supports Resource Council,* might consist of a high school and its feeder middle and elementary schools. It brings together one or two representatives from each school's resource team (see Guide 7.3).

Guide 7.3   Resource-oriented Mechanisms Across a Family of Schools

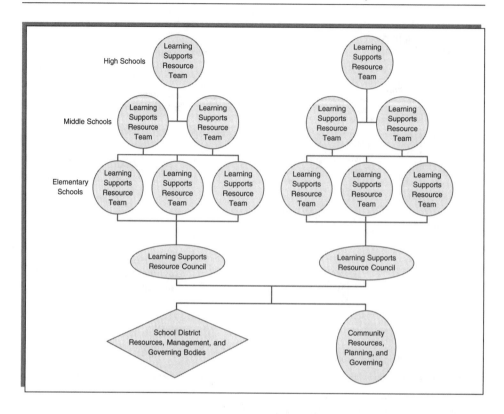

The council meets about once a month to help (a) coordinate and integrate programs serving multiple schools, (b) identify and meet common needs with respect to guidelines and staff development, and (c) create linkages and collaborations among schools and with community agencies. In this last regard, it can play a special role in community outreach both to create formal working relationships and to ensure that all participating schools have access to such resources.

More generally, the council provides a useful mechanism for leadership, communication, maintenance, quality improvement, and ongoing development of a comprehensive continuum of programs and services. Natural starting points for councils are the sharing of needs assessments, resource maps, analyses, and recommendations for reform and restructuring. Specific areas of initial focus would be on local, high priority concerns, such as addressing violence and developing prevention programs and safe-school and neighborhood plans.

Representatives from learning supports resource councils would be invaluable members of planning groups (e.g., service planning area councils, local management boards). They bring information about specific schools, clusters of schools, and local neighborhoods and do so in ways that reflect the importance of school-community partnerships.

ABOUT LEADERSHIP AND INFRASTRUCTURE

It is clear that building a Learning Supports or Enabling Component requires strong leadership and new positions to help steer systemic changes and construct the necessary infrastructure. Establishment and maintenance of the component requires continuous, proactive, and effective teaming and organization and accountability.

Administrative leadership *at every level* is vital to the success of any systemic change initiative in schools. Given that an Enabling or Learning Supports Component is one of the primary and essential components of school improvement, it is imperative to have designated administrative and staff leadership for the component at school and district levels. Everyone at the school site should be aware of who in the school district provides leadership for promotes, and is accountable for the development of the component. It is crucial that such leadership be at a high enough level to be at key decision-making tables when budget and other fundamental decisions are discussed.

At the school level, an administrative leader for the component may be created by redefining a percentage of an assistant principal's day (e.g., 50%). Or in schools that have only one administrator, the principal might delegate some administrative responsibilities to a coordinator (e.g., Title I coordinator or a center coordinator at schools with a family or parent center). The designated administrative leader must sit on the resource team and represent and advocate team recommendations at administrative and governance body meetings.

Besides facilitating initial development of a potent component to address barriers to learning, the administrative leader must guide and be accountable for daily implementation, monitoring, and problem solving. This individual is the natural link to component leaders in the family of schools and at the district level and should be a vital force for community outreach and involvement.

There is also the need for a staff leader to address daily operational matters. This may be one of the learning supports staff (e.g., a school counselor, psychologist, social worker, nurse) or a Title I coordinator, or a teacher with a special interest in learning supports.

In general, these leaders, along with other key staff, embody the vision for the component. Their job descriptions should be reframed to delineate specific functions related to their new roles, responsibilities, and accountabilities.[1]

CONCLUDING COMMENTS

The coming years will mark a turning point for how schools and communities address the problems of children and youth. Currently being determined are these issues: *In what direction should schools go? Who should decide this?*

Initiative: New Directions for Student Support*

The kickoff for the Initiative was held in October 2002 and was followed in March 2003 with an East Coast regional meeting, a Midwest regional in May, a six-state regional, and then by statewide summits. The plan over several years is to hold a statewide summit in every state. Discussion at each summit centers around four fundamental problems that must be addressed in moving in new directions: (1) reframing policy, (2) adopting comprehensive intervention frameworks, (3) rethinking infrastructure and personnel roles and functions, and (4) facilitating systemic change.

After each state summit, a statewide leadership infrastructure is established to move the initiative forward. Another key facet of the initiative is an information and outreach campaign. At an appropriate time, the leadership network for new directions will organize a policymakers' summit on student support to clarify new directions and encourage adoption of major recommendations.

Throughout the process, major efforts to move in new directions are being identified and showcased. Technical assistance and training are available to localities and states moving forward. And mutual-support networks are being developed for sharing of effective practices, lessons learned, and data on progress.

---

*For detailed information on the initiative, click on "New Directions Initiative" on the homepage of the Center for Mental Health in Schools' Web site, http://smhp.psych.ucla .edu/. It provides a list of the cosponsors, a concept paper, reports and recommendations from the summits, guidelines for a student support component at a school, resource aids for new directions, descriptions of trailblazing efforts, and much more. There are also guidelines for how to start the process for a statewide summit.

Those interested in being involved in developing a Summit for New Directions for Student Support in their state should contact the center at Box 951563, UCLA, Los Angeles, CA 90095-1563, Ph: (310) 825-3634, toll-free (866) 846-4843, Fax: (310) 206-8716, e-mail: smhp@ucla.edu.

Where education leaders and learning supports staff are not yet shaping the answers to these questions, they need to find places at the relevant tables. Their expertise is needed in shaping policy and mechanisms for developing schoolwide and classroom programs to address barriers to learning and promote healthy development. There is much work to be done as learning supports are redefined in the next decade.

No leader in education will argue against maximizing a school's capability for addressing barriers to student learning and teaching. And with increasing accountability for student outcomes and dwindling budgets, there is little choice about rethinking the use of existing resources for learning supports. As we have stressed, cornerstones of such thinking must be ways to end the marginalization of learning supports as a school enterprise, minimize fragmentation of intervention activity, and eliminate counterproductive competition.

Because leadership is so critical to moving schools forward in new directions, a nationwide initiative for *New Directions for Student Support* was embarked upon in 2002. This was done in response to widespread interest in mounting a strategic effort to move forward.

The initial emphasis has been on encouraging advocacy for new directions, building a leadership network, and supporting those who are pioneering the way. Leaders from across the country already are involved, and others are coming aboard every day. And at the time this is being written, over thirty associations and agencies are cosponsoring the initiative. Daily work related to the initiative is facilitated by our Center at UCLA (see information at the end of this chapter and in Chapter 17, *New Directions for Student Support Initiative Brief: Assuring That No Child Is Left Behind*).

Partly as a result of the initiative and because of the increasing pressures on schools to enhance test scores and close the achievement gap, interest in moving in new directions is growing at an exponential rate. At state and local levels, policymakers are beginning to formulate positions and legislation (see Chapter 18, *Examples of Policy Statements*).

With appropriate leadership, work will advance with respect to *restructuring,* transforming, and enhancing school-owned programs and services and community resources. In doing so, the focus needs to be on *all* school resources, including compensatory and special education, support services, adult education, recreation and enrichment programs, and facility use, and on *all* community *resources*—public and private agencies, families, businesses; services, programs, facilities; institutions of higher education; professionals-in-training; and volunteers, including professionals making pro bono contributions.

The long-range aim is to weave all resources together into the fabric of every school and evolve a comprehensive component that effectively addresses barriers to development, learning, and teaching. As leaders and policymakers recognize the essential nature of such a component, it will be easier to braid resources to address barriers. In turn, this will enhance efforts to foster healthy development.

When resources are combined properly, the *end product* can be cohesive and potent school-community partnerships. Such partnerships seem essential if we are to strengthen neighborhoods and communities and create caring and supportive environments that maximize learning and well-being. We turn to this topic in Chapter 8.

It is only those who don't care about where they end up who can afford not to be involved in which way they are going.

NOTE

1. As noted in Chapter 5, Note 1, the Center for Mental Health in Schools has available hard copy and online resources to guide development of resource-oriented teams and for rethinking how resources are used for learning support. Included are learning supports job descriptions for administrators and staff.

School-Family-Community Connections

8

With a Special Focus on School-Community Collaboratives

One of the most important, cross-cutting social policy perspectives to emerge in recent years is an awareness that no single institution can create all the conditions that young people need to flourish.

—Melaville and Blank (1998)

ORIENTING QUESTIONS

? What makes school-community collaboration imperative?
? What are the ranges of resources that could be woven into such a collaboration?
? What are the basic dimensions of school-community collaborative arrangements?

Never doubt that a small group of thoughtful, committed people can change the world. Indeed, it is the only thing that ever has.

—Margaret Mead

Recent years have seen an escalating expansion in school-community linkages (Center for Mental Health in Schools, 1999; Honig, Kahne, & McLaughlin, 2001; Southwest Educational Development Laboratory, 2001). Initiatives are sprouting in a rather dramatic and ad hoc manner.

Comprehensive linkages represent a promising direction for generating essential interventions to address barriers to learning, enhance healthy development, and strengthen families and neighborhoods. For schools, such links are seen as a way to provide more support for schools, students, and families. For agencies, connection with schools is seen as providing better access to families and youth and thus providing an opportunity to reach and have an impact on hard-to-reach clients. The interest in working together is bolstered by concern about widespread fragmentation of school and community interventions. The hope is that integrated resources will have a greater impact on risk factors and on promoting healthy development.

While informal school-community linkages are relatively simple to acquire, establishing major, long-term connections is complicated. They require vision, cohesive policy, and basic systemic reform. The difficulties are readily seen in attempts to evolve a comprehensive, multifaceted, and integrated continuum of school-community interventions. Such a comprehensive continuum involves more than connecting with the community to enhance resources to support instruction, provide mentoring, and improve facilities. It involves more than school-linked, integrated services and activities. It requires weaving school and community resources together in ways that can achieved only be through connections that are formalized and institutionalized, with major responsibilities shared.

School-community connections often are referred to as *collaborations*. The usual intent in forming a collaboration is to sustain the connection over time. Optimally, such collaborations formally blend together resources of at least one school and sometimes a group of schools or an entire school district with resources in a given neighborhood or the larger community.

Building an effective collaboration requires an enlightened vision, creative leadership, and new and multifaceted roles for professionals who work in schools and communities as well as for all who are willing to assume leadership. And in thinking about all this, it is essential not to overemphasize the topics of coordinating community services and co-locating services on school sites. Such thinking ignores the range of resources in a community, including human and social capital; businesses; community-based organizations; postsecondary institutions; faith-based and civic groups; parks and libraries; and facilities for recreation, learning, enrichment, and support. Also, the overemphasis on service agencies downplays the need to restructure the various education support programs and services that schools own and operate. As we have noted, some policymakers have the mistaken impression that community service agencies can effectively meet the needs of schools in addressing barriers to learning. Even when one adds together community and school assets, the total set of services in impoverished locales is woefully inadequate.

In general, collaboration among schools, families, and communities could improve schools, strengthen families and neighborhoods, and lead to a marked reduction in young people's problems. Poorly implemented collaboration, however, risks becoming another reform that promised a lot, did little good, and even did some harm. With hope for a promising future, this chapter briefly

- Underscores the "why" of school-family-community collaborations
- Highlights their key facets
- Sketches out the state of the art across the country

- Discusses steps for building and maintaining school-community partnerships
- Offers some recommendations for local school and community policymakers and other leaders

WHY CONNECT?

Schools are located in communities but often are islands with no bridges to the mainland. Families live in neighborhoods, often with little connection to each other or to the schools their youngsters attend. Neighborhood entities, such as agencies, youth groups, and businesses, have major stakes in the community. All these affect each other, for good or bad. Because of this and because they share goals related to education, socialization, and well-being of the young, schools, homes, and communities must collaborate with each other if they are to minimize problems and maximize results with respect to overlapping goals.

Dealing with multiple and interrelated problems, such as poverty, child development, education, violence, crime, safety, housing, and employment, requires multiple and interrelated solutions—and these solutions require collaboration. Promoting well-being, resilience, and protective factors and empowering families, communities, and schools also require the concerted effort of all stakeholders. And *all* means more than just service providers. As important as health and human services are, such services remain only one facet of a comprehensive, cohesive approach for strengthening families and neighborhoods. The community side of school-community collaborations must encompass more than representatives of service agencies. The school side must include more than student support staff. Teachers and families, in particular, have a major stake in school-community connections.

It seems evident that when schools are an integral and positive part of the community, they are better positioned to address barriers to learning; enhance opportunities for learning, development, and academic performance; reduce discipline problems; expand home involvement; increase staff morale; and improve use of resources. Indeed, *leaving no child behind is feasible only through well-designed collaborative efforts.*

Similarly, by working with schools, families and other community entities can enhance parenting and socialization, address psychosocial problems, and strengthen the fabric of family and community well-being and community self-sufficiency. Agencies, for example, can make services more accessible to youth and families by linking with schools and can connect better with and have an impact on hard-to-reach clients.

Interest in working together also is bolstered by concern about widespread fragmentation of school and community interventions. Clearly, appropriate and effective school-community collaboration should be part of any strategy for developing comprehensive, multifaceted, and integrated approaches to promote well-being and address barriers. Strong school-community connections are critical in impoverished communities where schools often are the largest pieces of public real estate and resources and also may be the single largest employer.

Comprehensive collaboration represents a promising direction for generating essential interventions to address barriers to learning, enhance healthy development, and strengthen families and neighborhoods. This is accomplished by weaving together a critical mass of resources and strategies that enables effective teaching and learning by supporting all youth, their families, and teachers.

DEFINING COLLABORATION AND ITS PURPOSES

As we have noted, some wit defined *collaboration* as "an unnatural act between nonconsenting adults." This captures the reality that establishing a "collaborative" is a snap compared to the task of turning the group into an effective, ongoing mechanism. Collaboration involves more than simply working together, and a collaborative is more than a process to enhance cooperation and coordination. Thus teachers who team teach are not a collaborative; they are a teaching team. Professionals who work as a multidisciplinary team to coordinate treatment are not a collaborative; they are a treatment team. Interagency teams established to enhance coordination and communication across agencies are not collaboratives; they are coordinating teams.

Coalitions are not collaboratives; they are a form of collaboration that involves multiple organizations that establish an *alliance* for sharing information and jointly pursuing policy advocacy or cohesive action in overlapping areas of concern. A collaborative is a form of collaboration that involves establishing an infrastructure for *working together to accomplish specific functions* related to developing and enhancing interventions and systems in arenas where the participants' agendas overlap.

One hallmark of authentic collaboration is a *formal agreement* among participants to establish mechanisms and processes to accomplish *mutually desired results*—usually outcomes that would be difficult to achieve by any of the stakeholders alone. Thus, while participants may have primary affiliations elsewhere, they commit to working together under specified conditions to pursue a shared vision and common set of goals.

Effective collaboratives are built with vision, policy, leadership, infrastructure, and capacity building. A collaborative structure requires shared governance (power, authority, decision making, accountability) and weaving together an adequate set of resources. It also requires establishing well-defined and effective *working* relationships that enable participants to overcome individual agendas. If this cannot be accomplished, the intent of pursuing a shared agenda and achieving a collective vision is jeopardized.

Growing appreciation of human and social capital has resulted in collaboratives expanding to include a wide range of stakeholders (individuals, groups, formal and informal organizations). Many who at best were silent partners in the past now are finding their way to the collaborative table and becoming key players. The political realities of local control have expanded collaborative bodies to encompass local policymakers, representatives of families, nonprofessionals, and volunteers. Families, of course, have always provided a direct connection between school and community, but now they are seeking a greater decision-making role. In addition, advocates for students with special needs have opened the way for increased parent and youth participation in forums making decisions about interventions. Clearly, any effort to connect home, community, and school resources must embrace a wide spectrum of stakeholders.

In the context of a collaborative, collaboration is both a desired process and an outcome. That is, the intent is to work together to establish strong working relationships that are enduring. However, family, community, and school collaboration is not an end in itself. It is a turning point meant to enable participants to pursue increasingly potent strategies for strengthening families, schools, and communities.

Effective collaboratives, then, attempt to weave the responsibilities and resources of participating stakeholders together to create a new form of unified entity. For our purposes here, any group designed to connect a school, its families, and other entities from the surrounding neighborhood is referred to as a "school-community" collaborative. This may include entities focused on providing programs for education, literacy, youth development, the arts, health and human services, juvenile justice, vocational education, economic development, and more. It may encompass various sources of human, social, and economic capital, including teachers, student support staff, youth, families, community-based and community-linked organizations such as public and private health and human service agencies, civic groups, businesses, faith-based organizations, institutions of postsecondary learning, and so forth.

Operationally, a collaborative is defined by its *functions.* That is, a collaborative is about accomplishing functions, not about establishing and maintaining a collaborative body. Major examples of *functions* include

- Facilitating communication, cooperation, coordination, and integration
- Operationalizing the vision of stakeholders into desired functions and tasks
- Enhancing support for and developing a policy commitment to ensure that necessary resources are dispensed for accomplishing desired functions
- Advocating, analyzing, priority setting, governance, planning, implementation, and evaluation related to desired functions
- Aggregating data from schools and neighborhood to analyze system needs

- Mapping, analyzing, managing, redeploying, and braiding available resources together to enable accomplishment of desired functions
- Establishing leadership and institutional and operational mechanisms (e.g., infrastructure) for guiding and managing the accomplishment of desired functions
- Defining and incorporating new roles and functions into job descriptions
- Building capacity for planning, implementing, and evaluating desired functions, including ongoing stakeholder development for continuous learning and renewal and for bringing new arrivals up to speed
- Defining standards and ensuring accountability
- Social marketing

Functions encompass specific tasks, such as mapping and analyzing resources; exploring ways to share facilities, equipment, and other resources; expanding opportunities for community service, internships, jobs, recreation, and enrichment; developing pools of nonprofessional volunteers and professional pro bono assistance; making recommendations about priorities for use of resources; raising funds and pursuing grants; and advocating for appropriate decision making.

In organizing a collaborative, the fundamental principle is that *structure follows function.* Based on clear functions, a differentiated infrastructure must be developed to enable accomplishment of functions and related tasks. At a minimum, the need is

> Much of the emerging theory and practice of family and community connections with schools encourages a rethinking of our understanding of how children develop and how the various people and contexts fit together to support that development.
>
> —Southwest Educational Development Laboratory (2001)

for infrastructure mechanisms to steer and do work on a regular basis. And since the work almost always overlaps with that of others, a collaborative needs to establish connections with those others.

COLLABORATION: A GROWING MOVEMENT

Most of us know how hard it is to work effectively with a group. In fact, we all can point to committees and teams that have drained our time and energy to little avail.

Nevertheless, the fact remains that no organization can be truly effective if too many staff work in isolation. The same is true when school and community entities do not work together. Thus calls for collaboration have increased, and initiatives for school-community collaboration and collaborative bodies are springing up everywhere. Moreover, increased federal funding for afterschool programs at school sites is enhancing opportunities for collaboration by expanding recreation, enrichment, academic supports, and child care programs.

Various levels and forms of school, community, and family collaboration are being tested, including statewide initiatives. Some cataloguing has begun, but there is no complete picture of the scope of activity.

From what is known, it is clear that many efforts to collaborate have not taken the form of collaboratives. Many demonstration projects are mainly efforts to incorporate health, mental health, and social services into *centers* established at or near a school and use terms such as school-linked or school-based services; coordinated services; wraparound services; one-stop shopping; health, family, and parent centers; full-service schools; systems of care; and community schools.[1]

When collaborations and collaboratives are developed as part of funded projects, the general aims are to improve coordination and eventually integrate many programs and enhance their linkages to school sites. The scope varies. Most of the projects want to improve access to health services (including immunizations, prevention programs for substance abuse, asthma, and pregnancy) and access to social service programs (including foster care, family preservation, and child care). In addition or as a primary focus, some are concerned with (a) expanding afterschool academic, recreation, and enrichment, including tutoring, youth sports and clubs, art, music, and museum programs; (b) building systems of care, including case management and specialized assistance; (c) reducing delinquency, including truancy prevention, conflict mediation, and violence reduction; (d) enhancing transitions to work, career, and postsecondary education, including mentoring, internships, career academies, and job shadowing and job placement programs; and (e) strengthening schools and community connections through adopt-a-school programs, use of volunteers and peer supports, and neighborhood coalitions.

Projects have been stimulated by diverse initiatives:

- Some are driven by school reform.
- Some are connected to efforts to reform community health and social service agencies.
- Some stem from the community school and youth development movements.
- A few stem from community development endeavors.

Currently, only a few projects are driven by school reform. Most stem from efforts to reform community health and social services with the aim of reducing redundancy and increasing access and effectiveness. These tend to focus narrowly on particular services. Projects initiated by schools connect schools and communities to enhance school-to-career opportunities, develop pools of volunteers and mentors, and expand afterschool recreation and enrichment programs.

The community school and youth development movements have spawned school-community collaboration that clearly goes beyond a narrow service emphasis. They encourage a view of schools not only as community centers where families can access services but as hubs for communitywide learning and activity. In doing so, they encompass concepts and practices aimed at promoting protective factors, asset building, wellness, and empowerment. Included are efforts to establish full-fledged community schools, programs for community and social capital mobilization, and initiatives to establish community policies and structures that enhance youth support, safety, recreation, work, service, and enrichment. Their efforts, along with adult education and training at neighborhood schools, are changing the old view that schools close when the youngsters leave. The concept of a second shift at a school site to respond to community needs is beginning to spread.

School-community linkages are meant to benefit a wide range of youngsters and their families. For example, considerable attention has been paid to linkages to enhance outcomes for students with emotional disturbance. This population is served by classrooms, counseling, day care, and residential and hospital programs. It is widely acknowledged that all involved need to work together in providing services, monitoring and maintaining care, and facilitating the transitions to and from services. To address these needs, considerable investment has been made in establishing what are called *wraparound services* and *systems of care*. The work has tended to be the focus of multidisciplinary teams, usually without the support of a collaborative body. Initial evaluations of systems of care have been discussed in terms of the difficulty of studying linkages and the policy issues that arise regarding appropriate outcomes and cost-effectiveness. We would add that the studies highlight the need for the involvement of a school-community collaborative.

> ## How many members of a collaborative does it take to change a lightbulb?
>
> - Four—to share similar experiences of changing lightbulbs and how the lightbulb could have been changed differently
> - Seven—to caution about the dangers of changing lightbulbs
> - Twenty-seven—to point out spelling or grammar errors in postings about changing lightbulbs
> - Fifty-three—to flame the spelling and grammar critics
> - Three—to correct the spelling and grammar in the spelling-grammar flames
> - Six—to argue whether it's "lightbulb" or "lightbulb."
>
> **Moral:** It's easy to get distracted from the task at hand. Working collaboratively takes strong leadership to get the job done.

While data are sparse, a reasonable inference from available research is that school-community collaboration can be successful and cost-effective over the long run. Moreover, school-community collaborations not only have potential for improving access to and coordination of interventions, but they also encourage schools to open their doors and enhance opportunities for community and family involvement.

Currently, as portrayed in the top section of Guide 8.1, schools and community entities usually function as separate agents, with a few discrete linkages designed to address highly circumscribed matters. Often the linkages are encouraged by or directed at parents of school-age children or both. The immediate goal of many school-family-community collaboratives is to bring the entities together to work in more cooperative ways and, where feasible, to integrate resources and activities when they are dealing with overlapping concerns (see the middle section of Guide 8.1). Some

Guide 8.1   School-Community Relationships: Current Situation and Goals for the Future

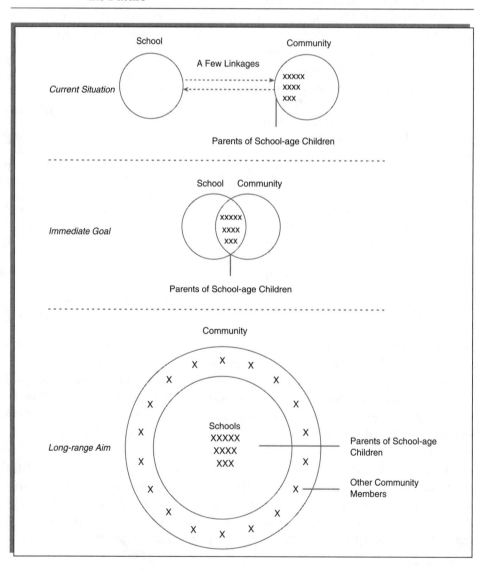

argue that ultimately it is all about community and that families should be understood and nurtured as the heart of any community and that schools should be completely embedded and not seen as separate agents (see the bottom section of Guide 8.1).

UNDERSTANDING KEY FACETS OF SCHOOL-COMMUNITY CONNECTIONS

As should be evident by now, school-community connections differ in terms of purposes adopted and functions pursued. They also differ in terms of a range of other dimensions. For example, they may vary in their degrees of formality, their time commitment, and the breadth of the connections, as well as the amount of systemic change required to carry out their functions and achieve their purposes.

Key Dimensions

Because family, community, and school collaboration can differ in so many ways, it is helpful to think in terms of categories of key factors relevant to such arrangements (see Guide 8.2).

Range of Resources

Guide 8.3 highlights the wealth of community resources that should be considered in establishing family, community, and school connections.

As mentioned, operationally, a collaborative is defined by its *focus* and *functions*. We have outlined the functions earlier in this chapter. The *focus* may be on

- *Improvement of direct delivery of services and programs* (improving interventions to promote healthy development, prevent and correct problems, meet client or consumer needs; improving processes for referral, triage, assessment, case management)

and/or

Family and Citizen Involvement

For various reasons, many collaboratives around the country consist mainly of professionals. Family and other citizen involvement may be limited to a few representatives of powerful organizations or token participants who are expected to sign off on decisions without active involvement in making them.

Genuine involvement of a wide range of representative families and citizens requires a deep commitment of collaborative organizers to recruit and build the capacity of such stakeholders so that they can competently participate as enfranchised and informed decision makers.

Collaboratives that proactively work to ensure that a broad range of stakeholders are participating effectively can establish an essential democratic base for their work. This also helps buffer against the inevitable mobility that results in participant turnover. Such an approach not only enhances family and community involvement, it may be essential to sustaining collaborative efforts over the long run.

Guide 8.2   Some Key Dimensions Relevant to Family-Community-School
Collaborative Arrangements

I. Initiation

    A. School-led

    B. Community-driven

II. Nature of Collaboration

    A. Formal
- Memorandum of understanding
- Contract
- Organizational or operational mechanisms

    B. Informal
- Verbal agreements
- Ad hoc arrangements

III. Focus

    A. Improvement of program and service provision
- For enhancing case management
- For enhancing use of resources

    B. Major systemic changes
- To enhance coordination
- For organizational restructuring
- For transforming system structure or function

IV. Scope of Collaboration

    A. Number of programs and services involved (from just a few up to a comprehensive, multifaceted continuum)

    B. Horizontal collaboration
- Within a school or agency
- Among schools and agencies

    C. Vertical collaboration
- Within a catchment area (e.g., school and community agency, family of schools, two or more agencies)
- Among different levels of jurisdictions (e.g., community, city, county, state, federal)

V. Scope of Potential Impact

    A. *Narrow-band:* A small proportion of youth and families can access what they need.

    B. *Broadband:* All in need can access what they need.

VI. Ownership and Governance of Programs and Services

    A. Owned and governed by a school

    B. Owned and governed by the community

    C. Shared ownership and governance

    D. Public-private venture—shared ownership and governance

VII. *Location of Programs and Services*

    A. Community-based, school linked
    B. School-based

VIII. *Degree of Cohesiveness Among Multiple Interventions Serving the Same Student and Family*

    A. Unconnected
    B. Communicating
    C. Cooperating
    D. Coordinated
    E. Integrated

IX. *Level of Systemic Intervention Focus*

    A. Systems for promoting healthy development
    B. Systems for prevention of problems
    C. Systems for early after onset of problems
    D. Systems of care for treatment of severe, pervasive, and chronic problems
    E. Full continuum, including all levels

X. *Arenas for Collaborative Activity*

    A. Health (physical and mental)
    B. Education
    C. Social services
    D. Work, career
    E. Enrichment, recreation
    F. Juvenile justice
    G. Neighborhood, community improvement

- *Improving major systemic concerns* (improving resource deployment and accessing more resources; moving from fragmented to cohesive approaches; developing a comprehensive, multifaceted continuum of integrated interventions; replicating innovations; scaling up)

An Example of Efforts to Establish Collaboratives Across an Entire State

In 1987, the governor of Maryland issued an executive order creating the Subcabinet for Children, Youth, and Families. In 1990, a statute (Chapter 419, 1991) was enacted requiring each local jurisdiction to establish a Local Governing Entity, now known as Local Management Boards (LMBs). By 1997, LMBs were operating in all twenty-four jurisdictions.

LMBs are the core entity established in each jurisdiction to stimulate joint action by state and local government, public and private providers,

Guide 8.3   Examples of the Range of Community Resources That Could Be Part of a Collaboration

County Agencies and Bodies

Depts. of Health, Mental Health, Children and Family Services, Public Social Services, Probation, Sheriff, Office of Education, Fire, Service Planning Area Councils, Recreation and Parks, Library, courts, housing

Municipal Agencies and Bodies

Parks and recreation, library, police, fire, courts, civic event units

Physical and Mental Health and Psychosocial Concerns Facilities and Groups

Hospitals, HMOs, clinics, guidance centers, Planned Parenthood, Aid to Victims, MADD, "Friends of" groups; family crisis and support centers, help lines, hotlines, shelters, mediation and dispute resolution centers, private practitioners

Mutual Support/Self-help Groups

Available for almost every problem and many other activities

Child Care/Preschool Centers

Postsecondary Education Institutions and Their Students

Community colleges, state universities, public and private colleges and universities, vocational colleges; specific schools within these, such as schools of law, education, nursing, dentistry

Service Agencies

PTA/PTSA, United Way, clothing and food pantries, Visiting Nurses Association, Cancer Society, Catholic Charities, Red Cross, Salvation Army, volunteer agencies, legal aid societies

Service Clubs and Philanthropic Organizations

Lions Club, Rotary Club, Optimists, Assistance League, men's and women's clubs, League of Women Voters, veterans' groups, foundations

Youth Agencies and Groups

Boys and Girls Clubs, Y, Scouts, 4-H, Woodcraft Rangers

Sports, Health, Fitness, Outdoor Groups

Sports teams, athletic leagues, local gyms, conservation associations, Audubon Society

Community-based Organizations

Neighborhood and homeowners' associations, Neighborhood Watch, block clubs, housing project associations, economic development groups, civic associations

Faith Community Institutions

Congregations and subgroups, clergy associations, Interfaith Hunger Coalition

Legal Assistance Groups and Practitioners

Public Counsel, schools of law, legal aid societies

Ethnic Associations

Committee for Armenian Students in Public Schools; Korean Youth Centers; United Cambodian Community; African American, Latino, Asian Pacific, Native American organizations

Special Interest Associations and Clubs

Future Scientists and Engineers of America, pet owner and other animal-oriented groups

Artists and Cultural Institutions

Museums, art galleries, zoos, theater groups, motion picture studios, TV and radio stations, writers' organizations, instrumental and choral groups, drawing and painting, technology-based arts, literary clubs, collectors' groups

Businesses, Corporations, Unions

Neighborhood business associations, chambers of commerce, local shops, restaurants, banks, AAA, Teamsters, school employee unions

Media

Newspapers, TV and radio, local access cable stations

Family Members, Local Residents, Senior Citizens Groups

business and industry, and community residents to build an effective system of services, supports, and opportunities that improve outcomes for children, youth, and families. An example is the partnership established in Anne Arundel County created by county government in December 1993.

As described by the Anne Arundel LMB, they are a collaborative board responsible for interagency planning; goal setting; resource allocation;

and developing, implementing, and monitoring interagency services to children and their families. Their mission is to enhance the well-being of all children and their families in the county. All their work focuses on making "children safe in their families and communities" with goals and priorities established by the board members through a community needs process completed in October 1997. The consortium consists of representatives of public and private agencies who serve children and families and of private citizens. Membership includes County Public Schools, Department of Social Services, Department of Juvenile Justice, Department of Health and Mental Health, County Mental Health Agency, Inc., County Recreation and Parks, county government, and private citizens (private providers, advocacy groups, parents, and other consumers). Private citizens can compose up to 49% of the membership. Board members are appointed by the county executive for a term of four years.

In pursuing their mission, the LMB (a) fosters collaboration among all public and private partners, (b) plans a wide array of services, (c) coordinates and pools resources, (d) monitors and evaluates the effectiveness of programs, and (e) provides a forum for communication and advocacy. For instance, it develops community plans for providing comprehensive interagency services with guidelines established by the Subcabinet for Children, Youth, and Families. Examples of program initiatives include

- Positive parenting programs
- Mom and tots support groups
- Safe Haven Runaway Shelter
- Youth and family services
- Mobile Crisis Team
- Success by 6 (preschool readiness to learn)
- Afterschool Middle School Programs for At-Risk Youth
- Kinship care support groups
- Police-sponsored teen opportunity programs
- Juvenile intervention programs
- Disruptive Youth Program
- Second Step Curriculum
- School-Community Centers Program

(For more info, see http://www.aacounty.org/lmb/default.htm.)

BARRIERS TO COLLABORATION

Collaboration is a developing process. It must be continuously nurtured, facilitated, and supported, and special attention must be given to overcoming institutional and personal barriers.

Years ago, former surgeon general Jocelyn Elders noted, "We all say we want to collaborate, but what we really mean is that we want to continue doing things as we have always done them while others change to fit what we are doing." More recently, some advocates for collaboration have cautioned that some collaborations amount to little more than groups of people sitting around engaging in "collabo-babble."

Barriers to collaboration arise from a variety of institutional and personal factors. A fundamental institutional barrier to family-community-school collaboration is the degree to which efforts to establish such connections are *marginalized* in policy and practice. The extent to which this is the case can be seen in how few resources most schools deploy to build effective collaboratives.

Institutional barriers are seen when existing policy, accountability, leadership, budget, space, time schedules, and capacity-building agendas do not address the effective and efficient use of collaborative arrangements to accomplish desired results. This may simply be a matter of benign neglect. More often, it reflects a lack of understanding, commitment, or capability related to establishing and maintaining a potent infrastructure for working together and for sharing resources. Occasionally, active forces are at work that mean to undermine collaboration.

Examples of institutional barriers include

- Policies that mandate collaboration but do not enable the process (e.g., a failure to reconcile differences among participants with respect to the outcomes for which they are accountable; inadequate provision for braiding funds across agencies and categorical programs)
- Policies for collaboration that do not provide adequate resources and time for leadership and stakeholder training and for overcoming barriers to collaboration
- Leadership that does not establish an effective infrastructure, especially mechanisms for steering and accomplishing tasks on a regular, ongoing basis
- Differences in the conditions and incentives associated with participation, such as setting meetings during the work day, which means that community agency and school personnel are paid participants while available family members are expected to volunteer their time

At the personal level, barriers mostly stem from practical deterrents, negative attitudes, and deficiencies of knowledge and skill. These vary for different stakeholders but often include problems related to work schedules, transportation, child care, communication skills, understanding differences in organizational culture, accommodations for language and cultural differences, and so forth.

Other barriers arise because of inadequate attention to factors associated with systemic change. How well an innovation such as a collaborative is implemented depends to a significant degree on the personnel doing the implementing and the motivation and capabilities of participants. Sufficient resources and time must be redeployed so they can learn and carry out new functions effectively. And when newcomers join, well-designed procedures must be in place to bring them up to speed.

When schools and community agencies are at the same table, it is a given that problems will arise related to the differences in organizational mission, functions, cultures, bureaucracies, and accountabilities. Considerable effort will be required to teach each other about these matters. When families are at the table, power differentials are common, especially when less-prepared families are involved and confronted with credentialed and titled professionals. And if the collaborative is not well-conceived and carefully developed, this generates additional barriers.

In too many instances, so-called school-community partnerships have amounted to little more than co-location of community agency staff onto school campuses. Services continue to function in relative isolation from each other, focusing on discrete problems and specialized services for individuals and small groups. Too little thought is given to the importance of meshing, as contrasted with simply linking, community services and programs with existing school-owned and school-operated activity. The result is that a small number of youngsters are provided services that they may not otherwise have received, but little connection is made with families, teachers, and other school staff and related programs. Because of this, a new form of fragmentation is emerging as community and school professionals engage in a form of parallel play at school sites.

As we have said earlier and want to stress, when outside professionals are brought into schools, district student support staff may view the move as discounting their skills and threatening their jobs. On the other side, the "outsiders" often feel unappreciated. Conflicts arise over turf, use of space, confidentiality, and liability. School professionals tend not to understand the culture of community agencies; agency staff are often naive about the culture of schools.

Working collaboratively requires overcoming barriers. Participants must be sensitive to a variety of human and institutional differences and learn strategies for dealing with them. These include differences in socio-cultural and economic background and current lifestyle, primary language spoken, skin color, sex, motivation, and capability. In addition, there are differences related to power, status, orientation, and organizational culture.

Differences can be complementary and helpful—as when staff from different disciplines work with and learn from each other. Differences become barriers when negative attitudes and inappropriate competition are allowed to prevail. Interpersonally, the general result is conflict and poor communication. For example, many individuals who have been treated unfairly, discriminated against, and deprived of opportunity and status at school, on the job, and in society use whatever means they can to seek redress and sometimes to strike back. Such individuals may promote conflict in hopes of correcting power imbalances or at least to call attention to injustice and inequality. However, because power differentials are so institutionalized, it is common for individual action to have little impact. This engenders growing frustration and a tendency to fight with anyone who seems to represent institutionalized power. Such fighting usually begins with words such as, "You don't understand," or worse, "You probably don't want to understand." Underlying all this may be the message, "You are my enemy."

It is unfortunate when barriers arise between those we are trying to help; it is a travesty when such barriers interfere with helpers working together effectively. The problem for a collaborative is how to keep such conflict from becoming counterproductive. Too much conflict among collaborative members interferes with accomplishing goals and contributes in a major way to burnout.

> Heard at a collaborative meeting where a member was talking on and on about too little:
> "Has he finished yet?"
> "Long ago, but he won't stop talking."

Overcoming barriers is easier to do when all stakeholders are committed to learning to do so. It means moving beyond naming problems to careful analysis of why the problem has arisen and then moving on to creative problem solving (see Guide 8.4).

Guide 8.4   *Overcoming Barriers Related to Differences*

Although workshops and presentations may be offered in an effort to increase specific cultural awareness, what can be learned in this way is limited, especially when one is in a community of many cultures. There also is a danger in prejudgments based on apparent cultural awareness. It is desirable to have the needed language skills and cultural awareness; it is also essential not to rush to judgment.

There are no easy solutions to overcoming deeply embedded negative attitudes. Certainly, a first step is to understand that the problem is not the differences per se but negative perceptions stemming from the politics and psychology of the situation. Such perceptions lead to (a) prejudgments that a person is bad because of an observed difference and (b) the view that there is little to be gained from working with that person.

In general, the task of overcoming negative attitudes interfering with a particular working relationship involves finding ways to counter negative prejudgments (to establish the credibility of those who have been prejudged) and demonstrate that there is something of value to be gained from working together.

In facilitating effective working relationships, collaborative leaders should

- Encourage all participants to defer negative judgments about those with whom they will be working.
- Enhance expectations that working together will be productive, with particular emphasis on establishing the value added by each participant in pursuing mutually desired outcomes.

Guide 8.4 (Continued)

- Ensure that there is appropriate time for making connections.
- Establish an infrastructure that provides support and guidance for effective task accomplishment.
- Provide active, task-oriented meeting facilitation that minimizes ego-oriented behavior.
- Ensure regular celebration of positive outcomes resulting from working together.

On a personal level, it is worth teaching participants that building relationships and effective communication involve the willingness and ability to

- *Convey Empathy and Warmth:* As a way of communicating understanding and appreciation of what others are thinking and feeling and transmitting a sense of liking
- *Convey Genuine Regard and Respect:* As a way of transmitting real interest and enabling others to maintain a feeling of integrity and personal control
- *Talk With, Not At, Others:* As a way of conveying that one is a good listener who avoids prejudgment, doesn't pry, and shares experiences only when appropriate and needed

---

Without dedicated commitment to creative problem solving, school-community collaboration can bog down and fade away.

BUILDING AND MAINTAINING EFFECTIVE COLLABORATIVES

It is commonly said that collaboration is about building relationships. That's fine, as long as the aim is to build potent, synergistic, *working* relationships, not simply to establish positive personal connections. Collaboratives built mainly on personal connections are vulnerable to the mobility of participants that characterizes many such groups and to exclusion of folks who are not already in the "inner circle." The intent must be to establish stable and sustainable working relationships and to recruit and involve all who are willing to contribute their talents. Remember: *It's not about having a collaborative—it's about collaborating to be effective. It involves more than meeting and talking—it's about working together in ways that produce effective interventions.*

Effective collaboration requires ensuring that participants have the training, time, support, and authority that enable them to carry out their roles and functions. Participants need well-delineated functions and defined tasks, clear roles, responsibilities, and an institutionalized infrastructure, including well-designed mechanisms for performing tasks, solving problems, and mediating conflict. Also needed are respected leaders and thoughtful, skilled, and content-focused facilitation.

In the absence of careful attention to the foregoing matters, collaboratives rarely live up to hopes and expectations. Participants often start out with great enthusiasm. But poorly facilitated working sessions quickly degenerate into another ho-hum meeting, lots of talk but little action, another burden, and a waste of time. Meeting and meeting but going nowhere are particularly likely to happen when the emphasis is mainly on the unfocused mandate to collaborate. Stakeholders must do more than embrace an important vision and mission. They need an infrastructure that ensures that effective work is done with respect to carefully defined functions and tasks.

As we've stressed, an optimal approach to building a school-community collaborative involves formally weaving together resources of at least one school and sometimes a group of schools or an entire school district with local family and community resources. The intent is to sustain connections over time. As indicated in Guide 8.3, the range of entities in a community can be extensive. Developing a comprehensive approach to shared school and community concerns requires expanding participation in a strategic manner and with a commitment to inclusion.

From a policy perspective, policymakers and other leaders must establish a foundation for building collaborative bridges connecting school, family, and community. Policy must be translated into authentic agreements. Although all this takes considerable time and other resources, the importance of building such bridges cannot be overemphasized. Failure to establish and successfully maintain effective collaboratives probably is attributable in great measure to the absence of clear, high level, and long-term policy support. For example, the primary agenda of community agencies in working with schools usually is to have better access to clients; this is a marginal item in the school accountability agenda for raising test scores and closing the achievement gap. Policy and leadership are needed to address the disparity in ways that integrate what the agency and school can contribute to each other's mission and elevate the work to a high priority.

When all major parties are committed to building an effective collaboration, the next step is to ensure that they understand that the process involves significant systemic changes and that they have the ability to facilitate such changes. Leaders in this situation must have both a vision for change and an understanding of how to effect and institutionalize the type of systemic changes needed to build an effective collaborative infrastructure. This encompasses changes related to governance, leadership, planning, implementation, sustainability, scale-up, and accountability. For example,

- Existing governance must be modified over time. The aim is shared decision making, involving school and community agency staff, families, students, and other community representatives. This involves equalizing power and sharing leadership so that decision making appropriately reflects and accounts for all stakeholder groups.

- High level leadership assignments must be designated to facilitate essential systemic changes and build and maintain family-community-school connections.
- Mechanisms must be established and institutionalized for analyzing, planning, coordinating, integrating, monitoring, evaluating, and strengthening collaborative efforts. All participants must share in the workload, pursuing clear functions.

Evidence of appropriate policy support is seen in the adequacy of funding for *capacity building* to accomplish desired systemic changes and ensure that the collaborative operates effectively over time. Accomplishing systemic changes requires the establishment of temporary facilitative mechanisms and the provision of incentives, supports, and training to enhance commitment to and capacity for essential changes. Ensuring effective collaboration requires institutionalized mechanisms, long-term capacity building, and ongoing support.

About Building From Localities Outward

Collaborations can be organized by any group of stakeholders. Connecting the resources of families and the community through collaboration with schools is essential for developing comprehensive, multi-faceted programs and services. At the multilocality level, efficiencies and economies of scale are achieved by connecting a complex (or family) of schools, such as a high school and its feeder schools. In a small community, such a complex often is the school district. Conceptually, it is best to think in terms of building from the local outward, but in practice, the process of establishing the initial collaboration may begin at any level.

As suggested in Chapter 7, developing an effective collaborative requires an infrastructure of organizational and operational mechanisms at all relevant levels for oversight, leadership, capacity building, and ongoing support. Such mechanisms are used to (a) make decisions about priorities and resource allocation, (b) maximize systematic planning, implementation, maintenance, and evaluation, (c) enhance and redeploy existing resources and pursue new ones, and (d) nurture the collaborative. At each level, such tasks require pursuing a proactive agenda.

Guide 8.5 provides a simplified illustration of the basic infrastructure needed. Guide 8.6 provides a more detailed picture.

An effective school-community collaborative must coalesce at the local level. Thus a school and its surrounding community are a reasonable focal point around which to build an infrastructure. Moreover, primary emphasis

Guide 8.5   About Basic Collaborative Infrastructure

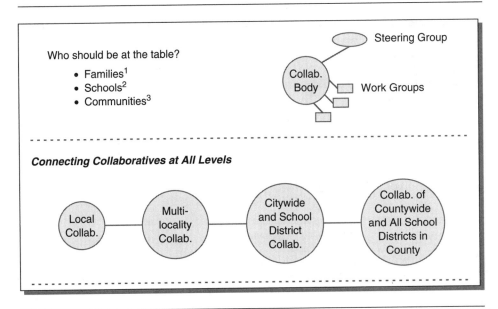

[1] *Families:* It is important to ensure that all who live in an area are represented, including, but not limited to, representatives of organized family advocacy groups. The aim is to mobilize all the human and social capital represented by family members and other home caretakers of the young.

[2] *Schools:* This encompasses all institutionalized entities that are responsible for formal education (pre-K, elementary, secondary, higher education). The aim is to draw on the resources of these institutions.

[3] *Communities:* This encompasses all the other resources (public and private money, facilities, human and social capital) that can be brought to the table at each level, such as health and social service agencies; businesses and unions; recreation, cultural, and youth development groups; libraries; juvenile justice and law enforcement; faith-based community institutions; service clubs; and the media. As the collaborative develops, additional steps must be taken to reach out to disenfranchised groups.

on this level meshes nicely with views that stress increased school-based and neighborhood control.

To maintain the focus on evolving a comprehensive continuum of intervention that plays out in an effective manner in *every locality,* it is a good idea to conceive the process from the local level outward. That is, first the focus is on mechanisms at the school-neighborhood level. Based on analyses of what is needed to facilitate and enhance efforts at a locality, mechanisms are conceived that enable several school-neighborhood collaboratives to work together for increased efficiency, effectiveness, and economies of scale. Then, systemwide mechanisms can be (re)designed to provide support for what each locality is trying to develop.

Guide 8.6   Comprehensive Collaborative Infrastructure

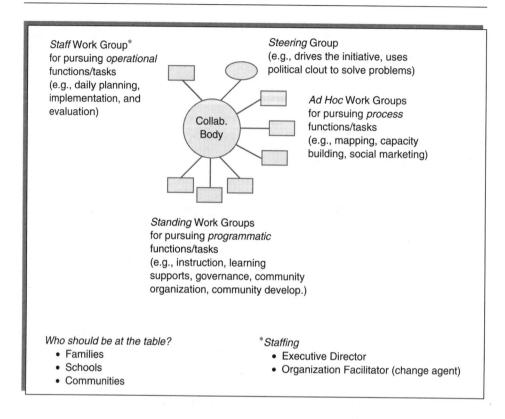

Staff Work Group*
for pursuing *operational*
functions/tasks
(e.g., daily planning,
implementation, and
evaluation)

Steering Group
(e.g., drives the initiative, uses
political clout to solve problems)

Collab.
Body

Ad Hoc Work Groups
for pursuing *process*
functions/tasks
(e.g., mapping, capacity
building, social marketing)

Standing Work Groups
for pursuing *programmatic*
functions/tasks
(e.g., instruction, learning
supports, governance, community
organization, community develop.)

Who should be at the table?
- Families
- Schools
- Communities

*Staffing
- Executive Director
- Organization Facilitator (change agent)

About Capacity Building

As noted, oversight, leadership, resource development, and ongoing support are required at all levels. With each of these functions in mind, specific mechanisms and their interrelationship with each other and with other planning groups can be developed. A well-designed infrastructure provides ways to (a) arrive at decisions about resource allocation, (b) maximize systematic and integrated planning, implementation, maintenance, and evaluation, (c) reach out to create formal working relationships with all concerned stakeholders, and (d) regularly upgrade and renew the collaborative.

A special concern of school-community partnerships involves what often is called diffusion, replication, rollout, or scale-up. The process of scale-up requires a separate capacity-building emphasis (see the discussion in Chapter 10).

A Few Lessons Learned

The following are lessons we learned the hard way and should be kept in mind by those who establish collaboratives. First, an obvious point: a collaborative needs financial support. The core operational budget can draw from direct funding and in-kind contributions from the resources of stakeholder groups. A good example is the provision of space for the collaborative. A school or community entity should be asked to contribute the necessary space. As specific functions and initiatives are undertaken that reflect overlapping arenas of concern for schools and community organizations, such as safe schools and neighborhoods, some portion of their respective funding streams can be braided together. Over time, there will be opportunities to supplement the budget with extramural grants.

A caution here: it is important not to pursue pernicious funding, funding for projects that will distract the collaborative from vigorously pursuing its vision in a cohesive, unfragmented manner. A related concern is the trend to try to expand resources through providing services reimbursed through third-party payments, such as Medicaid funds. This often results in further limiting the range of interventions offered and who receives them. Moreover, payments from third-party sources often do not adequately cover the costs of services rendered, and as the numbers receiving services increase markedly, third-party payers seek ways to cap costs.

A second lesson relates to how agreements are made: in marketing new ideas, it is tempting to accentuate their promising attributes and minimize complications. For instance, in negotiating agreements for school connections, decision makers frequently are asked simply to sign a memorandum of understanding, rather than involving them in processes that lead to a comprehensive, informed commitment. Sometimes their motivation mainly is to obtain extra resources; sometimes they are motivated by a desire to be seen by constituents as doing *something* to improve things. In both instances, the result may be premature implementation that produces the form rather than the substance of change.

Third, without careful planning, implementation, and capacity building, collaborative efforts rarely live up to the initial hopes. For example, formal arrangements for working together often take the form of meetings. To be effective, such sessions require thoughtful and skillful facilitation. Even when they begin with great enthusiasm, poorly facilitated working sessions quickly degenerate into more talk but little action, another burden, and a waste of time. This is particularly likely to happen when the primary emphasis is on the unfocused mandate to collaborate rather than on moving an important vision and mission forward through effective working relationships and well-defined functions and tasks.

Finally, given how hard it is to work effectively in a group, steps must be taken to ensure that work groups are formed in ways that maximize their effectiveness. This includes providing them with the training, time, support, and authority to carry out their role and functions. It also requires effective meeting facilitation.

SOME POLICY RECOMMENDATIONS

Any school-community collaborative agenda that addresses barriers to learning and development must focus on evolving a comprehensive, multifaceted, and cohesive approach. The agenda must encompass addressing the complex needs of all youngsters, their families, the participating schools, and the surrounding neighborhood.

The work must be resource-oriented so that existing resources are used in the most cost-effective manner. This includes braiding together many public and private resources.

To these ends, a cohesive, high priority policy commitment is required. This encompasses revisiting current policies to reduce redundancy and redeploy school and community resources that are used ineffectively.

> You know you are an education leader if
> - You want to slap the next person who says, "Must be nice to work 8 to 3:20 and have summers free."
> - You've ever had your profession slammed by someone who would "Never DREAM" of doing your job.
> - You think caffeine should be available in intravenous form.

Policy must be operationalized in ways that (a) support the strategic development of comprehensive approaches by weaving together school and community resources, (b) sustain partnerships, and (c) generate renewal. In communities, the need is for better ways of connecting agencies and other resources to each other and to schools. In schools, there is a need for restructuring to combine parallel efforts supported by general funds, compensatory and special education entitlement, safe-school and drug-free-school grants, and specially funded projects. This includes enhancing efficiency and effectiveness by connecting families of schools.

With all this in mind, Guides 8.7 and 8.8 outline some policy and practice guidelines for those leaders who are concerned with the development of effective school-community collaboratives.

CONCLUDING COMMENTS

Interest in connecting schools, communities, and families is growing at an exponential rate. Collaboratives often are established because of the desire to address a local problem or in the wake of a crisis. In the long run, however, school-community connections must be driven by a comprehensive vision about strengthening youngsters, families, schools, and neighborhoods. This encompasses a focus on safe schools and neighborhoods; positive development and learning; personal, family, and economic well-being; and more.

Collaboratives can weave together a critical mass of resources and strategies to enhance caring communities that support all youth and their families and enable success at school and beyond. Strong school-community connections are critical in impoverished communities where schools often are the largest pieces of public real estate and the single largest employer.

While it is relatively simple to make informal linkages, establishing major long-term collaborations is complicated. The complications are

Guide 8.7   Recommendations to Enhance and Sustain School-Community
Collaboratives

Effective school-community collaboratives require policies and leadership to

- Establish collaborative *governance* in ways that move toward shared decision making, with appropriate degrees of local control and private-sector involvement; a key
  facet of this is guaranteeing roles and providing incentives, supports, and training
  for effective involvement of all concerned stakeholders.
- Delineate high level *leadership assignments* and underwrite essential *leadership
  and management training* regarding vision for outcomes and collaboration, how to
  effect and institutionalize changes, and how to generate ongoing renewal.
- Establish *institutionalized mechanisms* (e.g., work groups) to carry out collaborative functions and tasks (analyzing, planning, coordinating, integrating, monitoring,
  evaluating, and strengthening ongoing efforts).
- Provide adequate funds for *capacity building* of collaborative participants to
  enhance operational quality over time; a key facet of this is a major investment in
  stakeholder recruitment and development using well-designed and technologically
  sophisticated strategies for dealing with the problems of frequent turnover and dif-
  fusing information updates; another facet is an investment in technical assistance
  at all levels and for all aspects and stages of the work.
- Encourage using some braided funds to hire two staff members to carry out the
  daily activities stemming from work group activity (e.g., an executive director and
  someone with organization facilitator/change agent capabilities).
- Require a sophisticated approach to *accountability* that calls for data that can help
  develop effective collaboration through initial focus on short-term benchmarks and
  evolve into evaluation on long-range indicators of impact.

Such a strengthened policy focus would allow collaborative participants to build the
continuum of interventions needed to make a significant impact in addressing learning,
behavior, emotional, and health concerns through strengthening youngsters, families,
schools, and neighborhoods.

readily seen in any effort to develop a comprehensive, multifaceted, and
integrated approach to promoting healthy development and addressing
barriers to development and learning. Such efforts necessitate major systemic changes involving formal and institutionalized sharing of a wide
spectrum of responsibilities and resources. The nature and scope of change
requires stakeholder readiness, an enlightened vision, cohesive policy,
creative leadership, basic systemic reforms, and new and multifaceted
roles for professionals who work in schools and communities, as well as
for family and other community members assuming leadership.

It is unwise to limit school-community connections to coordinating
community services, recreation, and enrichment activities and co-locating
some on school sites. As we have stressed, this downplays the need to
restructure the various education support programs and services that

Guide 8.8 Some Ways to Begin or Reinvigorate a Collaborative

1. *Adopt a Comprehensive Vision for the Collaborative:* Collaborative leadership builds consensus that the aim of those involved is to help weave together community and school resources to develop a comprehensive, multifaceted, and integrated continuum of interventions so that no child is left behind.

2. *Write a "Brief" to Clarify the Vision:* The collaborative establishes a writing team to prepare a brief concept paper, executive summary, and set of talking points clarifying the vision by delineating the rationale and frameworks that will guide development of a comprehensive, multifaceted, and integrated approach.

3. *Establish a Steering Committee to Move the Initiative Forward and Monitor Process:* The collaborative identifies and empowers a representative subgroup that will be responsible and accountable for ensuring that the vision/big picture is not lost and the momentum of the initiative is maintained through establishing and monitoring ad hoc work groups that are asked to pursue specific tasks.

4. *Start a Process for Translating the Vision Into Policy:* The steering committee establishes a work group to prepare a campaign geared to key local and state school and agency policy makers that focuses on (a) establishing a policy framework for the development of a comprehensive, multifaceted, and integrated approach and (b) ensuring that such policy has a high enough level of priority to end the current marginalized status such efforts have at schools and in communities.

5. *Develop a Five-year Strategic Plan:* The steering committee establishes a work group to draft a five-year strategic plan that delineates (a) the development of a comprehensive, multifaceted, and integrated approach and (b) the steps to be taken to accomplish the required systemic changes. The strategic plan will cover such matters as use of formulation of essential agreements about policy, resources, and practices; assignment of committed leadership; change agents to facilitate systemic changes; infrastructure redesign; enhancement of infrastructure mechanisms; resource mapping, analysis, and redeployment; capacity building; standards, evaluation, quality improvement, and accountability; and social marketing.

   - The steering committee circulates a draft of the plan (a) to elicit suggested revisions from key stakeholders and (b) as part of a process for building consensus and developing readiness for proceeding with its implementation.
   - Work groups make relevant revisions based on suggestions.

6. *Move the Strategic Plan to Implementation:* The steering committee ensures that key stakeholders finalize and approve strategic plan; submits plan on behalf of key stakeholders to school and agency decision makers to formulate formal agreements (e.g., MOUs, contracts) for start-up, initial implementation, and on-going revisions that can ensure institutionalization and periodic renewal of a comprehensive, multifaceted, and integrated approach; establishes a work group to develop action plans for start-up and initial implementation. The action plan identifies general functions and key tasks to be accomplished, necessary systemic changes, and how to get from here to there in terms of who, how, by when, who monitors, and so on.

schools own and operate, and it has led some policymakers to the mistaken impression that community resources can effectively meet the needs of schools in addressing barriers to learning. Policymakers must realize that increasing access to services is only one facet of any effort to establish a comprehensive, cohesive approach for strengthening students, schools, families, and neighborhoods.

Clearly, the myriad political and bureaucratic difficulties involved in making major institutional changes, especially with sparse financial resources, leads to the caution that such changes are not easily accomplished without a high degree of commitment and relentlessness of effort. Also, it should be remembered that systemic change rarely proceeds in a linear fashion. The success of school-community connections is first and foremost in the hands of policymakers. For increased connections to be more than another desired but underachieved aim of reformers, policymakers must understand the nature and scope of what is involved. They must deal with the problems of marginalization and fragmentation. They must support development of appropriately comprehensive and multifaceted school-community collaboratives. They must revise policy related to school-linked services because such initiatives are grossly inadequate responses to the many complex factors that interfere with development, learning, and teaching.

Focusing primarily on linking community services to schools downplays the role of existing school and other community and family resources. This perpetuates an orientation that overemphasizes individually prescribed services, results in further fragmentation of interventions, and undervalues the human and social capital indigenous to every neighborhood. And all this is incompatible with developing the type of comprehensive approaches needed to make statements such as *We want all children to succeed* and *No Child Left Behind* be more than rhetoric.

NOTE

1. In practice, the terms *school-linked* and *school-based* encompass two separate dimensions: (a) where programs or services are *located* and (b) who *owns* them. Taken literally, *school-based* should indicate activity carried out on a campus, and *school-linked* should refer to off-campus activity with formal connections to a school site. In either case, the services may be owned by a school or schools or a community-based organization or in some cases may be co-owned. As commonly used, the term *school-linked* refers to community-owned on-campus and off-campus services and is strongly associated with the notion of coordinated services.

REFERENCES

Center for Mental Health in Schools. (1999). *School-community partnership: A guide.* Los Angeles: Center for Mental Health in Schools at UCLA.

Chapter 419, Acts of 1990, Annotated Code of Maryland §11, Article 49D. (1991).

Honig, M. I., Kahne, J., & McLaughlin, M. W. (2001). School-community connections: Strengthening opportunity to learn and opportunity to teach. In V. Richardson (Ed.), *Handbook of research on teaching* (4th ed.). Washington, DC: American Educational Research Association.

Melaville, A., & Blank, M. J. (1998). *Learning together: The developing field of school-community initiatives.* Flint, MI: Mott Foundation.

Southwest Educational Development Laboratory. (2001). *Emerging issues in school, family, & community connections: Annual synthesis.* Austin, TX: Author.

Subcabinet for Children, Youth, and Families. (1987). Retrieved April 15, 2005, from www.mdarchives.state.md.us/msa/mdmanual/08conoff/cabinet/html/child.html.

Using and Extending   9
the Research Base for
Addressing Barriers
to Learning

*The science base for intervention is an essential building block.
However, we must extend it, and we must be careful that we don't limit
progress while we do so.*

The first step is to measure whatever can be easily measured.
That's okay as far as it goes.

The second step is to disregard that which can't be measured or give it
an arbitrary quantitative value. That's artificial and misleading.

The third step is to presume that what can't be measured
easily isn't very important. That's blindness.

The fourth step is to say
what can't be measured really
doesn't exist.   That's suicide.

SOURCE: Statement attributed to Yankelovich

ORIENTING QUESTIONS

? Why is it valuable to organize the research base around the six
arenas of an enabling or learning component?

? What is an expanded framework for school accountability?

? What is a framework for program evaluation that encompasses
planning, implementation, and results?

*I find myself looking at children and wondering how they'll impact the
average score of my class. I sometimes find myself doing calculations
where my students are not learners but assets and liabilities toward the
class average on a standardized exam.*

—Teacher, quoted in Intrator (2002)

Alll professional interveners need data to enhance the quality of their efforts and to monitor their outcomes in ways that promote appropriate accountability. This is especially the case for those who work with youngsters who manifest behavior, learning, and emotional problems. Sound planning, implementation, accountability, and advancement of the field necessitate amassing and analyzing existing information and gathering appropriate new evaluative data. In addition, the field is at a point in time when there is an intensive policy emphasis on the evidence base for instruction and interventions to promote healthy development, prevent problems, intervene early, counsel, collaborate, and so forth.

Commonly heard these days is the shibboleth,

In God we trust; from all others, demand data.

Increasingly, policymakers and others who make decisions are demanding,

Show me the data!

With respect to addressing barriers to learning and teaching, the policy emphasis on an evidence base is producing somewhat of a catch-22. Proposals to strengthen student support are consistently met with demands from policymakers for data showing that the additional effort will improve student achievement. The reality is that available direct evidence is sparse, and other relevant data must be appreciated in terms of addressing barriers that interfere with improving student achievement. Because the body of evidence showing a direct and immediate relationship is limited, many school districts shy away from investing in efforts to improve learning supports. And because policymakers do not invest in building the types of learning support systems that can produce the results they are looking for, it is unlikely that better data will be generated soon.

At this time, the field is a long way from having enough sound research to rely on as the sole basis for building truly comprehensive, multifaceted approaches that match the complexity of the problems we face in schools and communities. Moreover, because the need to address barriers to learning, development, and teaching covers so many different facets of intervention, it is hard even to summarize what has been found to date. Much of the literature focuses on only one facet, such as instruction, prevention, or treatment, and often only on narrow, person-focused interventions. Most collections of practice include a mixture of research projects and homegrown programs. And because schools and collaboratives do not have the resources for extensive data gathering, a great many local program evaluations are methodologically flawed.

The emphasis in this chapter is first on sharing the results of our center's effort to draw on the existing research base for support in developing comprehensive, multifaceted approaches to address barriers to learning and promote healthy development. Then we focus on the question of what constitutes appropriate evaluation data. In doing so, we (a) stress the need to expand the framework for current school accountability and (b) highlight the nature and scope of program evaluation as a tool for advancing the field. (Note: Because the list of references in the following section is so extensive, they are cited by number and listed that way at the end of this chapter.)

A USABLE RESEARCH BASE

As schools evolve their improvement plans in keeping with higher standards and expectations and increased accountability, most planners should recognize the need to include a comprehensive focus on addressing barriers to student learning and promoting healthy development.[1–15] Throughout this book, we have stressed the conceptual base for doing so. In this chapter, we highlight the extensive body of literature that supports the conceptual base. That literature includes a growing volume of research on the value of schools, families, and communities working together to provide supportive programs and services that enable students to learn and teachers to teach.[16–22] Findings include improved school attendance, fewer behavior problems, improved interpersonal skills, enhanced achievement, and increased bonding at school and at home.[23]

Most *formal* studies have focused on specific interventions (see Guide 9.1). This and other bodies of research indicate positive outcomes for school and society associated with a wide range of interventions. Because of the fragmented nature of the studies, the findings are best appreciated in terms of the whole being greater than the sum of the parts, and implications are best derived from the total theoretical and empirical picture. When such a broad perspective is adopted, schools have a larger science base to draw upon in addressing barriers to learning and enhancing healthy development.[24]

At the outset, we note that research on comprehensive approaches for addressing barriers to learning is still in its infancy. As we have mentioned, there are many "natural" experiments underscoring the promise of ensuring that all youngsters have access to a comprehensive, multifaceted continuum of interventions. These natural experiments play out in every school and neighborhood where families are affluent enough to purchase the additional programs and services they feel will maximize their youngsters' well-being. Those who can afford such interventions clearly understand their value. And not surprisingly, most indicators of well-being, including higher achievement test scores, are correlated with socioeconomic status. Available data highlight societal inequities that can be remedied through public financing for comprehensive programs.

Guide 9.1   Annotated Lists of Empirically Supported or Evidence-based Interventions for School-age Children and Adolescents

The following table provides a list of lists, with indications of what each list covers, how it was developed, what it contains, and how to access it.

I. Universal Focus on Promoting Healthy Development

A. *Safe and Sound. An Educational Leader's Guide to Evidence-based Social & Emotional Learning Programs.* (2002). The Collaborative for Academic, Social, and Emotional Learning (CASEL).

 1. *How It Was Developed:* Contacts with researchers and a literature search yielded 250 programs for screening; 81 programs were identified that met the criteria of being a multiyear program with at least eight lessons in one program year, designed for regular ed classrooms, and nationally available.

 2. *What the List Contains:* Descriptions (purpose, features, results) of the 81 programs.

 3. *How to Access:* CASEL at www.casel.org.

B. *Positive Youth Development in the United States: Research Findings on Evaluations of Positive Youth Development Programs.* (2002). Social Development Research Group, University of Washington.

 1. *How It Was Developed:* Seventy-seven programs that sought to achieve positive youth development objectives were reviewed. Criteria used: Research designs employed control or comparison group and had measured youth behavior outcomes.

 2. *What the List Contains:* Twenty-five programs designated as "effective" based on available evidence.

 3. *How to Access:* Online journal *Prevention & Treatment* at http://journals.apa.org/prevention/volume5/pre0050015a.html.

II. Prevention of Problems; Promotion of Protective Factors

A. *Blueprints for Violence Prevention.* (1998). Center for the Study and Prevention of Violence, Institute of Behavioral Science, University of Colorado, Boulder.

 1. *How It Was Developed:* Review of over 450 delinquency, drug, and violence prevention programs based on the criteria of a strong research design, evidence of significant deterrent effects, multiple site replication, and sustained effects.

 2. *What the List Contains:* Ten "model" programs and fifteen "promising" programs.

 3. *How to Access:* Center for the Study and Prevention of Violence at www.colorado. edu.

B. Exemplary Substance Abuse and Mental Health Programs (from the Substance Abuse and Mental Health Services Administration [SAMHSA]).

 1. *How It Was Developed:* These science-based programs underwent an expert consensus review of published and unpublished materials on eighteen criteria (e.g., theory, fidelity, evaluation, sampling, attrition, outcome measures, missing data, outcome data, analysis, threats to validity, integrity, utility, replications, dissemination, cultural and age appropriateness). The reviews have grouped them into "model," "effective," and "promising" programs.

2. *What the List Contains:* Prevention programs that may be adapted and replicated by communities.

3. *How to Access:* SAMHSA at http://www.modelprograms.samhsa.gov.

C. *Preventing Drug Use Among Children and Adolescents.* Research-based Guide. (1997). National Institute on Drug Abuse (NIDA).

1. *How It Was Developed:* NIDA and the scientists who conducted the research developed protocols. Each was tested in a family/school/community setting for a reasonable period with positive results.

2. *What the List Contains:* Ten programs that are universal, selective, or indicated.

3. *How to Access:* NIDA at www.nida.nih.gov/prevention/prevopen.html.

D. *Safe, Disciplined, and Drug-free Schools: Expert Panel Exemplary Programs.* (2001). U.S. Deptartment of Education Safe & Drug-free Schools.

1. *How It Was Developed:* A review was made of 132 programs submitted to the panel. Each program was reviewed in terms of quality, usefulness to others, and educational significance.

2. *What the List Contains:* Nine "exemplary" and thirty-three "promising" programs focusing on violence, alcohol, tobacco, and drug prevention.

3. *How to Access:* U.S. Department of Education at www.ed.gov/offices/OERI/ORAD/ KAD/expert_panel/drug-free.html.

III. Early Intervention: Targeted Focus on Specific Problems or At-risk Groups

A. *The Prevention of Mental Disorders in School-aged Children: Current State of the Field* (2001). Prevention Research Center for the Promotion of Human Development, Pennsylvania State University.

1. *How It Was Developed:* A review was made of scores of primary prevention programs to identify those with quasi-experimental or randomized trials and been found to reduce symptoms of psychopathology or factors commonly associated with an increased risk for later mental disorders.

2. *What the List Contains:* Thirty-four universal and targeted interventions that have demonstrated positive outcomes under rigorous evaluation and the common characteristics of these programs.

3. *How to Access:* Online journal *Prevention & Treatment.* Available from http://journals .apa.org/prevention/volume4/pre0040001a.html.

IV. Treatment for Problems

A. American Psychological Association's Society for Clinical Child and Adolescent Psychology, Committee on Evidence-based Practice List.

1. *How It Was Developed:* The committee reviewed outcome studies to determine how well each conformed to the guidelines of the Task Force on Promotion and Dissemination of Psychological Procedures (1996).

2. *What It Contains:* Reviews of the following:
   • *Depression (Dysthymia).* Analyses indicate that only one practice meets criteria for "well-established treatment" (best supported) and two practices meet criteria for "probably efficacious" (promising).

- *Conduct/Oppositional Problems.* Two meet criteria for "well-established" treatments: (a) videotape modeling parent training programs and (b) parent training program based on Living With Children. Ten practices identified as probably efficacious.
- *ADHD.* Behavioral parent training, behavioral interventions in the classroom, and stimulant medication meet criteria for "well-established" treatments. Two others meet criteria for "probably efficacious".
- *Anxiety Disorders.* For phobias, participant modeling and reinforced practice are "well-established", filmed modeling, live modeling, and cognitive behavioral interventions that use self-instruction training are "probably efficacious". For anxiety disorders, cognitive-behavioral procedures with and without family anxiety management, modeling, in vivo exposure, relaxation training, and reinforced practice are listed as "probably efficacious".

Caution: Reviewers stress the importance of (a) devising developmentally and culturally sensitive interventions targeted to the unique needs of each child and (b) a need for research informed by clinical practice.

   3. *How to Access:* www.effectivechildtherapy.com.

V. Review, Consensus Statements, and Compendia of Evidence-based Treatments

A. *School-based Prevention Programs for Children & Adolescents.* (1995). J. A. Durlak. Thousand Oaks, CA: Sage. Reports results from 130 controlled outcome studies that support "a secondary prevention model emphasizing timely intervention for subclinical problems detected early. . . . In general, best results are obtained for cognitive-behavioral and behavioral treatments and interventions targeting externalizing problems."

B. *Mental Health and Mass Violence.* Evidence-based early psychological intervention for victims/survivors of mass violence. A workshop to reach consensus on best practices (U.S. Departments of HHS, Defense, Veterans Affairs, and Justice, and the American Red Cross). Available at: www.nimh.nih.gov/publicat/massviolence.pdf.

C. Society of Pediatric Psychology, Division 54, American Psychological Association, *Journal of Pediatric Psychology.* Articles on empirically supported treatments in pediatric psychology related to obesity, feeding problems, headaches, pain, bedtime refusal, enuresis, encopresis, and symptoms of asthma, diabetes, and cancer.

D. *Preventing Crime: What Works, What Doesn't, What's Promising. A Report to the United States Congress.* (1997). L. W. Sherman, D. Gottfredson, et al. Washington, DC: U.S. Dept. of Justice. Reviews programs funded by the Office of Justice Programs (OJP) for crime, delinquency, and substance use at www.ncjrs.org/pdffiles/171676.pdf. Also see Denise Gottfredson's book *Schools and Delinquency* (2001). New York: Cambridge Press.

E. *School Violence Prevention Initiative Matrix of Evidence-based Prevention Interventions.* (1999). Center for Mental Health Services, SAMHSA. A synthesis of several lists cited earlier to highlight examples of programs that meet some criteria for a designation of evidence-based interventions for violence prevention and substance abuse prevention (i.e., synthesizes lists from the Center for the Study and Prevention of Violence, Center for Substance Abuse Prevention, Communities That Care, Dept. of Education, Department of Justice, Health Resources and Services Administration, National Assoc. of School Psychologists). Available at http://modelprograms.samhsa.gov/.

The research base supporting development of a comprehensive, multi-faceted approach to addressing barriers to learning and teaching is highlighted in the following discussion. To illustrate the value of a unifying framework, we have organized examples into the six arenas of an Enabling or Learning Supports Component. To reiterate, these are: (1) enhancing classroom teachers' capacity for addressing problems and for fostering positive social, emotional, intellectual, behavioral and physical development; (2) enhancing school capacity to handle transition concerns confronting students and families; (3) responding to, minimizing the impact of, and preventing crises; (4) enhancing home involvement; (5) reaching out to the community to build linkages and collaborations; and (6) providing special assistance to students and families.

Given how extensive the relevant research literature is, obviously the following in no way is meant to be exhaustive. We have chosen examples that make the point. There are many others that can be drawn upon, and many more will be forthcoming over the years.

Enhancing Teacher Capacity for Addressing Problems and Fostering Healthy Development

When a classroom teacher encounters difficulty in working with a youngster, the first step is to see whether there are ways to address the problem within the classroom and perhaps with added home involvement. It is essential to equip teachers to respond to garden-variety learning, behavior, and emotional problems using more than social control strategies for classroom management. Teachers must be helped to learn many ways to enable the learning of such students, and schools must develop schoolwide approaches to assist teachers in doing this fundamental work. The literature offers many relevant practices. A few prominent examples are prereferral intervention efforts, tutoring and other forms of one-to-one or small-group instruction, enhancing protective factors, and assets building (including use of curriculum-based approaches for promoting social-emotional development). Outcome data related to such matters indicate that they do make a difference. For instance,

- Many forms of *prereferral intervention programs* have shown success in reducing learning and behavior problems and unnecessary referrals for special assistance and special education.[25-31]
- Although only a few *tutoring programs* have been evaluated systematically, available studies report positive effects on academic performance when tutors are trained and appropriately used.[32-40]
- And some *programs that reduce class size* are finding increases in academic performance and decreases in discipline problems.[41-45]

Enhancing School Capacity to Handle the Variety of Transition Concerns Confronting Students and Their Families

It has taken a long time for schools to face up to the importance of establishing transition programs. In recent years, a beginning has been made. Transition programs are an essential facet of reducing levels of alienation and increasing levels of positive attitudes and involvement at school and in learning. Thus schools must plan, develop, and maintain a focus on the variety of transition concerns confronting students and their families. Examples of relevant practices are readiness-to-learn programs, beforeschool and afterschool programs to enrich learning and provide recreation in a safe environment, articulation programs for each new step in formal education, vocational and college counseling, and support in moving to and from special education, welcoming and social support programs, school-to-career programs, and programs to support moving to postschool living and work. Interventions to enable successful transitions have made a significant difference in how motivationally ready and able students are to benefit from schooling. For instance,

- Available evidence supports the positive impact of *early childhood programs* in preparing young children for school. The programs are associated with increases in academic performance and may even contribute to decreases in discipline problems in later school years.[46-54]
- There is enough evidence that *beforeschool and afterschool programs* keep kids safe and steer them away from crime, and there is some evidence suggesting that such programs can improve academic performance.[55-59]
- Evaluations show that well-conceived and implemented *articulation programs* can successfully ease students' transition between grades,[60-62] and preliminary evidence suggests the promise of programs that provide *welcoming and social support* for children and families transitioning into a new school.[63, 64]
- Initial studies of programs for transition *in and out of special education* suggest that the interventions can enhance students' attitudes about school and self and can improve their academic performance.[65-67]
- Finally, programs providing *vocational training and career education* are having an impact in terms of increasing school retention and graduation and show promise for successfully placing students in jobs following graduation.[68-72]

Responding to, Minimizing the Impact of, and Preventing Crises

The need for crisis response and prevention is constant in many schools. Such efforts ensure assistance when emergencies arise and follow-up care is provided as necessary and appropriate so that students can resume learning without undue delays. Prevention activity stresses creation of a safe and productive environment and development of student and family attitudes about and capacities for dealing with violence and other threats to safety. Examples include (a) systems and programs for emergency and crisis response and follow-up care at a site, throughout a family of schools, and communitywide and (b) prevention programs for school and community to address school safety and violence reduction, child abuse and suicide prevention, and so forth. Examples of relevant practices are establishment of a crisis team to ensure planning and implementation of crisis response and aftermath interventions, school environment changes and safety strategies, and curriculum approaches to preventing crisis events, such as violence, suicide, and physical/sexual abuse prevention. Current trends are stressing schoolwide and communitywide prevention programs. Most research in this area focuses on

- Programs designed to ensure a *safe and disciplined school environment* as a key to deterring violence and reducing injury
- *Violence prevention and resiliency curriculum* designed to teach children anger management, problem-solving skills, social skills, and conflict resolution

In both instances, the evidence supports a variety of practices that help reduce injuries and violent incidents in schools.[73–95]

Enhancing Home Involvement

In recent years, the trend has been to expand the school's focus on enhancing home involvement. Intervention practices encompass efforts for (a) addressing specific learning and support needs of adults in the home, such as mutual support groups and classes to enhance literacy, job skills, and English as a second language; (b) helping those in the home meet basic obligations to the student; (c) improving systems to communicate about matters essential to student and family; (d) strengthening the home-school connection and sense of community; (e) enhancing participation in making decisions essential to the student's well-being; (f) enhancing home support related to the student's basic learning and development; (g) mobilizing those at home to solve problems related to student needs; and (h) eliciting help from the home to meet classroom, school, and community needs. A few examples illustrate the growing research base for expanded home involvement:

- *Adult education* is a proven commodity in general and is beginning to be studied in terms of its impact on home involvement in schooling and on the behavior and achievement of youngsters in the family. For example, evaluations of adult education in the form of *family literacy* are reporting highly positive outcomes with respect to preschool children, and a summary of findings on family literacy reports highly positive trends into the elementary grades.[96, 97]

- Similarly, evaluations of *parent education* classes indicate the promise of such programs with respect to improving parent attitudes, skills, and problem-solving abilities; parent-child communication; and in some instances, the child's school achievement.[98–102] Data also suggest an impact on reducing children's negative behavior.[103–111]

- More broadly, programs to *mobilize the home in addressing students' basic needs* affect a range of behaviors and academic performance.[112, 113]

Reaching Out to the Community to Build Linkages and Collaborations

Currently, most school outreach to the community is designed to develop greater involvement in schooling and enhance support for efforts to enable learning. Outreach may be made to (a) public and private community agencies, colleges, organizations, and facilities; (b) businesses and professional organizations and groups; and (c) volunteer service programs, organizations, and clubs. Efforts in this area might include (a) programs to recruit and enhance community involvement and support; (b) systems and programs specifically designed to train, screen, and maintain volunteers; (c) outreach programs to hard-to-involve students and families; and (d) programs to enhance community-school connections and the sense of community.

The research base for involving the community is growing.

- A popular example is the variety of *mentoring and volunteer programs.* Available data support their value for both students and those from the community who offer to provide such supports. Student outcomes include positive changes in attitudes, behavior, and academic performance, including improved school attendance, reduced substance abuse, less school failure, and improved grades.[114–118]

- Another example is the group of efforts to reach out to the community to develop *school-community collaborations.* A reasonable inference from available data is that school-community collaborations can be successful and cost-effective over the long run. They not only improve access to services, they also seem to encourage schools to open their doors in ways that enhance recreational, enrichment, and remedial opportunities and family involvement. A few have encompassed concerns for economic development and have demonstrated the ability to increase job opportunities for young people.[119–123]

Another aim of outreach to the community is to collaborate to enhance the engagement of young people to directly strengthen youngsters, families, and neighborhoods. Across the country a dialogue has begun about how to both promote youth development and address barriers to development and learning. In this respect, increasing attention has been paid to interventions to promote healthy development, resiliency, and assets. There is widespread agreement that communities should integrate resources and strengthen opportunities for healthy, holistic development and learning in responsive environments.

- *Responsive and Caring Environments:* Engagement is fostered if the environment (a) creates an atmosphere where youngsters feel welcome, respected, and comfortable; (b) structures opportunities to develop caring relationships with peers and adults; (c) provides information, counseling, and expectations that enable them to determine what it means to care for themselves and to care for a definable group; and (d) provides opportunities, training, and expectations that encourage contributing to the greater good through service, advocacy, and active problem solving with respect to important matters.[124]
- *Facilitating Holistic Development:* Research has focused on interventions to provide for (a) basic needs—nutrition, shelter, health, and safety; (b) effective parenting and schooling using appropriate structure and expectations; and (c) more opportunities for recreation, enrichment, and creativity and for community, civic, and religious involvement. Findings indicate that features of positive developmental settings include physical and psychological safety; appropriate structure; supportive relationships; opportunities to belong; positive social norms; support for efficacy; opportunities for skill building; and integration of family, school, and community efforts.[125]

After evaluating programs designed to promote youth development, Catalano, Berglund, Ryan, Lonczak, and Hawkins (1998) report:

Effective programs addressed a range of positive youth development objectives yet shared common themes. All sought to strengthen social, emotional, cognitive and/or behavioral competencies, self-efficacy, and family and community standards for healthy social and person behavior. . . . The youth competency strategies varied among program from targeting youth directly with skills training sessions, to peer tutoring conducted by at-risk youth, to teacher training that resulted in better classroom management and instruction. The evidence showed an associated list of important outcomes including better school attendance, higher academic performance, healthier peer and adult interactions, improved decision-making abilities, and less substance use and risky sexual behavior.[126]

Providing Special Assistance for Students and Families

Some problems cannot be handled without a few special interventions, thus the need for student and family assistance. The emphasis is on providing special services in a personalized way to assist with a broad range of needs. School-owned, -based, and -linked interventions clearly provide better access for many youngsters and their families. Moreover, as a result of initiatives that enhance school-owned support programs and those fostering school-linked services and school-community connections, more schools have more to offer in the way of student and family assistance.

In current practice, available social, physical, and mental health programs in the school and community are used. Special attention is paid to enhancing systems for prereferral intervention, triage, case and resource management, direct services to meet immediate needs, and referral for special services and special education resources and placements as appropriate. A growing body of data indicates the current contribution and future promise of work in this area. For example,

- The more *comprehensive approaches* not only report results related to ameliorating health and psychosocial problems, but they are beginning to report a range of academically related improvements, such as increased attendance, improved grades, improved achievement, promotion to the next grade, reduced suspensions and expulsions, fewer dropouts, and increased graduation rates.[127–137]
- A rapidly increasing number of *targeted interventions* are reporting positive results related to the specific problems addressed, including reduced behavior, emotional, and learning problems; enhanced positive social-emotional functioning; reduced sexual activity; lower rates of unnecessary referral to special education; fewer visits to hospital emergency rooms; and fewer hospitalizations.[138–143]

Taken as a whole, the research base for initiatives to pursue a comprehensive focus on addressing barriers indicates a range of activity that can enable students to learn and teachers to teach. The findings also underscore the notion that addressing major psychosocial problems one at a time is unwise because the problems are interrelated and require multifaceted and cohesive solutions. In all, the literature offers information about learning supports and also stresses the importance of integrating such activities into a comprehensive, multifaceted approach.

EXPANDING THE ACCOUNTABILITY
FRAMEWORK FOR SCHOOLS

Systems are driven by what is measured for purposes of accountability. This is particularly so when systems are the focus of major reform. Under reform conditions, policymakers often want a quick and easy recipe to use. This leads to accountability measures aimed at holding program administrators and staff accountable for specific, short-term results. Little thought is given to the negative effects such a limited focus can have on achieving desired but more complex long-term outcomes. As a result, in too many instances, the tail wags the dog, the dog gets dizzy, and the citizenry doesn't get what it needs and wants.

School accountability is a good example of the problem. Accountability has extraordinary power to reshape schools—for good and for bad. The influence can be seen in classrooms every day. With the increasing demands for accountability, teachers quickly learn what will and will not be evaluated, and slowly but surely, greater emphasis is placed on teaching what will be on the tests. Over time, what is on the tests increasingly is viewed as the most important information to be taught. Because only so much time is available to the teacher, other things not only are de-emphasized, they also are dropped from the curriculum. If allowed to do so, accountability procedures have the power to reshape the entire curriculum.

What's wrong with that? Nothing—if what is being evaluated reflects all the important things we want youngsters to learn in school. This, of course, is not the case.

Current accountability pressures reflect values and biases that have led to evaluating a small range of basic skills and doing so in a narrow way. For students with learning, behavior, or emotional problems, this becomes a fundamental concern. Too often, it means their school programs mainly focus on improving skills they appear to lack. When this occurs, these students are cut off from participating in learning activities that might enhance their interest in overcoming their problems and that might open up opportunities and enrich their future lives.

Policymakers want schools, teachers, and administrators (and students and their families) held accountable for higher academic achievement. Moreover, as everyone involved in school reform knows, the only measure that really counts is achievement test scores. These tests drive school accountability, and what such tests measure has become the be-all and end-all of what is attended to by many decision makers. This produces a growing disconnection between the realities of what it takes to improve academic performance and where many policymakers and school reformers are leading the public.

The disconnection is especially evident in schools serving what are now being referred to as "low wealth" families. Such families and those who work in schools serving them have a clear appreciation of many barriers to learning that must be addressed so that students can benefit from the teacher's efforts to teach. These stakeholders stress that in many schools, major academic improvements are unlikely until comprehensive and multifaceted approaches to address these barriers are developed and pursued effectively.

At the same time, it is evident to anyone who looks that there is no direct accountability for whether these barriers are addressed. To the contrary, efforts essential for addressing barriers to development and learning often are devalued and cut when achievement test scores do not reflect an immediate impact.

Thus, rather than building the type of system that can produce improved academic performance, prevailing accountability measures are pressuring schools to pursue a direct route to improving instruction. The implicit underlying assumption is that students are motivationally ready and able each day to benefit from the teacher's instruction. The reality, of course, is that in too many schools, the *majority* of youngsters don't fit this picture. Students confronted with a host of external interfering factors usually are not in a position to benefit even from significant instructional improvements. The result is low test scores and an achievement gap.

Logically, well-designed, systematic efforts should be directed at addressing interfering factors. However, current accountability pressures override the logic and result in the marginalization of almost every initiative that is not seen as directly (and quickly) leading to academic gains. Ironically, not only does the restricted emphasis on achievement measures work against the logic of what needs to be done, it works against gathering evidence on how essential and effective it is to address barriers to learning in a direct manner.

All this leads to an appreciation of the need for an expanded framework for school accountability—a framework that includes direct measures of achievement and much more. We think this is a move toward

Guide 9.2   Expanding the Framework for School Accountability

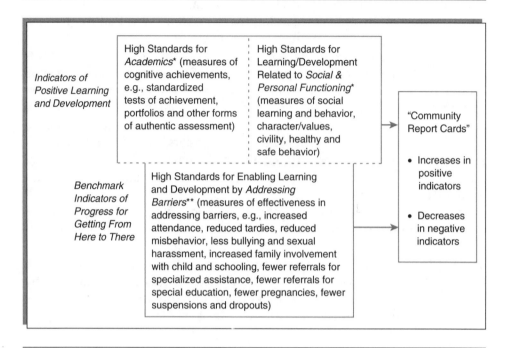

*Results of interventions for directly facilitating development and learning.

**Results of interventions for addressing barriers to learning and development.

what Michael Fullan (2005) has called *intelligent accountability.* Guide 9.2 highlights such an expanded framework.

As illustrated, there is no intent to deflect from the laserlike focus on accountability for meeting high standards related to academics. The debate will continue as to how best to measure academic outcomes, but clearly, schools must demonstrate that they effectively teach academics.

At the same time, it is important to acknowledge that schools also are expected to pursue high standards in promoting positive social and personal functioning, including teaching safe and healthy behavior and some form of character education. Every school we have visited has specific goals related to this facet of student development and learning. As well, it is evident that schools currently are not held accountable for goals in this arena. That is, there is no systematic evaluation or reporting of the work. As would be expected, then, schools direct few resources and too little attention to these unmeasured concerns. Yet society wants schools to attend to these matters, and most professionals understand that personal and social functioning are integrally tied to academic performance. From this perspective, it seems self-defeating not to hold schools accountable for improving students' social and personal functioning.

For schools where a large proportion of students are not doing well, it is also self-defeating not to attend to benchmark indicators of progress related to addressing barriers to learning. Teachers cannot teach children who are not in class. Therefore, increasing attendance, reducing tardiness, reducing problem behaviors, lessening suspension and dropout rates, and abating the large number of inappropriate referrals for special education are all essential indicators of school improvement and precursors of enhanced academic performance. Given this, the progress of school staff related to such matters should be measured and treated as a significant aspect of school accountability.

School outcomes, of course, are influenced by the well-being of the families and the neighborhoods in which they operate. The performance of any school must be judged within the context of the current status of indicators of community well-being, such as economic, social, and health measures. If those indicators are not improving or are declining, it is patently unfair to ignore these contextual conditions in judging school performance.

In sum, it is unlikely that the majority of students in economically depressed areas will perform up to high standards if schools and communities do not pursue a holistic, systemic, and collaborative approach that focuses not just on students but also on strengthening their families, schools, and surrounding neighborhoods. We are reminded of Ulric Neisser's (1976) dictum: "Changing the individual while leaving the world alone is a dubious proposition" (p. 43). A broader accountability framework is needed to encourage and support movement toward such an approach. Guide 9.3 presents a range of indicators on which an expanded accountability framework could focus measurement.

Guide 9.3   Indicators for a Broad Accountability Framework

Students	Families and Communities	Programs and Systems
Increased knowledge, skills, and attitudes to . enhance • Acceptance of responsibility (including attending school and following directions and agreed-upon rules/laws) • Self-esteem and integrity • Social and working relationships • Self-evaluation and self-direction/ regulation • Physical functioning • Health maintenance • Safe behavior Reduced barriers to school attendance and functioning by addressing problems related to • Health • Lack of adequate clothing • Dysfunctional families • Lack of home support for student improvement • Physical/sexual abuse • Substance abuse • Gang involvement • Pregnant/parenting minors • Dropouts • Need for compensatory learning strategies	Increased social and emotional support for families Increased family access to special assistance Increased family ability to reduce child risk factors that can be barriers to learning Increased bilingual ability and literacy of parents Increased family ability to support schooling Increased positive attitudes about schooling Increased home (family/ parent) participation at school Enhanced positive attitudes toward school and community Increased community participation in school activities Increased perception of the school as a hub of community activities Increased partnerships designed to enhance education and service availability in community Enhanced coordination and collaboration between community agencies and school programs and services Enhanced focus on agency outreach to meet family needs Increased psychological sense of community	Enhanced processes by which staff and families learn about available programs and services and how to access those they need Increased coordination among services and programs Increases in the degree to which staff work collaboratively and programmatically Increased services/programs at school site Increased amounts of school, family, and community collaboration Increases in quality of services and programs because of improved systems for requesting, accessing, and managing assistance for students and families (including overcoming inappropriate barriers to confidentiality) Establishment of a long-term financial base

UNDERSTANDING RESULTS:
A FRAMEWORK FOR PROGRAM EVALUATION

> *Evaluation practiced at the highest level of the state-of-the-art is one means of speeding up the processes that contribute to human and social progress.*

> —Rossi, Freeman, and Wright (1979)

Whatever the focus of accountability, the prevailing cry is for specific outcome evidence—usually in terms of readily measured immediate benefits—and for cost containment. Although understandable in light of the unfulfilled promise of so many programs and the insatiable demands on limited public finances, a narrow results emphasis can be counterproductive. This is because it ignores the state of the art related to complex interventions.

Intervention evaluation can aid efforts to (a) *make decisions* about whether to undertake, continue, modify, or stop an intervention and (b) *advance knowledge* about interventions in ways that can enhance understanding of and improve practices, training, and theory. Evaluation is useful in relation to a great variety of interventions as an aid in assessing efficiency, effectiveness, and impact.

Two unfounded presumptions are at the core of most current formal and informal evaluations in education and psychology. One premise is that an intervention in widespread use must be at a relatively evolved stage of development and therefore warrants the cost of summative evaluation. The other supposition is that major conceptual and methodological problems associated with evaluating intervention efficacy are resolved. The truth is that interventions are frequently introduced prior to adequate development, with a view to evolving them based on what is learned each day. Moreover, many well-institutionalized approaches remain relatively underfunded and underdeveloped. As to the process of evaluation, every review of the literature outlines major unresolved concerns. Given this state of affairs, accountability demands are often unreasonable and chronically reflect a naive view of research and theory.

Overemphasis on immediate evaluation of the efficacy of underdeveloped interventions draws resources and attention away from the type of intensive research programs necessary for advancing intervention knowledge and practice. Cost-effective outcomes cannot be achieved in the absence of costly development of interventions and related intervention research. *Premature* efforts to carry out comprehensive summative evaluations clearly are not cost-effective. Consequently, policies mandating naive accountability run the risk of generating evaluative practices that are neither cost-effective nor wise.

Essentially, evaluation involves determining the worth or value of something (Stake, 1967, 1976). For purposes of this discussion, *evaluation* is defined as a systematic process designed to describe and judge the overall impact and value of an intervention for purposes of making decisions and advancing knowledge.

More specifically, the goals and objectives of intervention evaluation include the following:

- To *describe* and *judge* an intervention's (a) rationale, including assumptions and intentions, and (b) standards for making judgments
- To *describe* and *judge* an intervention's (a) actual activity, including intended and unintended procedures and outcomes, and (b) costs (financial, negative effects)
- To *make decisions* about continuing, modifying, or stopping an intervention for an individual or for all those enrolled in a program
- To *advance knowledge* about interventions to improve (a) practices, (b) training, (c) theory, and (d) policy

The information needed to meet these purposes comes from comprehensive evaluations that include both immediate and long-term program data. The full range of data that may be gathered is suggested by the particular evaluation framework adopted.

A framework formulated by Robert Stake (1967) provides a useful specific example of the type of models used by evaluators concerned not just about results but also about understanding factors that influence outcomes. Stake's framework offers a graphic and comprehensive picture of various facets of evaluation and how they relate to each other (see Guide 9.4).

Guide 9.4   A Framework for Evaluation

| | Descriptive Matrix | | | Judgment Matrix | |
	Intents	Observations		Standards	Judgments
Underlying Intervention Rationale			Antecedents		
			Transactions		
			Outcomes		

SOURCE: R. Stake (1967). Reprinted with permission.

In brief, Stake (1967) emphasizes that "the two basic acts of evaluation" are description and judgment. Descriptions take the form of data gathered by formal or informal means. Judgments take the form of interpretive conclusions about the meaning of the data, such as whether a procedure is good or bad, a student is above or below norm, or a behavior is pathological or not. In practice, judgments are used for purposes of decision making. When it comes to deciding specifically what to describe and judge, evaluators often are guided by their understanding of decisions to be made at the conclusion of the evaluation. Stake stresses that proper program evaluation requires data and criteria for analyzing the degree to which

- Conditions anticipated prior to the program (antecedents), planned procedures (transactions), and intended outcomes are consistent with the program rationale and are logical in relation to each other.
- Intended antecedents, transactions, and outcomes actually occur.

In general, the types of data Stake's (1967) framework calls for can provide a wealth of information for use in describing and judging programs and making decisions about ways to improve them. As such, the data can be used not only for purposes of accountability but also to help build the research base. The data also can be used for purposes of social marketing (see Guide 9.5).

Systematic evaluation planning requires decisions about (a) the focus of evaluation (e.g., person or environment, immediate objectives vs. long-range aims); (b) whose perspective (e.g., client, intervener, program underwriter) is to determine the evaluation focus, methods, and standards used; and (c) the best way to proceed in gathering, analyzing, and interpreting information (e.g., specific measures, design). In making such decisions, concerns arise because what can be evaluated currently may be far less than what a program intends to accomplish. Furthermore, inappropriate bias and vested interests shape evaluation planning and implementation, thereby influencing whether a program is seen as good or bad.

Finally, remember that all aspects of evaluation have the potential to produce negative effects. For instance, over time, what is evaluated can reduce and reshape a program's intended aims. On a personal level, evaluation can lead to invasion of privacy and an undermining of the ability of those evaluated to self-evaluate.

In sum, evaluations of whether an intervention is any good must first address the question: *Is what the intervention is trying to accomplish appropriate?* The frame of reference for such evaluations may be the intervention rationale or what others think the program should be doing or both. After judging the appropriateness of what is wanted or expected, a program's intended breadth of focus should guide efforts to evaluate effectiveness. Because not everything is measurable in a technically

Guide 9.5   Using Data for Social Marketing

As Rossi and Freeman (1989) state,

> The mass communication and advertising industries use fundamentally the same approaches in developing media programs and marketing products; commercial and industrial corporations evaluate the procedures they use in selecting and promoting employees and organizing their work forces; political candidates develop their campaigns by evaluating the voter appeal of different strategies; . . . administrators in both the public and private sectors are continually assessing clerical, fiscal, and interpersonal practices of their organizations. The distinction between these uses of evaluation lies primarily in the intent of the effort to be evaluated . . . to benefit the human condition . . . [or] for other purposes, such as increasing profits or amassing influence and power.

Social marketing is a valuable tool for fostering a critical mass of stakeholder support for new directions to improve schools. Particularly important to effective marketing of change is the inclusion of the evidence base for moving in new directions. All data on a school or collaborative's positive impact should be packaged and widely shared.

Social marketing draws on concepts developed for commercial marketing. But in the context of school and community change, we are not talking about selling products. We are trying to build a consensus for ideas and new approaches that can strengthen youngsters, families, schools, and neighborhoods. So we need to reframe the concept to fit the aims, which are to create readiness for change and influence action by key stakeholders.

- To achieve these aims, essential information must be communicated to key stakeholders. Strategies must be used to help them understand that the benefits of change will outweigh the costs and are more worthwhile than competing directions for change.
- The strategies used must be personalized and accessible to the subgroups of stakeholders (e.g., they must be appealing, emphasize that costs are reasonable, and engage stakeholders in processes that build consensus and commitment).

One caution: Beware of thinking of social marketing as a one-time event. Because stakeholders and systems are continuously changing, social marketing is an ongoing process. It is tempting to plan a "big day" to bring people together to inform, share, involve, and celebrate. This can be a good thing if it is planned as one facet of a carefully thought-out strategic plan. It can be counterproductive if it is a one-shot activity that drains resources and energy and leads to a belief that "We did our social marketing."

sophisticated way, some things will be poorly measured or simply reviewed informally. Obviously, this is less than satisfactory. Still, from a rational perspective, continued emphasis on the entire gamut of what is intended is better than limiting an intervention to what can be measured readily or to naive accountability demands.

CONCLUDING COMMENTS

Gathering good evaluative data is a key to designing a promising future. It is a process that can improve programs, protect consumers, and advance knowledge. Doing so, however, is a difficult process, which many would prefer to avoid. Nevertheless, the need for professionals to improve their practices and be accountable is obvious.

The need to improve current evaluation practices seems equally obvious. Because evaluations can as easily reshape programs in negative as in positive directions, it is essential that such practices be improved and that accountability pressures not inappropriately narrow a program's focus. This is especially the case for programs designed to enable the learning of students who are not doing well at school. If the push for use of evidence-based practices is done in an unsophisticated way, there is a worry that it will narrow options for dealing with learning, behavior, and emotional problems. There is also the likelihood of further undermining efforts to deal with complex problems in a comprehensive, multifaceted way. The danger is that resources will be redeployed in ways that favor the current "evidence base"—no matter what its deficits.

Finding out if a program is any good is a necessity. But in doing so, it is wise to recognize that evaluation is not simply a technical process. Evaluation involves decisions about what to measure and how. It involves decisions about what standards to use in making judgments. These decisions are based in great part on values and beliefs.

As a result, limited knowledge, bias, vested interests, and ethical issues are constantly influencing the descriptive and judgmental processes that shape conclusions at the end of the evaluation. While researchers build a better evidence base over the next twenty years, rational judgments must temper the zeal to prematurely claim scientific validation. And everyone concerned about learning, behavior, and emotional problems must increase the efforts to bolster both the scientific and rational bases for enhancing learning supports.

As Dennie Wolf (2002), director of the Opportunity and Accountability Initiative at the Annenberg Institute for School Reform, notes, "Clearly, we know how to raise standards. However, we are less clear on how to support students in rising to meet those standards" (p. 20). Then she asks, "Having invested heavily in 'raising' both the standards and the stakes, what investment are we willing to make to support students in 'rising' to meet those standards?" (p. 21). Ultimately, the answer to that question will affect not only individuals with learning, behavior, and emotional problems but the entire society as well.

NUMBERED REFERENCES

1. Adelman, H. S., & Taylor, L. (1997). Addressing barriers to learning: Beyond school-linked services and full service schools. *American Journal of Orthopsychiatry, 67,* 408–421.
2. Adelman, H. S., & Taylor, L. (1998). Reframing mental health in schools and expanding school reform. *Educational Psychologist, 33,* 135–152.
3. Adelman, H. S., & Taylor, L. (2000). Looking at school health and school reform policy through the lens of addressing barriers to learning. *Children Services: Social Policy, Research, and Practice, 3,* 117–132.
4. Allensworth, D., Wyche, J., Lawson, E., & Nicholson, L. (Eds.). (1997). *Schools and health: Our nation's investment.* Washington, DC: National Academy Press.
5. Carnegie Council on Adolescent Development's Task Force on Education of Young Adolescents. (1989). *Turning points: Preparing American youth for the 21st century.* Washington, DC: Author.
6. Center for Mental Health in Schools. (1998). *Restructuring boards of education to enhance schools' effectiveness in addressing barriers to student learning.* Los Angeles: Author.
7. Center for Mental Health in Schools. (1999). *Policymakers' guide to restructuring student support resources to address barriers to learning.* Los Angeles: Author (at UCLA).
8. Comer, J. (1988). Educating poor minority children. *Scientific American, 259,* 42–48.
9. Dryfoos, J. (1998). *Safe passage: Making it through adolescence in a risky society.* New York: Oxford University Press.
10. Hargreaves, A. (Ed.). (1997). *Rethinking educational change with heart and mind (1997 ASCD Yearbook).* Alexandria, VA: ASCD.
11. Kirst, M. W., & McLaughlin, M. (1990). Rethinking children's policy: Implications for educational administration. In B. Mitchell & L. L. Cunningham (Eds.), *Educational leadership and changing context of families, communities, and schools: 89th yearbook of the National Society for the Study of Education* (Pt. 2, pp. 69–90). Chicago: University of Chicago Press.
12. Knitzer, J., Steinberg, Z., & Fleisch, B. (1990). *At the schoolhouse door: An examination of programs and policies for children with behavioral and emotional problems.* New York: Bank Street College.
13. Marx, E., & Wooley, S. F. (with Northrop, D.). (Eds.). *Health is academic: A guide to coordinated school health programs.* New York: Teachers College Press.
14. Schorr, L. B. (1988). *Within our reach: Breaking the cycle of disadvantage.* New York: Doubleday.
15. Schorr, L. B. (1997). *Common purpose: Strengthening families and neighborhoods to rebuild America.* New York: Anchor.
16. Adler, L., & Gardner, S. (Eds.). (1994). *The politics of linking schools and social services.* Washington, DC: Falmer.
17. Center for Mental Health in Schools. (1999). *School-community partnerships: A guide.* Los Angeles: Author (at UCLA).
18. Center for Mental Health in Schools. (1999). *Policymakers' guide to restructuring student support resources to address barriers to learning.* Los Angeles: Author (at UCLA).

19. Kretzmann, J. (1998). *Community-based development and local schools: A promising partnership.* Evanston, IL: Institute for Policy Research.

20. Lawson, H., & Briar-Lawson, K. (1997). *Connecting the dots: Progress toward the integration of school reform, school-linked services, parent involvement and community schools.* Oxford, OH: Danforth Foundation & Miami University, Institute for Educational Renewal.

21. Melaville, A., & Blank, M. J. (1998). *Learning together: The developing field of school-community initiatives.* Flint, MI: Mott Foundation.

22. Sailor, W., & Skrtic, T. M. (1996). School/community partnerships and educational reform: Introduction to the topical issue. *Remedial and Special Education, 17,* 267–270, 283.

23. Center for Mental Health in Schools. (2000). *A sampling of outcome findings from interventions relevant to addressing barriers to learning* (a compilation of research data). Los Angeles: Author (at UCLA).

24. Iowa Department of Education. (n.d.). *Developing Iowa's future—every child matters: Success4.* Des Moines: Author.

25. Bry, B. H. (1982). Reducing the incidence of adolescent problems through preventive intervention: One and five year follow-up. *American Journal of Community Psychology, 10,* 265–276.

26. Fuchs, D., Fuchs, L. S., & Bahr, M. W. (1990). Mainstream assistance teams: Scientific basis for the art of consultation. *Exceptional Children, 57,* 128–139.

27. O'Donnell, J., Hawkins, J. D., Catalano, R. F., Abbot, R. D., & Day, E. (1995). Preventing school failure, drug use, and delinquency among low-income children: Long-term intervention in elementary schools. *American Journal of Orthopsychiatry, 65,* 87–100.

28. Nelson, J. R., Carr, B. A., & Smith, D. J. (1997). Managing disruptive behaviors in school settings: The THINK TIME Strategy. *Communique, 25,* 24–25.

29. Shure, M. B. (1993). *Interpersonal problem solving and prevention: Five-year longitudinal study.* Prepared for Department of Health and Human Services, Public Health Service. Washington, DC: National Institute of Mental Health.

30. Smith, L. J., Ross, S. M., & Casey, J. P. (1994). *Special education analyses for Success for All in four cities.* Memphis, TN: University of Memphis, Center for Research in Educational Policy.

31. Sugai, G., & Horner, R. H. (1999). Discipline and behavioral support: Preferred processes and practices. *Effective School Practices, 7,* 10–22.

32. Cohen, P. A., Kuklik, J. A., & Kuklik, C.-L. C. (1982). Educational outcomes of tutoring: A meta analysis of findings. *American Educational Research Journal, 19,* 237–248.

33. Cooper, R., Slavin, R. E., & Madden, N. A. (1998). Success for All: Improving the quality of implementation of whole-school change through the use of a national reform network. *Education and Urban Society, 30*(3), 385–408.

34. Giesecke, D., Cartledge, G., & Gardner, R., III. (1993). Low-achieving students as successful cross-age tutors. *Preventing School Failure, 37,* 34–43.

35. Martino, L. R. (1994). Peer tutoring classes for young adolescents: A cost-effective strategy. *Middle School Journal, 25,* 55–58.

36. Ross, S. M., Nunnery, J., & Smith, L. J. (1996). *Evaluation of Title I reading programs: Amphitheater public schools. Year 1: 1995–96.* Memphis, TN: University of Memphis, Center for Research in Educational Policy.

37. Rossi, R. J. (1995). *Evaluation of projects funded by the School Dropout Demonstration Assistance Program: Final evaluation report, Volume I: Findings and recommendations.* Palo Alto, CA: American Institutes for Research.

38. Slavin, R. E., Madden, N. A., Dolan, L., Wasik, B. A., Ross, S. M., Smith, L. J., & Dianda, M. (1996). Success for All: A summary of research. *Journal of Education for Students Placed at Risk, 1,* 41–76.

39. Baker, S., Gersten, R., & Keating, T. (2000). When less may be more: A two-year longitudinal evaluation of a volunteer tutoring program requiring minimal training. *Reading Research Quarterly, 35*(4), 494–519.

40. Invernizzi, M., Rosemary, C., Juel, C., & Richards, H. C. (1997). At-risk readers and community volunteers: A three-year perspective. *Scientific Studies of Reading, 1*(3), 277–300.

41. Egelson, P., Harman, P., & Achilles, C. M. (1996). *Does class size make a difference? Recent findings from state and district initiatives.* Washington, DC: ERIC Clearinghouse. (ERIC Document Reproduction Services No. ED398644)

42. Molnar, A., Percy, S., Smith, P., & Zahorik, J. (1998, December). *1997–98 results of the Student Achievement Guarantee in Education (SAGE) program.* Milwaukee: University of Wisconsin.

43. Pritchard, I. (1999). *Reducing class size: What do we know?* Washington, DC: National Institute on Student Achievement, Curriculum and Assessment, Office of Educational Research and Improvement, U.S. Department of Education.

44. Robinson, G. E., & Wittebols, J. H. (1986). *Class size research: A related cluster analysis for decision-making.* Arlington, VA: Education Research Service.

45. Wright, E. N., Stanley M., Shapson, G. E., & Fitzgerald, J. (1977). *Effects of class size in the junior grades: A study.* Toronto: Ontario Institute for Studies of Education.

46. Cryan, J., Sheehan, R., Weichel, J., & Bandy-Hedden, I. G. (1992). Success outcomes of full-day kindergarten: More positive behavior and increased achievement in the years after. *Early Childhood Research Quarterly, 7,* 187–203.

47. Gomby, D. S., Larner, M. B., Stevenson, C. S., Lewit, E. M., & Behrman, R. E. (1995). Long-term outcomes of early childhood programs: Analysis and recommendations. *The Future of Children, 5,* 6–24.

48. U.S. Department of Education. (n.d.). *Even start: Evidence from the past and a look to the future. Planning and evaluation service analysis and highlights.* Washington, DC: Author. Retrieved April 15, 2005, from www.ed.gov/pubs/ EvenStart/highlights.html.

49. Caliber Associates, Ellsworth Associates, Westat, Mathematica Policy Research. (1997). *Head Start: First progress report on the Head Start program performance measures.* Washington, DC: Administration for Children and Families, Head Start Bureau. Retrieved April 15, 2005, from www2 .acf.dhhs.gov.

50. Karweit, N. (1992). The kindergarten experience. *Educational Leadership, 49,* 82–86.

51. Yoshikawa, H. (1995). Long-term effects of early childhood programs on social outcomes and delinquency. *The Future of Children, 5*(3), 51–75.

52. Henderson, A. T., & Mapp, K. L. (Eds.). (2002). *A new wave of evidence: The impact of school, family, and connections on student achievement, annual synthesis 2002.* Austin, TX: National Center for Family & Community Connections With Schools, Southwest Educational Development Laboratory.

53. Brigman, G. A., & Webb, L. D. (2003). Ready to learn: Teaching kindergarten students school success skills. *Journal of Educational Research, 96*(5), 286–292.

54. Reynolds, A. J., Temple, J. A., Robertson, D. L., & Mann, E. A. (2001). Long-term effects of an early childhood intervention on educational achievement and juvenile arrest. *JAMA, 285*(18), 2339–2346.

55. Lattimore, C. B., Mihalic, S. F., Grotpeter, J. K., & Taggart, R. (1998). *Blueprints for violence prevention, Book Four: The quantum opportunities program.* Boulder, CO: Center for the Study and Prevention of Violence.

56. Posner, J. K., & Vandell, D. L. (1994). Low-income children's after-school care: Are there beneficial effects of after-school programs? *Child Development, 65,* 440–456.

57. *Safe and Smart: Making after-school hours work for kids.* (1998). Retrieved April 15, 2005, from www.ed.gov/pubs/SafeandSmart/.

58. Seppanen, P. S, & others. (1993). *National study of before- and after-school programs: Final report.* Retrieved April 15, 2005, from www.eric.ed.gov.

59. Ferrin, D., & Amick, S. (2002). San Diego's 6 to 6: A community's commitment to out-of-school time. *New Directions for Youth Development, 94,* 109–117.

60. Felner, R. D., Ginter, M., & Primavera, J. (1982). Primary prevention during school transitions: Social support and environmental structure. *American Journal of Community Psychology, 10,* 277–289.

61. Greene, R. W., & Ollendick, T. H. (1993). Evaluation of a multidimensional program for sixth-graders in transition from elementary to middle school. *Journal of Community Psychology, 21,* 162–176.

62. Hellem, D. W. (1990). Sixth grade transition groups: An approach to primary prevention. *Journal of Primary Prevention, 10*(4), 303–311.

63. Felner, R. D., Brand, S., Adan, A. M., Mulhall, P. F., Flowers, N., Sartain, B., & DuBois, D. L. (1993). Restructuring the ecology of the school as an approach to prevention during school transitions: Longitudinal follow-ups and extensions of the School Transitional Environment Project (STEP). In L. A. Jason, K. E. Danner, & K. S. Kurasaki (Eds.), *Prevention and school transitions: Prevention in human services.* New York: Haworth.

64. Jason, L. A., Weine, A. M., Johnson, J. H., Danner, K. E., Kurasaki, K. S., & Warren-Sohlberg, L. (1993). The School Transitions Project: A comprehensive preventive intervention. *Journal of Emotional and Behavioral Disorders, 1,* 65–70.

65. Blalock, G. (1996). Community transition teams as the foundation for transition services for youth with learning disabilities. *Journal of Learning Disabilities, 29,* 148–159.

66. Smith, G., & Smith, D. (1985). A mainstreaming program that really works. *Journal of Learning Disabilities, 18,* 369–372.

67. Wang, M. C., & Birch, J. W. (1984). Comparison of a full-time mainstreaming program and a resource room approach. *Exceptional Children, 51,* 33–40.

68. Biller, E. F. (1987). *Career decision making for adolescents and young adults with learning disabilities: Theory, research and practice.* Springfield, IL: Charles C Thomas.

69. Hackett, H., & Baron, D. (1995). Canadian action on early school leaving: A description of the national stay-in-school initiative. *ERIC Digest.* (ERIC Document Reproduction Service No. ED399481)

70. Miller, J. V., & Imel, S. (1986). Some current issues in adult, career, and vocational education. In E. Flaxman (Ed.), *Trends and issues in education.*

Washington, DC: U.S. Department of Education. (ERIC Document Reproduction Service No. ED281897)

71. Naylor, M. (1987). Reducing the dropout rate through career and vocational education. Overview. *ERIC Digest.* (ERIC Document Reproduction Service No. ED282094)

72. Renihan, F., Buller, E., Desharnais, W., Enns, R., Laferriere, T., & Therrien, L. (1994). *Taking stock: An assessment of The National Stay-In-School Initiative.* Hull, PQ, Canada: Youth Affairs Branch, Human Resources Development Canada.

73. Altman, E. (1994). *Violence prevention curricula: Summary of evaluations.* Springfield: Illinois Council for the Prevention of Violence.

74. Bureau of Primary Health Care. (n.d.). *Healing fractured lives: How three school-based projects approach violence prevention and mental health care.* Washington, DC: U.S. Department of Health and Human Services.

75. Carter, S. L. (1994). Evaluation report for the New Mexico center for dispute resolution. *Mediation in the Schools Program, 1993–1994 school year.* Albuquerque, NM: Center for Dispute Resolution.

76. Davidson, L. L., Durkin, M. S., Kuhn, L., O'Connor, P., Barlow, B., & Heagarty, M. C. (1994). The impact of the Safe Kids/Health Neighborhoods Injury Prevention Program in Harlem, 1988–1991. *American Journal of Public Health, 84,* 580–586.

77. Embry, D. D., Flannery, D. J., Vazsonyi, A. T., Powell, K. E., & Atha, H. (1996). PeaceBuilders: A theoretically driven, school-based model for early violence prevention. *American Journal of Preventive Medicine* (Supp.), 12(5), 91–100.

78. Farrell, A. D., Meyer, A. L., & Dahlberg, L. L. (1996). The effectiveness of a school-based curriculum for reducing violence among urban sixth-grade students. *American Journal of Public Health, 87,* 979–984.

79. Farrell, A. D., Meyer, A. L., & Dahlberg, L. L. (1996). Richmond youth against violence: A school based program for urban adolescents. *American Journal of Preventive Medicine, 12,* 13–21.

80. Farrell, A. D., & Meyer, A. L. (in press). Social skills training to promote resilience in urban sixth grade students: One product of an action research strategy to prevent youth violence in high-risk environments. *Education and Treatment of Children.*

81. Grossman, D. C., Neckerman, H. J., Koepsell, T. D., Liu, P., Asher, K. N., Beland, K., Frey, K., & Rivara, F. P. (1997). Effectiveness of a violence prevention curriculum among children in elementary school: A randomized controlled trial. *Journal of the American Medical Association, 277*(20), 1605–1611.

82. Jason, L. A., & Burrows, B. (1983). Transition training for high school seniors. *Cognitive Therapy and Research, 7,* 79–91.

83. Klingman, A., & Hochdorf, Z. (1993). Coping with distress and self-harm: The impact of a primary prevention program among adolescents. *Journal of Adolescence, 16,* 121–140.

84. Knoff, H. M., & Batsche, G. M. (1995). Project ACHIEVE: Analyzing a school reform process for at-risk and underachieving students. *School Psychology Review, 24*(4), 579–603.

85. Orbach, I., & Bar-Joseph, H. (1993). The impact of a suicide prevention program for adolescents on suicidal tendencies, hopelessness, ego identity and coping. *Suicide and Life-Threatening Behavior, 23*(2), 120–129.

86. Poland, S. (1994). The role of school crisis intervention teams to prevent and reduce school violence and trauma. *School Psychology Review, 23,* 175–189.

87. Quinn, M. M., Osher, D., Hoffman, C. C., & Hanley, T. V. (1998*). Safe, drug-free, and effective schools for ALL students: What works!* Washington, DC: Center for Effective Collaboration and Practice, American Institutes for Research.

88. Tolan, P. H., & Guerra, N. G. (1994).*What works in reducing adolescent violence: An empirical review of the field.* Boulder, CO: Center for the Study and Prevention of Violence.

89. Walker, H. M., Colvin, G., & Ramsey, E. (1995). *Anti-social behavior in schools: Strategies and best practices.* Pacific Grove, CA: Brooks/Cole.

90. Walker, H. M., Severson, H. H., Feil, E. G., Stiller, B., & Golly, A. (1997). *First step to success: Intervening at the point of school entry to prevent antisocial behavior patterns.* Longmont, CO: Sopris West.

91. Walker, H. M., Stiller, B., Severson, H. H., Kavanagh, K., Golly, A., & Feil, E. G. (in press). First step to success: An early intervention approach for preventing school antisocial behavior. *Journal of Emotional and Behavioral Disorders, 5*(4).

92. Symons, C. W., Cinelli, B., James, T. C., & Groff, P. (1997). Bridging student health risk and academic achievement through comprehensive school health programs. *Journal of School Health, 67*(6), 220–227.

93. Nelson, R. J. (2001). Designing schools to meet the needs of students who exhibit disruptive behavior. In H. Walker & M. Epstein (Eds.), *Making schools safer and violence free: Critical issues, solutions, and recommended practices.* Austin, TX: PRO-ED.

94. Johnson, D. W., & Johnson, R. T. (1996). Conflict resolution and peer mediation programs in elementary and secondary schools: Review of the research. *Review of Educational Research, 66,* 459–506.

95. Rollin, S. A., Kaiser-Ulrey, C., Potts, I., & Creason, A. H. (2003). A school-based violence prevention model for at-risk eighth grade youth. *Psychology in the Schools, 40*(4), 403–415.

96. National Center for Family Literacy. (1997). *Even start: An effective literacy program helps families grow toward independence.* Louisville, KY: Author. Retrieved April 15, 2005, from www.famlit.org.

97. Jordan, G. E., Snow, C. E., & Porche, M. V. (2000). Project EASE: The effect of a family literacy project on kindergarten students' early literacy skills. *Reading Research Quarterly, 35*(4), 524–546.

98. Dishion, T. J., & Andrews, D. W. (1995). Preventing escalation in problem behaviors with high-risk young adolescents: Immediate and one-year outcomes. *Journal of Consulting and Clinical Psychology, 63,* 538–548.

99. Dishion, T. J., Andrews, D. W., Kavanagh, K., & Soberman, L. H. (1996). Preventive interventions for high-risk youth: The adolescent transitions program. In R. Peteres & R. McMahon (Eds.), *Preventing childhood disorders, substance abuse, and delinquency* (pp. 184–218). Thousand Oaks, CA: Sage.

100. Lally, J. R., Mangione, P. L., & Honig, A. S. (1988). The Syracuse University Family Development Research Program: Long-range impact on an early intervention with low-income children and their families. In D. R. Powell & I. E. Sigel (Eds.), *Parent education as early childhood intervention: Emerging direction in theory, research, and practice* (Annual advances in applied developmental psychology, Volume 3). Norwood, NJ: Ablex.

101. Spoth, R., Redmond, C., Haggerty, K., & Ward, T. (1995). A controlled parenting skills outcome study examining individual differences and attendance effects. *Journal of Marriage and the Family, 57,* 449.

102. Epstein, J. L., Simon, B. S., & Salinas, K. C. (1997). *Involving parents in homework in the middle grades.* Baltimore: Johns Hopkins.

103. Aktan, B. B., Kumpfer, K. L., & Turner, C. (1996). The Safe Haven Program: Effectiveness of a family skills training program for substance abuse prevention with inner city African-American families. *International Journal of the Addictions, 31,* 158–175.

104. Battistich, V., Schaps, E., Watson, M., & Solomon, D. (1996). Prevention effects of the Child Development Project: Early findings from an ongoing multisite demonstration trial. *Journal of Adolescent Research, 11,* 12–35.

105. Battistich, V., Solomon, D., Kim, D., Watson, M., & Schaps, E. (1995). Schools as communities, poverty levels of student populations, and student' attitudes, motives, and performance: A multilevel analysis. *American Educational Research Journal, 32,* 627–658.

106. Berrueta-Clement, J. R., Schweinhart, L. J., Barnett, W. S., Epstein, A. S., & Weikart, D. P. (1984). *Changed lives: The effects of the Perry Preschool Program on youths through age 19.* Ypsilanti, MI: High/Scope.

107. Epstein, A. S. (1993). *Training for quality: Improving early childhood programs through systematic inservice training.* Ypsilanti, MI: High/Scope.

108. McDonald, L., Billingham, S., Dibble, N., Rice, C., & Coe-Braddish, D. (1991, January). Families and Schools Together: An innovative substance abuse prevention program. *Social Work in Education: A Journal of Social Workers in School, 13,* 118–128.

109. O'Donnell, J., Hawkins, J. D., Catalano, R. F., Abbot, R. D., & Day, E. (1995). Preventing school failure, drug use, and delinquency among low-income children: Long-term intervention in elementary schools. *American Journal of Orthopsychiatry, 65,* 87–100.

110. Schweinhart, L. J., Barnes, H. V., & Weikart, D. P. (1993). Significant benefits: The High/Scope Perry Preschool Study through age 27. *Monograph of the High/Scope Educational Research Foundation, 10.*

111. Tremblay, R. E., Vitaro, F., Betrand, L., LeBlanc, M., Beauchesne, H., Bioleau, H., & David, L. (1992). Parent and child training to prevent early onset of delinquency: The Montreal Longitudinal Experimental Study. In J. McCord & R. Tremblay (Eds.), *Preventing antisocial behavior: Interventions from birth through adolescence.* New York: Guilford.

112. Epstein, J. (1995). School/family/community partnerships: Caring for the children we share. *Phi Delta Kappan, 76,* 701–713.

113. Gorman-Smith, D., Tolan, P. H., Henry, D. B., & Leventhal, A. (2002). Predictors of participation in a family-focused preventive intervention for substance use. *Psychology of Addictive Behaviors, 16* (Suppl. 4), S55.

114. Armstrong, P. M., Davis, P., & Northcutt, C. (1988). *Year end and final evaluation reports, Project years 1985–1986 and 1986–1987.* San Francisco: San Francisco Unified School District.

115. Carney, J. M., Dobson, J. E., & Dobson, R. L. (1987). Using senior citizen volunteers in the schools. *Journal of Humanistic Education and Development, 25*(3), 136–143.

116. Grossman, J. B., & Garry, E. M. (1997). *Mentoring: A proven delinquency prevention strategy.* Washington, DC: U.S. Department of Justice, Office of Juvenile Justice and Delinquency Prevention. Retrieved April 15, 2005, from www.ncjrs.org/txtfiles/164834.txt.

117. Davis, N. (1999). *Resilience: Status of the research and research-based programs.* Rockville, MD: Substance Abuse and Mental Health Administration Center for Mental Health Services Division of Program Development, Special Populations & Projects Special Programs Development Branch. Phone: (301) 443-2844.

118. Michael, B. (1990). *Volunteers in public schools.* Washington, DC: National Academy Press.

119. Cahill, M., Perry, J., Wright, M., & Rice, A. (1993). *A documentation report of the New York Beacons initiative.* New York: Youth Development Institute.

120. Davis, N. (1999). *Resilience: Status of the research and research-based programs.* Rockville, MD: Substance Abuse and Mental Health Administration Center for Mental Health Services Division of Program Development, Special Populations & Projects Special Programs Development Branch. Phone: (301) 443-2844.

121. Melaville, A., & Blank, M. (1998). *Learning together: The developing field of school-community initiatives.* Washington, DC: Institute for Educational Leadership & National Center for Community Education.

122. Shames, S. (1997). *Pursuing the dream: What helps children and their families succeed.* Chicago: Coalition.

123. Woodruff, D., Shannon, N., & Efimba, M. (1998). Collaborating for success: Merritt elementary extended school. *Journal of Education for Students Placed at Risk, 1*(1), 11–22.

124. Pittman, K., Irby, M., Tolman, J., Yohalem, N., & Ferber, T. (2001). *Prevention problems promoting development, encouraging engagement: Competing priorities or inseparable goals?* Washington, DC: Forum for Youth Investment.

125. Eccles, J., & Gootman, J. (Eds.). (2002). *Community programs to promote youth development.* Washington, DC: National Academies Press.

126. Catalano, R., Berglund, M., Ryan, J., Lonczak, H., & Hawkins, J. D. (1998). *Positive youth development in the United States: Research findings on evaluations of positive youth development programs.* Washington, DC: National Academies Press.

127. Botvin, G. J., Mihalic, S. F., & Grotpeter, J. K. (1998). *Blueprints for violence prevention, Book Five: Life skills training.* Boulder, CO: Center for the Study and Prevention of Violence.

128. Bureau of Primary Health Care. (1993). *School-based clinics that work* (HRSA Publication No. 93–248P). Washington, DC: Health Resources and Services Administration.

129. Caplan, M., Weissberg, R. P., Grober, J. S., Sivo, P. J., Grady, K., & Jacoby, C. (1992). Social competence promotion with inner-city and suburban young adolescents: Effects on social adjustment and alcohol use. *Journal of Consulting and Clinical Psychology, 60,* 56–63.

130. Catalano, R. F., Haggerty, K. P., Fleming, C. B., & Brewer, D. D. (in press). Focus on Families: Scientific findings from family prevention intervention research. *NIDA Research Monograph.*

131. Dryfoos, J. G., Brindis, C., & Kaplan, D. W. (1996, June) Research and evaluation in school-based health care. *Adolescent Medicine: State of the Art Reviews, 7*(2), 207–220.

132. Henggler, S. W. (1998). Mulitsystemic therapy. In D. S. Elliott (Ed.), *Blueprints for violence prevention.* Boulder, CO: Center for the Study and Prevention of Violence.

133. California Department of Education, Healthy Start and After School Partnerships Office. (1999, March). *Healthy Start works: A statewide profile of Healthy Start sites.* Sacramento, CA: Author. Contact (916) 657–3558.

134. Institute for At-Risk Infants, Children and Youth, and Their Families. (1994). *The effect of putting health services on site, Example 1. A full services school assembly.* Tallahassee, FL: Florida Department of Education.

135. Stroul, B. A. (1993, September). *From systems of care for children and adolescents with severe emotional disturbances: What are the results?* Washington, DC: CASSP Technical Assistance Center, Georgetown University Child Development Center, 3800 Reservoir Road, N.W., Washington, DC 20007, (202) 687-8635.

136. Warren, C. (1999). *Lessons from the evaluation of New Jersey's school-based Youth Services Program.* Prepared for the National Invitational Conference on Improving Results for Children and Families by Connecting Collaborative Services With School Reform Efforts. Washington, DC: Author.

137. Alexander, J., Barton, C., Gordon, D., Grotpeter, J., Hansson, K., Harrison, R., Mears, S., Mihalic, S., Parsons, B., Pugh, C., Schulman, S., Waldron, H., & Sexton, T. (1998). *Blueprints for violence prevention, Book Three: Functional family therapy.* Boulder, CO: Center for the Study and Prevention of Violence.

138. Ellickson, P. L. (1998). Preventing adolescent substance abuse: Lessons from the Project ALERT program. In J. Crane (Ed.), *Social programs that really work* (pp. 201–224). New York: Russell Sage.

139. Gillham, J. E., Reivich, K. J., Jaycox, L. H., & Seligman, M. E. P. (1995). Prevention of depressive symptoms in schoolchildren: Two-year follow-up. *Psychological Science, 6,* 343–351.

140. Lochman, J. E., Coie, J., Underwood, M., & Terry, R. (1993). Effectiveness of a social relations intervention program for aggressive and nonaggressive, rejected children. *Journal of Consulting and Clinical Psychology, 61,* 1053–1058.

141. Primary Mental Health Project, Inc. (1995, November). *An evaluation of the early mental health initiative's primary intervention program and enhanced primary intervention program for the 1994–95 academic year.* Rochester, NY: Author.

142. Prinz, R. J., Blechman, E. A., & Dumas, J. E. (1994). An evaluation of peer coping-skills training for childhood aggression. *Journal of Clinical Child Psychology, 23,* 193–203.

143. Gottfredson, D. C., & Wilson, D. B. (2003). Characteristics of effective school-based substance abuse prevention. *Prevention Science, 4*(1), 27–38.

GENERAL REFERENCES

Catalano, R., Berglund, M., Ryan, J., Lonczak, H., & Hawkins, J. D. (1998). *Positive youth development in the United States: Research findings on evaluations of positive youth development programs*. Washington, DC: National Academies Press.

Fullan, M. (2005). *Leadership & sustainability: System thinkers in action*. Thousand Oaks, CA: Corwin.

Intrator, S. (2002). *Stories of the courage to teach: Honoring the teacher's heart*. San Francisco: Jossey-Bass.

Neisser, U. (1976). *Cognition and reality: Principles and implications of cognitive psychology*. San Francisco: Freeman.

Rossi, P. H., & Freeman, H. E. (1989). *Evaluation: A systematic approach* (4th ed.). Newbury Park, CA: Sage.

Rossi, P. H., Freeman, H. E., & Wright, S. (1979). *Evaluation: A systematic approach* (3rd ed.). Beverly Hills, CA: Sage.

Stake, R. E. (1967). The countenance of educational evaluation. *Teachers College Record, 68,* 523–540.

Stake, R. E. (1976). *Evaluating educational programs: The need and the response*. Paris: Organization for Economic Cooperation and Development.

Wolf, D. P. (2002, December). When raising isn't rising. *The School Administrator Web Edition*. Arlington, VA: American Association of School Administrators. Retrieved April 15, 2005, from www.aasa.org/publications/.

Coda   **10**

Building Prototypes and Going-to-Scale

Ultimately, only three things matter about educational reform. Does it have depth: does it improve important rather than superficial aspects of students' learning and development? Does it have length: can it be sustained over long periods of time instead of fizzling out after the first flush of innovation? Does it have breadth: can the reform be extended beyond a few schools, networks or showcase initiatives to transform education across entire systems or nations?

—Andy Hargreaves and Dean Fink (2000)

The Problems of Prototype Implementation and Scale-up
It's About What Happens at the School and in the Classroom
Concluding Comment

SOURCE: Used with appreciation to an anonymous source.

ORIENTING QUESTIONS

? How does prototype implementation differ from scale-up?
? What ensures that a prototype for learning supports will play out at a school and in the classroom?

If we want to bring . . . quality, equity, and new life to our system—we must trust in a vision and a process of change.

—Dwight Allen (1993)

If our society truly means to provide the opportunity for all students to succeed at school, fundamental changes are needed so that teachers can personalize instruction and teachers along with other school staff can address barriers to learning. Policymakers can call for higher standards and greater accountability, improved curricula and instruction, increased discipline, reduced school violence, and on and on. None of it means much if the reforms enacted do not ultimately result in substantive changes in the classroom and throughout a school. Moreover, such reforms have to be sustained over time. And if the intent is to leave no child behind, then such reforms have to be replicated in all schools.

THE PROBLEMS OF PROTOTYPE
IMPLEMENTATION AND SCALE-UP

Well-conceived and implemented innovations are essential to strengthening students, schools, families, and communities. Many new initiatives, however, are pursued primarily as specially funded projects and demonstrations. When the funding ends, more often than not, much of what was put in place disappears. The history of schools is strewn with valuable innovations that were not sustained, never mind replicated. Naturally, financial considerations play a role, but a widespread "project mentality" also is culpable.

A common tendency is for those involved in a project to think about their work only as a project providing a discrete program or set of services. And it is common for others to view the work as temporary (e.g., "It will end when the grant runs out."). This mind-set leads to the view that new activities are time limited, and it contributes to fragmented approaches and the marginalization of the initiative. It also works against the systemic changes that sustain and expand innovations.

The consistent failure to sustain has increased interest in understanding how to institutionalize and diffuse effective innovations. Our interest in these matters has evolved over many years of implementing demonstrations and working to replicate innovations on a large scale (Adelman & Taylor, 1997, 2003; Taylor, Nelson, & Adelman, 1999). By now, we are fully convinced that advancing the field requires escaping project mentality and becoming sophisticated about sustainability and scale-up. As Fullan (2005) stresses, "What we need is leadership that motivates people to take on the complexities and anxieties of difficult change" (p. 104).

An initiative to improve schools requires a prototype for an improved approach. Such a prototype usually is developed and initially implemented as a pilot demonstration at one or more sites. Efforts to reform schooling, however, require much more than implementing a few demonstrations. Improved approaches are only as good as a school district's ability to develop and institutionalize them on a large scale. This process often is called *diffusion, replication, rollout,* or *scale-up.*

Guide 10.1 outlines major matters that must be considered related to planning, implementing, sustaining, and going to scale, as we see them. This tool can be used as a framework for thinking about these issues. It also can be used as a template for establishing benchmarks for purposes of formative evaluation.

As outlined, changes may encompass introducing one or more interventions, developing a demonstration at a specific site, or replicating a prototype on a large scale. Whatever the nature and scope of focus, all the *key facets* outlined come into play.

Each cell in the matrix warrants extensive discussion. Here, we must limit ourselves to highlighting some of the host of interacting concerns and activities involved in pursuing new directions for learning supports.

1. The *nature and scope of focus* raise such questions as
   - What specific functions will be implemented and sustained?
   - Will one or more sites or organizations be involved?
   - Is the intent to make systemwide changes?

2. With respect to *key facets,* whatever the nature and scope of the work, efforts begin with
   - Articulation of a clear, shared vision for the initiative
   - Ensuring that there is a major policy commitment from all participating partners
   - Negotiating partnership agreements and designating leadership

This is followed by processes for

   - Enhancing or developing an infrastructure based on a clear articulation of essential functions (e.g., mechanisms for governance

Guide 10.1   New Initiatives: Considerations Related to Planning, Implementing, Sustaining, and Going to Scale

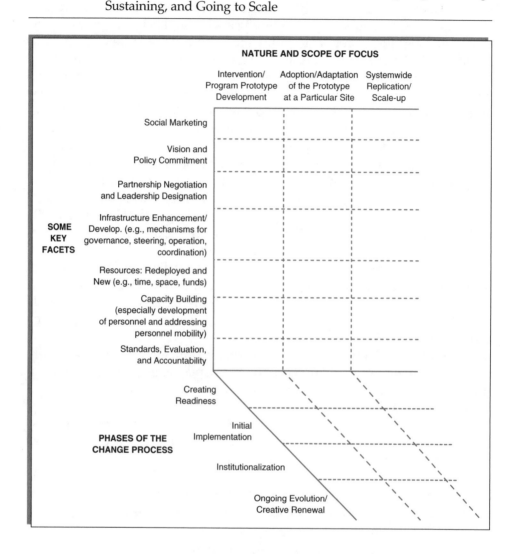

and priority setting, steering, operation, resource mapping and coordination)

Pursuing the work requires

- Strong facilitation related to all mechanisms
- Redeploying resources and establishing new ones
- Building capacity (especially personnel development and strategies for addressing personnel and other stakeholder mobility)
- Establishing standards, evaluation processes, and accountability procedures

And throughout, there must be an ongoing focus on social marketing.

3. Sustainability and scale-up processes must address each of the major phases of systemic change as has been described.

For the most part, education researchers and reformers have paid little attention to the complexities of large-scale diffusion. This is evident from the fact that the nation's research agenda does not include major initiatives to delineate and test models for widespread replication of education reforms. In addition, change agents are used who have relatively little specific training in facilitating large-scale systemic changes. Furthermore, leadership training has given short shrift to the topic of scale-up processes and problems (Elmore, 2004; Fullan, 2005; Glennan, Bodilly, Galegher, & Kerr, 2004; Thomas, 2002).

It is not surprising, then, that the pendulum swings characterizing shifts in the debate over how best to improve schools are not accompanied with sufficient resources to accomplish prescribed changes throughout a school district. A common deficiency is the failure to address the four phases of the change process outlined in Guide 10.2. Examples include failure to pursue adequate strategies for creating motivational readiness among a critical mass of stakeholders, especially principals and teachers, and for accommodating assignment changes. Moreover, time frames for building capacity to accomplish desired institutional changes usually are unrealistic. As Tom Vander Ark (2002), Executive Director of Education for the Bill and Melinda Gates Foundation, wisely notes, "Effective practices typically evolve over a long period in high-functioning, fully engaged systems" (p. 323).

For many years, our work revolved mainly around developing demonstration programs. Then we moved into the world of replicating new approaches to schooling on a large scale. Confronted with the problems and processes of scale-up, we analyzed a broad range of psychological and organizational literature and delineated the working framework for scale-up outlined in Guide 10.2.

To appreciate the point, think about the best model around for how schools can improve the way they address barriers to student learning. Assuming the model has demonstrated cost-effectiveness and that a school district wants to adopt or adapt it, the first problem becomes that of how to replicate it, and the next problem becomes that of how to do so at every school. Or in common parlance, the question is, *How do we get from here to there?*

Whether the focus is on establishing a prototype at one site or replicating it at many, the systemic changes can be conceived in terms of four overlapping phases: (1) *creating readiness*—increasing a climate and culture for change through enhancing the motivation and capability of a critical mass of stakeholders, (2) *initial implementation*—change is carried out in stages using a well-designed infrastructure to provide guidance and support, (3) *institutionalization*—accomplished by ensuring that there is an

Guide 10.2   Prototype Implementation and Scale-up: Phases and Parallel and Linked Tasks

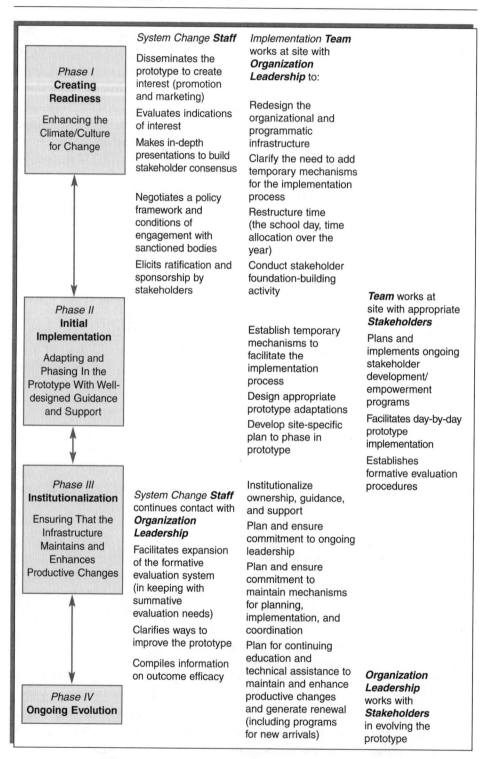

SOURCE: Adapted from Adelman and Taylor (1997).

infrastructure to maintain and enhance productive changes, and (4) *ongoing evolution*—through use of mechanisms to improve quality and provide continuing support in ways that enable stakeholders to become a community of learners and facilitate periodic creative renewal.

As indicated in Guide 10.2, a change *mechanism* is needed. One way to conceive such a mechanism is in terms of a *system implementation staff*. Such staff provides a necessary organizational base and skilled personnel for disseminating a prototype, negotiating decisions about replication, and dispensing the expertise to facilitate implementation of a prototype and eventual scale-up. They can dispense expertise by sending out a *team* consisting of personnel who, for designated periods of time, travel to the location in which the prototype is to be implemented or replicated. A core team of perhaps two to four staff works closely with a site throughout the process. The team is augmented whenever a specialist is needed to assist in replicating a specific element of the prototype design. Implementation and scaling up of a comprehensive prototype almost always require *phased-in* change and the addition of *temporary infrastructure mechanisms*.

Guides 10.1 and 10.2 briefly highlight key facets and specific tasks related to the four phases of prototype implementation and eventual scale-up. Note in particular the importance of

- Ongoing social marketing
- Articulation of a clear, shared vision for the work
- Ensuring that there is a major policy commitment from all participating partners
- Negotiating partnership agreements
- Designating leadership
- Enhancing or developing an infrastructure based on a clear articulation of essential functions (e.g., mechanisms for governance and priority setting, steering, operation, resource mapping and coordination, strong facilitation related to all mechanisms)
- Redeploying resources and establishing new ones
- Building capacity (especially personnel development and strategies for addressing personnel and other stakeholder mobility)
- Establishing standards, evaluation processes, and accountability procedures

Each facet and task requires careful planning based on sound intervention fundamentals. This means paying special attention to the problem of the match between intervention and those who are to change.

We do not mean to belabor all this. Our point simply is to make certain that there is a greater appreciation for and more attention paid to the problems of systemic change. As Seymour Sarason (1971) stressed a long time ago,

> Good ideas and missionary zeal are sometimes enough to change the thinking of individuals; they are rarely, if ever, effective in

changing complicated organizations (like the school) with traditions, dynamics, and goals of their own. (p. 213)

Those who set out to change schools and schooling are confronted with two enormous tasks. The first is to develop prototypes; the second involves large-scale replication. One without the other is insufficient. Yet considerably more attention is paid to developing and validating prototypes than to delineating and testing scale-up processes. Clearly, it is time to correct this deficiency.

IT'S ABOUT WHAT HAPPENS AT THE SCHOOL AND IN THE CLASSROOM

We want to stress a simple truth: if it doesn't play out at a school and in the classroom, it doesn't mean much. Improving test scores and closing the achievement gap require replication of good practices for every school in a district. Moreover, the type of innovations we have outlined requires avoiding the mistakes of past "district-centric" planning and resource allocation. For too long there has been a terrible disconnection between central office policy and operations and how programs and services evolve in classrooms and schools.

The time is opportune for schools and classrooms to truly become the center and guiding force for all planning. That is, planning should begin with a clear image of what the classroom and school must do to teach all students effectively. Then the focus can move to planning how a family of schools and the surrounding community can complement each other's efforts and achieve economies of scale. With all this clearly in perspective, central staff and state and national policy can be reoriented to the role of developing the best ways to support local efforts *as defined locally.*

At the same time, it is essential not to create a new mythology suggesting that every classroom and school are unique. There are fundamentals that permeate all efforts to improve schools and schooling and that should continue to guide policy, practice, research, and training. For example,

• The curriculum in every classroom must include a major emphasis on acquisition of basic knowledge and skills. However, such basics must be understood to involve more than the old "three R's" and cognitive development. There are many important areas of human development and functioning, and each contains basics that individuals may need help in acquiring. Moreover, any individual may require special accommodation in any of these areas.

- Every classroom must address student motivation as an antecedent, process, and outcome concern.

- Special assistance must be *added* to instructional programs for certain individuals, but only after the best nonspecialized procedures for facilitating learning have been tried. Moreover, such procedures must be designed to build on strengths and must not supplant continued emphasis on promoting healthy development.

- Beyond the classroom, schools must have policy, leadership, and mechanisms for developing schoolwide programs to address barriers to learning. Some of the work will need to be in partnership with other schools, and some will require weaving school and community resources together. The aim is to evolve a comprehensive, multifaceted, and integrated continuum of programs and services ranging from primary prevention through early intervention to treatment of serious problems. Our work suggests that at a school, this will require evolving programs to (a) enhance the ability of the classroom to enable learning, (b) provide support for the many transitions experienced by students and their families, (c) increase home involvement, (d) respond to and prevent crises, (e) offer special assistance to students and their families, and (f) expand community involvement, including volunteers.

- Leaders for education reform at all levels are confronted with the need to foster effective scale-up of promising reforms. This encompasses a major research thrust to develop efficacious demonstrations and effective models for replicating new approaches to schooling.

- Relatedly, policymakers at all levels must revisit current policy using the lens of addressing barriers to learning with the intent of both realigning existing policy to foster cohesive practices and enacting new policies to fill critical gaps.

CONCLUDING COMMENT

Clearly, there is ample direction for improving how schools address barriers to learning and teaching. The time to do so is now. Unfortunately, too many school professionals and researchers are caught up in the day-by-day pressures of their current roles and functions. Everyone is so busy "doing" that there is no time to introduce better ways. One is reminded of Winnie the Pooh who was always going down the stairs, bump, bump, bump, on his head behind Christopher Robin. He thinks it is the only way to go down stairs. Still, he reasons, there might be a better way if only he could stop bumping long enough to figure it out.

REFERENCES

Adelman, H. S., & Taylor, L. (1997). Toward a scale-up model for replicating new approaches to schooling. *Journal of Educational and Psychological Consultation, 8,* 197–230.

Adelman, H. S., & Taylor, L. (2003). On sustainability of project innovations as systemic change. *Journal of Educational and Psychological Consultation, 14,* 1–25.

Allen, D. W. (1993). *Schools for a new century: A conservative approach to radical school reform.* New York: Praeger.

Hargreaves, A., & Fink, D. (2000). The three dimensions of reform. *Educational Leadership, 57,* 30–34.

Elmore, R. F. (2004). *School reform from the inside out: Policy, practice, and performance.* Cambridge, MA: Harvard Educational Publishing Group.

Fullan, M. (2005). Leadership & sustainability: System thinkers in action. Thousand Oaks, CA: Corwin.

Glennan, T. K., Bodilly, S. J., Galegher, J., & Kerr, K. A. (Eds.). (2004). *Expanding the reach of education reforms: Perspectives from leaders in the scale-up of educational interventions.* Santa Monica, CA: RAND.

Sarason, S. (1971). *The culture of school and the problem of change.* Boston: Allyn & Bacon.

Taylor, L., Nelson, P., & Adelman, H. S. (1999). Scaling up reforms across a school district. *Reading & Writing Quarterly, 15,* 303–326.

Thomas, R. M. (2002). *Overcoming inertia in school reform: How to successfully implement change.* Thousand Oaks, CA: Corwin.

Vander Ark, T. (2002). Toward success at scale. *Phi Delta Kappan, 84,* 322–326.

PART III

Resources

B esides the resources included throughout the volume, we wanted to provide a few others that folks around the country have found useful. They are designed to

- Enhance understanding of points presented in the foregoing chapters
- Provide additional aids for use in planning, advocacy, and staff and other stakeholder development

Included here are

- More About Understanding and Labeling Student Problems
- Student Support and Behavior Problems
- Reframing the Roles and Functions of Student Support Staff
- About Surveying How a School Is Addressing Barriers to Student Learning
- Natural Opportunities to Promote Social and Emotional Learning and Well-being
- About Mental Health in Schools
- New Directions for Student Support Initiative Brief: Assuring That No Child Is Left Behind
- Examples of Policy Statements
- Our Published Works and Center-produced Resources on Addressing Barriers to Learning
- Internet Sites for a Sampling of Major Agencies and Organizations Relevant to Learning Supports

For more resources we have helped develop and for links to even more, go to the Quick Find Online Clearinghouse for the Center for Mental Health in Schools at UCLA, http://smhp.psych.ucla.edu.

More About Understanding and Labeling Student Problems

11

An increasing number of youngsters with common learning and behavior problems are misdiagnosed as having *learning disabilities* (LD) or *attention-deficit/hyperactivity disorder* (ADHD). As a result, leaders for new directions for learning supports must be prepared to discuss this matter and to clarify implications for systemic changes. This brief reading provides a resource for doing so.

We cannot perceive unless we anticipate, but we must not see only what we anticipate.

—Ulric Neisser (1976)

Or as one colleague noted,

She wouldn't have seen it, if she hadn't believed it!

In Chapter 2, we discussed the question, *What causes student problems?* There are several matters related to this question that are worth a bit more exploration.

THE PROBLEM OF COMPELLING CLUES

At one time, there was a tribe of South Pacific natives who believed that lice were responsible for keeping a person healthy (Chase, 1956). They had noticed that almost all the healthy people in the tribe had lice, while those who were sick had no lice. So it seemed reasonable to them that lice caused good health.

A teacher-in-training working with children with learning or behavior problems notices that most of them are easily distracted and more fidgety than students without such problems. They are also less likely to listen or to do assignments well, and they often flit from one thing to another. The new teacher concludes that there is something physically wrong with these youngsters.

Every day we puzzle over our experiences and, in trying to make sense of them, arrive at conclusions about what caused them to happen. It is a very basic and useful part of human nature for people to try to understand cause and effect. Unfortunately, sometimes we are wrong. The South Pacific Islanders didn't know that sick people usually have a high fever, and since lice do not like the higher temperature, they jump off!

The teacher-in-training is right in thinking that some children with learning problems may have a biological condition that makes it hard for them to pay attention. However, with further training and experience, teachers learn that there are a significant number of students whose attention problems stem from a lack of interest or from the belief that they really can't do the work or from any number of other psychological factors.

Errors in Logic

Whenever I read the obituary column, I can never understand how people always seem to die in alphabetical order.

Because it is so compelling to look for causes, and because people so often make errors in doing so, logicians and scientists have spent a lot of time discussing the problem. Logicians point out the fallacy of assuming (as the Islanders did) that one event (lice) causes another (good health) just because the first event preceded the second. People make this type of error every time they *presume* that a person's learning or behavior problems are due to a difficult birth, a divorce, poor nutrition, or other factors that preceded the problem.

Another kind of logical error occurs when one event may affect another but only in a minor way, as part of a much more complicated set of events. There is a tendency to think that people who behave nicely have been brought up well by their parents. We all know, however, of cases in which the parents' actions seem to have very little to do with the child's behavior. This can be especially true of teenagers, who are strongly influenced by their friends.

A third logical error can arise when two events repeatedly occur together. After a while, it can become impossible to tell whether one causes the other or whether both are caused by something else. For instance, children with learning problems also frequently have behavior problems. Did the learning problem cause the behavior problem? Did the behavior problem cause the learning problem? Did poor parenting or poor teaching or poor peer models cause both? The longer these problems coexist, the harder it is to know.

Causes and Correlates

In trying to understand learning and behavior problems, researchers and practitioners look for all sorts of clues, or *correlates*. When faced with compelling clues, it is important to understand the difference between causes and correlates. *Correlates* are simply events that have some relation to each other: lice and good health, no lice and sickness, learning and behavior problems. A *cause* and its effect show a special type of correlation, one in which the nature of the relationship is known. Some events that occur together (i.e., are correlates) fit so well with "common sense" that we are quick to believe they are cause and effect. However, we may overlook other factors important in understanding the actual connection.

Some correlates are particularly compelling because they fit with current theories, attitudes, or policies. In general, once a problem is seen as severe enough to require referral for treatment, any other problem or relatively unusual characteristic or circumstance attracts attention. Often these other problems, characteristics, or circumstances seem to be connected by some cause-effect relationship. The more intuitively logical the connection, the harder it is to understand that they may not be causally related. They are compelling clues, but they may be misleading.

LD AND ADHD: CENTRAL NERVOUS SYSTEM DYSFUNCTIONS

LD and ADHD provide prominent examples of how cause and effect become muddled. In contrast to common learning problems, LD and ADHD are defined in theory as stemming from central nervous system (CNS) dysfunctions. The neurological dysfunction, however, is seen as relatively subtle or minor. That is, the learning and behavior problems are not considered the result of *gross* brain damage or the kind of severe CNS dysfunction associated with major disorders, such as cerebral palsy. As you read on, remember that the factors discussed can, but do not *always*, cause CNS dysfunctions, and when they do, the effects may be so minimal that they do not even result in learning and behavior problems.

Factors Causing Central Nervous System Problems

Factors that can cause CNS problems and lead to LD and ADHD can be grouped into four categories: (1) genetic, (2) prenatal (before birth), (3) perinatal (during birth), and (4) postnatal (after birth).

Genetic

There is a tendency to believe that the problem is inherited when a child with a learning or behavior problem has a parent who also has a similar problem. This is unfortunate since more often than not similar environmental factors may have caused the problem for both the parent and the child. Research has not demonstrated that genetic defects are a frequent cause of LD or ADHD. Clearly, genetic influences play a role in anyone's development. At the same time, the learning experiences that determine subsequent learning and behavior often are very similar for parents and their children.

For example, children often go to schools similar to those their parents attended. Parents often recreate the home environments they experienced as children. If books and reading were not important in the home where the father and mother grew up, the parents may not make much of an effort to provide books or to encourage their children to spend much time reading. In general, parents' attitudes and beliefs are "taught" to children in daily encounters. If parents don't like to read or if they think of themselves as having a learning problem, their children may soon learn the same attitudes. A child may see these attitudes as family traits and may model or adopt them. What has been passed on in such cases often is a *learned* behavior and not a genetic trait.

A few relatively rare genetic syndromes (e.g., neurofibromatosis) do appear to have a high probability of leading to learning problems. The transmission of such genetic abnormalities may produce abnormal brain structures, dysfunctional patterns of CNS maturation, biochemical irregularities, or a high risk for diseases that can impair the brain. When any of these occur, whether genetically caused or not, learning and behavior problems may follow.

Prenatal (Before Birth)

More commonly than genetic transmission, events in the first stages of life can lead to problems. Factors suggested as resulting in CNS malfunctioning before birth include (a) Rh factor incompatibility; (b) exposure to disease, such as German measles; (c) deficiencies in the mother's diet, such as vitamin or mineral deficiencies; (d) illnesses of the mother, such as diabetes, kidney disease, hypothyroidism, emotional stress; (e) exposure to radiation, such as x-rays; (f) use of certain drugs and medication by the mother; and (g) excessive use of cigarettes and other substances by the mother that may produce a shortage of oxygen. Because many of these prenatal factors are seen as causing premature birth, premature infants (those less than 5 1/2 pounds) are seen as being especially at risk for a variety of illnesses that may affect CNS development.

Perinatal (During Birth)

During labor and delivery, a few events can occur that may result in physical damage or oxygen deficiency affecting brain tissue. Perinatal factors, however, are not seen as frequent primary causes of learning disabilities. Those perinatal events that may cause problems include (a) intracranial hemorrhaging during labor due to prolonged difficulty in passing through the birth canal, (b) injury from forceps delivery, (c) deprivation of oxygen when the umbilical cord is wrapped around the infant's throat, and (d) various negative effects from some drugs used to induce labor and control postnatal hemorrhaging.

Postnatal (After Birth)

Many factors in subsequent stages of life may instigate CNS malfunctions. To simplify things, they may be categorized as including events or conditions leading to (a) destruction or deterioration of brain tissue and (b) biochemical irregularities that cause poor connections between brain cells or result in abnormal brain development. Specific examples of these kinds of events and conditions are head injuries, strokes, tumors, ingestion of toxic substances, poor nutrition (such as vitamin deficiencies), hypoglycemia, severe and chronic emotional stress, glandular disorders (such as calcium and thyroid imbalances), and diseases and illnesses that cause prolonged high fevers (such as meningitis and encephalitis).

How the Central Nervous System
Is Affected and Learning Is Disrupted

Because it is relatively easy and particularly compelling to suggest a variety of ways in which the brain fails to function appropriately and thus causes learning disabilities, let's focus in on this topic. Many theories have been offered. However, the more that is learned about CNS functioning, the more some of the theories are seen as too simplistic. Any factor that leads to hormonal, chemical, or blood flow imbalances may instigate some degree of CNS trouble. Yet only a few factors are likely to have more than temporary effects. When the effects are more than temporary, they take the form of CNS destruction or deterioration, delayed neurological maturation, development of abnormal brain structures, or malfunction of connections between brain cells.

Brain Injury and Dysfunction

Nerve cells in the brain (neurons) that are destroyed cannot be restored. It is comforting to note, however, that the human brain is estimated to have 12 billion neurons, and that as many as 10,000 die a natural death every day without apparent negative effect on brain functioning. Therefore, a small amount of damage can occur without severe consequences. In cases of brain injury, the nature and scope of dysfunction appears to depend, in part, on the amount of tissue damage. For example, as long as enough cells remain undamaged, there are instances where nondamaged cells take over specific functions. Also important in determining the effects of brain injury are its location and the stage of CNS development.

Any malfunctions in the connections necessary for the cells to communicate with each other (i.e., neural impulse transmission) can cause learning, behavior, and emotional problems. Communication between brain cells is carried out through an electrochemical process and is essential to effective learning and performance. Impulse transmission problems occur when a neuron is prevented from communicating with others or when the speed of transmission is too rapid or too slow. Dysfunctions in neural impulse transmission can be the result of endocrine malfunctions and chemical imbalances.

Developmental Lag

Not all theories about neurological causes focus on CNS dysfunction. Any of the instigating factors from the environment or other persons, as cited in Guide 2.2, can delay the rate of CNS maturation. It is widely hypothesized that persons whose neurological development is disrupted or is comparatively slow will lag behind their peers, especially in the early formative years. This slow development often is referred to as *maturational or developmental lag*. According to this view, children whose neurological development is not the same as that of others their age are not ready to learn the same tasks as the majority of their peers. At school, children who are lagging considerably behind others find that most classrooms cannot wait for them to catch up. It is this fact, not the developmental lag itself, that is seen as the instigating factor leading to learning problems.

For instance, the first-grade reading curriculum begins with the assumption that all students have a certain level of auditory and visual perceptual capability. (Perception is the psychological process by which a person organizes and makes sense out of incoming sensory information.) A child may have 20/20 vision but not be able to discriminate (perceptually distinguish) differences among letters. Youngsters who have yet to develop certain capabilities at the expected level usually are unable to handle parts of reading lessons at the expected time. As the teacher moves on to the next lesson, such students fall farther behind. A year or so later, neurological development will likely have advanced to a point where the youngster has the necessary physiological capability. But important basic skills will not have been learned yet.

In such cases (and in many cases in which CNS malfunctions produce only temporary disruptions in learning), subsequent learning problems are no longer due to the initial CNS factors. They are caused by the fact that the individual is missing certain skills that are prerequisites for subsequent learning. In effect, the missing skills make the youngster vulnerable to subsequent learning problems. Whether long-term problems emerge depends on how the environment responds to accommodate the vulnerability.

The sequence of events discussed to this point, beginning with initial instigating factors, is diagramed in the following graphic.

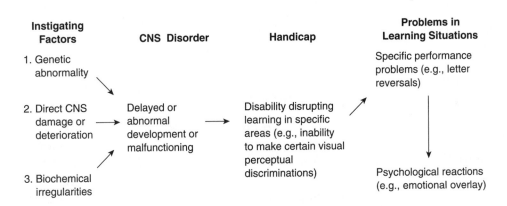

The sequence of events related to CNS disorders can be described as beginning with a *primary* instigating factor that produces the disorder (see diagram). In turn, the disorder can produce a handicap. In the case of disrupted learning resulting from a CNS disorder, such a handicap has come to be called a *learning disability*. Such a handicapping disability is seen as disrupting learning in specific areas (e.g., in associating meaning with symbols). As a result, learning problems become evident as the individual has trouble performing (e.g., during instruction at school).

The sequence of events becomes complicated after a CNS disorder causes learning problems. More often than not, the learning problems themselves cause more problems. Subsequent development, learning, and performance are disrupted. The impact on the individual can extend into all areas of learning and can be responsible for a variety of negative emotions, attitudes, and behaviors. The combination of performance problems and problems stemming from negative psychological effects often causes the learning problems to become worse. That is, these factors become secondary instigating factors leading to further handicapping conditions that cause specific learning problems to become wide-ranging performance and behavior problems.

In theory, then, it can be compelling to hypothesize that a youngster's learning and behavior problems were instigated initially by a CNS dysfunction. This tendency is abetted by the current state of the art related to diagnostic practices.

LIMITED BASES OF CURRENT LABELING PRACTICES

As illustrated in Guide 11.1, behaviors can be described in terms of normal variations or as common problems that do not warrant diagnosis as disorders. In contrast to this broad perspective, the thinking of those who study behavioral, emotional, and learning problems has long been dominated by models stressing *person* pathology. This is evident in discussions of cause, diagnosis, and intervention strategies. It is clearly reflected in the ways LD and ADHD are commonly described and defined.

Attention-deficit/Hyperactivity Disorder and Learning Disabilities

Efforts to describe ADHD often are considered too vague, fitting too many kids with commonplace problems. Moreover, because the widely used *Diagnostic and Statistical Manual of Mental Disorders, Fourth Edition* (*DSM-IV*, American Psychiatric Association [APA], 1994), emphasizes classifying person-based pathology (i.e., disorders and disabilities), the label often is applied without adequately accounting for psychosocial problems (see Guide 11.2).

The definition and diagnosis of *learning disabilities* also has been described as too vague. As currently stated in the 2004 reauthorization of the federal Individuals with Disabilities Education Act:

Guide 11.1 Developmental Variations and Problems

---

1. Developmental Variations: Behaviors Within the Range of Expected Behaviors for a Particular Age Group*

Developmental Variation

Hyperactive/Impulsive

Variation

Young children in infancy and in the preschool years are normally very active and impulsive and may need constant supervision to avoid injury. Their constant activity may be stressful to adults who do not have the energy or patience to tolerate the behavior.

During school years and adolescence, activity may be high in play situations, and impulsive behaviors may normally occur, especially in peer pressure situations.

High levels of hyperactive/impulsive behavior do not indicate a problem or disorder if the behavior does not impair functioning.

Common Developmental Variations

Infancy

Infants vary in their responses to stimulation. Some infants may be overactive to sensations such as touch and sound and may squirm away from the caregiver, while others may find it pleasurable to respond with increased activity.

Early Childhood

The child runs in circles, doesn't stop to rest, may bang into objects or people, and asks questions constantly.

Middle Childhood

The child plays active games for long periods. The child may occasionally do things impulsively, particularly when excited.

Adolescence

The adolescent engages in active social activities (e.g., dancing) for long periods and may engage in risky behaviors with peers.

Special Information

Activity should be thought of not only in terms of actual movement but also in terms of variations in responding to touch, pressure, sound, light, and other sensations. Also, for the infant and young child, activity and attention are related to the interaction between the child and the caregiver (e.g., when sharing attention and playing).

Activity and impulsivity often normally increase when the child is tired or hungry and decrease when sources of fatigue or hunger are addressed.

Activity may normally increase in new situations or when the child is anxious. Familiarity then reduces activity.

Both activity and impulsivity must be judged in the context of the caregiver's expectations and the level of stress experienced by the caregiver. When expectations are unreasonable, the stress level is high, and/or the parent has an emotional disorder (especially depression), the adult may exaggerate the child's level of activity/impulsivity.

Activity level is a variable of temperament. The activity level of some children is on the high end of normal from birth and continues to be high throughout their development.

2. Problems: Behaviors Serious Enough to Disrupt Functioning With Peers, at School, and at Home, But Not Severe Enough to Meet Criteria of a Mental Disorder*

Problem

Hyperactive/Impulsive

Behavior Problem

These behaviors become problems when they are intense enough to begin to disrupt relationships with others or to affect the acquisition of age-appropriate skills. The child displays some of the symptoms listed in the section on ADHD, predominantly hyperactive/impulsive subtype. However, the behaviors are not sufficiently intense to qualify for a behavioral disorder diagnosis, such as ADHD, or of a mood disorder (see section on Sadness and Related Symptoms) or anxiety disorder (see section on Anxiousness Symptoms).

A problem degree of this behavior is also likely to be accompanied by other behaviors, such as negative emotional behaviors or aggressive/oppositional behaviors.

Common Developmental Presentations

Infancy

The infant squirms and has early motor development with increased climbing. Sensory underreactivity and overreactivity as described in developmental variations can be associated with high activity levels.

Early Childhood

The child frequently runs into people or knocks things down during play, gets injured frequently, and does not want to sit for stories or games.

Middle Childhood

The child may butt into other children's games, interrupts frequently, and has problems completing chores.

Adolescence

The adolescent engages in "fooling around" that may annoy others and fidgets in class or while watching television.

Special Information

In infancy and early childhood, a problem level of these behaviors may be easily confused with cognitive problems, such as limited intelligence or specific developmental problems. However, cognitive problems and hyperactive/impulsive symptoms can occur simultaneously.

A problem level of these behaviors may also be seen from early childhood on, as a response to neglect, physical/sexual abuse, or other chronic stress, and this possibility should be considered.

SOURCE: *Adapted from American Academy of Pediatrics (1996).

Guide 11.2 Diagnostic Criteria for Attention-deficit/Hyperactivity Disorder

---

A. Either (1) or (2)

1. *Six (or more) of the following symptoms of inattention have persisted for at least six months to a degree that is maladaptive and inconsistent with developmental level:*

Inattention

    a. Often fails to give close attention to details or makes careless mistakes in school-work, work, or other activities
    b. Often has difficulty sustaining attention in tasks or play activities
    c. Often does not seem to listen when spoken to directly
    d. Often does not follow through on instructions and fails to finish schoolwork, chores, or duties in the workplace (not due to oppositional behavior or failure to understand instructions)
    e. Often has difficulty organizing tasks and activities
    f. Often avoids, dislikes, or is reluctant to engage in tasks that require sustained mental efforts (such as schoolwork or homework)
    g. Often loses things necessary for tasks or activities (e.g., toys, school assignments, pencils, books, or tools)
    h. Is often easily distracted by extraneous stimuli
    i. Is often forgetful in daily activities

2. *Six (or more) of the following symptoms of hyperactivity-impulsivity have persisted for at least six months to a degree that is maladaptive and inconsistent with developmental level:*

Hyperactivity

    a. Often fidgets with hands or feet or squirms in seat
    b. Often leaves seat in classroom in other situations in which remaining seated is expected
    c. Often runs about or climbs excessively in situations in which is it inappropriate
    d. Often has difficulty playing or engaging in leisure activities
    e. Is often "on the go" or often acts as if "driven by a motor"
    f. Often talks excessively

Impulsivity

    g. Often blurts out answers before questions have been completed
    h. Often has difficulty awaiting turn
    i. Often interrupts or intrudes on others (e.g., butts into conversations or games)

B. Some hyperactivity-impulsive or inattentive symptoms that caused impairment were present before age 7 years.

C. Some impairment from the symptoms is present in two or more settings (e.g., at school [or work] and at home).

D. There must be clear evidence of clinically significant impairment in social, academic, or occupational functioning.

SOURCE: From APA (1994).

a. *In General.* The term "specific learning disability" means a disorder in 1 or more of the basic psychological processes involved in understanding or in using language, spoken or written, which disorder may manifest itself in the imperfect ability to listen, think, speak, read, write, spell, or do mathematical calculations.

b. *Disorders Included.* Such term includes such conditions as perceptual disabilities, brain injury, minimal brain dysfunction, dyslexia, and developmental aphasia.

c. *Disorders Not Included.* Such term does not include a learning problem that is primarily the result of visual, hearing, or motor disabilities, of mental retardation, of emotional disturbance, or of environmental, cultural, or economic disadvantage.

Among the ongoing criticisms of this definition are: (a) the phrase "basic psychological processes" and that the list of inclusive conditions (e.g., perceptual handicaps, minimal brain dysfunction) are ill-defined and (b) the "exclusion" clause contributes to misconceptions (e.g., that LD cannot occur in conjunction with other handicapping conditions, environmental, cultural, or economic disadvantage).

Data from the National Center for Educational Statistics (U.S. Department of Education, 2000) indicate that 37% of fourth graders cannot read at a basic level. Best estimates suggest that at least 20% of elementary students in the United States have significant reading problems. Among those from poor families and those with limited English language skills, the percentage shoots up to 60%–70%. At the same time, best estimates suggest that minimally 95% of all children can be taught to read. Yet as noted in Chapter 2, by the late 1990s, about 50% of those students designated as in need of special education were labeled as LD.

These types of data have led to focusing on inadequate teaching as a cause of many learning problems, particularly reading problems. Not surprisingly, there is considerable controversy about this as well as about how to improve the situation. On one side are those who emphasize the instructional literature. They stress the use of direct reading instruction to ensure that students, especially in the early grades, learn to distinguish phonemic sounds, connect letters with the sounds they represent (phonics), decode words, and eventually learn to read fluently and with comprehension (National Institute of Child Health & Human Development [NICHD], 2000). With specific respect to LD, such direct instruction or "scientifically based reading instruction" is being advocated as the key to reducing the numbers labeled. The claim is that findings from early intervention and prevention studies suggest that "reading failure rates as high as 38–40 percent can be reduced to six percent or less" (Lyon, 1998). Thus, before a student is diagnosed, advocates want students provided with "well-designed and well-implemented early intervention." This approach to the problem of diagnosis is dubbed *response to intervention* (RTI). The notion has been included in the 2004 reauthorization of IDEA. It states that "in determining whether a child has a specific learning disability, a local educational agency may use a process that determines if the child responds to scientific, research-based intervention" as a part of the required evaluation procedures.

One controversy related to RTI stems from the emphasis on using the type of direct instruction described by the National Reading Panel sponsored by NICHD (2000). Direct instruction is heavily oriented to development of specific skills, with the skills explicitly laid out in lesson plans for teachers in published reading programs and with frequent testing to identify what has and hasn't been learned.

On the other side of the controversy are critics who argue that the evidence base for direct instruction is so limited that no one can be confident that the approach will produce the type of reading interest and abilities that college-bound students must develop. These professionals are especially critical of the work of the National Reading Panel, which they argue was overloaded with proponents of direct instruction and inappropriately relied on correlational data to infer causation.

Pathological Bias

Comprehensive *formal* systems used to classify youngsters experiencing problems tend to convey the impression that all behavioral, emotional, or learning problems are instigated by internal *pathology.* Most differential diagnoses of such problems are made by focusing on identifying one or more disorders (e.g., oppositional defiant disorder, attention-deficit/hyperactivity disorder, learning disabilities, or adjustment disorders), rather than first asking, *Is there a disorder?*

Bias toward classifying problems in terms of *personal* rather than *social causation* is bolstered by factors such as (a) attributional bias—a tendency for observers to perceive others' problems as rooted in stable personal dispositions (Miller & Porter, 1988) and (b) economic and political influences—whereby society's current priorities and other extrinsic forces shape professional practice (Becker, 1963; Byrnes, 2002; Coles, 1978; Hobbs, 1975; Prilleltensky & Nelson, 2002; Stainback & Stainback, 1995).

> There is a substantial community-serving component in policies and procedures for classifying and labeling exceptional children and in the various kinds of institutional arrangements made to take care of them. "To take care of them" can and should be read with two meanings: to give children help and to exclude them from the community.
>
> —Nicholas Hobbs (1975, pp. 20–21)

Overemphasis on classifying problems in terms of personal pathology skews theory, research, practice, and public policy. One example is seen in the fact that comprehensive classification systems do not exist for environmentally caused problems or for psychosocial problems caused by the transaction between internal and environmental factors. There is considerable irony in all this because so many practitioners who use prevailing diagnostic labels understand how many human problems result from the interplay of person and environment.

KEEPING LD AND ADHD IN PROPER PERSPECTIVE: TYPE I, II, AND III LEARNING AND BEHAVIOR PROBLEMS

Because of the scope of misdiagnosis, it is obvious that the assignment of the LD and ADHD labels is not a sufficient indication that an individual has an underlying dysfunction. Still, it remains scientifically valid to conceive of a subgroup (albeit a small subset) with neurologically based learning and behavior problems and to differentiate this subgroup from those with learning and behavior problems *caused* by other factors. A useful perspective for doing this is provided by the reciprocal determinist or transactional view of behavior described in Chapter 2. (Note that this view goes beyond taking an ecological perspective.)

Remember: a transactional perspective subsumes rather than replaces the idea that some learning and behavior problems stem from biological dysfunctions and differences. As we stressed, a transactional view acknowledges that there are cases in which an individual's disabilities predispose him or her to problems even in highly accommodating settings. At the same time, however, such a view accounts for instances in which the environment is so inadequate or hostile that individuals have problems despite having no disability. Finally, it recognizes problems caused by a combination of person and environment factors. One value of a broad transactional perspective, then, is that it shifts the focus from asking whether there is a biological deficit causing the problem to asking whether the causes are to be found in the person, the environment, or the reciprocal interplay of individual and environment.

In most cases, it is impossible to be certain what the cause of a specific individual's learning or behavior problem might be. Nevertheless, from a theoretical viewpoint, it makes sense to think of such problems as caused by different factors (see Guide 11.3 for a review or this point). And of course, a similar case can be made for a range of mental health and psychosocial concerns related to children and adolescents (Adelman, 1995; Adelman & Taylor, 1994).

Failure to differentiate LD and ADHD from other types of learning and behavior problems has caused a great deal of confusion and controversy. Currently, almost any individual with a learning or behavior problem

Guide 11.3   Placing LD and ADHD in Proper Perspective

By way of introduction, think about a random sample of students for whom learning or behavior problems are the *primary* problem (that is, the problem is not the result of seeing or hearing impairments, severe mental retardation, severe emotional disturbances, or autism). What makes it difficult for them to learn and behave appropriately? Theoretically, at least, it is reasonable to speculate that some may have a relatively minor internal disorder causing a *minor* CNS dysfunction that makes learning and behaving appropriately difficult even under good teaching circumstances. These are individuals for whom the terms *learning disabilities* and *ADHD* were created. In differentiating them from those with other types of learning and behavior problems, it may help if you visualize LD and ADHD as being at one end of a continuum. We call this group Type III problems.

Type III
Problems

Caused by internal factors,
such as minor CNS dysfunctioning
(e.g., LD, ADHD, other disorders)

At the other end of the continuum are individuals with problems that arise from causes outside the person. Such problems should not be called LD or ADHD. Obviously, some people do not learn or behave well when a learning situation is not a good one. It is not surprising that a large number of students who live in poverty and attend overcrowded schools manifest learning and psychosocial problems. Problems that are primarily the result of deficiencies in the environment in which learning takes place can be thought of as Type I problems.

Type I Problems	Type III Problems
Caused by factors outside the person	Caused by internal factors, such as minor CNS dysfunctioning (e.g., LD, ADHD, other disorders)

To provide a reference point in the middle of the continuum, we can conceive of a Type II learning problem group. This group consists of persons who do not learn or perform well in situations where their individual differences and vulnerabilities are poorly accommodated or are responded to with hostility. The learning problems of an individual in this group can be seen as a relatively equal product of the person's characteristics and the failure of the learning and teaching environment to accommodate to that individual.

Type I Problems	Type II Problems	Type III Problems
Caused by factors outside the person	Caused by person and environment factors	Caused by internal factors, such as minor CNS dysfunctioning (e.g., LD, ADHD, other disorders)

Primary Locus of Cause

stands a good chance of being diagnosed as having LD, ADHD, or both. As a result, many who do not have disabilities are treated as if they did. This leads to prescriptions of unneeded treatments for nonexistent or misidentified internal dysfunctions. It also interferes with efforts to clarify which interventions do and do not show promise for ameliorating different types of learning problems. Ultimately, keeping LD and ADHD in proper perspective is essential to improving both practice and research.

After the general groupings are identified, it becomes relevant to consider differentiating subgroups or subtypes. For example, subtypes for the Type III category might first differentiate learning, behavioral, and emotional problems arising from serious internal pathology (e.g., structural and functional malfunctioning within the person that cause disorders and disabilities and disrupt development). Then subtypes might be differentiated within each of these categories.

Such subtyping has long characterized discussions of LD (e.g., dyslexia, dyscalculia) and ADHD (e.g., inattentive, hyperactive-impulsive, combined subtypes). For broader illustrative purposes, Guide 11.4 presents some ideas for subgrouping Type I and III problems and Guide 11.5 presents ideas for further subtyping misbehavior within the Type I category. In formulating subtypes, basic dimensions, such as problem severity, pervasiveness, and chronicity, continue to play key roles as do considerations about development, gender, culture, and social class.

Our point in offering specific examples is not to argue for their adoption but to emphasize that discussion of classifying problems raises theoretical, practical, legal, and ethical matters of profound concern. The clearer the image people have of learning, behavior, and emotional problems, the sharper the discussion of cause and correction can be and the greater the chances are for advancing knowledge and preventing and correcting the full range of problems.

CONCLUDING COMMENTS

While it's good to give special help to those who need it, the tendency to ignore the fact that many commonplace learning, behavior, and emotional problems are misdiagnosed has compromised the integrity of practice and research. Confusion and controversy will reign supreme as long as some people use terms such as LD, ADHD, and depression to label common problems, and others think there is no such thing as an LD, ADHD, or clinical depression.

A broad understanding of what causes problems is essential, as is the need to approach all such problems in the context of fundamental ideas about learning and teaching. This is an essential key to enhancing efforts to address the multitude of problems confronting children and adolescents. And it will help avoid the type of backlash that came to a head during federal legislative reauthorization hearings in 2002 (see Guide 11.6).

Guide 11.4   A Categorization of Type I, II, and III Problems

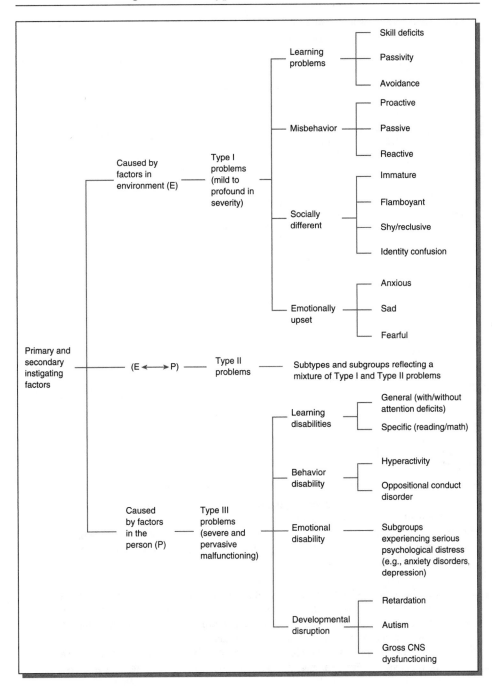

Guide 11.5 Subtyping Intentional Misbehavior: A Type I Problem

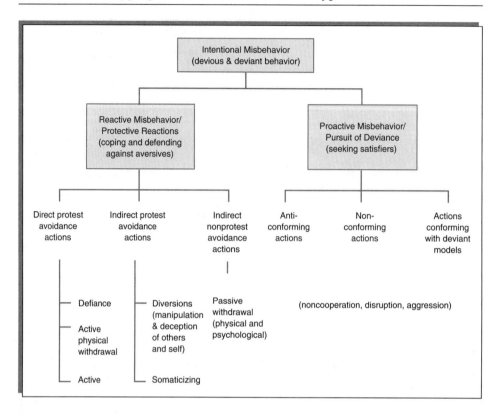

Guide 11.6 LD: The Backlash

With respect to reauthorization of IDEA, G. Reid Lyon (2002), Chief of the Child Development and Behavior Branch of the National Institute of Child Health and Human Development at the National Institutes of Health testified to Congress on June 6, 2002. He stated that the large and increasing number of individuals diagnosed as having learning disabilities stems from four factors:

First, the vague definition of LD currently in Federal law and the use of invalid eligibility criteria (e.g., IQ–achievement discrepancies) invite variability in identification procedures. For instance, LD identification processes, particularly with regard to how test scores are used, differ across states and even across local school districts within states. Thus the identification of students with LD is a highly subjective process. . . . For example, one state or local district may require a 22-point discrepancy between an IQ and an achievement test, while another state or district requires more or fewer points or does not require an IQ–achievement discrepancy calculation at all.

Second, and clearly related to increases in referral for assessment of LD, traditional approaches to reading instruction in the early grades have substantially underestimated the variability among children in their talent and preparation for learning to read. We have seen that many teachers have not been prepared to address and respond to the individual differences in learning that students bring to the classroom. A significant number of general education teachers report that their training programs did not prepare them to properly assess learner characteristics and provide effective reading instruction on the basis of these assessments, particularly to children with limited oral language and literacy experiences who arrive in the classroom behind in vocabulary development, print awareness abilities, and phonological abilities. Our data suggest that many of these youngsters have difficulties reading, not because they are LD but because they are initially behind and do not receive the classroom instruction that can build the necessary foundational language and early reading skills. If a student is not succeeding academically, general education teachers tend to refer them for specialized services. While some children require these services, many may only require informed classroom instruction from a wellprepared classroom teacher. . . .

Third, given that remediation of learning difficulties is minimally effective after the second grade, it is especially troubling that there has been a large increase in the identification of learning disabilities of students in the later grades. We have theorized that this is primarily due to students falling farther and farther behind in their academic progress because of reading difficulties and losing motivation to succeed rather than due to limitations in brain plasticity or the closing of "critical periods" in which learning can occur. Consider, during the time that students have been allowed to remain poor readers, they have missed out on an enormous amount of text exposure and reading practice compared to average readers. By one estimate, the number of words read by a middle school student who is a good reader approaches one million compared with 100,000 for a poor reader. In other words, reading failure seems to compound learning failure exponentially with every grade year passed. This difference places poor readers at a significant disadvantage with respect to vocabulary development, sight word development, and the development of reading fluency. In short, reading becomes an onerous chore, a chore that is frequently avoided.

Fourth, and related to the foregoing, the assessment and identification practices employed today under the existing definition of LD and the accompanying requirements of IDEA work directly against identifying children with LD before the second or even the third grade. Specifically, . . . the over reliance on the use of the IQ–achievement discrepancy criterion for the identification of LD means that a child must fail or fall below a predicted level of performance before he or she is eligible for special education services. Because achievement failure sufficient to produce a discrepancy from IQ cannot be reliably measured until a child reaches approximately nine years of age, the use of the IQ–achievement discrepancy literally constitutes a "wait to fail" model. Thus the youngster has suffered the academic and emotional strains of failure for two or three years or even more before potentially effective specialized instruction can be brought to bear. Thus it is not surprising that our NICHD longitudinal data show clearly that the majority of children who are poor readers at age nine or older continue to have reading difficulties into adulthood.

In summary, the increase in the incidence of LD over the past quarter century . . . particularly within the older age ranges, reflects the fact that federal policy as set out in the IDEA led to ineffective, inaccurate and frequently invalid identification practice . . . placing highly vulnerable children at further risk.

Given all this, Lyon (2002) recommended that the exclusionary criteria in the definition be replaced with evidence-based inclusionary criteria and the IQ discrepancy criterion be discontinued. This recommendation was included in the 2004 reauthorization of IDEA. It states that "a local educational agency shall not be required to take into consideration

Guide 11.6 (Continued)

whether a child has a severe discrepancy between achievement and intellectual ability in oral expression, listening comprehension, written expression, basic reading skill, reading comprehension, mathematical calculation, or mathematical reasoning." In addition, the reauthorized law states that "in determining whether a child has a specific learning disability, a local educational agency may use a process that determines if the child responds to scientific, research-based intervention" as a part of the required evaluation procedures.

REFERENCES

Adelman, H. S. (1995). Clinical psychology: Beyond psychopathology and clinical interventions. *Clinical Psychology: Science and Practice, 2,* 28–44.

Adelman, H. S., & Taylor, L. (1994). *On understanding intervention in psychology and education.* Westport, CT: Praeger.

American Academy of Pediatrics. (1996). *The classification of child and adolescent mental diagnoses in primary care.* Elk Grove Village, IL: Author.

American Psychiatric Association. (1994). *Diagnostic and statistical manual of mental disorders.* Washington, DC: Author.

Bandura, A. (1978). The self system in reciprocal determinism. *American Psychologist, 33,* 344–358.

Becker, H. S. (1963). *Outsiders: Studies in the sociology of deviance.* New York: Free Press.

Byrnes, M. A. (Ed.). (2002). *Taking sides: Clashing views on controversial issues in special education.* Guilford, CT: McGraw-Hill/Dushkin.

Chase, S. (1956). *Guides to straight thinking.* New York: Harper.

Coles, G. (1978). The learning-disabilities test battery: Empirical and social issues. *Harvard Educational Review, 48,* 313–340.

Hobbs, N. (1975). *The futures of children.* San Francisco: Jossey-Bass.

Lyon, G. R. (1998). *Testimony before the U.S. Senate Committee on Labor and Human Resources.* Retrieved March 12, 2005, from http://www.nichd.nih.gov/publications/pubs/jeffords.htm.

Lyon, G. R. (2002). *Testimony before the U.S. Senate Subcommittee for Educational Reform.* Retrieved March 12, 2005, from http://www.nih.gov.

Miller, D. T., & Porter, C. A. (1988). Errors and biases in the attribution process. In L. Y. Abramson (Ed.), *Social cognition and clinical psychology: A synthesis.* New York: Guilford.

National Center for Educational Statistics. (2000). *The digest of educational statistics.* Washington, DC: Institute of Education Sciences, U.S. Department of Education. Retrieved March 12, 2005, from www.nces.ed.gov/programs/digest.

National Institute of Child Health & Human Development. (2000). *Teaching children to read: An evidence-based assessment of the scientific research literature on reading and its implications for reading instruction* (National Reading Panel Report). Washington, DC: Retrieved April 20, 2005, from http://www.nichd.nih.gov/publications/nrp/report.pdf.

Neisser, U. (1976). *Cognition and reality: Principles and implications of cognitive psychology.* San Francisco: Freeman.

Prilleltensky, I., & Nelson, G. (2002). *Doing psychology critically: Making a difference in diverse settings.* New York: Palgrave Macmillan.

Stainback, W. C., & Stainback, S. B. (Eds.). (1995). *Controversial issues confronting special education: Divergent perspectives* (2nd ed.). Boston: Allyn & Bacon.

U.S. Department of Education, National Center for Educational Statistics. (2000). *The condition of education 2000* (NCES 2000–062). Washington, DC: U.S. Government Printing Office. Retrieved April 20, 2005, from http://nces.ed.gov/pubs2000/2000062_intro.pdf.

SUGGESTED READING

Brook-Gunn, J., & Duncan, G. J. (1997). The effects of poverty on children. *The Future of Children, 7*, 55–71.

Filipek, P. (1995). Neurobiologic correlates of developmental dyslexia: How do dyslexics' brains differ from those of normal readers? *Journal of Child Neurology, 10* (Suppl. 1), S62–S68.

Garbarino, J. (1995). *Raising children in a socially toxic environment.* San Francisco: Jossey-Bass.

Kibby, M., & Hynd, G. (2001). Neurological basis of learning disabilities. In D. Hallahan & B. Keogh (Eds.), *Research and global perspectives in learning disabilities: Essays in honor of William A. Cruickshank* (pp. 25–42). Mahwah, NJ: Erlbaum.

Pennington, B. (1995). Genetics of learning disabilities. *Journal of Child Neurology, 10* (Suppl. 1), S69–S77.

Rutter, M., & Maughan, B. (2002). School effectiveness findings. *Journal of School Psychology, 40*, 451–475.

Ryan, W. (1971). *Blaming the victim.* New York: Random House.

Scales, P. C., & Leffert, N. (1999). *Developmental assets.* Minneapolis: Search Institute.

Tallal, P., Miller, S., Jenkins, W., & Merzenich, M. (1997). The role of temporal processing in developmental language-based learning disorders: Research and clinical implications. In B. Blachman (Ed.), *Foundations of reading acquisition and dyslexia* (pp. 49–66). Mahwah, NJ: Erlbaum.

U.S. Census Bureau. (2000). *Households and families: Census 2000 Brief* (Issued September 2001). Washington, DC: U.S. Department of Commerce. Retrieved April 20, 2005, www.census.gov/prod/2001pubs/.

Zefferino, T., & Eden, G. (2000). The neural basis of developmental dyslexia. *Annals of Dyslexia, 50*, 3–30.

Student Support and Behavior Problems

12

As we have stressed, the welfare of those with learning, behavior, and emotional problems often depends on the ability of society, professionals, and parents to keep the difference between socialization and helping in perspective, to resolve conflicting interests appropriately, and to address behavior problems in ways that reengage students in classroom learning. This brief reading provides a resource for further clarifying such matters.

Discipline in the Classroom
Social Skills Training
About Addressing Underlying Motivation
     Misbehavior Can Reflect Proactive (Approach) or Reactive
       (Avoidance) Motivation
     Interventions for Reactive and Proactive Behavior Problems
       Begin With Major Program Changes
About Helping and Socialization

Because of the frequency with which a student may be misbehaving, teachers often feel they must deal with the behavior problem before they can work on the matters of engagement and accommodation. Let's take a close look at this concern.

In their effort to deal with deviant and devious behavior and create safe environments, teachers and other school staff increasingly have adopted social control practices. These include some *discipline* and *classroom management* practices that often model behavior that fosters (rather than counters) development of negative values.

To move beyond overreliance on punishment and social control strategies, there is ongoing advocacy for *social skills training* and new agendas for *emotional "intelligence" training* and *character education*. Relatedly, there are calls for greater home involvement, with emphasis on enhanced parent responsibility for their children's behavior and learning.

More comprehensively, there are efforts to transform classrooms and schools through the creation of an atmosphere of caring, cooperative learning, and a sense of community. This agenda allows for a holistic and family-centered orientation, with curricula that enhances personal responsibility (social and moral), integrity, self-regulation (self-discipline), a work ethic, diverse talents, and positive feelings about self and others.

DISCIPLINE IN THE CLASSROOM

Misbehavior disrupts; it may be hurtful; it may disinhibit others. When a student misbehaves, a natural reaction is to want that youngster to experience and other students to see the consequences of misbehaving. One hope is that public awareness of consequences will deter subsequent problems. As a result, the primary intervention focus in schools usually is on discipline—sometimes embedded in the broader concept of classroom management.

See Guide 12.1 for an overview of prevailing discipline practices.

Unfortunately, too many people see punishment as the only recourse in dealing with misbehavior. They use the most potent negative consequences available to them in a desperate effort to control an individual and make it clear to others that acting in such a fashion is not tolerated.

It is worth noting that a large literature points to the negative impact of various forms of parental discipline on internalization of values and of early harsh discipline on child aggression and formation of a maladaptive social information processing style. And a significant correlation has been found between corporal punishment of adolescents and depression, suicide, alcohol abuse, and wife beating.

In schools, short of suspending the individual, punishment essentially takes the form of doing something to the student that he or she does not want done. In addition, a demand for future compliance usually is made, along with threats of harsher punishment if compliance is not forthcoming. The discipline may be administered in ways that suggest that the student is seen as an undesirable person. As students get older, suspension increasingly comes into play. Indeed, suspension remains one of the most common disciplinary responses for the transgressions of secondary students.

As with many emergency procedures, the benefits of using punishment may be offset by many negative consequences. These include increased negative attitudes toward school and school personnel. These attitudes

Guide 12.1 Defining and Categorizing Discipline Practices

The two mandates that shape much of current practice are that (1) schools must teach self-discipline to students and (2) teachers must learn to use disciplinary practices effectively to deal with misbehavior.

Knoff (1987) offers three definitions of discipline as applied in schools:

(a) . . . punitive intervention; (b) . . . a means of suppressing or eliminating inappropriate behavior, of teaching or reinforcing appropriate behavior, and of redirecting potentially inappropriate behavior toward acceptable ends; and (c) . . . a process of self-control whereby the (potentially) misbehaving student applies techniques that interrupt inappropriate behavior, and that replace it with acceptable behavior. (p. 119)

In contrast to the first definition, which specifies discipline as punishment, Knoff sees the other two as nonpunitive or, as he calls, them "positive, best-practices approaches."

Hyman, Flannagan, and Smith (1982) categorize models shaping disciplinary practices into five groups: psychodynamic interpersonal models, behavioral models, sociological models, eclectic-ecological models, and human potential models.

Wolfgang and Glickman (1986) group disciplinary practices in terms of a process-oriented framework:

- Relationship-listening models (e.g., Gordon's Teacher Effectiveness Training, values clarification approaches, transactional analysis)
- Confronting-contracting models (e.g., Dreikurs' approach, Glasser's Reality Therapy)
- Rules/rewards-punishment (e.g., Canter's Assertive Discipline)

Bear (1995) offers three categories in terms of the goals of the practice, with a secondary nod to processes, strategies, and techniques used to reach the goals:

- Preventive discipline models (e.g., models that stress classroom management, prosocial behavior, moral/character education, social problem solving, peer mediation, affective education, and communication models)
- Corrective models (e.g., behavior management, Reality Therapy)
- Treatment models (e.g., social skills training, aggression replacement training, parent management training, family therapy, behavior therapy)

often lead to more behavior problems, antisocial acts, and various mental health problems. Disciplinary procedures also are associated with dropping out of school. It is not surprising, then, that some concerned professionals refer to extreme disciplinary practices as *pushout strategies.*

Most school guidelines for managing misbehavior stress that discipline should be reasonable, fair, and nondenigrating (e.g., it should be experienced by recipients as legitimate reactions that neither denigrate one's sense of worth nor reduce one's sense of autonomy). With this in

Guide 12.2   About Logical Consequences

In classrooms, there may be little ambiguity about the rules; unfortunately, the same cannot often be said about "logical" penalties. Even when the consequence for a particular rule infraction has been specified ahead of time, its logic may be more in the mind of the teacher than in the eyes of the students. In the recipient's view, any act of discipline may be experienced as punitive—unreasonable, unfair, denigrating, disempowering.

Basically, consequences involve depriving students of things they want or making them experience something they don't want. Consequences take the form of (a) removal or deprivation (e.g., loss of privileges, removal from an activity), (b) reprimands (e.g., public censure), (c) reparations (e.g., to compensate for losses caused by misbehavior), and (d) recantations (e.g., apologies, plans for avoiding future problems). For instance, teachers commonly deal with acting-out behavior by removing a student from an activity. To the teacher, this step (often described as "time-out") may be a logical way to stop the student from disrupting others by isolating him or her, or the logic may be that the student needs a cooling-off period. It may be reasoned that (a) by misbehaving, the student has shown that he or she does not deserve the privilege of participating (assuming the student likes the activity) and (b) the loss will lead to improved behavior in order to avoid future deprivation.

Most teachers have little difficulty explaining their reasons for using a consequence. However, if the intent really is to have students perceive consequences as logical and nondebilitating, it seems logical to determine whether the recipient sees the discipline as a legitimate response to misbehavior. Moreover, it is well to recognize the difficulty of administering consequences in a way that minimizes the negative impact on a student's perceptions of self. Although the intent is to stress that it is the misbehavior and its impact that are bad, the student can too easily experience the process as a characterization of her or him as a bad person.

Organized sports, such as youth basketball and soccer, offer prototypes of an established and accepted set of consequences administered with the recipients' perceptions given major consideration. In these arenas, the referee is able to use the rules and related criteria to identify inappropriate acts and apply penalties and is expected to do so with positive concern for maintaining the youngsters' dignity and engendering respect for all.

If discipline is to be perceived as a logical consequence, steps must be taken to convey that a response is not a personally motivated act of power (e.g., an authoritarian action) and, indeed, is a rational and socially agreed-upon reaction. Also, if the intent is long-term reduction in future misbehavior, it may be necessary to take time to help students learn right from wrong, to respect others' rights, and to accept responsibility.

From a motivational perspective, it is essential that logical consequences be based on understanding of a student's perceptions and used in ways that minimize negative repercussions. To these ends, motivation theorists suggest (a) establishing a publicly accepted set of consequences to increase the likelihood that they are experienced as socially just (e.g., reasonable, firm but fair) and (b) administering such consequences in ways that allow students to maintain a sense of integrity, dignity, and autonomy. These ends are best achieved under conditions where students are empowered (e.g., are involved in deciding how to make improvements and avoid future misbehavior and have opportunities for positive involvement and reputation building at school).

mind, classroom management practices usually emphasize establishing and administering *logical consequences*. Such an idea is generalized from situations where there are naturally occurring consequences (e.g., you touch a hot stove, you get burned). See Guide 12.2 for more on the topic of logical consequences.

SOCIAL SKILLS TRAINING

Suppression of undesired acts does not necessarily lead to desired behavior. It is clear that more is needed than classroom management and disciplinary practices.

Is the answer social skills training? After all, poor social skills are identified as a symptom (a correlate) and a contributing factor in a wide range of educational, psychosocial, and mental health problems.

Programs to improve social skills and interpersonal problem solving are described as having promise for both prevention and correction. However, reviewers tend to be cautiously optimistic because studies to date have found that the range of skills acquired is quite limited, and generalizability and maintenance of outcomes are poor. This is the case for training of specific skills (e.g., what to say and do in a specific situation), general strategies (e.g., how to generate a wider range of interpersonal problem-solving options), as well as efforts to develop cognitive-affective orientations (e.g., empathy training). Reviews of social skills training over the past two decades conclude that individual studies show effectiveness, but outcomes continue to lack generalizability and social validity. (While their focus is on social skills training for students with emotional and behavior disorders, their conclusions hold for most populations.) (For specific information on curriculum content areas for fostering social and emotional development, see Collaborative for Academic, Social, and Emotional Learning [CASEL] at www.casel.org.)

Specific discipline practices ignore the broader picture that every classroom teacher must keep in mind: *The immediate objective of stopping misbehavior must be accomplished in ways that maximize the likelihood that the teacher can engage or reengage the student in instruction and positive learning.*

From a prevention viewpoint, there is widespread awareness that program improvements can reduce behavior (and learning) problems significantly. It also is recognized that the application of consequences is an insufficient step in preventing future misbehavior. Therefore, as outlined in Guide 12.3, interventions for misbehavior should be conceived in terms of

- Efforts to prevent and anticipate misbehavior
- Actions to be taken during misbehavior
- Steps to be taken afterwards

ABOUT ADDRESSING UNDERLYING MOTIVATION

Beyond discipline and skills training is a need to address the roots of misbehavior, especially the underlying motivational bases for such behavior. Consider students who spend most of the day trying to avoid all or part of the instructional program. An intrinsic motivational interpretation of the

Guide 12.3   Intervention Focus in Dealing With Misbehavior

I. Preventing Misbehavior

A. Expand Social Programs.

1. Increase economic opportunity for low-income groups.

2. Augment health and safety prevention and maintenance (encompassing parent education and direct child services).

3. Extend quality day care and early education.

B. Improve Schooling.

1. Personalize classroom instruction (e.g., accommodating a wide range of motivational and developmental differences).

2. Provide status opportunities for nonpopular students (e.g., offer special roles as assistants and tutors).

3. Identify and remedy skill deficiencies early.

C. Follow Up All Occurrences of Misbehavior to Remedy Causes.

1. Identify underlying motivation for misbehavior.

2. For unintentional misbehavior, strengthen coping skills (e.g., social skills, problem-solving strategies).

3. If misbehavior is intentional but reactive, work to eliminate conditions that produce reactions (e.g., conditions that make the student feel incompetent, controlled, or unrelated to significant others).

4. For proactive misbehavior, offer appropriate and attractive alternative ways that the student can pursue a sense of competence, control, and relatedness.

5. Equip the individual with acceptable steps to take instead of misbehaving (e.g., options to withdraw from a situation or to try relaxation techniques).

6. Enhance the individual's motivation and skills for overcoming behavior problems (including altering negative attitudes toward school).

II. Anticipating Misbehavior

A. Personalize Classroom Structure for High Risk Students.

1. Identify underlying motivation for misbehavior.

2. Design curricula to consist primarily of activities that are a good match with the identified individual's intrinsic motivation and developmental capability.

3. Provide extra support and direction so the identified individual can cope with difficult situations (including steps that can be taken instead of misbehaving).

B. Develop Consequences for Misbehavior That Are Perceived by Students as Logical (i.e., perceived as reasonable, fair, and nondenigrating reactions that do not reduce one's sense of autonomy).

III. During Misbehavior

A. *Try to Base Response on Understanding of Underlying Motivation (if uncertain, start with assumption the misbehavior is unintentional).*

B. *Reestablish a Calm and Safe Atmosphere.*

1. Use understanding of student's underlying motivation for misbehaving to clarify what occurred (if feasible, involve participants in discussion of events).

2. Validate each participant's perspective and feelings.

3. Indicate how the matter will be resolved, emphasizing the use of previously agreed-upon logical consequences that have been personalized in keeping with understanding of underlying motivation.

4. If the misbehavior continues, revert to a firm but nonauthoritarian statement.

5. As a last resort, use crisis backup resources.
   a. If appropriate, ask student's classroom friends to help.
   b. Call for help from identified backup personnel.

6. Throughout the process, keep others calm by dealing with the situation with a calm and protective demeanor.

IV. After Misbehavior

A. *Implement Discipline: Logical Consequences.*

Remember:

1. Consequences
   a. Deprive a student of something he or she wants
   b. Make the student experience something he or she doesn't want

2. Consequences may take the form of
   a. Removing or depriving the student of something desired (e.g., loss of privileges, removal from activity)
   b. Reprimanding the student (e.g., public censure)
   c. Arranging for reparations to be made by the student (e.g., of damaged or stolen property)
   d. Asking for recantations (e.g., apologies, plans for avoiding future problems)

B. *Discuss the Problem With Parents.*

1. Explain how they can avoid exacerbating the problem.

2. Mobilize them to work preventively with the school.

C. *Work Toward the Prevention of Further Occurrences (see I & II).*

avoidance behavior of many of these youngsters is that it reflects their perception that school is not a place where they experience a sense of competence, autonomy, and or relatedness to others. Over time, these perceptions develop into strong motivational dispositions and related patterns of misbehavior.

Misbehavior Can Reflect Proactive
(Approach) or Reactive (Avoidance) Motivation

Noncooperative, disruptive, and aggressive behavior patterns that are *proactive* tend to be rewarding and satisfying to an individual because the behavior itself is exciting or because the behavior leads to desired outcomes (e.g., peer recognition, feelings of competence or autonomy). Intentional negative behavior stemming from such approach motivation can be viewed as pursuit of deviance.

Misbehavior in the classroom often also is *reactive*, stemming from avoidance motivation. This behavior can be viewed as a protective reaction. Students with learning problems can be seen as motivated to avoid and to protest against being forced into situations in which they cannot cope effectively. For such students, many teaching and therapy situations are perceived in this way. Under such circumstances, individuals can be expected to react by trying to protect themselves from the unpleasant thoughts and feelings that the situations stimulate (e.g., feelings of incompetence, loss of autonomy, negative relationships). In effect, the misbehavior reflects efforts to cope and defend against aversive experiences. The actions may be direct or indirect and include defiance, physical and psychological withdrawal, and diversionary tactics.

Interventions for Reactive and Proactive
Behavior Problems Begin With Major Program Changes

From a motivational perspective, the aims are to (a) prevent and overcome negative attitudes toward school and learning, (b) enhance motivational readiness for learning and overcoming problems, (c) maintain intrinsic motivation throughout learning and problem solving, and (d) nurture the type of continuing motivation that results in students' engaging in activities away from school that foster maintenance, generalization, and expansion of learning and problem solving. Failure to attend to motivational concerns in a comprehensive, normative way results in approaching passive and often hostile students with practices that instigate and exacerbate problems.

After making broad programmatic changes to the degree feasible, intervention with a misbehaving student involves remedial steps directed at underlying factors. For instance, with intrinsic motivation in mind, the following assessment questions arise:

- Is the misbehavior unintentional or intentional?
- If it is intentional, is it reactive or proactive?
- If the misbehavior is reactive, is it a reaction to threats to self-determination, competence, or relatedness?
- If it is proactive, are there other interests that might successfully compete with satisfaction derived from deviant behavior?

In general, intrinsic motivation theory suggests that corrective interventions for those misbehaving reactively require steps designed to reduce reactance and enhance positive motivation for participation. For youngsters highly motivated to pursue deviance (e.g., those who proactively engage in criminal acts), even more is needed. Intervention might focus on helping these youngsters identify and follow through on a range of valued, socially appropriate alternatives to deviant activity. Such alternatives must be capable of producing greater feelings of self-determination, competence, and relatedness than usually result from the youngster's deviant actions. To these ends, motivational analyses of the problem can point to corrective steps for implementation by teachers, clinicians, parents, or the students themselves.

ABOUT HELPING AND SOCIALIZATION

A concern arising when intervention focuses on deviant behavior is whether the agenda is to help or to socialize or both. The key to differentiating between helping and formal socialization interventions is determining primary intent with respect to whose interests are to be served (see Guide 12.4). Helping interventions are defined in terms of a primary intention to serve the client's interests; socialization through formal intervention primarily seeks to serve the interests of the society.

How does one know whose interests are served? This can be defined with reference to the nature of the consent and ongoing decision-making processes. That is, by definition, the individual's interests are served when he or she consents to intervention without coercion and has control over major intervention decisions. In contrast, socialization agendas usually are implemented under a form of social contract that allows society's agents to decide on certain interventions for the individual without asking for consent, and in the process, society maintains control over intervention decisions.

Situations arise when the intent is to serve the individual's interest, but it is not feasible to elicit truly informed consent or ensure that the individual has control. Then one is forced to operate in a gray area. This is quite likely to arise with young children and those with severe and profound learning and behavior problems. One also is working in a gray area when intervening at the request of a surrogate who sees the intervention as in a person's best interests despite the individual's protests to the contrary.

Conflict in the form of socialization versus helping can be expected whenever decisions are made about interventions to deal with behavior the majority of a social group find disruptive or view as inappropriate. Such a conflict can arise, for example, in dealing with children who misbehave at school.

One major reason for *compulsory* education is that society wants schools to act as socializing agencies. For example, when James misbehaved at

Guide 12.4   Helping and Socialization Interventions

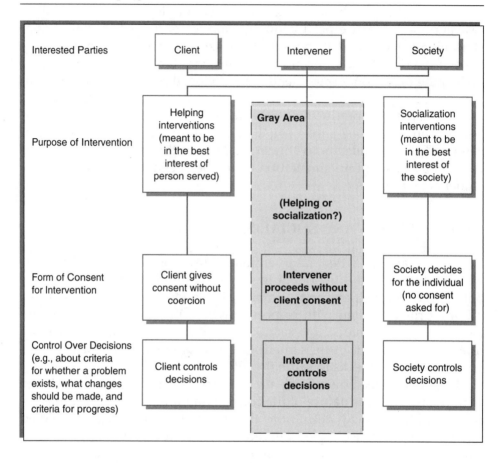

school, the teacher's job was to bring the deviant and devious behavior under control. Interventions were designed to convince James that he should conform to the proscribed limits of the social setting. His parents valued the school's socializing agenda but also wanted him to receive special help at school for what they saw as an emotionally based problem. James, like most children, did not appreciate the increasing efforts to control his behavior, especially since many of his actions were intended to enable him to escape such control. Under the circumstances, not only was there conflict among the involved parties, it is likely that the teacher's intervention efforts actually caused James to experience negative emotional and behavior reactions.

It is commonplace for practitioners to be confronted with situations where socialization and helping agendas are in conflict. Some resolve the conflict by clearly defining themselves as socializing agents and in that role pursue socialization goals. In such a context, it is understood that helping is not the primary concern. Others resolve the conflict by viewing individuals as clients and pursuing interventions that can be defined as helping. In such cases, the goal is to work with the consenting individual to resolve learning and behavior problems, including efforts designed to make environments more accommodative of individual differences. Some practitioners are unclear about their agendas or are forced by circumstances to try to pursue helping and socialization goals simultaneously, and this adds confusion to an already difficult situation.

The problem of conflicting agendas is particularly acute for those who work in institutional settings, such as schools and residential treatment centers. In such settings, the tasks confronting the practitioner often include both aspects: helping individuals overcome underlying problems and controlling misbehavior to maintain social order. At times, the two are incompatible. And although all interventions in the setting may be designated as "remediation" or "treatment," the need for social control can overshadow the concern for helping. Moreover, the need to control individuals in such settings has led to coercive and repressive actions. Ultimately, every practitioner must personally come to grips with what he or she views as morally proper in balancing the respective rights of the various parties when interests conflict.

REFERENCES

Bear, G. G. (1995). Best practices in school discipline. In A. Thomas & J. Grimes (Eds.), *Best practices in school psychology III.* Washington, DC: National Association of School Psychologists.

Hyman, I., Flannagan, D., & Smith, K. (1982). Discipline in the schools. In C. R. Reynolds & T. B. Gutkin (Eds.), *The handbook of school psychology.* New York: Wiley.

Knoff, H. M. (1987). School-based interventions for discipline problems. In C. A. Maher & J. Zins (Eds.), *Psychoeducational interventions in the schools.* New York: Pergamon.

Wolfgang, C. H., & Glickman, C. D. (1986). *Solving discipline problems: Strategies for classroom teachers* (2nd ed.). Boston: Allyn & Bacon.

Reframing the Roles and Functions of Student Support Staff

13

Moving in new directions for student support requires rethinking personnel roles and functions. The following analysis and framework were developed as part of a report stemming from work with a group convened by one state's school credentialing office.

The full report is online at http://smhp.psych.ucla.edu/pdfdocs/Report/framingnewdir.pdf.

Areas of Function, Levels of Professional Development, and Nature and Scope of Competencies

---

Many influences are reshaping the work of pupil services staff and other learning supports staff. Besides changes called for by the growing knowledge in various disciplines and fields of practice, initiatives to restructure education and community health and human services are creating new roles and functions. Clearly, staff for learning supports are needed to provide targeted direct assistance and support. At the same time, their roles as advocates, catalysts, brokers, and facilitators of systemic reform can be expected to expand. As a result, they will engage in an increasingly wide array of activity to promote academic achievement and healthy development and address barriers to student learning. In doing so, they must be prepared to improve intervention outcomes by enhancing coordination and collaboration within a school and with community resources to deal cohesively with the complex concerns confronting schools.

The trend in school improvement is toward less emphasis on intervention ownership and more attention to accomplishing desired outcomes through flexible and expanded roles and functions for staff. This trend recognizes underlying commonalities among a variety of school concerns and intervention strategies and is fostering increased interest in cross-disciplinary training and interprofessional education. All this has major implications for changing professional preparation and credentialing.

Efforts to capture key implications are illustrated in the framework outlined in Guide 13.1. This framework was sketched out by an expert panel convened by one state's credentialing commission to provide guidelines for revision of the state's standards for developing and evaluating pupil services personnel credential programs.

The following section should help to clarify major aspects of the framework.

AREAS OF FUNCTION, LEVELS OF PROFESSIONAL DEVELOPMENT, AND NATURE AND SCOPE OF COMPETENCIES

Three basic dimensions are outlined to guide the rethinking of preparation programs. As highlighted in Guide 13.2, the emphasis is on four major areas of staff function:

1. Direct interventions with students and families

2. Interventions to enhance systems within schools

3. Interventions to enhance school-community linkages and partnerships

4. Supervision and administration

Within each area are sets of generic and specialized competencies that are learned at various levels of professional development. There is a need to develop criteria with respect to each of these areas (see examples in Guide 13.2). Of course, the number of criteria and the standards used to judge performance vary with the specific job assignment and level of professional development.

Although some new knowledge, skills, and attitudes are learned, *specialized* competence is seen as emerging primarily from increasing one's breadth and depth related to generic competencies. Clearly, such specialized learning is shaped by one's field of specialization (e.g., school counselor, psychologist, social worker, nurse) as well as by prevailing views of job demands.

Note that most competencies for supervision and administration are left for development at Level IV. Also note that crosscutting all dimensions are foundational knowledge, skills, and attitudes related to such topics as (a) human growth, development, and learning; (b) interpersonal and group relationships, dynamics, and problem solving; (c) cultural competence; (d) group and individual differences; (e) intervention theory; (f) legal, ethical, and professional concerns; and (g) applications of advanced technology.

Guide 13.1   Areas of Function, Levels of Professional Development, and Nature and Scope of Competencies

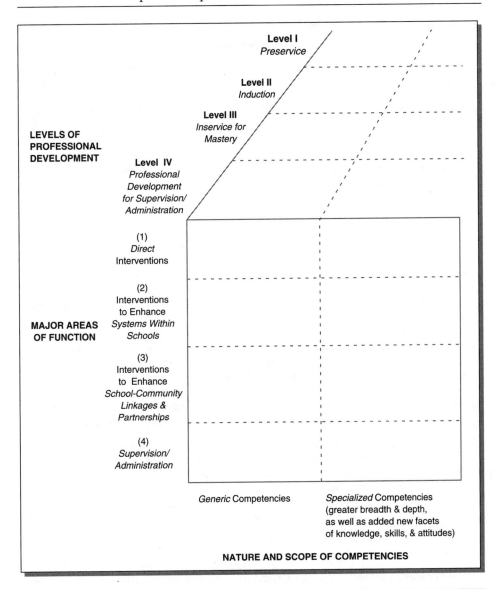

Notes: Crosscutting all dimensions are foundational knowledge, skills, and attitudes related to such topics as (a) human growth, development, and learning; (b) interpersonal and group relationships, dynamics, and problem solving; (c) cultural competence; (d) group and individual differences; (e) intervention theory; (f) legal, ethical, and professional concerns; and (g) applications of advanced technology.

a. *Direct* interventions = Implementing one-to-one, group, or classroom programs and services

b. Interventions to enhance *systems within schools* = Coordination, development, and leadership related to programs, services, resources, and systems

c. Interventions to enhance *school-community linkages and partnerships* = Connecting with community resources

d. *Supervision/Administration* = Responsibility for training pupil personnel and directing pupil personnel services and programs

Guide 13.2   Examples of Generic Criteria for Staff Performance in Each Area of Function

---

1. Direct Interventions With Students and Families

Student Support: Demonstrates the ability to plan, implement, and evaluate programs and services that equitably address barriers to learning and promote healthy development among a diverse range of students (e.g., developmental and motivational assessments of students, regular and specialized assistance for students in and outside the classroom, prereferral interventions, universal and targeted group interventions, safe and caring school interventions, academic and personal counseling, support for transitions)

Family Assistance: Demonstrates the ability to plan, implement, and evaluate programs and services for students' families whenever necessary to enhance student support (e.g., providing information, referrals, and support for referral follow-through; instruction; counseling; home involvement)

2. Interventions to Enhance *Systems Within Schools*

Coordination and Integration of Programs, Services, and Systems: Demonstrates the ability to plan, implement, and evaluate *mechanisms* for collaborating with colleagues to ensure that activities are carried out in the most equitable and cost-effective manner consistent with legal and ethical standards for practice (examples of mechanisms include case-oriented teams; resource-oriented teams; consultation, coaching, and mentoring mechanisms; triage, referral, and care monitoring systems; crisis teams)

Development of Programs, Services, and Systems: Demonstrates the ability to enhance development of a comprehensive, multifaceted, and integrated continuum of interventions for equitably addressing barriers to learning and promoting healthy development among a diverse range of students and their families (e.g., collaborates in improving existing interventions; collaborates to develop ways to fill gaps related to needed prevention programs, early-after-onset interventions, and assistance for students with severe or chronic problems; incorporates an understanding of legal and ethical standards for practice)

3. Interventions to Enhance School-Community Linkages and Partnerships

Coordination and Integration of School-Community Resources and Systems: Demonstrates the ability to plan, implement, and evaluate *mechanisms* for collaborating with community entities to weave together school and community resources and systems to enhance current activity and enhance development of a comprehensive, multifaceted, and integrated continuum of interventions for equitably addressing barriers to learning and promoting healthy development

4. Supervision and Administration

Supervision of Professionals-in-Training and Induction of New Staff: Demonstrates the ability to coach, mentor, and supervise professionals-in-training and newly hired pupil services personnel with respect to both generic and specialty functions

Administration of Pupil Services: Demonstrates the ability to design, manage, and build capacity of personnel and programs with respect to specialized pupil services activities and generic systemic approaches to equitably addressing barriers to learning and promoting healthy development

Administrative Leadership in the District: Demonstrates the ability to participate effectively in district decision making to advance an equitable and cost-effective role for pupil services personnel in addressing barriers to learning and promoting healthy development

In addition to the foregoing, each field (e.g., school psychology, counseling, social work, nursing) will want to add several specialized competencies.

About Surveying How a School Is Addressing Barriers to Student Learning

14

Addressing barriers to student learning and moving in new directions involve careful analyses of resource use in the context of needs and priorities. The process begins with mapping all existing learning supports activity.

This resource aid provides some tools and highlights some strategies for mapping what a school is doing to address barriers to learning. The findings can provide a data-driven basis for analyzing resource use and identifying gaps related to needs and priorities for enhancing learning supports.

> Mapping, Analyzing, and Enhancing Resources
> Some Tools to Aid Mapping

S chools already have a variety of programs and services to address barriers and promote development. These range from Title I programs, through extra help for low-performing students, to accommodations for special education students. In some places, the personnel and programs to support learning may account for as much as 25%–30% of the resources expended by a school. However, because school leaders have been so focused on instruction, too little attention is paid to the need for and potential impact of rethinking how these resources can be used to enable student learning.

Critical steps in enhancing learning supports involve (a) taking stock of the resources already being expended and (b) considering how these valuable resources can be used to the greatest effect. These matters involve a variety of functions and tasks we encompass under the theme of mapping, analyzing, and enhancing resources.

MAPPING, ANALYZING, AND ENHANCING RESOURCES

In most schools and community agencies, there is redundancy stemming from ill-conceived policies and lack of coordination. These facts do not translate into evidence that there are pools of unneeded personnel and programs; they simply suggest that there are resources that can be used in different ways to address unmet needs. Given that additional funding always is hard to come by, redeployment of resources is the primary answer to the ubiquitous question, *Where will we find the funds?* A primary and essential task in improving the current state of affairs, therefore, is to enumerate (map) existing school and community programs and services aimed at supporting students, families, and staff. Such mapping is followed by analyses of what is available, effective, and needed. The analysis provides a sound basis for formulating strategies to link with additional resources at other schools, district sites, and in the community and to enhance use of existing resources. Such analyses also can guide efforts to improve cost-effectiveness. In a similar fashion, mapping and analyses of a complex or family of schools provide information to guide strategies to enhance intervention effectiveness and garner economies of scale.

Carrying out the functions and tasks related to mapping, analyzing, and managing resources is, in effect, an intervention for systemic change. For example,

- A focus on these matters highlights the reality that the school's current infrastructure probably requires some revamping to ensure that there is a mechanism focusing on resources and ongoing development of a comprehensive approach to addressing barriers to learning.
- By identifying and analyzing existing resources (e.g., personnel, programs, services, facilities, budgeted dollars, social capital), awareness is heightened of their value and potential for playing a major role in helping students engage and reengage in learning at school.
- Analyses also lead to sophisticated recommendations for deploying and redeploying resources to improve programs, enhance cost-effectiveness, and fill programmatic gaps in keeping with well-conceived priorities.
- The products from mapping can be invaluable for social marketing efforts designed to show teachers, parents, and other community stakeholders all that the school is doing to address barriers to learning and promote healthy development.

Enhanced appreciation of the importance of resource mapping, analysis, and management may lead to a desire to move too quickly in doing the tasks in order to get on with the "real business." This is unwise. Resource mapping and management is real business and the tasks are ongoing.

Generally speaking, mapping usually is best done in stages, and the information requires constant updating and analysis. Most schools find it convenient to do the easiest forms of mapping first and build the capacity to do in-depth mapping over a period of months. Similarly, initial analyses and management of resources focus mostly on enhancing understanding of what exists and coordinating resource use. Over time, the focus is on spreadsheet-type analyses, priority recommendations, and braiding resources together to enhance cost-effectiveness and fill programmatic gaps. Guide 14.1 outlines matters related to mapping and managing resources. More on this topic is available in *Resource Mapping and Management to Address Barriers to Learning: An Intervention for Systemic Change*—a technical assistance packet developed by the Center for Mental Health in Schools at UCLA. (This document and the surveys reproduced on the following pages also can be downloaded at no cost from the Web site of the Center for Mental Health in Schools at UCLA: go to http://smhp .psych.ucla.edu/pdfdocs/Surveys/Set1.pdf.)

SOME TOOLS TO AID MAPPING

A gap analysis is generated when surveys of unmet needs of students, their families, and school staff are paired with resource mapping. The following set of self-study surveys was developed to aid school staff in mapping and analyzing current programs, services, and systems (see Guides 14.2–14.9). These surveys provide a starter tool kit to aid in mapping.

- The first survey provides an overview of System Status (see Guide 14.2).
- This is followed by a set of surveys related to each of the six content areas of an Enabling or Learning Supports Component:

  1. Classroom-based approaches to enable and reengage students in classroom learning (Guide 14.3)

  2. Crisis assistance and prevention (Guide 14.4)

  3. Support for transitions (Guide 14.5)

  4. Home involvement in schooling (Guide 14.6)

  5. Outreach to develop greater community involvement and support, including recruitment of volunteers (Guide 14.7)

  6. Prescribed student and family assistance (Guide 14.8)

Guide 14.1 About Resource Mapping and Management

A. Why Mapping Resources Is So Important

- To function well, every system has to fully understand and manage its resources. Mapping is a first step toward enhancing essential understanding, and done properly, it is a major intervention in the process of moving forward with enhancing systemic effectiveness.

B. Why Mapping Both School and Community Resources Is So Important

- Schools and communities share
  - Goals and problems with respect to children, youth, and families
  - The need to develop cost-effective systems, programs, and services to meet the goals and address the problems
  - Accountability pressures related to improving outcomes
  - The opportunity to improve effectiveness by coordinating and eventually integrating resources to develop a full continuum of systemic interventions

C. What Are Resources?

- Programs, services, real estate, equipment, money, social capital, leadership, infrastructure mechanisms, and more

D. What Do We Mean by Mapping, and Who Does It?

- A representative group of informed stakeholders is asked to undertake the process of identifying
  - What currently is available to achieve goals and address problems
  - What else is needed to achieve goals and address problems

E. What Does This Process Lead To?

- Analyses to clarify gaps and recommend priorities for filling gaps related to programs and services and deploying, redeploying, and enhancing resources
- Identifying needs for making infrastructure and systemic improvements and changes
- Clarifying opportunities for achieving important functions by forming and enhancing collaborative arrangements
- Social marketing

F. How to Do Resource Mapping

- Do it in stages (start simple and build over time).
  - A first step is to clarify people/agencies who carry out relevant roles/functions.
  - Next clarify specific programs, activities, and services (including information on how many students/families can be accommodated).
  - Identify the dollars and other related resources (e.g., facilities, equipment) that are being expended from various sources.
  - Collate the various policies that are relevant to the endeavor.
- At each stage, establish a computer file, and in the later stages create spreadsheet formats.
- Use available tools (see following examples).

G. Use Benchmarks to Guide Progress Related to Resource Mapping.

Finally, included is a survey focusing specifically on school-community collaboration (Guide 14.9).

The items on any of the surveys can help clarify

- What is currently being done and whether it is being done well
- What else is desired

At schools, this type of self-study is best done by teams. However, it is *not* about having another meeting or getting through a task. It is about moving on to better outcomes for students through (a) working together to understand what is and what might be and (b) clarifying gaps, priorities, and next steps. For example, a group of school staff (teachers, support staff, administrators) could use the items to discuss how the school currently addresses any or all of the areas. Members of a team initially might work separately in responding to survey items, but the real payoff comes from group work.

The purposes of the group's work are to

- Analyze whether certain activities should no longer be pursued (because they are not effective or not as high a priority as some others that are needed).
- Decide what resources can be redeployed to enhance current efforts that need embellishment.
- Identify gaps with respect to important areas of need.
- Establish priorities, strategies, and timelines for filling gaps.

Done right, mapping and analysis of resources can

- Counter fragmentation and redundancy.
- Mobilize support and direction.
- Enhance linkages with other resources.
- Facilitate effective systemic change.
- Integrate all facets of systemic change and counter marginalization of the component to address barriers to student learning.

Ongoing attention to all this provides a form of quality review.

- Now review the set of surveys and think about how to use them to enhance learning supports.
- See Guide 14.10 for a tool that can be used to facilitate priority setting and follow-up actions.

Guide 14.2   Survey of Learning Supports System Status

As a school sets out to enhance the usefulness of learning supports designed to address barriers to learning, it helps to clarify what you have in place as a basis for determining what needs to be done. You will want to pay special attention to

- Clarifying what resources already are available
- How the resources are organized to work in a coordinated way
- What procedures are in place for enhancing resource usefulness

This survey provides a starting point.

The first form provides a template that you can fill in to clarify the people and their positions at your school who provide services and programs related to addressing barriers to learning. This also is a logical group of people to bring together in establishing a resource-oriented team for learning supports at the school.

Following this is a survey designed to help you review how well systems for learning supports have been developed and are functioning.

Learning Supports Staff at the School

In a sense, each staff member is a special resource for every other. A few individuals are highlighted here to underscore some special functions.

Administrative Leader for Learning Supports _____

School Psychologist _____

Times at the school _____

- Provides assessment and testing of students for special services, counseling for students and parents, support services for teachers, prevention of crises, conflict resolution, and program modification for special learning and behavioral needs

School Nurse _____

Times at the school _____

- Provides immunizations, follow-up, communicable disease control, vision and hearing screening and follow-up, health assessments and referrals, and health counseling and information for students and families

Pupil Services and Attendance Counselor
_____

Times at the school _____

- Provides a liaison between school and home to maximize school attendance, provides transition counseling for returnees, and enhances attendance improvement activities

Social Worker _____

Times at the school _____

- Assists in identifying at-risk students and provides follow-up counseling for students and parents; refers families for additional services if needed

Counselor _____

Times at the school _____

Counselor _____

Times at the school _____

- Provides general and special counseling/ guidance services and consults with parents and school staff

Dropout Prevention Program Coordinator
_____

Times at the school _____

- Coordinates activity designed to promote dropout prevention

Title I and Bilingual Coordinators

_____

_____

- Coordinate categorical programs, provide services to identified Title I students, and implement bilingual master plan (supervising the curriculum, testing, and so forth)

Resource and Special Education Teachers

_____

_____

_____

Times at the school _____

- Provide information on program modifications for students in regular classrooms as well as providing services for special education

Other Important Resources:

School-based Crisis Team (list by name/title)
_____ / _____
_____ / _____
_____ / _____
_____ / _____
_____ / _____

School Improvement Program Planners
_____ / _____
_____ / _____
_____ / _____

Community Resources

- Providing school-linked or school-based interventions and resources

Who   What they do   When
_____ / _____ / _____
_____ / _____ / _____
_____ / _____ / _____
_____ / _____ / _____
_____ / _____ / _____
_____ / _____ / _____

Survey of Learning Supports System Status

Items 1–9 ask about what processes are in place.

Use the following ratings in responding to these items.

DK = Don't know

1 = Not yet

2 = Planned

3 = Just recently initiated

4 = Has been functional for a while

5 = Well-institutionalized (well-established with a commitment to maintenance)

1. Is someone at the school designated as the administrative leader for activity designed to address barriers to learning (e.g., learning supports, health and social services, the Enabling Component)?   DK 1 2 3 4 5

2. Is there a time and place when personnel involved in activity designed to address barriers to learning meet together?   DK 1 2 3 4 5

3. Is there a resource-oriented team (e.g., a Learning Supports Resource Team), as contrasted to a case-oriented team?   DK 1 2 3 4 5
    a. Does the team analyze data trends at the school with respect to
        - Attendance?   DK 1 2 3 4 5
        - Dropouts?   DK 1 2 3 4 5
        - Achievement?   DK 1 2 3 4 5
    b. Does the team map learning supports programs to determine whether
        - Identified priorities are being addressed adequately?   DK 1 2 3 4 5
        - Program quality is up to standards?   DK 1 2 3 4 5
        - Gaps have been identified, and priorities for the future are set? DK 1 2 3 4 5
    c. Which of the following areas of learning support are reviewed regularly?
        - Classroom-based approaches to enable and reengage students in classroom learning (see Guide 14.3)   DK 1 2 3 4 5
        - Crisis assistance and prevention (see Guide 14.4)   DK 1 2 3 4 5
        - Support for transitions (see Guide 14.5)   DK 1 2 3 4 5
        - Home involvement in schooling (see Guide 14.6)   DK 1 2 3 4 5
        - Community outreach for involvement and support (see Guide 14.7)   DK 1 2 3 4 5
        - Student and family assistance programs and services (see Guide 14.8)   DK 1 2 3 4 5

4. Are there *written descriptions* of learning supports programs available to give to
    a. Staff?   DK 1 2 3 4 5
    b. Families?   DK 1 2 3 4 5
    c. Students?   DK 1 2 3 4 5
    d. Community stakeholders?   DK 1 2 3 4 5

5. Are there case-oriented systems in place for
    a. Concerned parties to use in making referrals?   DK 1 2 3 4 5
    b. Triage (to decide how to respond when a referral is made)?   DK 1 2 3 4 5
    c. Case monitoring and management?   DK 1 2 3 4 5
    d. A student review team?   DK 1 2 3 4 5
    e. A crisis team?   DK 1 2 3 4 5

6. Are there *written descriptions* available to
    give to staff and others about
    a. How to make referrals?   DK 1 2 3 4 5
    b. The triage process?   DK 1 2 3 4 5
    c. The process for case monitoring and management?   DK 1 2 3 4 5
    d. The process for student review?   DK 1 2 3 4 5

7. Are there systems in place to support staff wellness?   DK 1 2 3 4 5

8. Are there processes by which staff and families learn
    a. What is available in the way of programs/services at school?   DK 1 2 3 4 5
    b. How to access programs/services they need?   DK 1 2 3 4 5

9. Has someone at the school been designated as a representative   DK 1 2 3 4 5
    to meet with the other schools in the feeder pattern to enhance
    coordination and integration of learning supports among the
    schools and with community resources?

The following items ask about the effectiveness of existing processes.

Use the following ratings in responding to these items.

    DK = Don't know

      1 = Hardly ever effective

      2 = Effective about 25% of the time

      3 = Effective about half the time

      4 = Effective about 75% of the time

      5 = Almost always effective

10. How effective are the processes for
    a. Planning, implementing, and evaluating learning   DK 1 2 3 4 5
        supports system improvements?
    b. Enhancing learning supports resources (e.g., through budget   DK 1 2 3 4 5
        decisions and staff development, developing or bringing new
        programs/services to the site, making formal linkages with
        programs/services in the community)?

11. How effective are the processes for ensuring that
    a. Resources are properly allocated and coordinated?   DK 1 2 3 4 5
    b. Community resources linked with the school are effectively   DK 1 2 3 4 5
        coordinated/integrated with related school activities?

12. How effective are the processes for ensuring that resources   DK 1 2 3 4 5
    available to the whole feeder pattern of schools are properly
    allocated and shared/coordinated?

13. How effective is the
    a. Referral system?   DK 1 2 3 4 5
    b. Triage system?   DK 1 2 3 4 5
    c. Case monitoring and management system?   DK 1 2 3 4 5
    d. Student review team?   DK 1 2 3 4 5
    e. Crisis team?   DK 1 2 3 4 5

14. List community resources with which you have formal relationships.
    a. Those that bring program(s) to the school site
    b. Those not at the school site but which have made a special
        commitment to respond to the school's referrals and needs

Guide 14.3   Classroom-based Approaches to Enable and Reengage Students in Classroom Learning: A Self-study Survey

This arena provides a fundamental example not only of how learning supports overlap regular instructional efforts but also how they add value to prevailing efforts to improve instruction. Classroom-based efforts to enable learning can (a) prevent problems, (b) facilitate intervening as soon as problems are noted, (c) enhance intrinsic motivation for learning, and (d) reengage students who have become disengaged from classroom learning. This is accomplished by increasing teachers' effectiveness so they can account for a wider range of individual differences, foster a caring context for learning, and prevent and handle a wider range of problems when they arise. Effectiveness is enhanced through personalized staff development and opening the classroom door to others who can help. One objective is to provide teachers with the knowledge and skills to develop a classroom infrastructure that transforms a big class into a set of smaller ones. Such a focus is essential for increasing the effectiveness of regular classroom instruction, supporting inclusionary policies, and reducing the need for specialized services.

Work in this arena requires programmatic approaches and systems designed to personalize the professional development of teachers and support staff, develop the capabilities of paraeducators and other paid assistants and volunteers, provide temporary out-of-class assistance for students, and enhance resources. For example, personalized help is provided to increase a teacher's array of strategies for accommodating, as well as teaching students to compensate for, differences, vulnerabilities, and disabilities. Teachers learn to use paid assistants, peer tutors, and volunteers in targeted ways to enhance social and academic support.

As appropriate, support *in the classroom* also is provided by resource and itinerant teachers and counselors. This involves restructuring and redesigning the roles, functions, and staff development of resource and itinerant teachers, counselors, and other pupil service personnel so they are able to work closely with teachers and students in the classroom and on regular activities.

Classroom-based Approaches

Indicate all items that apply.

	Yes	Yes, but more of this is needed.	No	If no, is this something you want?

I. Opening the Classroom Door

A. Are others invited into the classroom to assist in enhancing classroom approaches?

1. Aides (e.g., paraeducators, other paid assistants)?	___	___	___	___
2. Older students?	___	___	___	___
3. Other students in the class?	___	___	___	___
4. Volunteers?	___	___	___	___
5. Parents?	___	___	___	___
6. Resource teacher?	___	___	___	___
7. Specialists?	___	___	___	___
8. Other? (specify) _____	___	___	___	___

B. Are there programs to train aides, volunteers, and other assistants who come into the classrooms to work with students who need help? ___ ___ ___ ___

II. Redesigning Classroom Approaches to Enhance Teacher Capability to Prevent and Handle Problems and Reduce the Need for Out-of-class Referrals

A. Is instruction personalized (i.e., designed to match each student's motivation and capabilities)? ___ ___ ___ ___

B. When needed, is in-classroom special assistance provided? ___ ___ ___ ___

C. Are there small-group and independent learning options? ___ ___ ___ ___

D. Are behavior problems handled in ways designed to minimize a negative impact on student attitudes toward classroom learning? ___ ___ ___ ___

E. Is there a range of curricular and instructional options and choices? ___ ___ ___ ___

F. Are prereferral interventions used? ___ ___ ___ ___

G. Are materials and activities upgraded to

1. Ensure that there are enough basic supplies in the classroom?	___	___	___	___
2. Increase the range of high-motivation activities (keyed to the interests of students in need of special attention)?	___	___	___	___
3. Include advanced technology?	___	___	___	___
4. Other? (specify) _____	___	___	___	___

H. Are regular efforts to foster social and emotional development supplemented? ___ ___ ___ ___

	Yes	Yes, but more of this is needed.	No	If no, is this something you want?

I. Which of the following can teachers request as special interventions?

    1. Family problem-solving conferences? _____ _____ _____ _____

    2. Exchange of students to improve student-teacher match and for a fresh start? _____ _____ _____ _____

    3. Referral for specific services? _____ _____ _____ _____

    4. Other? (specify) _____ _____ _____ _____ _____

J. What programs are there for temporary out-of-class help?

    1. A family center providing student and family assistance? _____ _____ _____ _____

    2. Designated problem remediation specialists? _____ _____ _____ _____

    3. A time-out situation? _____ _____ _____ _____

    4. Other? (specify) _____ _____ _____ _____ _____

K. What is done to assist a teacher who has difficulty with limited-English-speaking students?

    1. Is the student reassigned? _____ _____ _____ _____

    2. Does the teacher receive professional development related to working with limited-English-speaking students? _____ _____ _____ _____

    3. Does a bilingual coordinator offer consultation? _____ _____ _____ _____

    4. Is a bilingual aide assigned to the class? _____ _____ _____ _____

    5. Are volunteers brought in to help (e.g., parents, peers)? _____ _____ _____ _____

    6. Other? (specify) _____ _____ _____ _____ _____

III. **Enhancing and Personalizing Professional Development**

A. Are teachers clustered for support and staff development? _____ _____ _____ _____

B. Are demonstrations provided? _____ _____ _____ _____

C. Are workshops and readings offered regularly? _____ _____ _____ _____

D. Is consultation available from persons with special expertise such as

    1. Learning supports staff (e.g., psychologist, counselor, social worker, nurse)? _____ _____ _____ _____

    2. Resource specialists and/or special education teachers? _____ _____ _____ _____

    3. Members of special committees? _____ _____ _____ _____

    4. Bilingual or other coordinators? _____ _____ _____ _____

    5. Other? (specify) _____ _____ _____ _____ _____

E. Is there a formal mentoring program? _____ _____ _____ _____

F. Is team teaching or coteaching used as an opportunity for teachers to learn on the job? _____ _____ _____ _____

G. Is the school creating a learning community? _____ _____ _____ _____

H. Is there staff social support? _____ _____ _____ _____

I. Is there formal conflict mediation/ resolution for staff? _____ _____ _____ _____

J. Is there a focus on learning how to integrate intrinsic motivation into teaching and classroom management? _____ _____ _____ _____

	Yes	Yes, but more of this is needed.	No	If no, is this something you want?
K. Is there assistance in learning to use advanced technology?	___	___	___	___
L. Other? (specify) _____	___	___	___	___

IV. Curricular Enrichment and Adjunct Programs

A. What types of technology are available to the classroom?

	Yes	Yes, but more of this is needed.	No	If no, is this something you want?
1. Are there computers in the classroom?	___	___	___	___
2. Is there a computer lab?	___	___	___	___
3. Is computer-assisted instruction offered?	___	___	___	___
4. Are there computer literacy programs?	___	___	___	___
5. Are computer programs used to address ESL needs?	___	___	___	___
6. Does the classroom have video recording capability?	___	___	___	___
7. Is instructional TV used in the classroom?	___	___	___	___
8. Is there a multimedia lab?	___	___	___	___
9. Other? (specify)	___	___	___	___

B. What curricular enrichment and adjunct programs do teachers use?

	Yes	Yes, but more of this is needed.	No	If no, is this something you want?
1. Are library activities used regularly?	___	___	___	___
2. Is music/art used regularly?	___	___	___	___
3. Is health education a regular part of the curriculum?	___	___	___	___
4. Are student performances regular events?	___	___	___	___
5. Are there several field trips a year?	___	___	___	___
6. Are there student council and other leaders opportunities?	___	___	___	___
7. Are there school environment projects such as				
a. Mural painting?	___	___	___	___
b. Horticulture/gardening?	___	___	___	___
c. School cleanup and beautification?	___	___	___	___
d. Other? (specify)	___	___	___	___
8. Are there special schoolwide events such as				
a. Sports?	___	___	___	___
b. Clubs and similar organized activities?	___	___	___	___
c. Publication of a student newspaper?	___	___	___	___
d. Sales events?	___	___	___	___
e. Poster contests?	___	___	___	___
f. Essay contests?	___	___	___	___
g. Book fairs?	___	___	___	___
h. Pep rallies/contests?	___	___	___	___
i. Attendance competitions?	___	___	___	___
j. Attendance awards/assemblies?	___	___	___	___
k. Other? (specify) _____	___	___	___	___
9. Are guest contributors used (e.g., outside speakers/performers)?	___	___	___	___
10. Other? (specify) _____	___	___	___	___

V. Classroom and Schoolwide Approaches Used to Create and Maintain a Caring and Supportive Climate

A. Are there schoolwide approaches for

	Yes	Yes, but more of this is needed.	No	If no, is this something you want?
1. Creating and maintaining a caring and supportive climate?	___	___	___	___

	Yes	Yes, but more of this is needed.	No	If no, is this something you want?
2. Supporting high standards for positive behavior?	____	____	____	____
3. Other? (specify) _____	____	____	____	____
B. Are there classroom approaches for				
1. Creating and maintaining a caring and supportive climate?	____	____	____	____
2. Supporting high standards for positive behavior?	____	____	____	____
3. Other? (specify) _____	____	____	____	____

VI. Capacity Building for Classroom-based Approaches

	Yes	Yes, but more of this is needed.	No	If no, is this something you want?
A. Are there programs to enhance broad stakeholder involvement in classroom-based approaches?	____	____	____	____
B. Programs used to meet the educational needs of personnel related to classroom-based approaches:	____	____	____	____
1. Is there ongoing training for learning supports staff with respect to classroom-based approaches?	____	____	____	____
2. Is there ongoing training for others involved in providing classroom-based approaches (e.g., teachers, peer buddies, office staff, administrators)?	____	____	____	____
3. Other? (specify) _____	____	____	____	____
C. Which of the following topics are covered in educating stakeholders?				
1. How others can work effectively in the classroom	____	____	____	____
2. Reengaging students who have disengaged from classroom learning	____	____	____	____
3. Personalizing instruction	____	____	____	____
4. Addressing learning, behavior, and emotional problems	____	____	____	____
5. Enriching options and facilitating student and family involvement in decision making	____	____	____	____
D. Indicate below other things you want the school to do to assist a teacher's efforts to address barriers to students' learning.				

Other matters relevant to classroom-based approaches are found in the surveys on

- Support for Transitions (Guide 14.5)
- Home Involvement in Schooling (Guide 14.6)
- Community Involvement and Support (Guide 14.7)

Guide 14.4   Crisis Assistance and Prevention: A Self-study Survey

Schools must respond to, minimize the impact of, and prevent school and personal crises. This requires schoolwide and classroom-based systems and programmatic approaches. Such activity focuses on (a) emergency/crisis response at a site, throughout a school complex, and communitywide (including a focus on ensuring follow-up care), (b) minimizing the impact of crises, and (c) prevention measures at school and in the community to address school safety and violence reduction, suicide prevention, child abuse prevention, and so forth.

Desired outcomes of crisis assistance include ensuring immediate emergency and follow-up care so students are able to resume learning without too much delay. Prevention outcome indices reflect a safe and productive environment where students and their families display the attitudes and capacities needed to deal with violence and other threats to safety.

A key mechanism in this arena often is the development of a crisis team. Such a team is trained in emergency response procedures, physical and psychological first aid, aftermath interventions, and so forth. The team also can take the lead in planning ways to prevent some crises by facilitating development of programs to mediate and resolve conflicts, enhance human relations, and promote a caring school culture.

Crisis Assistance and Prevention

Indicate all items that apply.

		Yes	Yes, but more of this is needed.	No	If no, is this something you want?
I.	**Ensuring Immediate Assistance in Emergencies/Crises**				
A.	Is there a plan that details a coordinated response				
	1. For all at the school site?	___	___	___	___
	2. With other schools in the complex?	___	___	___	___
	3. With community agencies?	___	___	___	___
B.	Are emergency/crisis plans updated appropriately with regard to				
	1. Crisis management guidelines (e.g., flowcharts, checklists)?	___	___	___	___
	2. Plans for communicating with homes/community?	___	___	___	___
	3. Media relations guidelines?	___	___	___	___
C.	Are stakeholders regularly provided with information about emergency response plans?	___	___	___	___
D.	Is medical first aid provided when crises occur?	___	___	___	___
E.	Is psychological first aid provided when crises occur?	___	___	___	___
F.	Other? (specify) _____	___	___	___	___
II.	**Providing Follow-up Assistance as Necessary**				
A.	Are there programs for *short-term* follow-up assistance?	___	___	___	___
B.	Are there programs for *longer-term* follow-up assistance?	___	___	___	___
C.	Other? (specify) _____	___	___	___	___
III.	**Crisis Team to Formulate Response and Prevention Plans**				
A.	Is there an active crisis team?	___	___	___	___
B.	Is the crisis team appropriately trained?	___	___	___	___
C.	Does the team focus on prevention of school and personal crises?	___	___	___	___
IV.	**Mobilizing Staff, Students, and Families to Anticipate Response Plans and Recovery Efforts**				
	With respect to planning and training for crisis response and recovery, are there programs to involve and integrate				
A.	Learning supports staff?	___	___	___	___
B.	Teachers?	___	___	___	___
C.	Other school staff?	___	___	___	___
D.	Students?	___	___	___	___
E.	Families?	___	___	___	___

	Yes	Yes, but more of this is needed.	No	If no, is this something you want?
F. Other schools in the vicinity?	_____	_____	_____	_____
G. Other concerned parties in the community?	_____	_____	_____	_____

V. Creating a Caring and Safe Learning Environment Through Programs to Enhance Healthy Development and Prevent Problems

	Yes	Yes, but more of this is needed.	No	If no, is this something you want?
A. Are there programs for				
1. Promoting healthy development?	_____	_____	_____	_____
2. Bullying and harassment abatement?	_____	_____	_____	_____
3. School and community safety/violence reduction?	_____	_____	_____	_____
4. Suicide prevention?	_____	_____	_____	_____
5. Child abuse prevention?	_____	_____	_____	_____
6. Sexual abuse prevention?	_____	_____	_____	_____
7. Substance abuse prevention?	_____	_____	_____	_____
8. Other? (specify) _____	_____	_____	_____	_____
B. Is there an ongoing emphasis on enhancing a caring and safe learning environment				
1. Schoolwide?	_____	_____	_____	_____
2. In classrooms?	_____	_____	_____	_____

VI. Capacity Building to Enhance Crisis Response and Prevention

	Yes	Yes, but more of this is needed.	No	If no, is this something you want?
A. Is there an ongoing emphasis on enhancing a caring and safe learning environment through programs to enhance the capacity of				
1. Learning supports staff?	_____	_____	_____	_____
2. Teachers?	_____	_____	_____	_____
3. Other school staff?	_____	_____	_____	_____
4. Students?	_____	_____	_____	_____
5. Families?	_____	_____	_____	_____
6. Other schools in the feeder pattern?	_____	_____	_____	_____
7. Other concerned parties in the community?	_____	_____	_____	_____
B. Is there ongoing training for learning supports staff with respect to the area of crisis assistance and prevention?	_____	_____	_____	_____
C. Is there ongoing training for others involved in crisis response and prevention (e.g., teachers, office staff, administrators)?	_____	_____	_____	_____
D. Which of the following topics are covered in educating stakeholders?				
1. Anticipating emergencies	_____	_____	_____	_____
2. How to respond when an emergency arises	_____	_____	_____	_____
3. How to access assistance after an emergency (including watching for posttraumatic psychological reactions)	_____	_____	_____	_____

	Yes	Yes, but more of this is needed.	No	If no, is this something you want?
4. Indicators of abuse and potential suicide and what to do	___	___	___	___
5. How to respond to concerns related to death, dying, and grief	___	___	___	___
6. How to mediate conflicts and minimize violent reactions	___	___	___	___
7. Other (specify) _____	___	___	___	___
E. Indicate below other things you want the school to do in responding to and preventing crises.	___	___	___	___

Other matters relevant to crises response are found in the survey on Student and Family Assistance (Guide 14.8).

Guide 14.5   Support for Transitions: A Self-study Survey

Students and their families are regularly confronted with a variety of transitions—changing schools, changing grades, encountering a range of other daily hassles and major life demands. Many of these can interfere with productive school involvement. A comprehensive focus on transitions requires schoolwide and classroom-based systems and programs designed to (a) enhance successful transitions, (b) prevent transition problems, and (c) use transition periods to reduce alienation and increase positive attitudes toward school and learning. Examples of programs include schoolwide and classroom-specific activities for welcoming new arrivals (students, their families, staff) and rendering ongoing social support; counseling and articulation strategies to support grade-to-grade and school-to-school transitions and moves to and from special education, college, and postschool living and work; and beforeschool, afterschool, and intersession activities to enrich learning and provide recreation in a safe environment.

Anticipated overall outcomes are reduced alienation, enhanced motivation, and increased involvement in school and learning activities. Examples of early outcomes include reduced tardies, resulting from participation in beforeschool programs, and reduced vandalism, violence, and crime at school and in the neighborhood, resulting from involvement in afterschool activities. Over time, articulation programs can reduce school avoidance and dropouts as well as enhancing the number who make successful transitions to higher education and postschool living and work. It is also likely that a caring school climate can play a significant role in reducing student transience.

Support for Transitions

Indicate all items that apply.

	Yes	Yes, but more of this is needed.	No	If no, is this something you want?

I. Programs Establishing a Welcoming and Socially Supportive School Community

   A. Supportive welcoming

      1. Are there welcoming materials and a welcoming decor? ____ ____ ____ ____

      2. Are there welcome signs? ____ ____ ____ ____

      3. Are welcoming information materials used? ____ ____ ____ ____

      4. Is a special welcoming booklet used? ____ ____ ____ ____

      5. Are materials translated into appropriate languages? ____ ____ ____ ____

      6. Is advanced technology used as an aid (e.g., a video or computerized introduction to the school and staff)? ____ ____ ____ ____

   B. Orientation and follow-up "induction"

      1. Are there orientation programs? ____ ____ ____ ____

      2. Are there introductory tours? ____ ____ ____ ____

      3. Are introductory presentations made? ____ ____ ____ ____

      4. Are new arrivals introduced to special people, such as the principal and teachers? ____ ____ ____ ____

      5. Are special events used to welcome recent arrivals? ____ ____ ____ ____

      6. Are different languages accommodated? ____ ____ ____ ____

   C. Is special assistance available to those who need help registering? ____ ____ ____ ____

   D. Social supports

      1. Are social support strategies and mechanisms used? ____ ____ ____ ____

      2. Are peer buddies assigned? ____ ____ ____ ____

      3. Are peer parents assigned? ____ ____ ____ ____

      4. Are special invitations used to encourage family involvement? ____ ____ ____ ____

      5. Are special invitations used to encourage students to join in activities? ____ ____ ____ ____

      6. Are advocates available when new arrivals need them? ____ ____ ____ ____

   E. Other (specify) _____ ____ ____ ____ ____

II. Daily Transition Programs for Before and After School and Lunch and Breaks

   A. Which of the following are available?

      1. Subsidized food program ____ ____ ____ ____

      2. Recreation program ____ ____ ____ ____

      3. Sports program ____ ____ ____ ____

      4. Drill team ____ ____ ____ ____

      5. Student and family assistance program ____ ____ ____ ____

      6. Youth groups such as

         a. Interest groups (e.g., music, drama, career) ____ ____ ____ ____

	Yes	Yes, but more of this is needed.	No	If no, is this something you want?
b. Service clubs	_____	_____	_____	_____
c. Organized youth programs (Y, Scouts)	_____	_____	_____	_____
d. Cadet Corps	_____	_____	_____	_____
e. Other (specify) _____	_____	_____	_____	_____
7. Academic support in the form of				
a. Tutors	_____	_____	_____	_____
b. Homework club	_____	_____	_____	_____
c. Study hall	_____	_____	_____	_____
d. Homework phone line	_____	_____	_____	_____
e. E-mail and Web assistance	_____	_____	_____	_____
f. Homework center	_____	_____	_____	_____
g. Other (specify) _____	_____	_____	_____	_____

III. Articulation Programs

Which of the following transition programs are in use for grade-to-grade and program-to-program articulation?

	Yes	Yes, but more of this is needed.	No	If no, is this something you want?
A. Are orientations to the new situation provided?	_____	_____	_____	_____
B. Is transition counseling provided?	_____	_____	_____	_____
C. Are students taken on warm-up visits?	_____	_____	_____	_____
D. Is there a "survival" skill training program?	_____	_____	_____	_____
E. Is information available from previous teachers?	_____	_____	_____	_____
F. Is the new setting primed to accommodate the individual's needs?	_____	_____	_____	_____
G. Other? (specify) _____	_____	_____	_____	_____

IV. Vacation and Intersession Programs

Which of the following programs are offered during vacation and/or intersession?

	Yes	Yes, but more of this is needed.	No	If no, is this something you want?
A. Recreation	_____	_____	_____	_____
B. Sports	_____	_____	_____	_____
C. Student and family assistance	_____	_____	_____	_____
D. Youth groups	_____	_____	_____	_____
E. Academic support	_____	_____	_____	_____
F. Enrichment opportunities (including classes)	_____	_____	_____	_____
G. Other? (specify) _____	_____	_____	_____	_____

V. Transitions to Higher Education/Career

Which of the following are used to facilitate transition to higher education and postschool living?

	Yes	Yes, but more of this is needed.	No	If no, is this something you want?
A. Vocational counseling	_____	_____	_____	_____
B. College counseling	_____	_____	_____	_____
C. A mentoring program	_____	_____	_____	_____
D. College prep courses and related activity	_____	_____	_____	_____
E. Job training	_____	_____	_____	_____
F. Job opportunities on campus	_____	_____	_____	_____
G. A work-study program	_____	_____	_____	_____
H. Life skills counseling	_____	_____	_____	_____
I. Other (specify) _____	_____	_____	_____	_____

	Yes	Yes, but more of this is needed.	No	If no, is this something you want?

VI. Capacity Building to Enhance Support for Transitions

A. Are there programs to enhance broad stakeholder involvement in transition activity?

B. With respect to programs used to meet the educational needs of personnel related to support for transitions,

    1. Is there ongoing training for learning supports staff with respect to providing supports for transitions?

    2. Is there ongoing training for others involved in providing supports for transitions (e.g., teachers, peer buddies, office staff, administrators)?

    3. Other? (specify) _____

C. Which of the following topics are covered in educating stakeholders?

    1. Understanding how to create a psychological sense of community

    2. Developing systematic social supports for students, families, and staff

    3. How to ensure successful transitions

    4. The value of and strategies for creating beforeschool and afterschool programs

    5. Other (specify) _____

D. Indicate below other things you want the school to do in providing support for transitions.

Other matters relevant to support for transitions are found in the surveys on

- Classroom-based Approaches (Guide 14.3)
- Home Involvement in Schooling (Guide 14.6)
- Community Involvement and Support (Guide 14.7)

Guide 14.6   Home Involvement in Schooling: A Self-study Survey

This arena expands concern for parent involvement to encompass anyone in the home who is influencing the student's life. In some cases, grandparents, aunts, or older siblings have assumed the parenting role. Older brothers and sisters often are the most significant influences on a youngster's life choices. Thus schools and communities must go beyond focusing on parents in their efforts to enhance home involvement.

This arena includes schoolwide and classroom-based efforts designed to strengthen the home situation, enhance family problem-solving capabilities, and increase support for student well-being. Accomplishing all this requires schoolwide and classroom-based systems and programs to (a) address the specific learning and support needs of adults in the home, such as offering them ESL, literacy, vocational, and citizenship classes, enrichment and recreational opportunities, and mutual support groups; (b) help those in the home improve how basic student obligations are met, such as providing guidance related to parenting and how to help with schoolwork; (c) improve forms of basic communication that promote the well-being of student, family, and school; (d) enhance the home-school connection and sense of community; (e) foster participation in making decisions essential to a student's well-being; (f) facilitate home support of student learning and development; (g) mobilize those at home to solve problems related to student needs; and (h) elicit help (support, collaborations, and partnerships) from those at home with respect to meeting classroom, school, and community needs. The context for some of this activity may be a *parent or family center* if one has been established at the site. Outcomes include indices of parent learning, student progress, and community enhancement specifically related to home involvement.

Home Involvement in Schooling

Indicate all items that apply.

	Yes	Yes, but more of this is needed.	No	If no, is this something you want?
I. Addressing Specific Learning and Support Needs of the Family				
A. Does the site offer adult classes focused on				
1. English as a Second Language (ESL)?	___	___	___	___
2. Basic literacy skills?	___	___	___	___
3. GED preparation?	___	___	___	___
4. Job preparation?	___	___	___	___
5. Citizenship preparation?	___	___	___	___
6. Other? (specify) _____	___	___	___	___
B. Are there groups for				
1. Mutual support?	___	___	___	___
2. Discussion?	___	___	___	___
C. Are adults in the home offered assistance in accessing outside help for personal needs?	___	___	___	___
D. Which of the following are available to help those in the home meet basic survival needs and basic obligations to the student?				
1. Is help provided for addressing special family needs for				
a. Food?	___	___	___	___
b. Clothing?	___	___	___	___
c. Shelter?	___	___	___	___
d. Health and safety?	___	___	___	___
e. School supplies?	___	___	___	___
f. Other? (specify) _____	___	___	___	___
2. Are education programs offered on				
a. Child rearing/parenting?	___	___	___	___
b. Creating a supportive home environment for students?	___	___	___	___
c. Reducing factors that interfere with a student's school learning and performance?	___	___	___	___
3. Are guidelines provided for helping a student deal with homework?	___	___	___	___
4. Other? (specify) _____	___	___	___	___
II. Improve Mechanisms for Communication and Connecting School and Home				
A. Are there periodic general announcements and meetings such as				
1. Advertising for incoming students?	___	___	___	___
2. Orientation for incoming students and families?	___	___	___	___
3. Bulletins/newsletters?	___	___	___	___
4. Web site?	___	___	___	___

	Yes	Yes, but more of this is needed.	No	If no, is this something you want?
5. Back-to-school night/open house?	_____	_____	_____	_____
6. Parent-teacher conferences?	_____	_____	_____	_____
7. Other? (specify) _____	_____	_____	_____	_____
B. Is there a system to inform the home on a regular basis (e.g., regular letters, newsletters, e-mail, computerized phone messages, Web site)				
1. About general school matters?	_____	_____	_____	_____
2. About opportunities for home involvement?	_____	_____	_____	_____
3. Other? (specify) _____	_____	_____	_____	_____
C. To enhance home involvement in the student's program and progress, are interactive communications used, such as				
1. Sending notes home regularly?	_____	_____	_____	_____
2. A computerized phone line?	_____	_____	_____	_____
3. E-mail?	_____	_____	_____	_____
4. Frequent in-person conferences with the family?	_____	_____	_____	_____
5. Other? (specify) _____	_____	_____	_____	_____
D. Which of the following are used to enhance the home-school connection and sense of community:				
1. Does the school offer orientations and open houses?	_____	_____	_____	_____
2. Does the school have special receptions for new families?	_____	_____	_____	_____
3. Does the school regularly showcase students to the community through				
a. Student performances?	_____	_____	_____	_____
b. Award ceremonies?	_____	_____	_____	_____
c. Other? (specify) _____	_____	_____	_____	_____
4. Does the school offer the community				
a. Cultural and sports events?	_____	_____	_____	_____
b. Topical workshops and discussion groups?	_____	_____	_____	_____
c. Health fairs?	_____	_____	_____	_____
d. Family preservation fairs?	_____	_____	_____	_____
e. Work fairs?	_____	_____	_____	_____
f. Newsletters?	_____	_____	_____	_____
g. Community bulletin boards?	_____	_____	_____	_____
h. Community festivals and celebrations?	_____	_____	_____	_____
i. Other? (specify) _____	_____	_____	_____	_____
5. Is there outreach to families that are hard to involve, such as				
a. Making home visits?	_____	_____	_____	_____
b. Offering support networks?	_____	_____	_____	_____
c. Other? (specify) _____	_____	_____	_____	_____
6. Other? (specify) _____	_____	_____	_____	_____

	Yes	Yes, but more of this is needed.	No	If no, is this something you want?

III. Involving Homes in Making Decisions Essential to the Student

A. Are families invited to participate through personal

　1. Letters?

　2. Phone calls?

　3. E-mail?

　4. Other? (specify) _____

B. Are families informed about schooling choices through

　1. Letters?

　2. Phone calls?

　3. E-mail?

　4. Conferences?

　5. Other? (specify) _____

C. Are families taught skills to participate effectively in decision making?

D. With respect to mobilizing problem solving at home related to student needs,

　1. Is instruction provided to enhance family problem-solving skills (including increased awareness of resources for assistance)?

　2. Is good problem solving modeled at conferences with the family?

E. Other? (specify) _____

IV. Enhancing Home Support for Student Learning and Development

A. Are families instructed on how to provide opportunities for students to apply what they are learning?

B. Are families instructed on how to use enrichment opportunities to enhance youngsters' social and personal and academic skills and higher-order functioning?

C. Are family field trips organized?

D. Are families provided space and facilitation for meeting together as a community of learners?

E. Are family literacy programs available?

F. Are family homework programs offered?

G. Other? (specify) _____

V. Recruiting Families to Strengthen School and Community

A. For which of the following are those in the home recruited and trained to help meet school/community needs?

　1. Improving schooling for students by assisting

　　a. Administrators

	Yes	Yes, but more of this is needed.	No	If no, is this something you want?
b. Teachers	_____	_____	_____	_____
c. Other staff	_____	_____	_____	_____
d. Others in the community	_____	_____	_____	_____
e. With lessons or tutoring	_____	_____	_____	_____
f. On class trips	_____	_____	_____	_____
g. In the cafeteria	_____	_____	_____	_____
h. In the library	_____	_____	_____	_____
i. In computer labs	_____	_____	_____	_____
j. With homework help lines	_____	_____	_____	_____
k. In the front office, to welcome visitors and new enrollees and their families	_____	_____	_____	_____
l. With phoning/e-mailing home regarding absences	_____	_____	_____	_____
m. Outreach to the home	_____	_____	_____	_____
n. Other (specify) _____	_____	_____	_____	_____
2. Improving school operations by assisting with				
a. School and community upkeep and beautification	_____	_____	_____	_____
b. Improving school-community relations	_____	_____	_____	_____
c. Fundraising	_____	_____	_____	_____
d. PTA	_____	_____	_____	_____
e. Enhancing public support by increasing political awareness about the contributions and needs of the school	_____	_____	_____	_____
f. School governance	_____	_____	_____	_____
g. Advocacy for school needs	_____	_____	_____	_____
h. Advisory councils	_____	_____	_____	_____
i. Program planning	_____	_____	_____	_____
j. Other (specify) _____	_____	_____	_____	_____
3. Establishing home-community networks to benefit the community	_____	_____	_____	_____
4. Other? (specify) _____	_____	_____	_____	_____

VI. Capacity Building to Enhance Home Involvement

A. Are there programs to enhance broad stakeholder involvement in efforts to enhance home involvement in schools?   _____ _____ _____ _____

B. With respect to programs used to meet the educational needs of personnel related to home involvement,

1. Is there ongoing training for learning supports staff with respect to enhancing home involvement?   _____ _____ _____ _____

2. Is there ongoing training for others involved in enhancing home involvement (e.g., teachers, parent peer buddies, office staff, administrators)?   _____ _____ _____ _____

3. Other? (specify) _____   _____ _____ _____ _____

	Yes	Yes, but more of this is needed.	No	If no, is this something you want?
C. Which of the following topics are covered in educating stakeholders?				
1. How to facilitate family participation in decision-making meetings	___	___	___	___
2. Designing an inclusionary parent center	___	___	___	___
3. Overcoming barriers to home involvement	___	___	___	___
4. Developing group-led mutual support groups	___	___	___	___
5. Developing families as a community of learners	___	___	___	___
6. Available curriculum for parent education	___	___	___	___
7. Teaching parents to be mentors and leaders at the school	___	___	___	___
8. Other (specify) _____	___	___	___	___
D. Indicate below other things you want the school to do to enhance home involvement.	___	___	___	___

Other matters relevant to home involvement are found in the surveys on

- Classroom-based Approaches (Guide 14.3)
- Support for Transitions (Guide 14.5)
- Community Involvement and Support (Guide 14.7)
- Student and Family Assistance (Guide 14.8)

Guide 14.7   Community Outreach for Involvement and Support:
A Self-study Survey

Schools can do their job better when they are an integral and positive part of the community. For example, it is a truism that learning is neither limited to what is formally taught nor to time spent in classrooms. It occurs whenever and wherever the learner interacts with the surrounding environment. All facets of the community provide learning opportunities, not just the school. *Anyone in the community who wants to facilitate learning might be a contributing teacher.* This includes aides, volunteers, parents, siblings, peers, mentors in the community, librarians, recreation staff, college students, and so forth. They all constitute what can be called *the teaching community.* When a school successfully joins with its surrounding community, everyone has the opportunity to learn and to teach.

Another key facet of community involvement is opening up school sites as places where parents, families, and other community residents can engage in learning, recreation, and enrichment and can find services they need. This encompasses an outreach to the community to collaborate and enhance the engagement of young people to directly strengthen youngsters, families, and neighborhoods. In this respect, increasing attention is paid to interventions to promote healthy development, resiliency, and assets.

For schools to be seen as an integral part of the community, outreach steps must be taken to create and maintain linkages and collaborations. The intent is to maximize mutual benefits, including better student progress, an enhanced sense of community, community development, and more. In the long run, the aims are to strengthen students, schools, families, and neighborhoods. Outreach focuses on public and private agencies, organizations, universities, colleges, and facilities; businesses and professional organizations and groups; and volunteer service programs, organizations, and clubs. Greater volunteerism on the part of parents, peers, and others from the community can break down barriers and increase home and community involvement in schools and schooling. Over time, this area can include systems and programs designed to (a) recruit a wide range of community involvement and support; (b) train, screen, and maintain volunteers; (c) reach out to students and families who don't come to school regularly—including truants and dropouts; (d) connect school and community efforts to promote child and youth development; and (e) enhance community-school connections and sense of community.

Community Outreach for Involvement and Support

Indicate all items that apply.

	Yes	Yes, but more of this is needed.	No	If no, is this something you want?

I. Planning and Implementing Outreach to Recruit a Wide Range of Community Resources

A. From which of the following sources are participants recruited?

	Yes	Yes, but more of this is needed.	No	If no, is this something you want?
1. Public community agencies, organizations, facilities, and providers	___	___	___	___
2. Private community agencies, organizations, facilities, and providers	___	___	___	___
3. Business sector	___	___	___	___
4. Professional organizations and groups	___	___	___	___
5. Volunteer service programs, organizations, and clubs	___	___	___	___
6. Universities and colleges	___	___	___	___
7. Other (specify) _____	___	___	___	___

B. Indicate current types of community involvement at the school:

	Yes	Yes, but more of this is needed.	No	If no, is this something you want?
1. Mentoring for students and families	___	___	___	___
2. Volunteer functions	___	___	___	___
3. A community resource pool that provides expertise as requested, such as				
a. Artists	___	___	___	___
b. Musicians	___	___	___	___
c. Librarians	___	___	___	___
d. Health and safety programs	___	___	___	___
e. Other (specify) _____	___	___	___	___
4. Formal agency and program linkages that result in community health and social services providers coming to the site, such as				
a. Afterschool programs coming to the site	___	___	___	___
b. Services programs providing direct access to referrals from the site	___	___	___	___
c. Other (specify) _____	___	___	___	___
5. Formal arrangements that involve community agents in				
a. School governance	___	___	___	___
b. Advocacy for the school	___	___	___	___
c. Advisory functions	___	___	___	___
d. Program planning	___	___	___	___
e. Fundraising	___	___	___	___
f. Sponsoring activity (e.g., adopt-a-school)	___	___	___	___
g. Creating awards and incentives	___	___	___	___
h. Providing job-shadowing opportunities	___	___	___	___

		Yes	Yes, but more of this is needed.	No	If no, is this something you want?
	i. Creating jobs	___	___	___	___
	j. Other (specify) ___	___	___	___	___
6.	Formal arrangements that connect school and community for enhancing child and youth development	___	___	___	___
C.	With specific respect to volunteers,				
1.	What types of volunteers are used at the site?	___	___	___	___
	a. Nonprofessionals	___	___	___	___
	b. Parents	___	___	___	___
	c. College students	___	___	___	___
	d. Senior citizens	___	___	___	___
	e. Businesspeople	___	___	___	___
	f. Peer and cross-age tutors	___	___	___	___
	g. Peer and cross-age counselors	___	___	___	___
	h. Paraprofessionals	___	___	___	___
	i. Professionals-in-training (specify) ___	___	___	___	___
	j. Professionals (pro bono) (specify) ___	___	___	___	___
	k. Other (specify) ___	___	___	___	___
2.	Who do volunteers assist?				
	a. Administrators	___	___	___	___
	b. Teachers	___	___	___	___
	c. Other staff	___	___	___	___
	d. Others (specify) ___	___	___	___	___
3.	In which of the following ways do volunteers participate?				
	a. Providing general classroom assistance	___	___	___	___
	b. Assisting with targeted students	___	___	___	___
	c. Assisting after school	___	___	___	___
	d. Providing special tutoring	___	___	___	___
	e. Helping students with attention problems	___	___	___	___
	f. Helping with bilingual students	___	___	___	___
	g. Helping to address other diversity matters	___	___	___	___
	h. Helping in the cafeteria	___	___	___	___
	i. Helping in the library	___	___	___	___
	j. Helping in the computer lab	___	___	___	___
	k. Helping on class trips	___	___	___	___
	l. Helping with homework help lines	___	___	___	___
	m. Working in the front office	___	___	___	___
	n. Welcoming visitors	___	___	___	___
	o. Welcoming new enrollees and their families	___	___	___	___
	p. Phoning or e-mailing home about absences	___	___	___	___
	q. Helping with outreach to the home	___	___	___	___
	r. Acting as mentors or advocates for students, families, staff	___	___	___	___

	Yes	Yes, but more of this is needed.	No	If no, is this something you want?
s. Assisting with school upkeep and beautification efforts	___	___	___	___
t. Helping enhance public support by increasing political awareness about the contributions and needs of the school	___	___	___	___
u. Other (specify) _____	___	___	___	___

II. Systems to Recruit, Screen, Prepare, and Maintain Community Resource Involvement

A. Are there systems and programs specifically designed to

	Yes	Yes, but more of this is needed.	No	If no, is this something you want?
1. Recruit community stakeholders?	___	___	___	___
2. Orient and welcome community stakeholders who have been recruited for school involvement and support?	___	___	___	___
3. Enhance the volunteer pool?	___	___	___	___
4. Screen volunteers?	___	___	___	___
5. Train volunteers?	___	___	___	___
6. Maintain volunteers?	___	___	___	___

III. Reaching Out to Students and Families Who Don't Come to School Regularly, Including Truants and Dropouts

A. Which of the following are used to enhance school involvement of hard-to-involve students and families?

1. Home visits to assess and plan ways to overcome barriers to

	Yes	Yes, but more of this is needed.	No	If no, is this something you want?
a. Student attendance	___	___	___	___
b. Family involvement in schooling	___	___	___	___

2. Support networks connecting hard-to-involve

	Yes	Yes, but more of this is needed.	No	If no, is this something you want?
a. Students with peers and mentors	___	___	___	___
b. Families with peers and mentors	___	___	___	___

3. Special incentives for

	Yes	Yes, but more of this is needed.	No	If no, is this something you want?
a. Students	___	___	___	___
b. Families	___	___	___	___
4. Other (specify) _____	___	___	___	___

IV. Connecting School and Community Efforts to Promote Child and Youth Development and a Sense of Community

A. Which of the following are used to enhance community-school connections and sense of community?

1. Orientations and open houses for

	Yes	Yes, but more of this is needed.	No	If no, is this something you want?
a. Newly arriving students	___	___	___	___
b. Newly arriving families	___	___	___	___
c. New staff	___	___	___	___
2. Student performances for the community	___	___	___	___

3. School-sponsored

	Yes	Yes, but more of this is needed.	No	If no, is this something you want?
a. Cultural and sports events for the community	___	___	___	___
b. Community festivals and celebrations	___	___	___	___
c. Topical workshops and discussion groups	___	___	___	___

	Yes	Yes, but more of this is needed.	No	If no, is this something you want?
d. Health fairs	_____	_____	_____	_____
e. Family preservation fairs	_____	_____	_____	_____
f. Work fairs	_____	_____	_____	_____
4. Other (specify) _____	_____	_____	_____	_____

V. Capacity Building to Enhance Community Involvement and Support

A. Are there programs to enhance broad stakeholder involvement in enhancing community involvement and support?   _____ _____ _____ _____

B. With respect to programs used to meet the educational needs of personnel related to community involvement and support,

    1. Is there ongoing training for learning supports staff with respect to enhancing community involvement and support?   _____ _____ _____ _____

    2. Is there ongoing training for others involved in enhancing community involvement and support (e.g., teachers, administrators, volunteers)?   _____ _____ _____ _____

    3. Other? (specify) _____   _____ _____ _____ _____

C. Which of the following topics are covered in educating stakeholders?

    1. Understanding the local community: culture, needs, resources   _____ _____ _____ _____

    2. How to recruit, train, and retain community resources and volunteers

        a. In general   _____ _____ _____ _____

        b. For special roles   _____ _____ _____ _____

    3. How to move toward collaborations with community resources   _____ _____ _____ _____

    4. How to outreach to hard-to-involve students and families   _____ _____ _____ _____

    5. Understanding how to create a psychological sense of community   _____ _____ _____ _____

    6. Developing systematic social supports for students, families, and staff   _____ _____ _____ _____

    7. Other (specify) _____   _____ _____ _____ _____

D. Indicate below other things you want the school to do in enhancing community involvement and support.   _____ _____ _____ _____

Other matters relevant to enhancing community involvement and support are found in the surveys on

- Classroom-based Approaches (Guide 14.3)
- Home Involvement in Schooling (Guide 14.6)
- School-Community Collaboration (Guide 14.9)

Guide 14.8   Student and Family Assistance Programs and Services:
                         A Self-study Survey

Specialized assistance for students and their families is for the relatively few problems that cannot be handled without adding special interventions. The emphasis is on providing special services in a personalized way to assist with a broad range of needs. To begin with, social, physical, and mental health assistance available in the school and community are used. As community outreach brings in other resources, these are linked to existing activity in an integrated manner. Additional attention is paid to enhancing systems for triage, case and resource management, direct services for immediate needs, and referral for special services and special education as appropriate. Ongoing efforts are made to expand and enhance resources. While any office or room can be used, a valuable context for providing such services is a center facility, such as a family, community, health, or parent resource center.

A programmatic approach in this arena requires systems designed to provide special assistance in ways that increase the likelihood that a student will be more successful at school while also reducing the need for teachers to seek special programs and services. The work encompasses providing all stakeholders with information clarifying available assistance and how to access help, facilitating requests for assistance, handling referrals, providing direct service, implementing case and resource management, and interfacing with community outreach to assimilate additional resources into current service delivery. It also involves ongoing analyses of requests for services as a basis for working with school colleagues to design strategies that can reduce inappropriate reliance on special assistance. Thus major outcomes are enhanced access to special assistance as needed, indices of effectiveness, *and* the reduction of inappropriate referrals for such assistance.

Student and Family Assistance Programs and Services

Indicate all items that apply.

	Yes	Yes, but more of this is needed.	No	If no, is this something you want?
I. Providing Extra Support as Soon as a Need Is Recognized and Doing So in the Least Disruptive Ways				
A. Are there classroom-based approaches to reduce the need for teachers to seek special programs and services (e.g., prereferral interventions in classrooms; problem-solving conferences with parents; open access to school, district, and community support programs—see the Survey on Classroom-based Approaches, Guide 14.3)?	____	____	____	____
II. Timely Referral Interventions for Students and Families With Problems Based on Response to Extra Support				
A. What activity is there to facilitate and evaluate requests for assistance?				
1. Does the site have a directory that lists services and programs?	____	____	____	____
2. Is information circulated about services/programs?	____	____	____	____
3. Is information circulated clarifying how to make a referral?	____	____	____	____
4. Is information about services, programs, and referral procedures updated periodically?	____	____	____	____
5. Is a triage process used to assess				
a. Specific needs?	____	____	____	____
b. Priority for service?	____	____	____	____
6. Are procedures in place to ensure use of prereferral interventions?	____	____	____	____
7. Do inservice programs focus on teaching the staff ways to prevent unnecessary referrals?	____	____	____	____
8. Other? (specify) _____	____	____	____	____
III. Enhancing Access to Direct Interventions for Health, Mental Health, and Economic Assistance				
A. After triage, how are referrals handled?				
1. Is detailed information provided about available services (e.g., is an annotated community resource system available)?	____	____	____	____
2. Is there a special focus on facilitating effective decision making?	____	____	____	____
3. Are students/families helped to take the necessary steps to connect with a service or program to which they have been referred?	____	____	____	____
4. Is there a process to ensure referral follow-through?	____	____	____	____

	Yes	Yes, but more of this is needed.	No	If no, is this something you want?

B. What types of direct interventions are provided?

1. Which medical services and programs are provided?

		Yes	Yes, but more of this is needed.	No	If no, is this something you want?
a.	Immunizations	___	___	___	___
b.	First aid and emergency care	___	___	___	___
c.	Crisis follow-up medical care	___	___	___	___
d.	Health and safety education and counseling	___	___	___	___
e.	Health and safety prevention programs	___	___	___	___
f.	Screening for vision problems	___	___	___	___
g.	Screening for hearing problems	___	___	___	___
h.	Screening for health problems (specify) ___	___	___	___	___
i.	Screening for dental problems (specify) ___	___	___	___	___
j.	Treatment of some acute problems (specify) ___	___	___	___	___
k.	Medication monitoring	___	___	___	___
l.	Medication administration	___	___	___	___
m.	Home outreach	___	___	___	___
n.	Other (specify) ___	___	___	___	___

2. Which psychological services and programs are provided?

		Yes	Yes, but more of this is needed.	No	If no, is this something you want?
a.	Psychological first aid	___	___	___	___
b.	Crisis follow-up counseling	___	___	___	___
c.	Crisis hotlines	___	___	___	___
d.	Conflict mediation	___	___	___	___
e.	Alcohol and other drug abuse programs	___	___	___	___
f.	Pregnancy prevention program	___	___	___	___
g.	Programs for pregnant and parenting students	___	___	___	___
h.	Gang prevention program	___	___	___	___
i.	Gang intervention program	___	___	___	___
j.	Dropout prevention program	___	___	___	___
k.	Physical and sexual abuse prevention and response	___	___	___	___
l.	Individual counseling	___	___	___	___
m.	Group counseling	___	___	___	___
n.	Family counseling	___	___	___	___
o.	Mental health education	___	___	___	___
p.	Home outreach	___	___	___	___
q.	Other (specify) ___	___	___	___	___

3. Which of the following are provided to meet basic survival needs?

		Yes	Yes, but more of this is needed.	No	If no, is this something you want?
a.	Emergency food	___	___	___	___
b.	Emergency clothing	___	___	___	___
c.	Emergency housing	___	___	___	___
d.	Transportation support	___	___	___	___
e.	Welfare services	___	___	___	___
f.	Language translation	___	___	___	___
g.	Legal aid	___	___	___	___

		Yes	Yes, but more of this is needed.	No	If no, is this something you want?
h.	Protection from physical abuse	_____	_____	_____	_____
i.	Protection from sexual abuse	_____	_____	_____	_____
j.	Child care	_____	_____	_____	_____
k.	Employment assistance	_____	_____	_____	_____
l.	Other (specify) _____	_____	_____	_____	_____

4. Which of the following special education, Special Eligibility, and independent study programs and services are provided?

		Yes	Yes, but more of this is needed.	No	If no, is this something you want?
a.	Early education program	_____	_____	_____	_____
b.	Special day classes (specify) _____	_____	_____	_____	_____
c.	Speech and language therapy	_____	_____	_____	_____
d.	Adaptive PE	_____	_____	_____	_____
e.	Occupational and physical therapy	_____	_____	_____	_____
f.	Special assessment	_____	_____	_____	_____
g.	Resource Specialist Program	_____	_____	_____	_____
h.	Title I	_____	_____	_____	_____
i.	School Readiness Language Development Program	_____	_____	_____	_____
j.	Other (specify) _____	_____	_____	_____	_____

5. Which of the following adult education programs are provided?

		Yes	Yes, but more of this is needed.	No	If no, is this something you want?
a.	ESL	_____	_____	_____	_____
b.	Citizenship classes	_____	_____	_____	_____
c.	Basic literacy skill	_____	_____	_____	_____
d.	Parenting	_____	_____	_____	_____
e.	Helping children do better at school	_____	_____	_____	_____
f.	Other (specify) _____	_____	_____	_____	_____

6. Are services and programs provided to enhance school readiness? (Specify) _____

_____ _____ _____ _____

7. Which of the following are provided to address attendance problems?

		Yes	Yes, but more of this is needed.	No	If no, is this something you want?
a.	Absence follow-up	_____	_____	_____	_____
b.	Attendance monitoring	_____	_____	_____	_____
c.	First-day calls	_____	_____	_____	_____

8. Are discipline proceedings carried out regularly?

_____ _____ _____ _____

9. Other? (specify) _____

_____ _____ _____ _____

IV. **Care Monitoring, Management, Information Sharing, and Follow-up Assessment**

A. Which of the following are used to manage cases and resources?

		Yes	Yes, but more of this is needed.	No	If no, is this something you want?
1.	Is a student information system used?	_____	_____	_____	_____
2.	Is a system used to trail the progress of students and their families?	_____	_____	_____	_____
3.	Is a system used to facilitate communication for				
a.	Case management?	_____	_____	_____	_____
b.	Resource and system management?	_____	_____	_____	_____

	Yes	Yes, but more of this is needed.	No	If no, is this something you want?

4. Are there follow-up systems to determine
    a.   Referral follow-through? ____ ____ ____ ____
    b.   Consumer satisfaction with referrals? ____ ____ ____ ____
    c.   The need for more help? ____ ____ ____ ____
5. Other? (specify) _____ ____ ____ ____ ____

B. Which of the following are used to help enhance the quality and quantity of services and programs?
    1.   Is a quality improvement system used? ____ ____ ____ ____
    2.   Is a mechanism used to coordinate and integrate services/programs? ____ ____ ____ ____
    3.   Is there outreach to link up with community services and programs? ____ ____ ____ ____
    4.   Is a mechanism used to redesign current activity as new collaborations are developed? ____ ____ ____ ____
    5.   Other? (specify) _____ ____ ____ ____ ____

V. Mechanisms for *Resource* Coordination and Integration

A. Is there a resource-oriented mechanism (e.g., a Learning Supports Resource Team) that focuses on
    1.   Coordinating and integrating resources? ____ ____ ____ ____
    2.   Braiding resources? ____ ____ ____ ____
    3.   Pursuing economies of scale? ____ ____ ____ ____
    4.   Filling gaps? ____ ____ ____ ____
    5.   Linking with community providers (e.g., to fill gaps)? ____ ____ ____ ____

B. Is there a special facility to house student and family assistance programs and services (e.g., health center, family or parent center, counseling center)? ____ ____ ____ ____

VI. Enhancing Stakeholder Awareness of Programs and Services

A. Are there *written descriptions* of available learning supports programs? ____ ____ ____ ____

B. Are there written descriptions about
    1.   How to make referrals? ____ ____ ____ ____
    2.   The triage process? ____ ____ ____ ____
    3.   The process for case monitoring and management? ____ ____ ____ ____
    4.   The process for student review? ____ ____ ____ ____

C. Are there communication processes that inform stakeholders about available learning supports programs and how to navigate the systems? ____ ____ ____ ____

VII. Capacity Building to Enhance Student and Family Assistance

A. Are there programs to enhance broad stakeholder involvement in enhancing student and family assistance? ____ ____ ____ ____

B. With respect to programs used to meet the educational needs of personnel related to student and family assistance,

		Yes	Yes, but more of this is needed.	No	If no, is this something you want?
	1. Is there ongoing training for learning supports staff with respect to student and family assistance?	_____	_____	_____	_____
	2. Is there ongoing training for others involved in enhancing student and family assistance (e.g., teachers, administrators, volunteers)?	_____	_____	_____	_____
	3. Other? (specify) _____	_____	_____	_____	_____
C.	Which of the following topics are covered in educating stakeholders?				
	1. Broadening understanding of causes of learning, behavior, and emotional problems	_____	_____	_____	_____
	2. Broadening understanding of ways to ameliorate (prevent, correct) learning, behavior, and emotional problems	_____	_____	_____	_____
	3. Developing systematic academic supports for students in need	_____	_____	_____	_____
	4. What classroom teachers and the home can do to minimize the need for special interventions	_____	_____	_____	_____
	5. Enhancing resource quality, availability, and scope	_____	_____	_____	_____
	6. Enhancing the referral system and ensuring effective follow-through	_____	_____	_____	_____
	7. Enhancing the case management system in ways that increase service efficacy	_____	_____	_____	_____
	8. Other (specify) _____	_____	_____	_____	_____
D.	Indicate below other things you want the school to do in providing student and family assistance.	_____	_____	_____	_____

Other matters relevant to enhancing student and family assistance are found in the surveys on

- Learning Supports System Status (Guide 14.2)
- Home Involvement in Schooling (Guide 14.6)
- School-Community Collaboration (Guide 14.9)

Guide 14.9   School-Community Collaboration: A Self-study Survey

---

Formal efforts to create school-community collaboration to improve schools and neighborhoods encompass building formal relationships to connect resources involved in pre-K–12 schooling and resources in the community. (This includes collaboration among formal and informal organizations such as (a) schools; (b) the home; (c) agencies involved in providing health and human services, religion, policing, justice, economic development, fostering youth development, recreation, and enrichment; (c) businesses; (e) unions; (f) governance bodies; and (g) institutions of higher education.)

As you work toward enhancing such collaboration, it helps to clarify what you have in place as a basis for determining what needs to be done. You will want to pay special attention to

- The mechanisms used to enhance collaboration
- Clarifying what resources already are available
- How the resources are organized to work together
- What procedures are in place for enhancing resource usefulness

The following survey is designed as a self-study instrument related to school-community collaboration. Stakeholders can use such surveys to map and analyze the current status of their efforts.

This type of self-study is best done by teams. For example, a group of stakeholders could use the items to discuss how well specific processes and programs are functioning and what's not being done. Members of the team initially might work separately in filling out the items, but the real payoff comes from discussing them as a group. The instrument also can be used as a form of program quality review.

In analyzing the status of their school-community collaboration, the group may decide that some existing activity is not a high priority and that the resources should be redeployed to help establish more important programs. Other activity may be seen as needing to be embellished so that it is effective. Finally, decisions may be made regarding new desired activities, and since not everything can be added at once, priorities and timelines can be established.

I. **List Current School-Community Collaboration**
Make two lists:
1. Activities and collaborators that are focused on improving the *school*
2. Those focused on improving the *neighborhood* (through enhancing links with the school, including use of school facilities and resources)

II. **Overview: Areas for School-Community Collaboration**
Indicate the status of collaboration between a given school or family of schools and community with respect to each of the following areas:
Indicate all items that apply.

	Yes	Yes, but more of this is needed.	No	If no, is this something you want?
A. Improving the school (name of school(s): _____)	____	____	____	____
1. The instructional component of schooling	____	____	____	____
2. The governance and management of schooling	____	____	____	____
3. Financial support for schooling	____	____	____	____
4. Stakeholder development	____	____	____	____
5. School-based programs and services to address barriers to learning	____	____	____	____
B. Improving the neighborhood (through enhancing linkages with the school, including use of school facilities and resources)	____	____	____	____
1. Youth development programs	____	____	____	____
2. Youth and family recreation and enrichment opportunities	____	____	____	____
3. Physical health services	____	____	____	____
4. Mental health services	____	____	____	____
5. Programs to address psychosocial problems	____	____	____	____
6. Basic living needs services	____	____	____	____
7. College prep programs	____	____	____	____
8. Work/career programs	____	____	____	____
9. Social services	____	____	____	____
10. Crime and juvenile justice programs	____	____	____	____
11. Legal assistance	____	____	____	____
12. Support for development of neighborhood organizations	____	____	____	____
13. Economic development programs	____	____	____	____

III. Overview: System Status for Enhancing School-Community Collaboration

Items A–F ask about what processes are in place. Use the following ratings in responding to these items.

DK = Don't Know
1 = Not yet
2 = Planned
3 = Just recently initiated
4 = Has been functional for a while
5 = Well-institutionalized (well-established with a commitment to maintain)

A.	Is there a stated policy for enhancing school-community collaboration (e.g., from the school, community agencies, government bodies)?	DK	1	2	3	4	5
B.	Is there a designated leader or leaders for enhancing school-community collaboration?	DK	1	2	3	4	5
C.	With respect to each entity involved in the school-community collaboration, have specific persons been designated as representatives to meet with each other?	DK	1	2	3	4	5
D.	Do personnel involved in enhancing school-community collaboration meet regularly as a team to evaluate current status and plan next steps?	DK	1	2	3	4	5
E.	Is there a written plan for capacity building related to enhancing the school-community collaboration?	DK	1	2	3	4	5
F.	Are there written descriptions available to give to all stakeholders regarding current school-community collaboration efforts?	DK	1	2	3	4	5

Use the following ratings in responding to these items.

DK = Don't know
1 = Hardly ever effective
2 = Effective about 25% of the time
3 = Effective about half the time
4 = Effective about 75% of the time
5 = Almost always effective

G.	Are there effective processes by which stakeholders learn						
	1. What is available in the way of programs/services?	DK	1	2	3	4	5
	2. How to access programs/services they need?	DK	1	2	3	4	5
H.	In general, how effective are your local efforts to enhance school-community collaboration?	DK	1	2	3	4	5
I.	With respect to enhancing school-community collaboration, how effective are each of the following?						
	1. Current policy	DK	1	2	3	4	5
	2. Designated leadership	DK	1	2	3	4	5
	3. Designated representatives	DK	1	2	3	4	5
	4. Team monitoring and planning of next steps	DK	1	2	3	4	5
	5. Capacity-building efforts	DK	1	2	3	4	5

IV. School-Community Collaboration to Improve the School

Indicate the status of collaboration between a given school or family of schools and community (name of school(s): _____)

Indicate all items that apply.

	Yes	Yes, but more of this is needed.	No	If no, is this something you want?
A. Collaboration to improve *school*				
1. The instructional component of schooling				
a. Kindergarten readiness programs	_____	_____	_____	_____
b. Tutoring	_____	_____	_____	_____
c. Mentoring	_____	_____	_____	_____
d. School reform initiatives	_____	_____	_____	_____
e. Homework hotlines	_____	_____	_____	_____
f. Media/technology	_____	_____	_____	_____
g. Service learning	_____	_____	_____	_____
h. Career mentoring	_____	_____	_____	_____
i. Career academy programs	_____	_____	_____	_____
j. Adult education, ESL, literacy, citizenship classes	_____	_____	_____	_____
k. Others _____	_____	_____	_____	_____
2. The governance and management of schooling				
a. PTA/PTSA	_____	_____	_____	_____
b. Shared leadership	_____	_____	_____	_____
c. Advisory bodies	_____	_____	_____	_____
d. Others _____	_____	_____	_____	_____
3. School-based programs and services to address barriers to learning				
a. Student and family assistance programs/services*	_____	_____	_____	_____
b. Transition programs*	_____	_____	_____	_____
c. Crisis response and prevention programs*	_____	_____	_____	_____
d. Home involvement programs*	_____	_____	_____	_____
e. Community involvement programs*	_____	_____	_____	_____
f. Classroom-based approaches*	_____	_____	_____	_____
g. Preservice and inservice staff development programs	_____	_____	_____	_____
h. Others _____	_____	_____	_____	_____
4. Stakeholder development				
a. School staff	_____	_____	_____	_____
b. Staff from community programs and services	_____	_____	_____	_____
c. Family members	_____	_____	_____	_____
d. Others _____	_____	_____	_____	_____

	Yes	Yes, but more of this is needed.	No	If no, is this something you want?
5. Financial support for schooling				
a. Adopt-a-school	___	___	___	___
b. Grant programs and funded projects	___	___	___	___
c. Donations/fundraising	___	___	___	___
d. Others _____	___	___	___	___
B. Collaboration to improve *neighborhood*				
1. Youth development programs				
a. Home visitation programs	___	___	___	___
b. Parent education	___	___	___	___
c. Infant and toddler programs	___	___	___	___
d. Child care/children's centers/ preschool programs	___	___	___	___
e. Community service programs	___	___	___	___
f. Public health and safety programs	___	___	___	___
g. Leadership development programs	___	___	___	___
h. Others _____	___	___	___	___
2. Youth and family recreation and enrichment opportunities				
a. Art/music/cultural programs	___	___	___	___
b. Park programs	___	___	___	___
c. Youth clubs	___	___	___	___
d. Scouts	___	___	___	___
e. Youth sports leagues	___	___	___	___
f. Community centers	___	___	___	___
g. Library programs	___	___	___	___
h. Faith community activities	___	___	___	___
i. Camping programs	___	___	___	___
j. Others _____	___	___	___	___
3. Physical health services				
a. School-based/linked clinics for primary care	___	___	___	___
b. Immunization clinics	___	___	___	___
c. Communicable disease control programs	___	___	___	___
d. Early periodic screening, diagnosis, and treatment (EPSDT) programs	___	___	___	___
e. Pro bono/volunteer programs	___	___	___	___
f. AIDS/HIV programs	___	___	___	___
g. Asthma programs	___	___	___	___
h. Pregnant and parenting minors programs	___	___	___	___
i. Dental services	___	___	___	___
j. Vision and hearing services	___	___	___	___
k. Referral facilitation	___	___	___	___
l. Emergency care	___	___	___	___
m. Others _____	___	___	___	___
4. Mental health services				
a. School-based/linked clinics with mental health component	___	___	___	___
b. EPSDT mental health focus	___	___	___	___
c. Pro bono/volunteer programs	___	___	___	___
d. Referral facilitation	___	___	___	___

	Yes	Yes, but more of this is needed.	No	If no, is this something you want?
e. Counseling	_____	_____	_____	_____
f. Crisis hotlines	_____	_____	_____	_____
g. Others _____	_____	_____	_____	_____
5. Programs to address psychosocial problems				
a. Conflict mediation/resolution	_____	_____	_____	_____
b. Substance abuse	_____	_____	_____	_____
c. Community/school safe havens	_____	_____	_____	_____
d. Safe passages	_____	_____	_____	_____
e. Youth violence prevention	_____	_____	_____	_____
f. Gang alternatives	_____	_____	_____	_____
g. Pregnancy prevention and counseling	_____	_____	_____	_____
h. Case management of programs for high-risk youth	_____	_____	_____	_____
i. Child abuse and domestic violence programs	_____	_____	_____	_____
j. Others _____	_____	_____	_____	_____
6. Basic living needs services				
a. Food_____	_____	_____	_____	
b. Clothing	_____	_____	_____	_____
c. Housing	_____	_____	_____	_____
d. Child care	_____	_____	_____	_____
e. Transportation assistance	_____	_____	_____	_____
f. Others _____	_____	_____	_____	_____
7. Work/career/higher education programs				
a. College prep programs	_____	_____	_____	_____
b. Job mentoring	_____	_____	_____	_____
c. Job shadowing	_____	_____	_____	_____
d. Job programs and employment opportunities	_____	_____	_____	_____
e. Others _____	_____	_____	_____	_____
8. Social services				
a. School-based/linked family resource centers	_____	_____	_____	_____
b. Integrated services initiatives	_____	_____	_____	_____
c. Budgeting/financial management counseling	_____	_____	_____	_____
d. Family preservation and support	_____	_____	_____	_____
e. Foster care school transition programs	_____	_____	_____	_____
f. Case management	_____	_____	_____	_____
g. Immigration and cultural transition assistance	_____	_____	_____	_____
h. Language translation	_____	_____	_____	_____
i. Others _____	_____	_____	_____	_____
9. Crime and juvenile justice programs				
a. Camp returnee programs	_____	_____	_____	_____
b. Children's court liaison	_____	_____	_____	_____
c. Truancy mediation	_____	_____	_____	_____
d. Juvenile diversion programs with school	_____	_____	_____	_____

		Yes	Yes, but more of this is needed.	No	If no, is this something you want?
e.	Probation services at school	___	___	___	___
f.	Police protection programs	___	___	___	___
g.	Others ___	___	___	___	___
10.	**Legal assistance**				
a.	Legal aid programs	___	___	___	___
b.	Others ___	___	___	___	___
11.	**Support for development of neighborhood organizations**				
a.	Neighborhood protective associations	___	___	___	___
b.	Emergency response planning and implementation	___	___	___	___
c.	Neighborhood coalitions and advocacy groups	___	___	___	___
d.	Volunteer services	___	___	___	___
e.	Welcoming clubs	___	___	___	___
f.	Social support networks	___	___	___	___
g.	Others ___	___	___	___	___
12.	**Economic development and housing programs**				
a.	Empowerment zones	___	___	___	___
b.	Urban village programs	___	___	___	___
c.	Accessing affordable housing	___	___	___	___
d.	Others ___	___	___	___	___

*See surveys for each of these arenas of school intervention.

Guide 14.10   Analyzing Gaps, Reviewing Resources, Planning Action

Based on the mapping you have done, make an analysis of

1. Which programs address barriers that your district/school has identified as the most significant factors interfering with students learning and teachers teaching effectively

2. Which of the significant factors are not being addressed (these are gaps to be filled)

3. Your priorities with respect to filling gaps

4. Any programs that you think are not effective and probably should be discontinued so that the resources can be redeployed to fill your high-priority gaps

5. Who in the community you can establish a collaboration with to fill your high priority gaps

6. Other sources of funds available at this time to fill the gaps

7. What steps you will take to act upon the analysis

Natural Opportunities to Promote Social and Emotional Learning and Well-being

15

Natural opportunities for learning are authentic, teachable moments.

What Are Natural Opportunities?
    Daily Opportunities
    Yearly Patterns
    Transitions
    Early After the Onset of Student Problems
Some Key Principles Underlying Efforts to Use Teachable Moments
Making It Happen
Concluding Comments

In some form or another, every school has goals emphasizing a desire to enhance students' personal and social functioning. Such goals reflect views that social and emotional growth are important in

- Enhancing the daily smooth functioning of schools and the emergence of a safe, caring, and supportive school climate
- Facilitating students' holistic development
- Enabling student motivation and capability for academic learning
- Optimizing life beyond schooling

Sadly, the stated goals too often are not connected to daily practices. This seems even more the case as increasing accountability demands mount for quick academic gains on achievement tests. So just as calls for attending to social and emotional learning are increasing and research findings grow promising, the focus on such matters widely remains marginalized in schools.

Some schools do provide prominent demonstrations of curriculum-based approaches to promote social-emotional learning and incorporate character education, including programs designed to address risk factors and prevent problems. Others have programs that pair students with mentors, or engage students in helping peers, or encourage participation in service learning activity, and so forth. Districtwide, however, a full-scale commitment to such programs is rare. And the situation is unlikely to change as long as the focus on social and emotional learning is viewed as taking time away from efforts to increase achievement test scores.

Given the last point, those concerned with promoting social-emotional learning and minimizing transactions that interfere with positive growth need to place greater emphasis on strategies that can capitalize on *natural* opportunities at schools. In keeping with this notion, this resource briefly (a) outlines a range of natural opportunities, (b) highlights key principles underlying efforts to use such opportunities, and (c) suggests who might take the lead in developing strategies for capitalizing on them.

WHAT ARE NATURAL OPPORTUNITIES?

Guide 15.1 offers examples of natural opportunities at schools for promoting personal and social growth. They are grouped into four categories:

- Daily opportunities
- Yearly patterns
- Transitions
- Early after the onset of student problems

In effect, natural opportunities are one of the most authentic examples of "teachable moments." A few comments about each will help clarify this point.

Daily Opportunities

Schools are social milieus. Each day in the classroom and around the school, students interact with their peers and various adults in formal and informal ways. Every encounter, positive and negative, represents a potential learning experience. All school staff, and especially teachers, can learn ways to use the encounters to minimize transactions that work against positive growth and capitalize on many opportunities to enhance social-emotional learning.

Appreciation of what needs attention can be garnered readily by looking at the school day through the lens of goals for personal and social functioning. Is instruction carried out in ways that strengthen or hinder development of interpersonal skills and connections and student understanding of self and others? Are cooperative learning and sharing promoted? Is inappropriate competition minimized? Are interpersonal conflicts mainly suppressed or are they used as learning opportunities? Are roles provided for all students to be positive helpers throughout the school and community?

Of course, appreciating problems and opportunities is not enough. Preservice and inservice education must focus on teaching those working in schools how to minimize what's going wrong and enable personal and social growth.

Yearly Patterns

The culture of most schools yields fairly predictable patterns over the course of the year. The beginning of the school year, for example, typically is a period of hope. As the year progresses, a variety of stressors are encountered. Examples include increasingly difficult homework assignments, interpersonal conflicts, and testing and grading pressures. There also are special circumstances associated with holidays, social events, sports, grade promotions, and graduation.

Each month, strategies can be implemented that encourage school staff to minimize stressors and enhance coping through social-emotional learning and shared problem solving. To support such efforts, the Center for Mental Health in Schools at UCLA has developed a set of monthly themes as examples for schools to draw upon and go beyond. (See the Center Web site for a description of how to pursue such themes, at http://smhp.psych.ucla.edu.) One set of examples is listed in Guide 15.1; other themes are readily generated. The point is to establish a focus each month and build the capacity of school staff to evolve the school culture in ways that reduce unnecessary stressors and naturally promote social and emotional development.

Transitions

Students are regularly confronted with a variety of transitions: changing schools, changing grades, and encountering a range of other minor and major transitory demands. Such transitions are ever present and usually are not a customary focus of institutionalized efforts to support students. Every transition can exacerbate problems or can be used as a natural opportunity to promote positive learning and attitudes and reduce alienation.

Guided by their goals for enhancing personal and social functioning, schools need to build their capacities to address transitions proactively. Examples of schoolwide and classroom-specific opportunities include a focus on welcoming new arrivals (e.g., students, their families, staff,

Guide 15.1   Examples of Natural Opportunities at School to Promote
Social-Emotional Learning

I. Daily Opportunities

   1. In the classroom (e.g., as students relate to each other and to staff during class and group instruction, as essential aspects of cooperative learning and peer sharing and tutoring, as one facet of addressing interpersonal and learning problems)

   2. Schoolwide (e.g., providing roles for all students to be positive helpers and leaders throughout the school and community; engaging students in strategies to enhance a caring, supportive, and safe school climate; as essential aspects of conflict resolution and crisis prevention)

II. In Response to Yearly Patterns. Schools have a yearly rhythm, changing with the cycle and demands of the school calendar. The following are examples of monthly themes the center has developed for schools to draw upon and go beyond. The idea is to establish focal points for minimizing potential problems and pursuing natural opportunities to promote social-emotional learning.

September: *Getting Off to a Good Start*

October: *Enabling School Adjustment*

November: *Responding to Referrals in Ways That Can Stem the Tide*

December: *Reengaging Students: Using a Student's Time Off in Ways That Pay Off!*

January: *New Year's Resolutions—A Time for Renewal: A New Start for Everyone*

February: *The Midpoint of a School Year—Report Cards and Conferences: Another Barrier or a Challenging Opportunity?*

March: *Reducing Stress; Preventing Burnout*

April: *Spring Can Be a High Risk Time for Students*

May: *Time to Help Students and Families Plan Successful Transitions to a New Grade or School*

June: *Summer and the Living Ain't Easy*

July: *Using "Down Time" to Plan Better Ways to Work Together in Providing Learning Supports*

August: *Now Is the Time to Develop Ways to Avoid Burnout*

III. During Transitions

   1. Daily (e.g., capturing opportunities before school, during breaks, lunch, after school)

   2. With newcomers (e.g., as part of welcoming and social support processes; in addressing school adjustment difficulties)

   3. Grade to grade (e.g., preparing students for the next year; addressing adjustment difficulties as the year begins)

IV. At the First Indication That a Student Is Experiencing Problems. Enhancing social and emotional functioning is a natural focus of early-after-onset interventions for learning, behavior, and emotional problems.

volunteers); providing ongoing social supports as students adjust to new grades, new schools, and new programs; and using beforeschool, afterschool, and intersession activities as times for facilitating generalization and enrichment of such learning.

Early After the Onset of Student Problems

Stated simply, every student problem represents a need and an opportunity for learning—and often what needs to be learned falls into the social-emotional arena. Whatever the first response when a problem arises, the second response should include a focus on promoting personal and social growth.

SOME KEY PRINCIPLES UNDERLYING EFFORTS TO USE TEACHABLE MOMENTS

A natural focus on social and emotional learning at school is built on the same fundamental principles advocated in discussions of good schooling and teaching in a democracy. This means, first and foremost, addressing principles reflecting overlapping concerns about distributive justice (equity and fairness) and empowerment. Adherence to such concerns requires that school staff have

- Clarity about the respective rights and obligations of all stakeholders
- The time, training, skills, and institutional and collegial support necessary to build relationships of mutual trust, respect, equality, and appropriate risk taking
- The motivation and skill to create an accepting, caring, and safe environment and to account for distinctive needs, assets, and other forms of diversity

At a minimum, when designing and implementing instruction, practices must not have a negative impact on social and emotional growth. To this end, the aim is for teachers to

- Tailor processes so that they are a good fit for the learner in terms of *both* motivation and capability (i.e., meet learners where they are).
- Deal with students holistically and developmentally, as individuals and as part of a family, neighborhood, and community.

With a view to designing academic instruction in ways that will also enhance social and emotional learning, the aim is for teachers to

- Offer real choices and involve students in meaningful decision making.
- Contextualize and make learning authentic, including the use of real-life situations as well as mentors.
- Foster joint student learning activities and products.

And all the foregoing also are applicable when pursuing the teachable moments that arise during other natural opportunities.

MAKING IT HAPPEN

Increasing a school's focus on natural opportunities for personal and social growth requires advocacy, planning, and building the capacity of school staff. At most schools, learning supports staff represent natural leaders for pursuing all this. As a starting point, such staff can form a small work group dedicated to moving the agenda forward.

The functions for the work group include

- Developing a map of natural opportunities for promoting social-emotional development
- Delineating ways in which students experience transactions that interfere with positive growth
- Clarifying ways for staff to minimize negative experiences and maximize use of opportunities to promote positive growth
- Providing a variety of learning opportunities for staff related to each of the foregoing

CONCLUDING COMMENTS

Teachers and other school staff have been described as prisoners of time. Those concerned about social and emotional learning at school understand this all too well. Proposals for adding new programs are rejected because there is sparse time available for teaching anything but standards-based academic subjects. Even when nonacademic programs are added, requests for time to train teachers are given short shrift because there is little time available for anything besides inservice related to academic instruction. The bottom line is that competition for classroom and teacher time is fierce. As a result, efforts to add a curriculum for social-emotional learning and train a district's teachers to implement it with fidelity usually are stymied.

Given sparse time and resources, hard choices must be made. How much should be invested in curricular approaches to social-emotional learning? How much should be invested in pursuing natural opportunities to promote a school's goals for personal and social functioning? Making such decisions at this point is difficult because so little research has been done on the latter approach or on the comparative impact of the two. All this underscores the problem of basing practice only on approaches for which there already is evidence. Here is an instance where specific data exist on one approach (i.e., teaching a formal curriculum) but not directly on the other, and there is no comparative research. Questions cannot be satisfactorily answered about the *respective* or *complementary* range of impact, maintenance, generalization, and iatrogenic effects (e.g., negative outcomes to individuals, families, schools) or about costs versus benefits. A bit of data exists, however, that warrants the attention of decision makers. The data are that most districts have not moved to adopt curriculum for social-emotional learning. And in many schools, not only are natural opportunities to promote such growth not taken, current practices are having deleterious effects.

About Mental   16
Health in Schools

In many schools, the need for enhancing mental health is a common topic. Moreover, efforts to transform the mental health system in the United States are looking at the schools as an essential partner. A perspective on all this is offered here.

The theme throughout is

> Advancing mental health in schools is about much more than expanding services and creating full-service schools. It is about becoming part of a comprehensive, multifaceted approach that strengthens students, families, schools, and neighborhoods and does so in ways that maximize learning, caring, and well-being. This means fully integrating mental health agendas into the school's learning supports component.

Mental Health in Schools: Where We Are
A Shared Agenda: Where We Need to Go
Concluding Comments

Because schools are not in the mental health business, they tend to shy away from the term, especially since it usually is viewed as only about treating mental disorders. Isolated mental health agendas always are marginalized at schools. Nevertheless, a variety of agendas are pursued. And ironically, available research suggests that for some youngsters, schools are the main providers of mental health services. As Burns and her colleagues (1995) found, "the major player in the de facto system of care was the education sector—more than three-fourths of children receiving mental health services were seen in the education sector, and for many this was the sole source of care" (p. 152).

MENTAL HEALTH IN SCHOOLS: WHERE WE ARE

While mental health in schools is widely discussed, what's being talked about often differs in fundamental ways. This not only contributes to a degree of confusion, it seems to be a source of increasing conflict. The fact is that various enterprises are being pursued; therefore, there are divergent policy, practice, research, and training agendas.

Agendas for mental health in schools can be grouped in terms of the *primary* interests of various parties. For our purposes here, we categorize seven major interests, each of which can be subdivided. While some are complementary, many are not. So it is not surprising that competing interests come into conflict with each other:

1. Efforts to use schools to increase *access* to youngsters and their families for purposes of
   a. Conducting research related to mental health concerns
   b. Providing services related to mental health concerns

2. Efforts to increase *availability* of mental health interventions
   a. Through expanded use of school resources
   b. Through co-locating community resources on school campuses
   c. Through finding ways to combine school and community resources

3. Efforts to get schools to adopt or enhance specific programs and approaches
   a. For treating specific individuals
   b. For addressing specific types of problems in targeted ways
   c. For addressing problems through schoolwide, "universal" interventions
   d. For promoting healthy social and emotional development

4. Efforts to *improve specific processes and interventions* related to mental health in schools (e.g., improve systems for identifying and referring problems and for case management, enhancing prereferral and early-intervention programs)

5. Efforts to enhance *economic interests* of specific disciplines, contractors, businesses, and so forth that are
   a. Already part of school budgets
   b. Seeking to be part of school budgets

6. Efforts to *change how student supports are conceived* at schools (e.g., rethink, reframe, reform, restructure) through
   a. Enhanced focus on multidisciplinary team work (e.g. among school staff, with community professionals)
   b. Enhanced coordination of interventions (e.g., among school programs and services, with community programs and services)

    c. Appropriate integration of interventions (e.g., that schools own, that communities base or link with schools)

    d. Modifying the roles and functions of various student support staff

    e. Developing a comprehensive, multifaceted, and cohesive component for systematically addressing barriers to student learning at every school

7. Efforts to *reduce school involvement* in mental health programs and services (e.g., to maximize the focus on instruction, to use the resources for youth development, to keep the school out of areas where family values are involved)

As a result of so many agendas, a wide range of school-based and school-linked mental health programs have appeared, and conflicts are common.

Agendas for mental health in schools are manifested through five major *delivery mechanisms and formats* (see Guide 16.1). However, despite this range of activity, it is common knowledge that few schools come close to having enough resources to deal with a large number of students with mental health and psychosocial problems. School staff whose functions overlap with mental health concerns have a variety of other roles and responsibilities, and mental health providers who come into the school usually are part-time employees.

Clearly, mental health activity is going on in schools with competing agendas vying for the same dwindling resources. Naturally, all advocates want to advance their agendas. And to do so, the temptation usually is to keep the agendas problem-focused and rather specific and narrow. Politically, this makes some sense. But in the long run, it may be counterproductive since it fosters piecemeal, fragmented, and redundant policies and practices. Diverse school and community resources are attempting to address complex, multifaceted, and overlapping psychosocial and mental health concerns in highly fragmented and marginalized ways. This has led to redundancy, counterproductive competition, and inadequate results.

One response to this state of affairs is the call for realigning policy and practice around a cohesive framework based on well-conceived models and the best available scholarship. In particular, it is stressed that initiatives for mental health in schools must connect in major ways with the missions of schools and integrate with a restructured system of education support programs and services. This theme permeates this book.

A SHARED AGENDA: WHERE WE NEED TO GO

As we have stressed, it has long been acknowledged that psychosocial and mental health concerns must be addressed if schools are to function

Guide 16.1   Delivery Mechanisms and Formats

The five mechanisms and related formats are

I. School-financed Student Support Services

Most school districts employ support services or pupil services professionals, such as school psychologists, counselors, and social workers. These personnel perform services connected with mental health and psychosocial problems (including related services designated for special education students). The format for this delivery mechanism usually is a combination of centrally based and school-based services.

II. School District Mental Health Unit

A few districts operate specific mental health (MH) units that encompass clinic facilities, as well as providing services and consultation to schools. Some others have started financing their own school-based health centers with MH services as a major element. The format for this mechanism tends to be centralized clinics with the capability for outreach to schools.

III. Formal Connections With Community Mental Health Services

Increasingly, schools have developed connections with community agencies, often as the result of the school-based health center movement, school-linked services initiatives (e.g., full-service schools, family resource centers), and efforts to develop systems of care (e.g., wraparound services for those in special education). Four formats have emerged:

- Co-location of community agency personnel and services at schools—sometimes in the context of school-based health centers partly financed by community health organizations
- Formal linkages with agencies to enhance access and service coordination for students and families at an agency, at a nearby satellite clinic, or in a school-based or school-linked family resource center
- Formal partnerships between a school district and community agencies to establish or expand school-based or school-linked facilities that include provision of MH services
- Contracting with community providers to provide needed student services

IV. Classroom-based Curricula and Special "Pullout" Interventions

Most schools include in some facet of their curricula a focus on enhancing social and emotional functioning. Specific instructional activities may be designed to promote healthy social and emotional development or to prevent psychosocial problems, such as behavior and emotional problems, school violence, and drug abuse. And of course, special education classrooms always are supposed to have a constant focus on mental health concerns. Three formats have emerged:

- Integrated instruction as part of the regular classroom content and processes
- Specific curricula or special interventions implemented by personnel specially trained to carry out the processes
- A curriculum approach as part of a multifaceted set of interventions designed to enhance positive development and prevent problems

V. Comprehensive, Multifaceted, and Integrated Approaches

A few school districts have begun the process of reconceptualizing their piecemeal and fragmented approaches to addressing barriers that interfere with students' having an equal opportunity to succeed at school. They are starting to restructure their student support services and weave them together with community resources and integrate all this with instructional efforts that effect healthy development. The intent is to develop a full continuum of programs and services encompassing efforts to promote positive development, prevent problems, respond as early after onset as is feasible, and offer treatment regimens. Mental health and psychosocial concerns are a major focus of the continuum of interventions. Efforts to move toward comprehensive, multifaceted approaches are likely to be enhanced by initiatives to integrate schools more fully into systems of care and the growing movement to create community schools. Three formats are emerging:

- Mechanisms to coordinate and integrate school and community services
- Initiatives to restructure support programs and services and integrate them into school reform agendas
- Community schools

satisfactorily and students are to learn and perform effectively. The need is articulated nicely by the Carnegie Council Task Force on Education of Young Adolescents (1989):

> School systems are not responsible for meeting every need of their students. But when the need directly affects learning, the school must meet the challenge. (p. 61)

This necessity is reflected in the aims of the No Child Left Behind Act and the Individuals with Disabilities Education Act. And it is consonant with the goals and recommendations of the president's New Freedom Commission on Mental Health. Indeed, these initiatives reflect a shared agenda and must integrate school improvement policies and initiatives in ways that more wisely invest sparse resources.

With a shared agenda in mind, mental health in schools is conceived as (a) *part of* essential learning supports systems that enable students to learn so that schools can achieve their mission and (b) a fundamental facet of the initiative to transform the mental health system. In pursuit of a shared agenda, existing resources can be deployed and redeployed in ways that enhance equity with respect to availability, access, and effectiveness. The focus of mental health in schools is on

- Promoting social-emotional development, preventing mental health and psychosocial problems, and enhancing resiliency and protective buffers
- Intervening as early after the onset of emotional, behavior, and learning problems as is feasible and to address severe and chronic problems

- Addressing systemic matters at schools that affect student and staff well-being, such as practices that engender bullying, alienation, and student disengagement from classroom learning
- Establishing guidelines, standards, and accountability for mental health in schools in ways that confront equity considerations
- Building the capacity of all school staff to address emotional, behavioral, and learning problems and promote healthy social-emotional development
- Drawing on all empirical evidence as an aid in developing a comprehensive, multifaceted, and cohesive continuum of school-community interventions to address emotional, behavioral, and learning problems (again, see Guide 3.1)

CONCLUDING COMMENTS

Those concerned with enhancing mental health in schools must approach the matter under a more comprehensive umbrella and with an agenda that meshes with the basic mission of schools. As discussed throughout this book, the umbrella is that of addressing barriers to learning and the agenda is to develop essential systems that enable students to learn in ways that assure that schools achieve their mandates. In this respect, we point again to the comprehensive and multifaceted guidelines outlined in Guide 5.6.

What's involved in pursuing a shared agenda? It calls for braiding resources and interventions with a view to ensuring that there is a cohesive component rather than separate programs and services. Coordinated efforts naturally are part of this, but the key is developing an integrated whole that meets overlapping needs. (For more on this, see the description of the work of the Center for Mental Health in Schools at UCLA in Guide 16.2, found at the end of this chapter.)

In a real sense, enhancing mental health in schools requires support staff to accept the idea that the school is the client. This does not mean that the needs of individuals are ignored. Rather, it recognizes that the goal is not to just respond to a few specific students with problems but rather to ensure that all students engage and reengage in classroom learning and that schools become healthier and health-promoting places for all concerned. And all this, of course, involves major systemic changes that addresses complications stemming from the scale of public education in the United States.

Clearly, enhancing mental health in schools is not an easy task. Indeed, it is likely to remain an insurmountable task until those advocating for mental health in schools pursue their agenda under the umbrella of a cohesive learning supports component and school reformers accept the reality that such activity is essential and does not represent an agenda separate from a school's instructional mission. For this to happen, those concerned with mental health in schools must encourage reformers to view the difficulty of raising achievement test scores through the complementary lenses of addressing barriers to learning and promoting healthy development. When this is done, it is more likely that mental health in schools will be understood as essential to the aim of leaving no child behind.

Guide 16.2 About the School Mental Health Project's Center for Mental Health in Schools at UCLA

In an effort to advance the field, the School Mental Health Project was established in 1986 in the Department of Psychology at UCLA to pursue theory, research, practice, and training related to addressing mental health and psychosocial concerns through school-based interventions. Under the auspices of the project, the national Center for Mental Health in Schools was funded in l995 and in October 2000 began a second five-year cycle of operation. The center is one of two national centers focusing directly on mental health in schools.* Its goals are to enhance *in strategic ways* (a) availability of and access to resources to improve and advance MH in schools, (b) the capacity of systems and personnel, and (c) the role of schools in addressing MH, psychosocial, and related health concerns.

From the perspective of the guiding frameworks described in various works generated by the project/center staff, addressing MH of youngsters involves ensuring that

- Mental illness is understood within the broader perspective of psychosocial and related health problems and in terms of strengths as well as deficits
- The roles of schools, communities, and homes are enhanced and pursued jointly
- Equity considerations are confronted
- The marginalization and fragmentation of policy, organizations, and daily practice are countered
- The challenges of evidence-based strategies and achieving results are addressed

Thus the center's work aims not only at improving practitioners' competence, but also at fostering changes in the systems with which they work. Such activity also addresses the varying needs of locales and the problems of accommodating diversity among those trained and among populations served.

Given the number of schools across the country, resource centers such as ours must work in well-conceived strategic ways. Thus our emphasis is on expanding programmatic efforts that enable all students to have an equal opportunity to succeed at school and on accomplishing essential systemic changes for sustainability and scale-up through (a) enhancing resource availability and the systems for delivering resources, (b) building state and local capacity, (c) improving policy, and (d) developing leadership.

The strategies for accomplishing all this include

- Connecting with major initiatives of foundations, federal government and policy bodies, and national associations
- Connecting with major initiatives of state departments and policy bodies, counties, and school districts
- Collaborating and network building for program expansion and systemic change
- Providing catalytic training to stimulate interest in program expansion and systemic change
- Catalytic use of technical assistance, the Internet, publications, resource materials, and regional meetings to stimulate interest in program expansion and systemic change

> Because we know that schools are not in the mental health business, all of our work strives to approach mental health and psychosocial concerns in ways that integrally connect with school reform. We do this by integrating health and related concerns into the broad perspective of addressing barriers to learning and promoting healthy development. We stress the need to restructure current policy and practice to enable development of a comprehensive and cohesive approach that is an essential and primary component of school reform, without which many students cannot benefit from instructional reforms, and thus achievement scores will not rise in the way current accountability pressures demand.

*The other national center, the Center for School Mental Health Assistance, is located at the University of Maryland at Baltimore and is directed by Mark Weist. Both centers are partially supported by the U.S. Dept. of Health and Human Services through the Office of Adolescent Health, Maternal and Child Health Bureau (Title V, Social Security Act), Health Resources and Services Administration, with cofunding from the Center for Mental Health Services, Substance Abuse and Mental Health Services Administration. The UCLA Center Web site is: http://smhp .psych.ucla.edu.

REFERENCES

Burns, B. J., Costello, E. J., Angold, A., Tweed, D., Stangl, D., Farmer, E., & Erkanli, A. (1995). Children's mental health service use across service sectors. *Health Affairs, 14*, 147–159.

Carnegie Council on Adolescent Development's Task Force on Education of Young Adolescents. (1989). *Turning points: Preparing American youth for the 21st century.* Washington, DC: Author.

New Directions for Student Support Initiative Brief

17

Assuring That No Child Is Left Behind

As part of the nationwide *New Direction for Student Support Initiative* described in the text, efforts are under way in various states to develop a brief overview statement to circulate widely about moving forward in the state.

With input from groups steering their state's initiative, the following generic brief was developed as a resource for others to adapt to fit their locality.

New Directions for Student Support Initiative*

Assuring That No Child Is Left Behind**

Enhancing Our Learning Support System by Building a Comprehensive Approach That Closes the Achievement Gap and Ensures That Every Student Has an Equal Opportunity to Succeed at School

School systems are not responsible for meeting every need of their students. But when the need directly affects learning, the school must meet the challenge.

—Carnegie Council on Education Task Force (1989)

As schools pursue their mission to educate and as communities pursue the aim of improving the quality of life of their residents, major initiatives have been introduced and progress is being made. At the same time, it is evident that there remains considerable fragmentation and significant gaps in some of our efforts to assure that no child is left behind. Fortunately, we have the opportunity and are at a place where we can take the next steps in strengthening our systems for addressing barriers to development and learning and promoting healthy development.

---

*The *New Directions for Student Support Initiative* was established in October 2002 in response to widespread interest in mounting a strategic effort to move in new directions. It is designed to encourage advocacy for and establishment of new directions and is building a leadership network to accomplish this. The initiative is hosted and facilitated by the Center for Mental Health in Schools at UCLA, and the list of cosponsoring associations and agencies has grown to over thirty. After holding one national and three regional summits, the emphasis is now on statewide summits, to be followed by the establishment of steering and work groups to guide the state's initiative.

**The following statement is intended to provide a template that can be adapted by schools, districts, and state educational agencies. It reflects input from various states where a summit for the *New Directions for Student Support Initiative* has been held and work on developing a statewide initiative is under way. It also incorporates pioneering work from Hawaii and Iowa and proposed legislation in California. To provide feedback or request additional copies of this document, contact ltaylor@ucla.edu.

Our schools strive for excellence in education, with strong parent and communitywide support. No community can be satisfied, however, until all its young people are healthy and socially competent, successful in school, and have an equal opportunity to grow into productive and contributing citizens.

The Challenge	In recent years, there has been increasing concern about a decline in standardized achievement test scores in reading and math and about dropout rates. And now the accountability requirements of the federal No Child Left Behind Act (2002) challenge us to develop ways to raise academic achievement levels of all students.

As the 2002 mission statement of the Council of Chief State School Officers stresses:

> It is not enough to say that all children can learn or that no child will be left behind; the work involves ... achieving the vision of an American education system that enables all children to succeed in school, work, and life.

*A system that **enables** all children to succeed*

Our schools recognize the essential nature and challenge of providing effective learning supports to enable the learning and development of all students by preventing and reducing barriers to student success. Given achievement gaps and recent evidence of a plateau effect in many schools, it seems evident that meeting the challenge will require not only improving how we teach but also will necessitate developing better ways for schools and communities to address factors that interfere with learning and teaching.

Reports from across the country verify earlier predictions that key facets of the No Child Left Behind reforms would result in modest immediate test score increases followed by a longer-term plateau. Data show that states reporting a steady few years' climb in achievement test scores during the 1990s now indicate faltering levels of achievement (e.g., Florida, Michigan, Texas). California is the most recent example of such a fade-out; the state's chief school officer recently confirmed that a majority of California's schools have hit a plateau or worse.

Building on Our History: Using What We've Learned

We understand the need, and we have examples and a science base upon which to build.

Every day, a wide range of learning, behavioral, physical, and emotional problems interfere with the ability of students to participate effectively and fully benefit from the instruction teachers provide. Even the best schools find that *too many* youngsters are growing up in situations where significant barriers regularly interfere with their reaching full potential.

The notion of *barriers to learning* encompasses both external and internal factors. Some children bring with them a wide range of problems stemming from restricted opportunities associated with poverty, difficult and diverse family conditions, high rates of mobility, lack of English language skills, violent neighborhoods, problems related to substance abuse, inadequate health care, and lack of enrichment opportunities. Some youngsters also bring with them intrinsic conditions that make learning and performing difficult. As a result, at every grade level there are students who come to school each day not quite ready to perform and learn in the most effective manner. And students' problems are exacerbated as they internalize the frustrations of confronting barriers to learning and the debilitating effects of performing poorly at school. All this interferes with the teacher's efforts to teach. (Clearly, addressing barriers is not at odds with the paradigm shift that emphasizes strengths, resilience, assets, and protective factors. Efforts to enhance positive development and improve instruction certainly can improve readiness to learn. However, it is frequently the case that preventing problems also requires direct action to remove or at least minimize the impact of barriers such as hostile environments and intrinsic problems. Without effective direct intervention, such barriers can continue to get in the way of development and learning.)

Our schools have a long history of assisting teachers in dealing with problems that interfere with school learning. Prominent examples are seen in the range of counseling, psychological, and social service programs and in initiatives for enhancing students' assets and resiliency. A great deal is done, but efforts are fragmented and often marginalized. As a result, they are less effective than they can be. It is time to establish as a priority the development of a comprehensive, multifaceted, and cohesive approach for addressing barriers to student learning and promoting healthy development.

Previous initiatives for enhancing student supports, in our schools and around the country, provide a foundation upon which we can build in our efforts to close the achievement gap and ensure that all students have equal educational opportunities. Fortunately, the science base provides evidence about what needs to be changed and what new directions hold promise.

Educators recognize and research supports the understanding that barriers to learning demand consistent, systemwide attention. The need is for a focused, cohesive, research-based effort that engages schools and their communities in collaboratively addressing all major barriers to learning and teaching.

Learning Supports: The Logic and the Science Base

We are committed to strengthening learning supports for all students. The aim is to enhance our system of learning supports. The specific focus is on developing a comprehensive and adaptable learning supports framework that can be fully integrated with efforts to improve instruction and management of resources. Such a framework will guide us in pursuing essential new directions for establishing a systemic approach to enhance outcomes for students, families, schools, and neighborhoods.

The logic for policy and systemic changes to enhance learning supports stems from the following basic premises:

Schools Must Address Barriers to Learning and Teaching in Order to Accomplish Their Instructional Mission.

- The mission of education includes a fundamental commitment to and accountability for academic achievement.
- Children/youth must be healthy, safe, and supported if they are to achieve academically and succeed in school.
- Some students experience significant barriers to learning.
- Student achievement is improved and barriers to learning are alleviated through a system of learning supports that incorporates a full continuum of evidence-based programs and services that ensure safe, health-promoting, supportive, and inclusive learning environments.

School-Community-Family Collaboration Is Essential.

- A full continuum of programs and services transcends what any one system can provide and requires a combination of school and community changes.
- Youngsters thrive and overcome barriers to learning when families are strengthened and assisted to find pathways to support their children's education and to pursue their own learning.
- Schools are strengthened when the efforts of community organizations and institutions are results-oriented and include policies, programs, practices, and resources that are aligned with those of schools to improve student achievement.
- Efforts to address barriers to learning are enhanced when interveners are willing to coordinate and integrate their efforts to support academic achievement.

The logic is clear . . .

Cohesive Leadership and Aligned Policy Are Needed at Every Level.

- Systems of learning supports require quality leaders at all levels who use effective systems of communication and data management, efficient and effective organization of resources, and well-articulated planning.
- Cohesive, aligned policies and practices within a district and among its community partners are essential to effect system changes at schools.
- The role of state, regional, and local agencies is to align, assist, and support local-level changes.

Beyond the logic, data show both a clear need and a science base for learning supports. In addition to lagging reading and math scores, the need is reflected in achievement gaps and high dropout rates for subpopulations of students, such as African Americans and Hispanics, students eligible for free or reduced-priced lunch, English language learners, and students with disabilities. The increased accountability and related timelines set by the No Child Left Behind Act (2002) places increasing pressure on schools where the population of students is diverse.

. . . the science base is expanding in volume and positive results.

The science base for learning supports is gleaned from a growing volume of research on the value of schools, families, and communities working together to provide supportive programs and services that enable students to learn and teachers to teach. Findings include improved school attendance, fewer behavior problems, improved interpersonal skills, enhanced student engagement and reengagement in classroom learning, enhanced achievement, and increased bonding at school and at home.

All this leads to the following conclusion:

Schools must implement and sustain a fully integrated system of learning supports into school improvement programs and practices. When a comprehensive range of learning supports is provided in a timely and effective manner, fewer students will require more intensive and expensive services. And the learning, achievement, and performance of all children and youth will improve in ways that enable them to become self-sufficient and successful members of a community and workforce.

Meeting the Challenge

The challenge, then, is to create a comprehensive, multifaceted, and cohesive system that supports student learning and healthy development and addresses barriers. Developing such a system of learning supports necessitates working in ways that reduce marginalization and fragmentation and minimize counterproductive competition for sparse resources. Toward these ends, we must rethink and redesign our current approach to learning supports with respect to

- Policies
- Intervention frameworks, standards, and accountability indicators
- Infrastructure design at the school level and at the district level for a feeder pattern (to achieve economies of scale) and for providing support from the district and community, intermediate regional agencies, and the state's department of education and its agency partners

In proceeding, we can draw upon and become part of pioneering initiatives emerging around the country that are rethinking how schools and communities meet the challenge of addressing persistent barriers to student learning. These initiatives reflect a fundamental commitment to a three-component framework for school improvement (see the figure that follows). Such a framework encompasses an agenda for developing intervention *systems* to (a) promote healthy development and prevent problems, (b) provide assistance as early as feasible after the onset of problems, and (c) address the needs of students with chronic and severe problems.

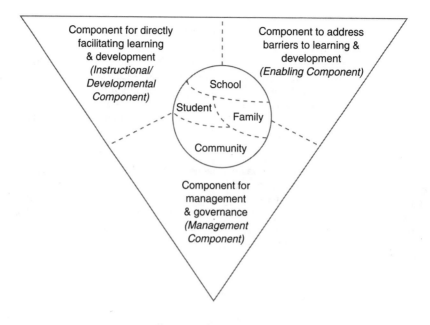

Component for directly facilitating learning & development (*Instructional/Developmental Component*)

Component to address barriers to learning & development (*Enabling Component*)

School

Student

Family

Community

Component for management & governance (*Management Component*)

A component to address barriers to learning and teaching

In developing a component to address barriers to learning and development, a major emphasis is on improving neighborhood, home, school, and classroom environments to prevent problems and enhance youngsters' strengths. At the same time, essential supports and assistance are provided those who need something more to address barriers and engage or reengage them in schooling and *enable* learning. This has led to calling this facet of school-community improvement an *Enabling Component*. The usefulness of the concept of an Enabling Component as a broad, unifying focal point for policy and practice is evidenced in its adoption by various states and localities around the country. These include the California and Iowa Departments of Education, whose version is called a *Learning Supports Component*, and the Hawaii Department of Education, whose version is called a *Comprehensive Student Support System*. Others have used terms such as *supportive learning environment*.

Whatever the component is called, the goals are the same:

- Providing students with comprehensive, multifaceted, and integrated learning supports that are accessible, timely, and strength-based so students can achieve in school, be confident and caring, and become contributing citizens in their communities
- Involving families, fellow students, educators, and community members as integral partners in the provision of a supportive, respectful learning environment
- Integrating the human and financial resources of public and private agencies to create caring communities at each school

The focus of such a component begins in the classroom, with differential classroom practices as the base of support for each student that extends beyond the classroom to include school and community resources. Specifically, each school is to have programs to

Comprehensive, multifaceted, and cohesive

- Enhance the ability of the classroom teacher and others to facilitate learning through prevention and early intervention.
- Increase family involvement in schools and schooling.
- Provide support for the many transitions experienced by students and their families.
- Expand community involvement through volunteers, businesses, agencies, faith-based organizations, and so on.
- Respond to and prevent crises, violence, bullying, substance abuse, and so on.
- Provide specialized student and family assistance.

The foregoing elements are essential to a school's ability to accomplish its instructional mission; it does not represent an agenda separate from that mission. Moreover, the emphasis on such programs and activities creates a schoolwide culture of caring and nurturing. Such an atmosphere helps students, families, staff, and the community at large feel that a school is a welcoming and supportive place that accommodates diversity and is committed to promoting equal opportunities for all students to succeed at school.

A school committed to promoting equal opportunities for all students to succeed at school

To pursue the functions involved in developing a learning supports component at a school, each school should establish

- An administrative leader who guides and is accountable for daily implementation, monitoring, problem solving, and long-term development of the learning supports component
- A team of learning supports staff (e.g., pupil services personnel) who ensure that all relevant resources are woven together to install, maintain, and evolve a comprehensive, multifaceted, and cohesive continuum of interventions over a period of years
- Mechanisms for identifying and responding to specific students' problems based on the principle of using the least intervention necessary

CONCLUDING COMMENTS

For some youngsters, regular development and improvement in school performance and academic achievement are hampered because of the absence of comprehensive, multifaceted, and cohesive approaches for addressing barriers to development and learning. At this stage in the ongoing development of our schools and communities, it is essential to take the next steps toward ensuring that such approaches are in place. By doing so, we move closer to fulfilling the intent of assuring that every child reaches full potential and no child is left behind.

Learn More About the New Directions for Student Support Initiative

For detailed information on the initiative, click on "Summits on New Directions" on the homepage of the Center for Mental Health in Schools' Web site: http://smhp.psych.ucla.edu/. It provides a list of the cosponsors, a concept paper, reports and recommendations from the summits, guidelines for a student support component at a school, resource aids for new directions, descriptions of trailblazing efforts, and much more. There are also guidelines for how to start the process for a statewide summit.

Those interested in being involved in developing a Summit for New Directions for Student Support in their state should contact the center at Box 951563, UCLA, Los Angeles, CA 90095–1563, Phone (310) 825-3634; Toll-free (866) 846-4843; Fax: (310) 206-8716; E-mail: smhp@ucla.edu.

REFERENCES

Carnegie Council on Adolescent Development's Task Force on Education of Young Adolescents. (1989). *Turning points: Preparing American youth for the 21st century.* Washington, DC: Author.

No Child Left Behind Act of 2001, Pub. L. No. 107–110, § 2, 115 Stat. 1425. (2002).

Examples of Policy Statements

18

With respect to new directions for student support, leaders recognize that substantially enhancing the well-being of young people involves addressing key policy concerns. As stressed in a policy report prepared by the Center for Mental Health in Schools (1999):

> Policy must be developed around well-conceived models and the best available information. Policy must be realigned horizontally and vertically to create a cohesive framework and must connect in major ways with the mission of schools. Attention must be directed at restructuring the education support programs and services that schools own and operate and weave school-owned resources and community-owned resources together into comprehensive, integrated approaches for addressing problems and enhancing healthy development. Policy makers also must deal with the problems of "scale-up" (e.g., underwriting model development and capacity building for systemwide replication of promising models and institutionalization of systemic changes). And in doing all this, more must be done to involve families and to connect the resources of schools, neighborhoods, and institutions of higher education.

This Appendix provides examples from the following:

The Urban Learning Center Comprehensive School Reform Model
An Example of an Early Legislative Proposal
Policy Resolution Proposed to and Passed by the Los Angeles
    Unified School District's Board of Education in 1998
Hawaii's Legislation for Its Comprehensive Student Support System
Proposed Legislation for a Comprehensive Student Learning
    Support System in California, 2004
Standards for an Enabling or Learning Supports Component

Guide 18.1 The Urban Learning Center Comprehensive School Reform
Model

In the 1990s, the New American Schools Development Corporation set out to develop "break the mold" models for comprehensive school reform. One of the eight prototypes that emerged is now called the Urban Learning Center model. A major demonstration of this model was developed at the Elizabeth Learning Center in Cudahy, California, which is now a K–12 school. The Urban Learning Center model incorporated and implemented the concept of a component to address barriers to learning as primary and essential and has been involved in replicating it as one of the comprehensive school reforms specified in the federal legislation for comprehensive school reform.

To clarify its commitment to learning supports, the governance body for the Elizabeth Learning Center adopted the following policy statement:

We recognize that for some of our students, improvements in Instruction/curricula are necessary but not sufficient. As the school's governance body, we commit to enhancing activity that addresses barriers to learning and teaching. This means the Elizabeth Learning Center will treat the Enabling Component on a par with its Instructional/Curriculum and Management/Governance Components. In policy and practice, the three components are seen as essential and primary if all students are to succeed.

Guide 18.2 An Example of an Early Legislative Proposal

California took an early lead in focusing attention on the need to develop policy for a component to address barriers to student learning. In 1995, California assembly member Juanita McDonald brought together a set of task forces to develop an Urban Education Initiative package of legislation. One major facet focused on overcoming barriers to pupil learning and called on school districts to ensure that schools within their jurisdictions had an enabling component in place. On the following pages is the draft of that part of the bill. Just before the legislation was to go to the Education Committee for review, McDonald was elected to Congress.

CALIFORNIA LEGISLATURE—1995–96 REGULAR SESSION

ASSEMBLY BILL No. 784 AMENDED IN ASSEMBLY APRIL 25, 1995

Introduced by Assembly Member McDonald

(Principal coauthor: Assembly Member Alpert)

(Coauthors: Assembly Members Archie-Hudson, Baca, Ducheny, Kuehl, and Napolitano)

(Coauthor: Senator Watson)

February 22, 1995

An act to add Part 29.5 (commencing with Section 55000) to the Education Code, relating to urban school districts.

LEGISLATIVE COUNSEL'S DIGEST

AB 784, as amended, McDonald. Education: urban school districts: equal opportunity to learn: teacher credentialing reform.

CHAPTER 5. OVERCOMING BARRIERS TO PUPIL LEARNING

Article 1. Enabling Pupils to Overcome Learning Barriers

55040. (a) It is the intent of the Legislature that on or before the commencement of the 1996–97 school year, each school district ensure that the schools within their jurisdiction have an enabling component in place. The enabling component shall enable pupils to overcome barriers that interfere with their ability to learn and to benefit from instructional and management reforms made at schools. For the purposes of this chapter, an "enabling component" means a comprehensive, integrated continuum of school-based and school-linked activity designed to enable schools to teach and pupils to learn. That continuum shall include prevention, including promotion of wellness, early-age and early-after-onset intervention, and treatments for severe, pervasive, and chronic conditions.

(b) Each enabling component developed by each school shall include, but not necessarily be limited to, the following:

(1) A plan for restructuring school education support programs and services.
(2) A plan for coordinating school district and community resources.
(3) A plan for coordinating school district enabling activities with health and human services provided by the state and by local government.
(4) A plan for enhancing the performance of persons involved in the delivery of education services to pupils.
(5) Strategies for replicating promising innovations.
(6) Strategies for the improvement of the quality of education and accountability of the school.

55041. The department shall develop and report to the Legislature on a plan for the implementation of the enabling components consistent with requirements set forth in subdivision (b) of Section 55040 and with any other requirements determined to be necessary by the department to enable pupils to overcome barriers to learning. The report shall include specific recommendations on coordinating school-based enabling activities with community resources and the ways in which the parents and guardians of pupils may be included in enabling activities. The report shall include specific recommendations on changes necessary to existing laws and on any new legislation that is necessary to implement the plan. The department shall report the plan to the Legislature not later than December 31, 1996. It is the intent of the Legislature that any necessary implementing legislation be enacted for the 1997–98 school year.

55042. School districts may request assistance from the department in the development of the enabling component described in Section 55040. The department shall assist school districts that have demonstrated readiness to develop enabling components to coordinate school-based enabling activities with community resources and to involve the parents and guardians of pupils in those activities.

Article 2. Restructuring Education Programs and Coordinating With Other Support Programs

55045. (a) For the purpose of enabling pupils to overcome barriers to learning, the department shall develop a strategic plan to guide and stimulate restructuring of education support programs and services operated by schools for pupils and their parents and guardians. The department shall include within that plan methods of coordinating school services with community services that are made available to pupils and their families by local government agencies or private nonprofit groups. The department shall also develop a plan for those programs and services that are operated by school districts and by the department. The plan shall include, but not be limited to, the following:

  (1) Moving from fragmented, categorical and single discipline-oriented services toward a comprehensive, integrated, cross-disciplinary approach.

  (2) Moving from activity that is viewed as supplementary toward a full-fledged integrated component that is understood to be primary and essential to enabling learning.

  (3) Involving pupils and their parents and guardians, and communities in the education process in a manner that capitalizes on their strengths and the many ways in which they can contribute to the education process.

  (4) Restructuring education support programs and services offered at schoolsites.

  (5) Coordinating services offered by school districts with other services available in the community.

  (6) Coordinating enabling components with health and human services offered by the state and by local government.

  (7) Involving all persons having an interest in the education process in developing the enabling component.

  (8) Strategies for replicating at school sites innovations to improve pupil learning that are successful at other school sites.

  (9) Strategies for improving the quality of education and for improving school accountability.

 (10) Establishing a comprehensive, integrated, cross-disciplinary approach to teaching.

 (11) Establishing an integrated component that is understood to be essential to learning.

 (12) Involving all persons having an interest in the education process in a manner that best utilizes their various strengths.

 (13) Integrating the enabling component with the instructional and management components of the education process.

 (14) Developing leadership to effectively operate and implement the enabling component.

 (15) Developing and incorporating integrated planning for the use of advanced multifaceted technology, to assist pupils and their parents or guardians in the learning process, to provide responses to and prevention of emergencies and other crises, to support transitions, and to provide for community and volunteer outreach.

(16) Facilitating teacher recruitment, continuing education for teachers, and retention of teachers.

(17) Infrastructure changes, particularly those related to operation space at schoolsites, allocation and maximization of fiscal resources, administrative and staff leadership, and mechanisms for effective coordination of essential system elements and resources.

(18) Strategies for phasing in the restructuring of education programs.

(19) Strategies to ensure the long-term success of planned changes.

(20) The types of leadership, infrastructure, and specific mechanisms that can be established at a schoolsite for high schools and their feeder schools, and in communities to facilitate coordinated and integrated governing, planning, and implementation of enabling components.

(21) Methods for schoolsites to ensure significant roles and leadership training for parents and guardians of pupils and for other community residents, representatives of community-based organizations, and, when appropriate, pupils.

(22) Methods to seek waivers of state and federal laws and regulations thereto when necessary to facilitate efforts to evolve a comprehensive, integrated approach to learning.

(23) Evaluating the progress of schools in implementing reforms and enhancing outcomes.

(24) Methods to provide professional preparation and continuing education programs that focus on the type of interprofessional collaborations necessary for the development of a comprehensive, integrated approach to enabling pupil learning.

(b) The department shall disseminate the strategic plan adopted pursuant to this section to school districts on or before December 31, 1996. The department shall also report the strategic plan to the Legislature not later than December 31, 1996, along with specific recommendations on any changes to existing law that are necessary to implement the plan and on any new legislation required to implement the plan. It is the intent of the Legislature that any necessary implementing legislation be enacted for the 1997–98 school year.

55046. (a) The department shall assist urban school districts or schools that demonstrate readiness to restructure their education support programs and services in a manner consistent with the strategic plan developed pursuant to Section 55045.

(b) The department may provide assistance to schools by any of the following methods:

(1) Informational guidelines and guidebooks.

(2) Leadership training.

(3) Regional workshops.

(4) Demonstrations of effective methods of restructuring education.

(5) Opportunities for interchanges.

(6) Technical assistance in developing plans.

Article 3. Models of Strategies to Enable Pupil Learning

55050. On or before December 31, 1996, the department shall develop a plan to enable schools to replicate methods of overcoming barriers to pupil learning that have been successfully implemented at the school site level. The plan shall include recommendations on the following:

(a) Guidelines and procedures for identifying successful innovations that are designed to address barriers to pupil learning and implemented at the school site or school district level.

(b) Procedures for analyzing new initiatives and promising innovations to identify possible redundancy and fragmentation of methods.

(c)   Disseminating successful innovations that are designed to overcome barriers to learning and, in doing so, reduce redundancy and fragmentation of methods.

(d)   Using demonstrations of innovative methods of overcoming pupil learning barriers as catalysts to stimulate interest in reform.

(e)   Developing replication models that can be adopted for use at the school site level.

(f)   Providing technical assistance for implementing replication strategies for school districts implementing innovations designed to address barriers to pupil learning.

55051. The department shall make the plan developed pursuant to Section 55050 available to school districts on or before December 31, 1996.

Guide 18.3   Policy Resolution Proposed to and Passed by the Los Angeles Unified School District's Board of Education in 1998

In the mid-1990s, the Los Angeles Unified School District began the task of restructuring its student support services. In 1998, the district's board of education resolved that a component to address barriers to student learning and enhance healthy development is one of the primary and essential components of the district's educational reform. In keeping with the California Department of Education's adoption of the unifying concept of *Learning Support,* the board adopted this term to encompass efforts related to its component of addressing barriers to student learning and enhancing healthy development.

Whereas, in its "Call to Action," the Los Angeles Unified School District has made clear its intent to create a learning environment in which all students succeed;

Whereas, new governance structures, higher standards for student performance, new instructional strategies, and a focus on results are specified as essential elements in attaining student achievement;

Whereas, a high proportion of students are unable to fully benefit from such reforms because of learning barriers related to community violence, domestic problems, racial tension, poor health, substance abuse, and urban poverty;

Whereas, teachers find it especially difficult to make progress with the high proportion of youngsters for whom barriers to learning have resulted in mild-to-moderate learning and behavior problems;

Whereas, many of these youngsters end up referred for special services and often are placed in special education;

Whereas, both the Los Angeles Unified School District and various community agencies devote resources to addressing learning barriers and initial processes have been implemented to reform and restructure use of their respective resources—including exploring strategies to weave District and community efforts together—in ways that can overcome key barriers to student achievement;

Whereas, a comprehensive, integrated partnership between all District support resources and community resources will provide the LEARNING SUPPORT necessary to effectively break down the barriers to student achievement; now, therefore, be it

Resolved, that the Board of Education should adopt the following recommendations made by the Standing Committee on Student Health and Human Services:

1. The Board should resolve that a component to address barriers to student learning and enhance healthy development be fully integrated with efforts to improve the instructional and management/governance components and be pursued as a primary and essential component of the District's education reforms in classrooms, schools, complexes/clusters, and at the central office level.

2. In keeping with the California Department of Education's adoption of the unifying concept of **Learning Support,** the Board should adopt this term to encompass efforts related to its component for addressing barriers to student learning and enhancing healthy development.

3. In adopting the concept of **Learning Support,** the Board should adopt the seven area framework currently used by the Division of Student Health and Human Services to guide coordination and integration of existing programs and activities related to school, home, and community.

4. The Board should direct the Superintendent to convene a working group to develop a plan that promotes coordination and integration of the **Learning Support** component with instruction and management reform efforts at every school site. This plan would also clarify ways for complex/cluster and central office operations to support school site efforts (e.g. helping schools achieve economics of scale and implement practices that effectively improve classroom operations and student learning). The plan would also focus on ways to further promote collaboration with communities at the classroom, school, complex/cluster, and central office levels. Such a plan should be ready for implementation by Spring 1998.

5. To counter fragmentation stemming from the way programs are organized and administered at the central office, the Board should restructure the administrative organization so that all programs and activity related to the Learning Support including Special Education are under the leadership of one administrator. Such an administrator would be charged with implementing the strategic plan developed in response to recommendation #4.

6. The Board should direct those responsible for professional and other stakeholder development activity throughout the District to incorporate a substantial focus on the **Learning Support** component into all such activity (e.g., all teacher professional education, training activity related to LEARN, the Chanda Smith Special Education Consent Decree, early literacy programs).

7. To facilitate continued progress related to the restructuring of student health and human services, the Board should encourage all clusters and schools to support the development of Cluster/Complex Resource Coordinating Councils and School-Site Resource Coordinating Teams, Such Councils and Teams provide a key mechanism for enhancing the **Learning Support** component by ensuring that resources are mapped and analyzed and strategies are developed for the most effective use of school, complex, and Districtwide resources and for appropriate school-community collaborations.

Guide 18.4 Hawaii's Legislation for Its Comprehensive Student Support System

Paralleling the work in California, Hawaii's legislature passed an act establishing a *Comprehensive Student Support Systems* (CSSS) in 1999.

S.B. NO. 519–TWENTIETH LEGISLATURE, 1999 STATE OF HAWAII

A Bill for an Act Relating to a Comprehensive Student Support System

DESCRIPTION: Requires the department of education to establish a comprehensive student support system (CSSS) in all schools to create a school environment in which every student is cared for and respected.

BE IT ENACTED BY THE LEGISLATURE OF THE STATE OF HAWAII:

SECTION 1. The legislature finds that the goal of the superintendent of education's success compact program is total support for every student, every time; every school, every time; and every community, every time. This integrated model focuses on the student and identifies the importance of literacy for every student, every time. To fulfill government's obligation to the children of this State, the superintendent, the board of education, the governor, and the legislature must reach every student, school, and community by realigning and redefining existing services and programs into a comprehensive student support system that systematically strengthens students, schools, and communities rather than by impulsively responding to crisis after crisis. It is the legislature's intention to create the comprehensive student support system from existing personnel and programmatic resources, i.e., without the need for additional or new appropriations.

The comprehensive student support system is a coordinated array of instructional programs and services that, as a total package, will meet the needs of traditional and nontraditional learners in school and community settings. This package takes what works, improves on others, and creates new avenues to services. The result will be customized support throughout a student's K-12 educational career. These services will include developmental, academic core, preventive, accelerated, correctional, and remedial programs and services. Linkages with other organizations and agencies will be made when services needed are beyond the purview of the department of education.

To achieve in school, students need to be wanted and valued. They need a positive vision of the future. They need safe, orderly schools, strong community support, high-quality care, and adults they can trust. Students often become alienated because they may not feel worthy, they may not have a supportive home or opportunities to learn to care, or they may not be successful in handling frustrations, or have good experiences in school. They may not see relevance to their education or have positive role models or may not have access to support services. Consequently, the superintendent, the board of education, the governor, and the legislature need to ensure that each student can read, write, and relate effectively, has self-worth, has meaning-based learning opportunities, and has positive support networks from other students, teachers, and members of the school community.

The legislature finds that the generalized school support groups and individualized student support teams created by the comprehensive student support system can give parents what they and their children want most from government—schools that are safe, and where the environment is focused on teaching and learning. The educational climate in Hawaii's public schools, as measured by average class and school size, absenteeism, tardiness, classroom misbehavior, lack of parental involvement, and other indicators, suggests that the time to implement the success compact program and the comprehensive student support system is today—not tomorrow when the State's economy might improve. According to the 1999 "Education Week, Quality Counts" survey, the educational climate in the State's public schools, given the grade of "F" (as in failed), would be hard pressed to get any worse than it already is.

The legislature's objective is to ensure that every student will become literate, confident, and caring, and be able to think critically, solve problems, communicate effectively, and function as a contributing member of society. The purpose of this Act is to authorize the department of education to establish a comprehensive student support system to meet this objective.

SECTION 2. Chapter 302A, Hawaii Revised Statutes, is amended by adding a new part to be appropriately designated and to read as follows:

PART. COMPREHENSIVE STUDENT SUPPORT SYSTEM

A. General Provisions

§§302A-A Establishment of comprehensive student support system. There is established within the department and for all schools the comprehensive student support system. §§302A-B Description of the comprehensive student support system.

(a) The comprehensive student support system establishes a school environment in which every student is cared for and respected. The comprehensive student support system is teacher-driven because teachers know students better than anyone in the department. The foundation of the comprehensive student support system is the school support group, in which groups of teachers and students become familiar with each other and share experiences, ideas, problems, and concerns that allow them to support one another. Every student shall belong to a group of teachers and students who will care about them and who will be the first to respond to their support needs.

(b) When students are deemed by their teachers and counselors in the school support groups to need special services and programs, supports shall be customized to address each student's needs so the individual can satisfactorily benefit from classroom instruction.

(c) A coordinated and integrated student support system:

(1) Avoids duplication and fragmentation of services, and ensures that services are timely; (2) Involves the use of formal and informal community supports such as churches and ethnic and cultural resources unique to the student and family.

(d) The comprehensive student support system shall be focused on the strength of the student and the student's family, and create a single system of educational and other support programs and services that is student-, family-, and community-based.

(e) The comprehensive student support system shall allow for the integration of:

(1) Personal efforts by teachers and students to support each other within the school support groups, including the support of parents and counselors where needed;

(2) Educational initiatives such as alternative education, success compact, school-to-work opportunities, high schools that work, after-school instructional program, and the middle school concept; and

(3) Health initiatives such as early intervention and prevention, care coordination, coordinated service planning, nomination, screening, and evaluation, staff training, service array, and service testing.

This integration shall work to build a comprehensive and seamless educational and student support system from kindergarten through high school.

§§302A-C Student support array.

(a) A student's social, personal, or academic problems shall be initially addressed through the school support group structure that involves interaction between student and student, student and adult, or adult and adults. Teachers, family, and other persons closely associated with a student may be the first to begin the dialogue if the student has needs that can be addressed in the classroom or home.

(b) Through dialogue within the school support group or with parents, or both, the teacher shall implement classroom accommodations or direct assistance shall be provided to address students' needs. Other teachers and school staff shall also provide support and guidance to assist families and students. These activities shall be carried out in an informal, supportive manner.

(c) School programs shall be designed to provide services for specific groups of students. Parents and families, teachers, and other school personnel shall meet as the student's support team to discuss program goals that best fit the individual student's needs. Regular program evaluations shall be used to keep the regular teacher and parents involved.

(d) When a student's needs require specialized assessment or assistance, a request form shall be submitted to the school's core team. One of the identified members of the core team shall serve as the interim coordinator who will organize and assemble a student support team. A formal problem solving session shall be held and a plan developed. Members of this student support team may include teachers, counselors, parents and family, and other persons knowledgeable about the student or programs and services. One or more members may assist in carrying out the plan. For the purposes of this section, "core team" refers to the faculty members comprising a school support group. "Core team" does not include persons who are only physically located at a school to facilitate the provision of services to the school complex.

(e) When the needs of the student and family require intensive and multiple supports from various agencies, the student support team shall develop a coordinated service plan. A coordinated service plan shall also be developed when two or more agencies or organizations are involved equally in the service delivery. A care coordinator shall be identified to coordinate and integrate the services.

(f) The comprehensive student support system shall recognize and respond to the changing needs of students, and shall lend itself to meet the needs of all students to promote success for each student, every time.

§§302A-D Mission and goals of the comprehensive student support system.

(a) The mission of the comprehensive student support system shall be to provide all students with a support system so they can be productive and responsible citizens.

(b) The goals of the comprehensive student support system shall be to:

(1) Involve families, fellow students, educators, and community members as integral partners in the creation of a supportive, respectful, learning environment at each school;

(2) Provide students with comprehensive, coordinated, integrated, and customized supports that are accessible, timely, and strength-based so they can achieve in school; and

(3) Integrate the human and financial resources of relevant public and private agencies to create caring communities at each school.

§§302A-E Classroom instruction component of the comprehensive student support system.

(a) "Classroom instruction" includes education initiatives and programs directed to all students such as success compact, school-to-work opportunities, high schools that work, after-school instructional program, and general counseling and guidance activities.

(b) Classroom instruction shall emphasize literacy development through hands-on, contextual learning that recognizes diversity in student needs, and shall be provided through coordinated and integrated instructional programs and services that are articulated among teachers in all grade levels in the school.

(c) Classroom instruction shall be guided by the Hawaii content and performance standards, assessed by student performances, and guided by teachers and other service providers who clearly exhibit caring and concern towards students. The ultimate outcome of classroom instruction shall be students who can read, compute, think, communicate, and relate.

(d) Students shall learn from each other and build a community of learners who care about each other. All schools shall incorporate success compact and the teaming of teachers with students into groups that result in a greater caring environment in a more personalized group setting. Every student shall belong to a group of teachers and students who care about them. These groups shall be the first to respond to students in need of support.

§§302A-F Management component of the comprehensive student support system. Management functions, for example, planning, budgeting, staffing, directing, coordinating, monitoring, evaluating, and reporting, shall organize the instructional and student support components to maximize the use of limited resources. The comprehensive student support system, management component, shall be consistent with and complement school/community-based management. The management of resources and services shall be integrated and collaborative.

§§302A-G Classroom, school, family, and community settings under the comprehensive student support system.

(a) Teachers shall work with students to provide informal assistance as needed.

(b) Other caring adults in the school shall be available to work together and provide support and assistance to students, parents, and teachers. The student support team shall convene when a student requires support for more complex needs.

(c) Family strengths, resources, and knowledge shall be an integral part of a student support team.

(d) Resources with expertise in various areas of child development shall be included in providing services that enhance the quality of customized services when needed.

§§302A-H Student support team.

(a) "Student support team" includes the student, family, extended family, close family friends, school, and other related professionals and agency personnel who are knowledgeable about the student or appropriate teaching methods, and programs and services and their referral processes. "Student support team" includes the parent and family at the outset of the planning stage and throughout the delivery of support.

(b) If community programs and services become necessary to address needs that are not being met by existing supports within the school, then professionals with specific expertise who are not located at the school shall be contacted by a designated student support team member, and may become additional members of the student support team.

(c) A student support team's general responsibilities shall include functions such as assessing student and family strengths and needs, identifying appropriate services, determining service and program eligibility, and referring to or providing services, or both. A student support team shall have the authority and resources to carry out decisions and follow-up with actions. The responsibilities of the student support team shall be determined by the issues involved and the supports and services needed.

(d) Each profession or agency involved shall adhere to its particular ethical responsibilities. These responsibilities shall include:

    (1) The ability to work as members of a team;

    (2) Actively listen;

    (3) Develop creative solutions; enhance informal supports;

    (4) Arrive at a mutually acceptable plan; and

    (5) Integrate and include the family's views, input, and cultural beliefs into the decision-making process and plan itself.

(e) Student support teams may focus on the following activities:

    (1) Working with the classroom teacher to plan specific school-based interventions related to specific behavior or learning needs, or both;

    (2) Participating in strength-based assessment activities to determine appropriate referrals and eligibility for programs and services;

    (3) Ensuring that preventive and developmental, as well as intervention and corrective, services are tailored to the needs of the student and family, and provided in a timely manner;

    (4) Facilitating the development of a coordinated service plan for students who require support from two or more agencies. The service plan shall incorporate other plans such as the individualized education plan, modification plan, individual family service plan, and treatment plan. A designated care coordinator shall monitor the coordination and integration of multi-agency services and programs, delivery of services, and evaluation of supports; and

    (5) Including parents and families in building a community support network with appropriate agencies, organizations, and service providers.

B. Implementation

§§302A-I School level implementation of the comprehensive student support system.

(a) School-communities may implement the comprehensive student support system differently in their communities; provided that, at a minimum, the school-communities shall establish both school support groups and student support teams in which all students are cared for.

(b) All school-communities shall design and carry out their own unique action plans that identify items critical to the implementation of the comprehensive student support system at the school level using the state comprehensive student support system model to guide them. The local action plan may include:

    (1) Information about school level policies, guidelines, activities, procedures, tools, and outcomes related to having the comprehensive student support system in place;

    (2) Roles of the school support group and student support team;

    (3) Roles of the school level cadre of planners;

    (4) Partnerships and collaboration;

    (5) Training;

(6) Identification, assessment, referral, screening, and monitoring of students;

(7) Data collection; and

(8) Evaluation.

(c) If there are existing action plans, projects, or initiatives that similarly address the comprehensive student support system goals, then the cadre of planners shall coordinate and integrate efforts to fill in the gaps and prevent duplication.

(d) The action plan shall be an integral part of the school's school improvement plan, not separated but integrated.

§§302A-J Complex level implementation of the comprehensive student support system. The comprehensive student support system shall be supported at the school complex level. A school-complex resource teacher shall provide staff support, technical assistance, and training to school-communities in each school complex in the planning and implementation of comprehensive student support system priorities and activities.

§§302A-K State level implementation of the comprehensive student support system.

(a) The department shall facilitate the process of bringing other state departments, community organizations, and parent groups on board with the department and allow line staff to work collaboratively in partnerships at the school level.

(b) The department, at the state level in partnership with other agencies, shall provide on-going professional development and training that are especially crucial in this collaborative effort.

(c) The department shall facilitate the procurement of needed programs and services currently unavailable or inaccessible at school sites.

(d) The department shall be responsive to complex and individual school needs.

C. Evaluation

§§302A-L Purpose of evaluating the comprehensive student support system.

(a) The department shall evaluate the comprehensive student support system to:

(1) Improve the further development and implementation of the comprehensive student support system;

(2) Satisfy routine accountability needs; and

(3) Guide future replication and expansion of the comprehensive student support system.

(b) Successful program development and implementation shall result in:

(1) Improved prevention and early intervention support;

(2) Coordinated services made possible through cross-discipline, cross-agency teams with a problem-solving, collaborating orientation;

(3) Promotion of pro-social skills;

(4) Increased family involvement in collaborative planning to meet the needs of students;

(5) Development of schools' capacity to assess and monitor progress on the program's objectives through the use of specially developed educational indicators; and

(6) Successful long and short-term planning integrated with school improvement plans.

§§302A-M Outcomes expected of the comprehensive student support system. The outcomes expected of the comprehensive student support system are:

    (1) Increased attendance;

    (2) Improved grades;

    (3) Improved student performance, as measured by established content and performance standards;

    (4) A substantial increase in parental participation; and

    (5) At the secondary level, increased participation in extracurricular activities.

SECTION 3. If any provision of this Act, or the application thereof to any person or circumstance is held invalid, the invalidity does not affect other provisions or applications of the Act which can be given effect without the invalid provision or application, and to this end the provisions of this Act are severable.

SECTION 4. In codifying the new sections added to chapter 302A, Hawaii Revised Statutes, by section 2 of this Act, the revisor of statutes shall substitute appropriate section numbers for the letters used in the new sections' designations in this Act.

SECTION 5. This Act shall take effect on January 1, 2000.

Online at: http://www.capitol.hawaii.gov/session1999/bills/sb519_.htm

Guide 18.5   Proposed Legislation for a Comprehensive Student Learning
Support System in California, 2004

BILL NUMBER: AB 2569

CALIFORNIA LEGISLATURE—2003–03 REGULAR SESSION

AMENDED IN ASSEMBLY MAY 4, 2004

AMENDED IN ASSEMBLY APRIL 14, 2004

INTRODUCED BY Assembly Member Yee

FEBRUARY 20, 2004

An act to add Chapter 6.4 (commencing with Section 52060) to Part 28 of the Education
Code, relating to pupils.

LEGISLATIVE COUNSEL'S DIGEST

AB 2569, as amended, Yee. Comprehensive Pupil Learning Support System.

Existing law establishes various educational programs for pupils in elementary,
middle, and high school to be administered by the State Department of Education.

This bill would establish the Comprehensive Pupil Learning Support System to provide each pupil with a support system to ensure that each pupil will be a productive and
responsible learner and citizen. The bill would require the State Department of Education
to administer and implement the program through existing resources that are available to
the department for the purposes of the program. The bill would require the department to
adopt regulations to implement the program.

The bill would require each elementary, middle, and high school to develop a school
action plan, as specified, based on guidelines to be developed by the State Department of
Education. The bill would require each school action plan to, among other things, enhance
the capacity of each school to handle transition concerns confronting pupils and their
families, enhance home involvement, provide special assistance to pupils and families, and
incorporate outreach efforts to the community. By imposing additional duties on school
districts, this bill would impose a state-mandated local program.

The California Constitution requires the state to reimburse local agencies and school
districts for certain costs mandated by the state. Statutory provisions establish procedures
for making that reimbursement, including the creation of a State Mandates Claims Fund to
pay the costs of mandates that do not exceed $1,000,000 statewide and other procedures
for claims whose statewide costs exceed $1,000,000.

This bill would provide that, if the Commission on State Mandates determines that the
bill contains costs mandated by the state, reimbursement for those costs shall be made
pursuant to these statutory provisions.

THE PEOPLE OF THE STATE OF CALIFORNIA DO ENACT AS FOLLOWS:

SECTION 1. The Legislature hereby finds and declares all of the following:

(a) The UCLA Center for Mental Health in Schools, the WestEd Regional Educational
Laboratory, the State Department of Education, and other educational entities have

adopted the concept of learning support within ongoing efforts to address barriers to pupil learning and to enhance healthy development.

(b) Learning supports are the resources, strategies, and practices that provide physical, social, emotional, and intellectual supports intended to enable all pupils to have an equal opportunity for success at school. To accomplish this goal, a comprehensive, multifaceted, and cohesive learning support system should be integrated with instructional efforts and interventions provided in classrooms and schoolwide to address barriers to learning and teaching.

(c) There is a growing consensus among researchers, policymakers, and practitioners that stronger collaborative efforts by families, schools, and communities are essential to pupil success.

(d) An increasing number of American children live in communities where caring relationships, support resources, and a profamily system of education and human services do not exist to protect children and prepare them to be healthy, successful, resilient learners.

(e) Especially in those communities, a renewed partnership of schools, families, and community members must be created to design and carry out system improvements to provide the learning support required by each pupil in order to succeed.

(f) Learning support is the collection of resources, strategies and practices, and environmental and cultural factors extending beyond the regular classroom curriculum that together provide the physical, emotional, and intellectual support that every pupil needs to achieve high-quality learning.

(g) A school that has an exemplary learning support system employs internal and external supports and services needed to help pupils become good parents, good neighbors, good workers, and good citizens of the world.

(h) The overriding philosophy is that educational success, physical health, emotional support, and family and community strength are inseparable.

(i) To implement the concept of learning supports, the state must systematically realign and redefine existing resources into a comprehensive system that is designed to strengthen pupils, schools, families, and communities rather than continuing to respond to these issues in a piecemeal and fragmented manner.

(j) Development of learning supports at every school is essential in meeting the needs arising from the federal No Child Left Behind Act and the Individuals with Disabilities Education Act. The state needs to ensure that each pupil is able to read, write, and relate effectively, has self-worth, has meaning-based learning opportunities, and has positive support networks from their peers, teachers, pupil support professionals, family members, and other school and community stakeholders.

(k) It is essential that each pupil becomes literate, confident, caring, and capable of thinking critically, solving problems, communicating effectively, and functioning as a contributing member of society.

(l) The education climate in the public schools of the state, as measured by overcrowded schools, absenteeism, increasing substance and alcohol abuse, school violence, sporadic parental involvement, dropouts, and other indicators, suggest that the state is in immediate need of learning supports.

(m) A learning support system needs to be developed at every school to ensure that pupils have essential support for learning, from kindergarten to high school.

(n) A learning support system should encompass school-based and school-linked activities designed to enable teachers to teach and pupils to learn. It should include a continuum of interventions that promote learning and development, prevent and respond early after the onset of problems, and provide correctional, and remedial programs and services. In the aggregate, a learning support system should create a supportive and respectful learning environment at each school.

(o) A learning support system is a primary and essential component at every school, designed to support learning and provide each pupil with an equal opportunity to succeed at school. The learning support system should be fully integrated into all school improvement efforts.

(p) The State Department of Education, other state agencies, local school districts, and local communities all devote resources to addressing learning barriers and promoting healthy development. Too often these resources are deployed in a fragmented, duplicative, categorical manner that results in misuse of sparse resources and failure to reach all the pupils and families in need of support. A learning support system will provide a unifying concept and context for linking with other organizations and agencies as needed and can be a focal point for braiding school and community resources into a comprehensive, multifaceted, and cohesive component at every school.

(q) It is the intent of the Legislature that the CPLSS is fully integrated with other efforts to improve instruction and focuses on maximizing the use of resources at individual schools and at the district level. Collaborative arrangements with community resources shall be developed with a view to filling any gaps in CPLSS components.

SECTION 2. Chapter 6.4 (commencing with Section 52060) is added to Part 28 of the Education Code, to read:

CHAPTER 6.4. COMPREHENSIVE PUPIL LEARNING SUPPORT SYSTEM

52060. (a) There is hereby established the Comprehensive Pupil Learning Support System (CPLSS). The CPLSS shall be implemented with existing personnel and program resources, without the need for additional or new appropriations.

(b) It is the intent of the Legislature in establishing the CPLSS to provide all pupils with a support system to ensure that they will be productive and responsible learners and citizens. It is further the intent of the Legislature that the CPLSS ensure that pupils have an equal opportunity to succeed at school and to do so in a supportive, caring, respectful, and safe learning environment.

(c) These goals shall be accomplished by involving pupils, teachers, pupil support professionals, family members, and other school and community stakeholders in the development, daily implementation, monitoring, and maintenance of a learning support system at every school and by braiding together the human and financial resources of relevant public and private agencies.

52061. The department shall facilitate the establishment of the CPLSS by doing all of the following:

(a) Developing standards and strategic procedures to guide the establishment of the CPLSS component at each school.

(b) Providing ongoing technical assistance, leadership training, and other capacity building supports.

(c) Rethinking the roles of pupil services personnel and other support staff for pupils and integrating their responsibilities into the educational program in a manner that meets the needs of pupils, teachers, and other educators.

(d) Detailing procedures for establishing infrastructure mechanisms between schools and school districts.

(e) Coordinating with other state agencies that can play a role in strengthening the CPLSS.

(f) Ensuring that the CPLSS is integrated within the organization of the department in a manner that reflects the school action plans developed by schools pursuant to subdivision (a) of Section 52062.

(g) Enhancing collaboration with state agencies and other relevant resources to facilitate local collaboration and braiding of resources.

(h) Including an assessment of the CPLSS of each school in all future school reviews and accountability reports.

52062. (a) Each elementary, middle, and high school shall develop a CPLSS component by developing a school action plan based on the guidelines developed by the department pursuant to Section 52061.

(b) Each school action plan shall be developed with the purpose of doing all of the following:

(1) Enhance the capacity of teachers to address problems, engage and re-engage pupils in classroom learning, and foster social, emotional, intellectual, and behavioral development. The component of the school action plan required by this paragraph shall emphasize ensuring that teacher training and assistance includes strategies for better addressing learning, behavior, and emotional problems within the context of the classroom. Interventions may include, but not be limited to, all of the following:

    (A) Addressing a greater range of pupil problems within the classroom through an increased emphasis on strategies for positive social and emotional development, problem prevention, and accommodation of differences in the motivation and capabilities of pupils.

    (B) Classroom management that emphasizes re-engagement of pupils in classroom learning and minimizes over-reliance on social control strategies.

    (C) Collaboration with pupil support staff and the home in providing additional assistance to foster enhanced responsibility, problem solving, resilience, and effective engagement in classroom learning.

(2) Enhance the capacity of schools to handle transition concerns confronting pupils and their families. The component of the school action plan required by this paragraph shall emphasize ensuring that systems and programs are established to provide supports for the many transitions pupils, their families, and school staff encounter. Interventions may include, but are not limited to, all of the following:

    (A) Welcoming and social support programs for newcomers.

    (B) Before, during, and afterschool programs to enrich learning and provide safe recreation.

    (C) Articulation programs to support grade transitions.

    (D) Addressing transition concerns related to vulnerable populations, including, but not limited to, those in homeless education, migrant education, and special education programs.

    (E) Vocational and college counseling and school-to-career programs.

    (F) Support in moving to postschool living and work.

    (G) Outreach programs to re-engage truants and dropouts in learning.

(3) Respond to, minimize the impact of, and prevent crises. The component of the school action plan required by this paragraph shall emphasize ensuring that systems and programs are established for emergency, crisis, and follow-up responses and for preventing crises at a school and throughout a complex of schools. Interventions may include, but are not limited to, all of the following:

(A) Establishment of a crisis team to ensure immediate response when emergencies arise, and to provide aftermath assistance as necessary and appropriate so that pupils are not unduly delayed in re-engaging in learning.

(B) Schoolwide and school-linked prevention programs to enhance safety at school and to reduce violence, bullying, harassment, abuse, and other threats to safety in order to ensure a supportive and productive learning environment.

(C) Classroom curriculum approaches focused on preventing crisis events, including, but not limited to, violence, suicide, and physical or sexual abuse.

(4) Enhance home involvement. The component of the school action plan required by this paragraph shall emphasize ensuring there are systems, programs, and contexts established that lead to greater involvement to support the progress of pupils with learning, behavior, and emotional problems. Interventions may include, but are not limited to, all of the following:

(A) Interventions that address specific needs of the caretakers of a pupil, including, but not limited to, providing ways for them to enhance literacy and job skills and meet their basic obligations to the children in their care.

(B) Interventions for outreaching and re-engaging homes that have disengaged from school involvement.

(C) Improved systems for communication and connection between home and school.

(D) Improved systems for home involvement in decisions and problem solving affecting the pupil.

(E) Enhanced strategies for engaging the home in supporting the basic learning and development of their children to prevent or at least minimize learning, behavior, and emotional problems.

(5) Outreach to the community in order to build linkages. The component of the school action plan required by this paragraph shall emphasize ensuring that there are systems and programs established to provide outreach to and engage strategically with public and private community resources to support learning at school of pupils with learning, behavior, and emotional problems. Interventions may include, but are not limited to, all of the following:

(A) Training, screening, and maintaining volunteers and mentors to assist school staff in enhancing pupil motivation and capability for school learning.

(B) Job shadowing and service learning programs to enhance the expectations of pupils for postgraduation opportunities.

(C) Enhancing limited school resources through linkages with community resources, including, but not limited to, libraries, recreational facilities, and postsecondary education institutions.

(D) Enhancing community and school connections to heighten a sense of community.

(6) Provide special assistance for pupils and families as necessary. The component of the school action plan required by this paragraph shall ensure that there are systems and programs established to provide or connect with direct services when necessary to address barriers to the learning of pupils at school. Interventions may include, but are not limited to, all of the following:

    (A) Special assistance for teachers in addressing the problems of specific individuals.

    (B) Processing requests and referrals for special assistance, including, but not limited to, counseling or special education.

    (C) Ensuring effective case and resource management when pupils are receiving direct services.

    (D) Connecting with community service providers to fill gaps in school services and enhance access for referrals.

(c) The development, implementation, monitoring, and maintenance of the school action plan shall include, but not be limited to, all of the following components:

    (1) Ensuring effective school mechanisms for assisting individuals and families with family decisionmaking and timely, coordinated, and monitored referrals to school and community services when indicated.

    (2) A mechanism for an administrative leader, support staff for pupils, and other stakeholders to work collaboratively at each school with a focus on strengthening the school action plan.

    (3) A plan for capacity building and regular support for all stakeholders involved in addressing barriers to learning and promoting healthy development.

    (4) Compliance with the guidelines developed by the department pursuant to Section 52061.

    (5) Accountability reviews.

    (6) Minimizing duplication and fragmentation between school programs.

    (7) Preventing problems and providing a safety net of early intervention.

    (8) Responding to pupil and staff problems in a timely manner.

    (9) Connecting with a wide range of school and community stakeholder resources.

    (10) Recognizing and responding to the changing needs of all pupils while promoting the success and well-being of each pupil and staff member.

    (11) Creating a supportive, caring, respectful, and safe learning environment.

52063. Each school shall integrate the CPLSS school action plan with other programs to improve instruction. Each school shall focus on maximizing its use of available resources at the individual school level and the school district level in order to implement this program. The school action plan shall be integrated into any existing school improvement plans and shall reflect all of the following:

(a) School policies, goals, guidelines, priorities, activities, procedures, and outcomes relating to implementing the CPLSS.

(b) Effective leadership and staff roles and functions for the CPLSS.

(c) A thorough infrastructure for the CPLSS.

(d) Appropriate resource allocation.

(e) Integrated school/community collaboration.

(f) Regular capacity building activity.

(g) Delineated standards, quality and accountability indicators, and data collection procedures.

52064. (a) For the purposes of this section, "complex of schools" means a group of elementary, middle, or high schools associated with each other due to the natural progression of attendance linking the schools.

    (b) To ensure that the CPLSS is developed cohesively, efficiently uses community, and capitalizes on economies of scale, CPLSS infrastructure mechanisms shall be established at the school and district level.

(c) Complexes of schools are encouraged to designate a pupil support staff member to facilitate a family complex CPLSS team consisting of representatives from each participating school.

(d) Each school district shall establish mechanisms designed to build the capacity of CPLSS components at each school, including, but not limited to, providing technical assistance and training for the establishment of effective CPLSS components.

52065. (a) The department shall evaluate the success of the CPLSS component of each school according to the following criteria:

(1) Improved systems for promoting prosocial pupil behavior and the well-being of staff and pupils, preventing problems, intervening early after problems arise, and providing specialized assistance to pupils and families.

(2) Increasingly supportive, caring, respectful, and safe learning environments at schools.

(3) Enhanced collaboration between the school and community.

(4) The integration of the CPLSS component with all other school improvement plans.

(5) Fewer inappropriate referrals of pupils to special education programs or other special services.

(b) The department shall consider all of the following in evaluating the success of the CPLSS component:

(1) Pupil attendance.

(2) Pupil grades.

(3) Academic performance.

(4) Pupil behavior.

(5) Home involvement.

(6) Teacher retention.

(7) Graduation rates.

(8) Literacy development.

(9) Other indicators required by the federal No Child Left Behind Act of 2001 (20 U.S.C. Sec. 6301 et seq) and included in the California Healthy Kids Survey.

SECTION 3. A local educational agency shall use funds made available pursuant to Title I of the No Child Left Behind Act of 2001 (20 U.S.C. Sec. 6301 et seq) for the purposes of implementing this act.

SECTION 4. Notwithstanding Section 17610 of the Government Code, if the Commission on State Mandates determines that this act contains costs mandated by the state, reimbursement to local agencies and school districts for those costs shall be made pursuant to Part 7 (commencing with Section 17500) of Division 4 of Title 2 of the Government Code. If the statewide cost of the claim for reimbursement does not exceed one million dollars ($1,000,000), reimbursement shall be made from the State Mandates Claims Fund.

Guide 18.6   Standards for an Enabling or Learning Supports Component

---

An *Enabling* or *Learning Supports Component* is an essential facet of a comprehensive school design. This component is intended to enable *all* students to benefit from instruction and achieve high and challenging academic standards. This is accomplished by providing a comprehensive, multifaceted, and integrated continuum of support programs and services at every school. The district is committed to supporting and guiding capacity building to develop and sustain such a comprehensive approach in keeping with these standards.

All personnel in the district and other stakeholders should use the standards to guide development of such a component as an essential facet of school improvement efforts. In particular, the standards should guide decisions about direction and priorities for redesigning the infrastructure, resource allocation, redefining personnel roles and functions, stakeholder development, and specifying accountability indicators and criteria.

The following are five major standards for an effective Enabling or Learning Supports Component:

Standard 1   *The Enabling or Learning Supports Component encompasses an evolving range of research-based programs and services designed to enable student learning and well-being by addressing barriers to learning and promoting healthy development.*

Standard 2   *The Enabling or Learning Supports Component is developed, coordinated, and fully integrated with all other facets of each school's comprehensive school improvement plan.*

Standard 3   *The Enabling or Learning Supports Component draws on all relevant resources at a school, in a family of schools, districtwide, and in the home and community to ensure that sufficient resources are mobilized for capacity building, implementation, filling gaps, and enhancing essential programs and services to enable student learning and well-being and strengthen families and neighborhoods.*

Standard 4   *Learning supports are applied in ways that promote the use of the least restrictive and nonintrusive forms of intervention required to address problems and accommodate diversity.*

Standard 5   *The Enabling or Learning Supports Component is evaluated with respect to its impact on enabling factors, as well as increased student achievement.*

Meeting these standards is a shared responsibility. District and school leaders, staff, and all other concerned stakeholders work together to identify learning supports needs and how best to meet them. The district and schools provide necessary resources, implement policies and practices to encourage and support appropriate interventions, and continuously evaluate the quality and impact of the Enabling/Learning Supports Component.

Guidelines and Quality Indicators for Each Standard

Standard 1 encompasses a guideline emphasizing the necessity of having a full continuum of programs and services in order to ensure that all students have an equal opportunity for success at school. Included are programs designed to promote and maintain safety, programs to promote and maintain physical and mental health, school readiness and early school adjustment services, expansion of social and academic supports, interventions prior to referral for special services, and provisions to meet specialty needs.

Quality Indicators for Standard 1

- All programs and services implemented are based on state-of-the-art best practices for addressing barriers to learning and promoting positive development.
- The continuum of programs and services ranges from prevention and early-age intervention—through responding to problems soon after onset—to partnerships with the home and other agencies in meeting the special needs of those with severe, pervasive, or chronic problems.
- Routine procedures are in place to review the progress of the component's development and the fidelity of its implementation.

Standard 2 encompasses a guideline that programs and services should be evolved within a framework of delineated areas of activity (e.g., five or six major areas) that reflect basic functions schools must carry out in addressing barriers to student learning and promoting healthy development. A second guideline stresses that a school-based lead staff member and team should be in place to steer development of these areas at each school and to ensure that all activities are implemented in an interdisciplinary, well-coordinated manner that ensures full integration into the instructional and management plan.

Quality Indicators for Standard 2

- All programs/services are established with a delineated framework of areas of activity that reflect basic functions a school must have in place for addressing barriers to learning and promoting healthy development.
- At the school level, a resource-oriented team is functioning effectively as part of the school's infrastructure with responsibility for ensuring that resources are deployed appropriately and used in a coordinated way. In addition, the team is facilitating (a) capacity building; (b) development, implementation, and evaluation of activity; and (c) full integration with all facets of the instructional and governance/management components.
- Routine procedures are in place to ensure that all activities are implemented in a manner that coordinates them with each other and integrates them fully into the instructional and governance/management components.
- Ongoing professional development is (a) provided for all personnel implementing any aspect of the Enabling/Learning Supports Component and (b) is developed and implemented in ways that are consistent with the district's Professional Development Standards.

Standard 3 encompasses a guideline underscoring that necessary resources must be generated by redeploying current allocations and building collaborations that weave together, in common purpose, families of schools, centralized district assets, and various community entities.

Quality Indicators for Standard 3

- Each school has mapped and analyzed the resources it allocates for learner support activity and routinely updates its mapping and analysis.
- All school resources for learner supports are allocated and redeployed based on careful analysis of cost-effectiveness.
- Collaborative arrangements for each family of schools are in place to (a) enhance effectiveness of learner supports and (b) achieve economies of scale.

- Centralized district assets are allocated in ways that directly aid capacity building and effective implementation of learner supports programs and services at school sites and by families of schools.
- Collaborative arrangements are in place with a variety of community entities to (a) fill gaps in the Enabling/Learning Supports Component, (b) enhance effectiveness, and (c) achieve economies of scale.

Standard 4 encompasses guidelines that highlight that enabling or learner supports activity should be applied in all instances where there is need and should be implemented in ways that ensure that needs are addressed appropriately, with as little disruption as feasible of a student's normal involvement at school.

Quality Indicators for Standard 4

- Procedures are in routine use for gathering and reviewing information on the need for specific types of learning supports activities and for establishing priorities for developing/implementing such activity.
- Whenever a need is identified, learning supports are implemented in ways that ensure that needs are addressed appropriately and with as little disruption as feasible of a student's normal involvement at school.
- Procedures are in routine use for gathering and reviewing data on how well needs are met; such data are used to inform decisions about capacity building, including infrastructure changes and personnel development.

Standard 5 encompasses a guideline for accountability that emphasizes a focus on the progress of students with respect to the direct enabling outcomes each program and service is designed to accomplish as well as by enhanced academic achievement.

Quality Indicators for Standard 5

- Accountability for the learning supports activity focuses on the progress of students at a school site with respect to both the direct enabling outcomes a program/service is designed to accomplish (measures of effectiveness in addressing barriers, such as increased attendance, reduced tardies, reduced misbehavior, less bullying and sexual harassment, increased family involvement with child and schooling, fewer referrals for specialized assistance, fewer referrals for special education, fewer pregnancies, fewer suspensions, and fewer dropouts) as well as academic achievement.
- All data are disaggregated to clarify impact as related to critical subgroup differences (e.g., pervasiveness, severity, and chronicity of identified problems).
- All data gathered on learning supports activity are reviewed as a basis for decisions about how to enhance and renew the Enabling/Learning Supports Component.

REFERENCE

Center for Mental Health in Schools. (1999). *Expanding policy leadership for mental health in schools*. Los Angeles: Center for Mental Health in Schools at UCLA.

Our Published Works and Center-produced Resources on Addressing Barriers to Learning

19

PUBLICATIONS SINCE 1990

Motivational readiness and minors' participation in psychoeducational decision making. Adelman, H. S., MacDonald, V. M., Nelson, P., Smith, D. C., & Taylor, L. (1990). *Journal of Learning Disabilities, 23*, 171–176.

School avoidance behavior: Motivational bases and implications for intervention. Taylor, L., & Adelman, H. S. (1990). *Child Psychiatry and Human Development, 20*, 219–233.

Intrinsic motivation and school misbehavior: Some intervention implications. Adelman, H. S., & Taylor, L. (1990). *Journal of Learning Disabilities, 23*, 541–550.

Issues and problems related to the assessment of learning disabilities. Adelman, H. S., & Taylor, L. (1991). In H. L. Swanson (Ed.), *Handbook on the assessment of learning disabilities: Theory, research, and practice.* Pro-ed.

Perceived control, causality, expectations, and help seeking behavior. Simoni, J. M., Adelman, H. S., & Nelson, P. (1991). *Counseling Psychology Quarterly, 4*, 37–44.

Mental health facets of the School-based Health Center movement: Need and opportunity for research and development. Adelman, H. S., & Taylor, L. (1991). *Journal of Mental Health Administration, 18*, 272–283.

Early school adjustment problems: Some perspectives and a project report. Adelman, H. S., & Taylor, L. (1991). *American Journal of Orthopsychiatry, 61*, 468–474.

The classification problem. Adelman, H. S. (1992). In W. Stainback & S. Stainback (Eds.), *Controversial issues confronting special education: Divergent perspectives.* Boston: Allyn & Bacon.

LD: The next 25 years. Adelman, H. S. (1992). *Journal of Learning Disabilities, 25,* 17–22.

Two studies of low income parents' involvement in schooling. Klimes-Dougan, B., Lopez, J., Adelman, H. S., & Nelson, P. (1992). *The Urban Review, 24,* 185–202.

Learning problems and learning disabilities: Moving forward. Adelman, H. S., & Taylor, L. (1993). Pacific Grove, CA: Brooks/Cole.

School-based mental health: Toward a comprehensive approach. Adelman, H. S., & Taylor, L. (1993). *Journal of Mental Health Administration, 20,* 32–45.

A study of a school-based clinic: Who uses it and who doesn't? Adelman, H. S., Barker, L. A., & Nelson, P. (1993). *Journal of Clinical Child Psychology, 22,* 52–59.

Utilization of a school-based clinic for identification & treatment of adolescent sexual abuse. McGurk, S. R., Cárdenas, J., & Adelman, H. S. (1993). *Journal of Adolescent Health, 14,* 196–201.

School-based mutual support groups for low-income parents. Simoni, J., & Adelman, H. S. (1993). *The Urban Review, 25,* 335–350.

Learning disabilities: On interpreting research translations. Adelman, H. S. (1994). In N.C. Jordan & J. Goldsmith-Phillips (Eds.), *Learning disabilities: New directions for assessment and intervention.* Boston: Allyn & Bacon.

Transition support for immigrant students. Cárdenas, J., Taylor, L., & Adelman, H. (1993). *Journal of Multicultural Counseling & Development, 21,* 203–210.

School-linked mental health interventions: Toward mechanisms for service coordination and integration. Adelman, H. S. (1993). *Journal of Community Psychology, 21,* 309–319.

Mental health status and help-seeking among ethnic minority adolescents. Barker, L. A., & Adelman, H. S. (1994). *Journal of Adolescence, 17,* 251–263.

On intervening to enhance home involvement in schooling. Adelman, H. S. (1994). *Intervention in School and Clinic, 29,* 276–287.

On understanding intervention in psychology and education. Adelman, H. S., & Taylor, L. (1994). Westport, CT: Praeger.

Clinical psychology: Beyond psychopathology and clinical interventions. Adelman, H. S. (1995). *Clinical Psychology: Science and Practice, 2,* 28–44.

Welcoming: Facilitating a new start at a new school. DiCecco, M. B., Rosenblum, L., Taylor, L., & Adelman, H. S. (1995). *Social Work in Education, 17,* 18–29.

Upgrading school support programs through collaboration: Resource Coordinating Teams. Rosenblum, L., DiCecco, M. B., Taylor, L., & Adelman, H. (1995). *Social Work in Education, 17,* 117–124.

Education reform: Broadening the focus. Adelman, H. S. (1995). *Psychological Science, 6,* 61–62.

Appreciating the classification dilemma. Adelman, H. S. (1996). In W. Stainback & S. Stainback (Eds.), *Controversial issues confronting special education: Divergent perspectives.* Boston: Allyn & Bacon.

Mobility and school functioning in the early grades. Nelson, P. S., Simoni, J. M., & Adelman, H. S. (1996). *Journal of Educational Research, 89,* 365–369.

Mental health in the schools: Promising directions for practice. Taylor, L., & Adelman, H. S. (1996). *Adolescent Medicine: State of the Art Reviews, 7,* 303–317.

Restructuring education support services: Toward the concept of an enabling component. Adelman, H. S. (1996). Kent, OH: American School Health Association.

Restructuring education support services and integrating community resources: Beyond the full service school model. Adelman, H. S. (1996). *School Psychology Review, 25,* 431–445.

Toward a scale-up model for replicating new approaches to schooling. Adelman, H. S., & Taylor, L. (1997). *Journal of Educational and Psychological Consultation, 8,* 197–230.

Addressing barriers to learning: Beyond school-linked services and full service schools. Adelman, H. S., & Taylor, L. (1997). *American Journal of Orthopsychiatry, 67,* 408–421.

Establishing school-based collaborative teams to coordinate resources: A case study. Lim, C., & Adelman, H. S. (1997). *Social Work in Education, 19,* 266–278.

Involving teachers in collaborative efforts to better address barriers to student learning. Adelman, H. S., & Taylor, L. (1998). *Preventing School Failure, 42,* 55–60.

School counseling, psychological, and social services. Adelman, H. S. (1998). In E. Marx & S. F. Wooley (with D. Northrop) (Eds.), *Health is academic: A guide to coordinated school health programs.* New York: Teachers College Press.

Psychosocial screening. Adelman, H. S., & Taylor, L. (1998). Scarborough, ME: National Association of School Nurses.

A policy and practice framework to guide school-community connections. Taylor, L., & Adelman, H. S. (1998). *Rural Special Education Quarterly, 17,* 62–70.

Mental health in schools: Moving forward. Adelman, H. S., & Taylor, L. (1998). *School Psychology Review, 27,* 175–190.

Confidentiality: Competing principles, inevitable dilemmas. Taylor, L., & Adelman, H. (1998). *Journal of Educational and Psychological Consultation, 9,* 267–275.

Reframing mental health in schools and expanding school reform. Adelman, H. S., & Taylor, L. (1998). *Educational Psychologist, 33,* 135–152.

Mental health in schools: A federal initiative. Adelman, H. S., Taylor, L., Weist, M., Adelsheim, S., et al. (1999). *Children Services: Social Policy, Research, and Practice, 2,* 99–119.

Mental health in schools and system restructuring. Adelman, H. S., & Taylor, L. (1999). *Clinical Psychology Review, 19,* 137–163.

Addressing barriers to student learning: Systemic changes at all levels. Adelman, H. S., & Taylor, L. (1999). Introduction to thematic section for *Reading & Writing Quarterly, 15,* 251–254.

Personalizing classroom instruction to account for motivational and developmental differences. Taylor, L., & Adelman, H. S. (1999). *Reading & Writing Quarterly, 15,* 255–276.

A school-wide component to address barriers to learning. Adelman, H. S., Taylor, L., & Schnieder, M. (1999). *Reading & Writing Quarterly, 15,* 277–302.

Scaling-up reforms across a school district. Taylor, L., Nelson, P., & Adelman, H. S. (1999). *Reading & Writing Quarterly, 15,* 303–326.

Fundamental concerns about policy for addressing barriers to student learning. Adelman, H., Reyna, C., Collins, R., Onghai, J., & Taylor, L. (1999). *Reading & Writing Quarterly, 15,* 327–350.

Keeping reading and writing problems in broad perspective. Adelman, H. S., & Taylor, L. (1999). Coda to thematic section for *Reading & Writing Quarterly, 15,* 351–354.

Moving prevention from the fringes into the fabric of school improvement. Adelman, H., & Taylor, L. (2000). *Journal of Educational and Psychological Consultation, 11,* 7–36.

Shaping the future of mental health in schools. Adelman, H. S., & Taylor, L. (2000). *Psychology in the Schools, 37,* 49–60.

Looking at school health and school reform policy through the lens of addressing barriers to learning. Adelman, H., & Taylor, L. (2000). *Children Services: Social Policy, Research, and Practice, 3,* 117–132.

Promoting mental health in schools in the midst of school reform. Adelman, H. S., & Taylor, L. (2000). *Journal of School Health, 70,* 171–178.

Toward ending the marginalization of mental health in schools. Taylor, L., & Adelman, H. S. (2000). *Journal of School Health, 70,* 210–215.

Connecting schools, families, and communities. Taylor, L., & Adelman, H. S. (2000). *Professional School Counseling, 3,* 298–307.

School learning. Adelman, H. S. (2000). In W. E. Craighead & C. B. Nemeroff (Eds.), *The Corsini encyclopedia of psychology and behavioral science* (3rd ed.). New York: John Wiley.

Enlisting appropriate parental cooperation & involvement in children's mental health treatment. Taylor, L., & Adelman, H. S. (2001). In E. R. Welfel & R. E. Ingersoll (Eds.), *The mental health desk reference.* New York: John Wiley.

Impediments to enhancing availability of mental health services in schools: Fragmentation, overspecialization, counterproductive competition, and marginalization. Adelman, H. S., & Taylor, L. (2002). Paper commissioned by the National Association of School Psychologists and the ERIC Clearinghouse on Counseling and Student Services (ERIC/CASS). Published by the *ERIC/CASS Clearinghouse.* Available online at http://smhp.psych.ucla.edu/.

Building comprehensive, multifaceted, and integrated approaches to address barriers to student learning. Adelman, H. S., & Taylor, L. (2002). *Childhood Education, 78,* 261–268.

Lessons learned from working with a district's mental health unit. Taylor, L., & Adelman, H. S. (2002). *Childhood Education, 78,* 295–300.

Lenses used determine lessons learned. Adelman, H., & Taylor, L. (2002). *Journal of Educational and Psychological Consultation, 13,* 227–236.

School-community relations: Policy and practice. Taylor, L., & Adelman, H. S. (2003). In Fishbaugh et al. (Eds.), *Ensuring safe school environments: Exploring issues—seeking solutions.* Mahwah, NJ: Lawrence Erlbaum.

Creating school and community partnerships for substance abuse prevention programs. (Commissioned by SAMHSA's Center for Substance Abuse Prevention.) Adelman, H. S., & Taylor, L. (2003). *Journal of Primary Prevention, 23,* 331–310.

Toward a comprehensive policy vision for mental health in schools. Adelman, H. S., & Taylor, L. (2002). In M. Weist, S. Evans, & N. Lever (Eds.), *School mental health handbook.* Norwell, MA: Kluwer.

Aligning school accountability, outcomes, and evidence-base practices. Adelman, H. S., & Taylor, L. (2002). *Data Matters, 5,* 16–18.

So you want higher achievement test scores? It's time to rethink learning supports. Adelman, H. S., & Taylor, L. (2002). *The State Education Standard, Autumn,* 52–56.

School counselors and school reform: New directions. Adelman, H. S., & Taylor, L. (in press). *Professional School Counseling.*

Advancing mental health in schools: Guiding frameworks and strategic approaches. Taylor, L., & Adelman, H. S. (in press). In K. Robinson (Ed.), *Advances in school-based mental health.* Creative Research Institute.

MATERIALS PRODUCED BY THE CENTER
FOR MENTAL HEALTH IN SCHOOLS AT UCLA

All the following resources can be downloaded at no cost from the Web site of the School Mental Health Project and its Center for Mental Health in Schools (see http://smhp.psych.ucla.edu).

The following documents represent a variety of resources, including

1. *Introductory Packets:* These provide overview discussions; descriptions of model programs; references to publications; access information to other relevant centers, agencies, organizations, advocacy groups, and Internet links; and a list of consultation cadre members ready to share expertise.
2. *Resource Aid Packets* (designed to complement the Introductory Packets): These are in the form of a tool kit for fairly circumscribed areas of practice. They contain overviews, outlines, checklists, instruments, and other resources that can be reproduced and used as information handouts and aids for training and practice.
3. *Technical Aid Packets:* These are designed to provide basic understanding of specific practices and tools.
4. *Technical Assistance Samplers:* These provide basic information for accessing a variety of resources on a specific topic, such as agencies, organizations, Web sites, individuals with expertise, relevant programs, and library resources.
5. *Guides to Practice:* These translate ideas into practice.
6. *Continuing Education Modules, Training Tutorials, and Quick Training Aids:* These provide learning opportunities and resources for use in inservice training.
7. *Special Reports and Center Briefs*

Some Resources Focused on Psychosocial Problems

- *Affect and Mood Problems Related to School-aged Youth* (Introductory Packet)
- *Anxiety, Fears, Phobias, and Related Problems: Intervention and Resources for School-aged Youth* (Introductory Packet)
- *Attention Problems: Intervention and Resources* (Introductory Packet)
- *Behavioral Problems at School* (Quick Training Aid)
- *Bullying Prevention* (Quick Training Aid)

- *Common Psychosocial Problems of School-aged Youth: Developmental Variations, Problems, Disorders, and Perspectives for Prevention and Treatment* (Guide to Practice)
- *Conduct and Behavior Problems in School-aged Youth* (Introductory Packet)
- *Dropout Prevention* (Introductory Packet)
- *Learning Problems and Learning Disabilities* (Introductory Packet)
- *Sexual Minority Students* (Technical Aid Packet)
- *School Interventions to Prevent Youth Suicide* (Technical Aid Packet)
- *Social and Interpersonal Problems Related to School-aged Youth* (Introductory Packet)
- *Substance Abuse* (Resource Aid Packet)
- *Suicide Prevention* (Quick Training Aid)
- *Teen Pregnancy Prevention and Support* (Introductory Packet)
- *Violence Prevention* (Quick Training Aid)

Some Resources Focused on Program/Process Concerns

- *Addressing Barriers to Learning: New Directions for Mental Health in Schools* (Continuing Education Modules)
- *Addressing Barriers to Learning: Overview of the Curriculum for an Enabling (or Learning Supports) Component* (Quick Training Aid)
- *Afterschool Programs and Addressing Barriers to Learning* (Technical Aid Packet)
- *Assessing to Address Barriers to Learning* (Introductory Packet)
- *Assessing & Screening* (Quick Training Aid)
- *Behavioral Initiatives in Broad Perspective* (Technical Assistance Sampler)
- *Classroom Changes to Enhance and Reengage Students in Learning* (Training Tutorial)
- *Case Management in the School Context* (Quick Training Aid)
- *Community Outreach: School-Community Resources to Address Barriers to Learning* (Training Tutorial)
- *Confidentiality* (Quick Training Aid)
- *Confidentiality and Informed Consent* (Introductory Packet)
- *Creating the Infrastructure for an Enabling (Learning Supports) Component to Address Barriers to Student Learning* (Training Tutorial)
- *Crisis Assistance and Prevention: Reducing Barriers to Learning* (Training Tutorial)
- *Cultural Concerns in Addressing Barriers to Learning* (Introductory Packet)
- *Early Development and Learning From the Perspective of Addressing Barriers* (Introductory Packet)
- *Early Development and School Readiness From the Perspective of Addressing Barriers to Learning* (Center Brief)

- *Enhancing Classroom Approaches for Addressing Barriers to Learning: Classroom-focused Enabling* (Continuing Education Modules With Accompanying Readings and Tool Kit)
- *Financing Strategies to Address Barriers to Learning* (Quick Training Aid)
- *Financial Strategies to Aid in Addressing Barriers to Learning* (Introductory Packet)
- *Financing Mental Health for Children & Adolescents* (Center Brief and Fact Sheet)
- *Guiding Parents in Helping Children Learn* (Technical Aid)
- *Home Involvement in Schooling* (Training Tutorial)
- *Least Intervention Needed: Toward Appropriate Inclusion of Students With Special Needs* (Introductory Packet)
- *Mental Health and School-based Health Centers* (Guide to Practice)
- *Mental Health in Schools: New Roles for School Nurses* (Continuing Education Modules)
- *Parent and Home Involvement in Schools* (Introductory Packet)
- *Protective Factors (Resiliency)* (Technical Assistance Sampler)
- *Reengaging Students in Learning* (Quick Training Aid)
- *Responding to Crisis at a School* (Resource Aid Packet)
- *School-based Client Consultation, Referral, and Management of Care* (Technical Aid Packet)
- *School-based Crisis Intervention* (Quick Training Aid)
- *School-based Health Centers* (Technical Assistance Sampler)
- *School-based Mutual Support Groups (For Parents, Staff, and Older Students)* (Technical Aid Packet)
- *Screening/Assessing Students: Indicators and Tools* (Resource Aid)
- *Students & Family Assistance Programs and Services to Address Barriers to Learning* (Training Tutorial)
- *Students and Psychotropic Medication: The School's Role* (Resource Aide Packet)
- *Support for Transitions to Address Barriers to Learning* (Training Tutorial)
- *Sustaining School-Community Partnerships to Enhance Outcomes for Children and Youth* (Guidebook and Tool Kit)
- *Understanding and Minimizing Staff Burnout* (Introductory Packet)
- *Using Technology to Address Barriers to Learning* (Technical Assistance Sampler)
- *Violence Prevention and Safe Schools* (Introductory Packet)
- *Volunteers to Help Teachers and Schools Address Barriers to Learning* (Technical Aid Packet)
- *Welcoming and Involving New Students and Families* (Technical Aid Packet)
- *What Schools Can Do to Welcome and Meet the Needs of All Students and Families* (Guide to Practice)

- *Where to Get Resource Materials to Address Barriers to Learning* (Resource Aid Packet)
- *Where to Access Statistical Information Relevant to Addressing Barriers to Learning: An Annotated Reference List* (Resource Aid Packet)

Some Resources Focused on Systemic Concerns

- *About Mental Health in Schools* (Introductory Packet)
- *Addressing Barriers to Learning: A Set of Surveys to Map What a School Has and What It Needs* (Resource Aid Packet)
- *Addressing Barriers to Student Learning: Closing Gaps in School/Community Policy and Practice* (Center Report)
- *Addressing Barriers to Student Learning & Promoting Healthy Development: A Usable Research-Base* (Center Brief)
- *Evaluation and Accountability: Getting Credit for All You Do!* (Introductory Packet)
- *Evaluation and Accountability Related to Mental Health in Schools* (Technical Aid Sampler)
- *Expanding Educational Reform to Address Barriers to Learning: Restructuring Student Support Services and Enhancing School-Community Partnerships* (Center Report)
- *Framing New Directions for School Counselors, Psychologists, & Social Workers* (Center Report)
- *Guides for the Enabling Component—Addressing Barriers to Learning and Enhancing Healthy Development* (Guides to Practice)
- *Integrating Mental Health in Schools: Schools, School-based Centers, and Community Programs Working Together* (Center Brief)
- *Introduction to a Component for Addressing Barriers to Student Learning* (Center Brief)
- *Mental Health in Schools: Guidelines, Models, Resources, & Policy Considerations* (Center Report)
- *New Directions in Enhancing Educational Results: Policymakers' Guide to Restructuring Student Support Resources to Address Barriers to Learning* (Guide to Practice)
- *New Directions for School & Community Initiatives to Address Barriers to Learning: Two Examples of Concept Papers to Inform and Guide Policy Makers* (Center Report)
- *New Initiatives: Considerations Related to Planning, Implementing, Sustaining, and Going to Scale* (Center Brief)
- *Organization Facilitators: A Change Agent for Systemic School and Community Changes* (Center Report)
- *Pioneer Initiatives to Reform Education Support Programs* (Center Report)
- *Policies and Practices for Addressing Barriers to Learning: Current Status and New Directions* (Center Report)

- *Resource Mapping and Management to Address Barriers to Learning: An Intervention for Systemic Change* (Technical Assistance Packet)
- *Resource-oriented Teams: Key Infrastructure Mechanisms for Enhancing Education Supports* (Center Report)
- *Restructuring Boards of Education to Enhance Schools' Effectiveness in Addressing Barriers to Student Learning* (Center Report)
- *Sampling of Outcome Findings From Interventions Relevant to Addressing Barriers to Learning* (Technical Assistance Sampler)
- *School-Community Partnerships: A Guide*
- *Thinking About and Accessing Policy Related to Addressing Barriers to Learning* (Technical Assistance Sampler)
- *Working Together: From School-based Collaborative Teams to School-Community-Higher Education Connections* (Introductory Packet)

Internet Sites for a Sampling of Major Agencies and Organizations Relevant to Learning Supports

20

There are many agencies and organizations that help and advocate for those with learning, behavior, and emotional problems. The following is a list of major links on the World Wide Web that offer information and resources related to such matters. This list is not exhaustive; it is meant to highlight some premier resources and serve as a beginning for your search. Many of the Web sites will have links to others that cover similar topics. In general, the Internet is an invaluable tool when looking for information on learning, behavior, and emotional problems.

American Academy of Child & Adolescent Psychiatry

www.aacap.org

Site serves both AACAP members and parents and families. Provides information to aid understanding and treatment of the developmental, behavioral, and mental disorders, including fact sheets for parents and caregivers, current research, practice guidelines, managed care information, and more. Provides fact sheets and other information.

American Academy of Pediatrics

www.aap.org

Site has a variety of reports, publications, aids, and links about the academy's various programs and initiatives. Also provides information about their policies and practice guidelines.

American Psychiatric Association

www.psych.org

Site has a variety of reports, publications, and fact sheets.

American Psychological Association

www.apa.org

Site provides news, reports, publication information, a consumer help center, information on continuing education, and more.

American School Counselor Association

www.schoolcounselor.org

Cosponsor of the New Directions for Student Support Initiative. Partners with Learning Network to provide school-counseling-related content for parents, including age- and grade-specific information to help enhance learning and overall development both inside and outside school. FamilyEducation.com offers twenty free e-mail newsletters, expert advice on education and child rearing, and home learning ideas. Includes materials for kids with special needs, gifted children, and homeschooling families.

American School Health Association

www.ashaweb.org

Cosponsor of the New Directions for Student Support Initiative. Multidisciplinary organization of administrators, counselors, dentists, health educators, physical educators, school nurses, and school physicians; advocates high-quality school health instruction, health services, and a healthful school environment.

Association for Supervision and Curriculum Development

www.ascd.org

Cosponsor of the New Directions for Student Support Initiative. Addresses all aspects of effective teaching and learning, such as professional development, educational leadership, and capacity building; offers broad, multiple perspectives—across all education professions—in reporting key policies and practices. Focus is solely on professional practice within the context of "Is it good for the children?" rather than what is reflective of a specific educator role.

California Association of School Psychologists

www.casponline.org

Cosponsor of the New Directions for Student Support Initiative. Provides liaison with state boards and commissions, represents school psychology to governmental officials and other policymakers; provides continuing professional development; publishes a quarterly magazine and annual research journal.

California Department of Education

www.cde.ca.gov

Cosponsor of the New Directions for Student Support Initiative. A state agency; has established a division for learning supports and has resources relevant to a school's focus on addressing barriers to learning.

Center for Community School Partnerships

education.ucdavis.edu/cress/ccsp

Cosponsor of the New Directions for Student Support Initiative. Originally the Healthy Start Field Office; serves community-school partnership across California and provides national and international consultation in

education reform and collaborative partnership policy.

Center for Cooperative Research and Extension Services for Schools

education.ucdavis.edu/cress

Cosponsor of the New Directions for Student Support Initiative. Brings together K–12 educators with university faculty, education extension specialists, and graduate students. Focuses on educational research, curriculum design, and new modes of professional development.

Center for Effective Collaboration and Practice

www.air.org/cecp

Identifies promising programs and practices, promotes information exchanges, and facilitates collaboration among stakeholders and across service system disciplines with a focus on the development and adjustment of children with or at risk of developing serious emotional disturbances.

Center for Mental Health in Schools

smhp.psych.ucla.edu

Approaches mental health and psychosocial concerns from the broad perspective of addressing barriers to learning and promoting healthy development. Its mission: to improve outcomes for young people by enhancing policies, programs, and practices relevant to mental health in schools. Web site has extensive online resources accessible at no cost.

Center for Prevention of Youth Violence, Johns Hopkins University

www.jhsph.edu/ PreventYouth Violence/

Cosponsor of the New Directions for Student Support Initiative. Brings together academic institutions, city and state agencies and organizations, community groups, schools, youth groups, and faith organizations to collaborate on both positive youth development and prevention of violence. Integrates research with education, professional development, and practice efforts, providing an infrastructure facilitating academic-community collaborations, thus translating research into improved professional practice.

Center for School Mental Health Assistance

csmha.umaryland.edu

Cosponsor of the New Directions for Student Support Initiative. Focuses on the concept of *expanded school mental health,* offers technical assistance and training, holds annual conferences to advance mental health in schools.

Center for Social and Emotional Education

www.csee.net

Cosponsor of the New Directions for Student Support Initiative. A multidisciplinary educational and professional development organization; works with educators, parents, schools, and communities to develop proactive ways to promote academic achievement as well as to prevent youth violence and other at-risk behaviors by fostering effective social and emotional education and character education for children and adolescents.

Center for the Study & Prevention of Violence

www.colorado.edu/cspv

At the Institute of Behavioral Sciences, University of Colorado at Boulder; provides informed assistance to groups committed to understanding and preventing violence.

Coalition for Community Schools

www.communityschools.org

Cosponsor of the New Directions for Student Support Initiative. Alliance of national, state, and local organizations in education K–16, youth development, community planning and development, family support, health and human services, government and philanthropy as well as community school networks. Advocates for community schools as the vehicle for strengthening schools, families, and communities so that together they can improve student learning.

Collaborative for Academic, Social, and Emotional Learning (CASEL)

www.casel.org

Cosponsor of the New Directions for Student Support Initiative. Located at University of Illinois at Chicago; an international collaborative of educators, scientists, policymakers, foundations, and concerned citizens promoting social and emotional educational and development in schools. Online resources include publications, reports, news, and links.

Connect for Kids

www.connectforkids.org

Information for those who want to make their communities better places for kids. Through radio, print, and TV ads, a weekly e-mail newsletter and a discussion forum, provides tools to help people become more active citizens— from volunteering to voting—on behalf of kids.

Council for Exceptional Children

www.cec.sped.org

Largest international professional organization dedicated to

improving educational outcomes for individuals with exceptionalities, students with disabilities, and/or the gifted. Has divisions focused on LD and behavioral disorders.

Education Development Center

main.edc.org

Cosponsor of the New Directions for Student Support Initiative. An international, nonprofit organization with more than 335 projects dedicated to enhancing learning, promoting health, and fostering a deeper understanding of the world.

Education World

www.educationworld.com

Education-based resource and Internet search site designed especially for teachers, students, administrators, and parents.

ERIC: Educational Resources Info Center

www.eric.ed.gov

Provides extensive information on all topics relevant to education.

Family Resource Coalition of America

www.familysupportamerica.org

For community-based providers, school personnel, those who work in human services, trainers, scholars, and policymakers. Provides resources, publications, technical assistance, and consulting, as well as public education and advocacy.

Federal Consumer Information Center

www.pueblo.gsa.gov

Publishes a catalog listing booklets from several federal agencies, including works related to learning, behavior, and emotional problems.

Federal Resource Center for Special Education

www.dssc.org/frc

Supports a national technical assistance network that responds quickly to the needs of students with disabilities, especially students from underrepresented populations.

Higher Education and the Handicapped

www.heath.gwu.edu

National clearinghouse offering statistics and information on post-high school education for individuals with disabilities.

Indiana Department of Education

www.doe.state.in.us

Cosponsor of the New Directions for Student Support Initiative. Provides leadership, vision, and advocacy to secure optimum educational opportunity and benefit to the citizens of Indiana.

Johns Hopkins University Graduate Division of Education

www.spsbe.jhu.edu/ programs/grad_edu.cfm

Cosponsor of the New Directions for Student Support Initiative. Committed to the preparation and support of a new generation of educators prepared to meet the challenges of high academic standards, expanding technology, and increasingly diverse student populations. Offers graduate programs providing innovative, research-based alternatives for the initial preparation and continuing development of teachers, administrators, specialists, and school and community counselors.

LD Online

www.ldonline.org

Focuses on the education and welfare of individuals with learning disabilities. Geared toward parents, teachers, and other professionals.

Learning Disabilities Association of America

www.ldanatl.org

National nonprofit advocacy organization. Site includes information on the association, upcoming conferences, legislative updates, and links to other related resources.

Mental Health Net (MHN)

mentalhelp.net

Guide to mental health topics, with more than 3,000 individual resources listed. Topics range from disorders such as depression, anxiety, and substance abuse to professional journals and self-help magazines available online.

Minnesota Department of Education

education.state.mn.us

Cosponsor of the New Directions for Student Support Initiative. Focuses on improving educational achievement by establishing clear standards, measuring performance, assisting educators, and increasing opportunities for lifelong learning.

National Alliance of Pupil Service Organizations

www.napso.org

Cosponsor of the New Directions for Student Support Initiative. A coalition of national professional organizations whose members provide a variety of school-based prevention and intervention services to assist students in becoming effective learners and productive citizens.

National Association of Pupil Service Administrators

www.napsa.com

Cosponsor of the New Directions for Student Support Initiative. Provides a network of professionals who can assist in the development of programs designed to meet locally identified needs. Has information on current trends and changes in legal and regulatory standards.

National Association of School Nurses

www.nasn.org

Cosponsor of the New Directions for Student Support Initiative. Core purpose is to advance delivery of professional school health services to promote optimal health and learning in students. Site has a variety of publications, training aids, and links.

National Association of School Psychologists

www.nasponline.org

Cosponsor of the New Directions for Student Support Initiative. Promotes the rights, welfare, education, and mental health of children and youth and advancing the profession of school psychology.

National Association of Secondary School Principals

nasspcms.principals.org

Cosponsor of the New Directions for Student Support Initiative. National voice for middle school and high school principals, assistant principals, and aspiring school leaders from across the United States and more than forty-five other countries. Site offers news, publications, research, professional development, and job opportunities.

National Association of Social Workers

www.naswdc.org

Cosponsor of the New Directions for Student Support Initiative. Works to enhance the professional growth and development of its members, to create and maintain professional standards, and to advance sound social policies. Site describes publications, resources, research, and so forth.

National Association of State Boards of Education

www.nasbe.org

Cosponsor of the New Directions for Student Support Initiative. Works to strengthen state leadership in educational policy making, promote excellence, advocate equality of access to educational opportunity, and ensure continued citizen support for public education. Site offers information, news, technical assistance, and links.

National Association of State Directors of Special Education

www.nasdse.org

Promotes and supports education programs for students with disabilities.

National Center for Community Education

www.nccenet.org

Cosponsor of the New Directions for Student Support Initiative. Promotes community and educational change emphasizing community schools by providing state-of-the-art leadership development, training, and technical assistance.

National Clearinghouse for Alcohol and Drug Information

www.health.org

Information service of the Substance Abuse and Mental Health Services Administration's (SAMHSA) Center for Substance Abuse Prevention (CSAP). World's largest resource for current information and materials concerning substance abuse. Has both English- and Spanish-speaking information specialists.

National Clearinghouse on Child Abuse and Neglect

http://nccanch.acf.hhs.gov/

U.S. Department of Health and Human Services' resource for professionals, with information on the prevention, identification, and treatment of child abuse.

National Dropout Prevention Center

www.dropoutprevention.org

Offers clearinghouse and professional development on

issues related to dropout prevention and strategies designed to increase the graduation rates.

National Information Center for Children and Youth With Disabilities

www.nichcy.org

National information and referral center for families, educators, and other professionals. Has a Spanish version accessible from the main Web page.

National Institute of Mental Health (NIMH)

www.nimh.nih.gov

Conducts and supports research nationwide on mental illness and mental health, including studies of the brain, behavior, and mental health services.

National Mental Health Information Center: Substance Abuse and Mental Health Services Administration (SAMHSA)

www.mentalhealth.samhsa.gov

Federal Center for Mental Health Services; provides a national, one-stop source of information and resources on prevention, treatment, and rehabilitation services for mental illness via toll-free telephone services and publications. Developed for users of mental health services and their

families, the general public, policymakers, providers, and the media. P.O. Box 42557, Washington, DC 20015. Ph: 800-789-CMHS (2647) M-F (8:30–5:00 ET). TDD: 866-889-2647.

National Middle School Association

www.nmsa.org

Cosponsor of the New Directions for Student Support Initiative. Offers news and views, bookstore, position papers, professional development, and research.

National Technical Assistance Center for Children's Mental Health

http://gucchd.georgetown.edu/ programs/ta_center/index.html

Provides technical assistance to improve service delivery and outcomes for children and adolescents with, or at risk of, serious emotional disturbance and their families. Assists states and communities in building systems of care that are child- and family-centered, culturally competent, coordinated, and community-based.

National Youth Gang Center

www.iir.com/nygc

Purpose is to expand and maintain the body of critical knowledge about youth gangs and effective responses to them. Assists state and local jurisdictions in the collection, analysis, and exchange of information on gang-related demographics, legislation, literature, research, and promising program strategies.

Office of Special Education and Rehabilitative Services

*www.ed.gov/about/
offices/list/osers/index.htm*

Supports programs that assist in educating children with special needs, provides for the rehabilitation of youth and adults with disabilities, and supports research to improve the lives of individuals with disabilities.

Partnerships Against Violence Network

http://www.pavnet.org

"Virtual library" of information about violence and youth at risk, representing data from seven different federal agencies. It is a one-stop, searchable information resource to help reduce redundancy in information management and provide clear and comprehensive access to information for states and local communities.

Public Citizen

www.citizen.org

Consumer organization (founded by Ralph Nader). Fights for the consumer in Washington. The group's Health Research Group

may be useful when researching learning, behavior, and emotional problems.

Region VII Comprehensive Center

region7.ou.edu

Cosponsor of the New Directions for Student Support Initiative. Promotes the learning of all students in its region (Indiana, Kansas, Illinois, Missouri, Nebraska, Oklahoma); provides technical assistance to local education agencies, schools, tribes, state education agencies, and community-based organizations.

School Social Work Association of America

www.sswaa.org

Cosponsor of the New Directions for Student Support Initiative. Dedicated to promoting the profession of school social work and the professional development of school social workers in order to enhance the educational experience of students and their families.

Teaching Learning Disabilities

www.teachingld.org

Provides up-to-date resources about teaching students with learning disabilities (a service of the Division for Learning Disabilities of the Council for Exceptional Children).

Urban Special Education Leadership Collaboration

www.urbancollaborative.org

Network of special and general education leaders working together to improve outcomes for students with disabilities in the nation's urban schools. Emphasis on mutual support, sharing of information and resources, and planning/problem-solving partnerships to strengthen each member district.

What Works Clearinghouse

www.whatworks.ed.gov

Gathers studies of the effectiveness of educational interventions (programs, products, practices, and policies), reviews the studies that have the strongest design, and reports on the strengths and weaknesses of those studies against the WWC Evidence Standards.

Wisconsin Department of Public Instruction

www.dpi.state.wi.us

Cosponsor of the New Directions for Student Support Initiative. Web site has information on various programs and initiatives supported by the department as well as updates and recent news for parents and educators alike.

Regional Education Laboratories

www.ed.gov/prog_info/Labs

With support from the U.S. Department of Education, Office of Educational Research and Improvement (OERI), this network of ten Regional Educational Laboratories serves geographic regions that span the nation. They work to ensure that those involved in educational improvement at the local, state, and regional levels have access to the best available information from research and practice. This site is one of many ways that the network reaches out to make that information accessible. While each laboratory has distinctive features tailored to meet the special needs of the geographic region it serves, they also have common characteristics—one of which is promoting widespread access to information regarding research and best practice.

Northeast and Islands Regional Educational Laboratory at Brown University (LAB at Brown U.)

- www.lab.brown.edu
- Serves CT, MA, ME, NH, NY, RI, VT, Puerto Rico, Virgin Islands

Laboratory for Student Success (LSS)

- www.temple.edu/lss
- Serves DC, DE, MD, NJ, PA

Appalachia Educational
Laboratory (AEL)

- www.ael.org
- Serves KY, TN, VA, WV

SERVE

- www.serve.org
- Serves AL, FL, GA, MS, NC,
  SC

North Central Regional
Educational Laboratory (NCREL)

- www.ncrel.org
- Serves IA, IL, IN, MI, MN,
  OH, WI

Southwest Educational
Development Laboratory (SEDL)

- www.sedl.org
- Serves AR, LA,
  NM, OK, TX

Mid-continent Research for
Education and Learning (McREL)

- www.mcrel.org
- Serves CO, KS, MO, NB,
  ND, SD, WY

WEST ED

- www.wested.org
- Serves AZ, CA, NE, UT

Northwest Regional Educational
Laboratory (NWREL)

- www.nwrel.org
- Serves AK, ID, MT, OR, WA

Pacific Resources for Education
and Learning (PREL)

- www.prel.org
- Serves American Samoa,
  Commonwealth of the
  Northern Mariana Islands,
  Federated States of
  Micronesia, Guam, HI,
  Republic of the Marshall
  Islands, Republic of Palau

Special Education Regional Resource Centers

The following six regional centers offer tools and strategies for achieving effective education and human services delivery systems: coordinating information, providing technical assistance, linking research with practice, facilitating interagency collaboration.

Northeast Regional Resource
Center

- www.wested.org/nerrc
- Serves CT, MA, ME, NH,
  NJ, NY, RI, VT

Mid-South Regional Resource
Center

- www.ihdi.uky.edu/msrrc
- Serves DC, DE, KY,
  MD, NC, SC, TN, VA, WV

Southeast Regional Resource Center

- edla.aum.edu/serrc/serrc.html
- Serves AL, AR, FL, GA, LA, MS, NM, OK, TX, Puerto Rico

North Central Regional Resource Center

- www.dssc.org/frc/ncrrc.htm
- Serves IA, IL, IN, MI, MN, MO, OH, PA, WI

Mountain Plains Regional Resource Center

- www.usu.edu/~mprrc
- Serves AZ, Bureau of Indian Affairs, CO, KS, MT, NB, ND, NM, SD, UT, WY

Western Regional Resource Center

- interact.uoregon.edu/wrrc/wrrc.html
- Serves AK, AZ, CA, HI, ID, NE, OR, WA, and the Pacific Islands

Comprehensive Regional Assistance Centers

The U.S. Department of Education established the fifteen Comprehensive Centers (CCs) to provide technical assistance services focused on the implementation of reform programs. The CCs work primarily with states, local education agencies, tribes, schools, and other recipients of funds under the Improving America's Schools Act of 1994 (IASA). Priority for services is given to high-poverty schools and districts, Bureau of Indian Affairs schools, and IASA recipients implementing schoolwide programs.

Region I

- www.edc.org/NECAC
- Serves CT, MA, ME, NH, RI, VT

Region II

- www.nyu.edu/education/metrocenter/NYTAC.html
- Serves NY

Region III

- http://ceee.gwu.edu
- Serves DC, DE, MD, NJ, OH, PA

Region IV

- www.ael.org/page.htm?&-pd=abo6721&pc=2
- Serves KY, NC, SC, TN, VA, WV

Region V

- www.sedl.org/secac
- Serves AL, AR, GA, LA, MS

Region VI

- www.wcer.wisc.edu/ccvi
- Serves IA, MI, MN, NC, SC, WI

Region VII

- region7.ou.edu
- Serves IL, IN, KS, MO, NE, OK

Region VIII

- http://www.starcenter.org
- Serves TX

Region IX

- www.cesdp.nmhu.edu
- Serves AZ, CO, NM, NV, UT

Region X

- www.nwrac.org
- Serves ID, MT, OR, WA, WY

Region XI

- www.wested.org
- Serves Northern CA

Region XII

- sccac.lacoe.edu
- Serves Southern CA

Region XIII

- http://www.serrc.org/akrac/
- Serves AK

Region XIV

- www.ets.org/ccxiv
- Serves FL, Puerto Rico, Virgin Islands

Region XV

- www.prel.org
- Serves American Samoa, Guam, HI, Federated States of Micronesia, Commonwealth of the Northern Mariana Islands, Republic of the Marshall Islands, Republic of Palau

Index

**CORWIN
PRESS**

The Corwin Press logo—a raven striding across an open book—represents the union of courage and learning. Corwin Press is committed to improving education for all learners by publishing books and other professional development resources for those serving the field of PreK–12 education. By providing practical, hands-on materials, Corwin Press continues to carry out the promise of its motto: **"Helping Educators Do Their Work Better."**